INTRODUCTION TO COGNITIVE REHABILITATION
Theory and Practice

INTRODUCTION TO COGNITIVE REHABILITATION
Theory and Practice

McKay Moore Sohlberg, M.Sc., C.C.C.
Catherine A. Mateer, Ph.D.

Good Samaritan Center for Cognitive Rehabilitation,
Puyallup, Washington

THE GUILFORD PRESS
New York   London

© 1989 The Guilford Press
A Division of Guilford Publications, Inc.
72 Spring Street, New York, NY 10012

Printed in the United States of America

Last digit is print number: 9 8 7 6 5 4 3 2 1

Library of Congress Cataloging-in-Publication Data

Sohlberg, McKay Moore.
  Introduction to cognitive rehabilitation.

  Includes bibliographies and index.
  1. Brain damage—Patients—Rehabilitation.
2. Cognition disorders—Patients—Rehabilitation.
I. Mateer, Catherine A. II. Title. [DNLM: 1. Brain
Injuries—rehabilitation. 2. Cognition Disorders—
rehabilitation. WL 354 S682p]
RC387.5.S64 1989   617.481044   88-24415
ISBN 0-89862-738-9

This book is dedicated to
our husbands
Olof Erick Sohlberg and Don Polly

Foreword

Cognitive rehabilitation is an emerging specialty. Hardly a decade has passed since it was born of mixed parentage—counting neuropsychology, occupational therapy, speech and language pathology, and special education among its forebears. From these diverse roots the young field has grown with an energy occasionally broaching unruliness. Sibling rivalry—discord from within—has been more threatening than challenges from without. Indeed, consumers of services have at times been uncritical in their eagerness for help.

Those of us who participated in the development of cognitive rehabilitation have learned that practical tools and techniques, such as computer software, have played an important role in the nurturance of this specialty. Likewise, this textbook will be readily adopted because it will be an important tool for use in educating the next generation of cognitive rehabilitation practitioners. Unlike most other book-length works in this field, this is not a collection of articles; rather, it is a cohesive, carefully planned exposition of the entire field. Its raison d'être is to teach.

However, the field is young enough for us still to recognize that there are few, if any, textbook answers. For instance, this writer would urge professionals to keep an open mind regarding the value of restorative approaches to memory rehabilitation. My own clinical experience with severely amnesic individuals who have engaged in intensive and protracted memory exercise regimens suggests that it is premature to write off restoration. I am concerned that this emerging specialty stands to lose far more by closing off inquiry and trial than it does from an excess of snake oil remedy.

Further, assisting individuals to engage in exercise directed toward restoration of function is often a more successful starting point for a clinical therapeutic relationship than focusing on compensation and conservation. If exercise does not lead to improved function, the individual will begin to welcome and appreciate compensatory methods, such as the ones described by Sohlberg and Mateer.

While this book will be used because it will serve an important need, it has far more than utility to recommend it, as it masterfully integrates theory with clinical practice. Each of the important domains of cognitive function is analyzed and explained with respect to underlying cognitive processes. These expositions are based on an appreciation of the state of the art in cognitive science, recognizing that an understanding of mental function in the neurologically intact individual is prerequisite to understanding pathology.

The best in scientific methodology for the clinical setting is conveyed through descriptions of single-case experimental design studies, e.g., Sohlberg and Mateer's study of process-specific interventions for attention disorders. These presentations will serve as models for students and should encourage scientific evaluation of efficacy. Such rigor is especially important in an emerging specialty, drawn by the urgency of unmet needs and swayed by appreciation for anything that seems helpful, or at least well-intentioned.

Clinical experience and sensitivity shine through this volume and the reader will find many useful concepts and techniques which can be put to immediate use. Without doubt, Sohlberg and Mateer have produced a textbook that will foster high standards for the education of scientist-practitioners of cognitive rehabilitation.

ROSAMOND GIANUTSOS, PH.D.

Preface

Rehabilitation professionals are finding that their case loads contain increasing numbers of head-injured patients. Depending on factors such as the location and organization of the rehabilitation facility, a variety of disciplines are called on to treat the cognitive disorders of head-injured patients. Speech/language pathologists, clinical psychologists, occupational therapists, and neuropsychologists may all have primary responsibility for cognitive rehabilitation, depending on their particular place of employment. In spite of expectations that these clinicians will manage the cognitive remediation within their clinical case work, their respective training programs do not provide the necessary background to serve this relatively new and special population.

Currently, there is no single discipline adequately prepared to assess and treat the cognitive impairments associated with head injury. Ideally, a graduate training program should be created which combines information from neuropsychology, cognitive psychology, educational psychology, and the rehabilitation specialties relevant to cognitive rehabilitation. However, since this is not currently the practice, it is the responsibility of those professionals treating cognitive impairments to seek the background needed to provide their patients with quality, state-of-the-art care. This text, written by a speech/language pathologist and a neuropsychologist, is designed to assist these efforts. Its primary purpose is to educate current and future rehabilitation professionals in the theory and practice of cognitive rehabilitation for head-injured adults.

This text is unique in its comprehensive attention to cognitive rehabilitation practices. It provides a theoretically based set of cognitive rehabilitation prescriptions that will allow effective remediation of impairments in cognitive function. Because this text is solely devoted to rehabilitation practice, it assumes some basic knowledge of neuroanatomy, neurophysiology, neuropathology, and the general phenomenon of head injury. It is best supplemented with a basic course in neurogenics. More general reviews of head injury have been provided elsewhere (e.g., Adamovich, Henderson, &

Auerbach, 1985; Goldstein & Ruthven, 1983; Levin, Benton, & Grossman, 1982; Prigatano, 1986).

The authors' clinical experience and results of experimental studies have demonstrated that it is possible to improve cognitive functioning with theoretically based rehabilitation exercises that systematically target specific processes—even when they are implemented well beyond the period of spontaneous recovery. This general approach to cognitive rehabilitation is termed the Process-Specific Approach and is detailed in Chapter 2. It does not exclude more functional approaches to training; rather, it embraces them as a necessary component of rehabilitation. Cognition cannot be addressed effectively in isolation from real-world activities, yet isolated training in activities of daily living will not result in generalizable cognitive improvements. The Process-Specific Approach combines these approaches by providing the opportunity to apply retrained cognitive skills in functional settings.

Although many of the treatment approaches described in this text were developed in the context of postacute outpatient brain-injury programs, all of them have been utilized with patients in earlier phases of recovery. The breadth, theoretical underpinnings, and systematic nature of the Process-Specific Approach make it very suitable to implementation even in the acute rehabilitation setting. The reaction of many practitioners who work in the field of head injury rehabilitation may be that the Process-Specific Approach and the outcomes of experimental studies reported in this text are only relevant to higher-level patients. Yet all of the individuals we have seen for postacute rehabilitation required acute rehabilitative care following their injuries. It is sometimes difficult to envision the long-term potential of patients when they are only seen in the acute setting. It is not naive optimism that drives us but our experience with well over a hundred head-injury cases (some of whom represent profound levels of impairment) whose vocational and living options were significantly changed by cognitive rehabilitation.

The text is divided into three parts. The first reviews general issues related to the practice of cognitive rehabilitation. It gives the reader a foundation in the basic principles of rehabilitation and places cognitive rehabilitation within the context of current practice. The second part is devoted to remediation of specific cognitive functions. These chapters each begin with a review of relevant neuropsychological principles, followed by descriptions of retraining methods. The last part discusses other disciplines and issues related to cognitive rehabilitation. The text should give the clinician the proper tools to assist clients in achieving maximum levels of vocational and independent-living abilities. This book's ambitious (and perhaps presumptuous) goal is to develop a discipline where previously one has not existed.

REFERENCES

Adamovich, B., Henderson, J., & Auerbach, S. (1985). *Cognitive rehabilitation of closed head injured patients: A dynamic approach.* San Diego: College Hill Press.

Goldstein, G., & Ruthen, L. (1983). *Rehabilitation of the brain damaged adult.* New York: Plenum.

Levin, N., Benton, A. L., & Grossman, R. G. (1982). *Neurobehavioral consequences of closed head injury.* New York: Oxford University Press.

Prigatano, G. (1986). *Neuropsychological rehabilitation after brain injury.* Baltimore: Johns Hopkins University Press.

Acknowledgments

This book would be incomplete without a special acknowledgment of those who have helped this field evolve to the point where the rehabilitation of cognitive deficits secondary to brain trauma can begin to be discussed. Ten years ago, the overriding notion within the medical community was that, beyond the initial spontaneous recovery period, residual brain damage was permanent; the dominant theme was that brain cells do not regenerate. Today, we are seeing patients more than 10 years post-injury (for whom there was no such field as cognitive rehabilitation at the time of their accident) demonstrate excellent neuropsychological progress as a result of treatment. Ultimately most of these patients return to gainful employment and independent living. While we admonish ourselves to generate more theoretically based, data-driven treatment and to encourage professionals in the field to adopt more rigorous scientific practices, we must stop now and again to appreciate the progress that has been realized. Our patients *are* getting better.

We would first and foremost like to acknowledge the contribution of our patients to this volume and to thank them for their courage and determination. In spite of facing such grim sentences as the loss of a hard-earned career or giving up a beloved sport, they have pushed on and maximized their residual abilities. We have learned much from them about the brain, about recovery, and about life in general. For this, we are deeply grateful. We would also like to thank those special professionals who believed that persons with head injury were capable of much, much more if provided with appropriate rehabilitation opportunities. Such individuals as Jack Geringer, the Director of Good Samaritan Hospital's Center for Cognitive Rehabilitation, and the entire CCR staff dedicate themselves to creating a system that knows no limitations in efforts to improve rehabilitation services. These are the individuals who are never too busy to have lunch with a patient or to provide assistance with the move into an independent apartment for the first time since an accident. Special thanks go to Mark Corey, Suzanne Geyer, Jane Lynch, Kristin Metzelaar, Kathi Miller, Jim Riggs, Karyn Ottolino, and Holly Sprunk. Finally, we would like to acknowledge the major contribution of Mary Ann Muenks who devoted endless hours to typing the manuscript—always with enthusiasm—and Terry Eberle who ably assisted her.

Certain projects are products of the heart and soul and not just of the intellect. McKay would like to thank her family, especially her parents (Brian and Sue) and siblings (Blake, Erika, and Michael), for creating an environment that encouraged careful thinking, education, and achievement in a way that could be applied to help others. Most of all, she would like to thank her husband, Olof, for sacrificing domestic tranquility in order for her to pursue a goal, as well as for providing a model of the true giving of oneself.

Katy would like to thank her dedicated and talented office staff, including Trudy Hustead and Sharon Eilers. Special thanks go to Dennis Williams for his clinical insights and commitment and to Julie Barber for her valuable editorial assistance. Katy would also like to thank her parents, who have provided such uncompromising support, and her husband, Don, for his understanding and patience, his late-night gourmet specialties, and his always reviving humor.

McKay Moore Sohlberg
Catherine Ann Mateer

Contents

PART II.   COGNITIVE PROCESS AREAS

Part I
GENERAL ISSUES

1
Current Perspectives
in Cognitive Rehabilitation

Cognitive rehabilitation is a very new field, with a limited research base and a lack of professional consensus in terminology, theoretical foundations, and treatment approaches. This first chapter offers an introduction to this evolving discipline as it is discussed throughout this text. The topics covered include definition of cognitive rehabilitation as used in this book, limitations on current research into the efficacy of treatment, general review of mechanisms of head injury, spontaneous recovery mechanisms of the brain and their implication for cognitive rehabilitation, Luria's model of brain organization, and the five stages of rehabilitation.

DEFINITIONS

Perhaps the most fundamental question to be answered in a text on cognitive rehabilitation is "What is it?" Unfortunately, the answer is not at all clear-cut. As with many fields, the vocabulary includes of a plethora of overlapping and poorly defined terms. Labels such as *cognitive rehabilitation, cognitive therapy, neurotraining, cognitive remediation, cognitive retraining,* and *mediation of brain–behavior relationships* are used interchangeably by some professionals, but to others, they denote very different phenomena. Currently, neither *cognitive rehabilitation* nor its counterpart terms conjures up a specific set of treatment protocols or even a general treatment approach in the minds of professionals working in this area. It is important that the field begin to better define its terms, since the question that usually follows "What is it?" is "Does it work?" Before a conclusive statement can be made regarding efficacy, we must first define our terms.

 Cognitive rehabilitation, as used in this text, refers to the therapeutic process of increasing or improving an individual's capacity to process and use incoming information so as to allow increased functioning in everyday life. This includes both methods to restore cognitive function and compensatory techniques. The term cognitive rehabilitation has also been used to denote certain neuropharmacologic interventions, psychotherapeutic approaches, and behavior management programs. Although these might be effective means of treating certain sequelae of damaged neurologic function, they do not provide direct retraining of cognitive processes. As used in this text, cognitive rehabilitation applies to therapy methods that actually retrain or alleviate problems caused by deficits in attention, visual processing, language, memory, reasoning/problem solving, and executive functions. Like Goldstein and Ruthven's (1983) term "rational rehabilitation," it refers to rehabilitation that is (1) based on solid, scientific knowledge of brain–behavior relationships and (2) designed to meet specifically defined treatment goals.

An example of a cognitive rehabilitation program is Attention Process Training (APT), described in Chapter 6. This program consists of hierarchically organized treatment tasks that target five theoretical components of attention, including Focused Attention, Sustained Attention, Alternating Attention, Selective Attention, and Divided Attention. Exercises require repetitive use of the impaired cognitive system in a graded, progressively more demanding sequence. As in "rational rehabilitation," these techniques are based on established principles from the cognitive sciences and are directed at remediating specific components of particular cognitive processes.

TREATMENT EFFICACY

Having briefly addressed the definitional issue, it is appropriate to consider the question, "Does it work?" Throughout this text, the reader is provided with the available data supporting the efficacy of treatment techniques. It should be recognized, however, that efficacy studies in the area of cognitive rehabilitation are at an embryonic stage at best. Several factors explain the dearth of studies evaluating treatment success.

Perhaps the most fundamental obstacle to assessing treatments arises from individual differences in spontaneous recovery from head injury. The individual differences most relevant to recovery include intraspecies differences in brain organization (e.g., cerebral dominance), location of lesion, extent or magnitude of neurologic damage, time post-onset, age at injury, rate of improvement immediately following injury, and premorbid level of functioning (e.g., socioeconomic factors and external factors such as presence of drugs or alcohol abuse). Such differences are easily confounded with treatment effects, making it difficult to evaluate treatment outcomes.

In addition to the heterogeneity of factors relating to damage and recovery, there is an ethical dilemma inherent in conducting traditional clinical experimental studies. The bulk of experimental work is conducted using group designs that require use of a control or no-treatment group. Since withholding treatment is not a reasonable clinical practice, many have been discouraged from carrying out efficacy treatment studies. One solution has been the use of single-subject designs (e.g., Gianutsos & Gianutsos, 1979; Sohlberg & Mateer, 1987; Sohlberg, Sprunk, & Metzelaar, 1988). Single-subject methodology has gained increasing respect as a means to evaluate treatment efficacy and has the advantage of allowing the investigator to evaluate changes longitudinally (see Chapter 3). A second solution that has been proposed is the use of matched head-injury controls using persons on rehabilitation programs' waiting lists. Results from studies using this model are yet to appear in the literature. In the past five years, there has been a tremendous increase in the number of studies that examine treatment effects. The field has begun to evolve from a purely descriptive discipline to one with practices that are data-based and grounded in sound theory from the cognitive sciences.

MECHANISMS OF TRAUMATIC BRAIN INJURY

The National Head Injury Foundation (1985) defines head injury as a traumatic insult to the brain capable of producing physical, intellectual, emotional, social, and vocational changes. This definition implies brain damage and associated dysfunction. This brain damage can compromise many functions, including the ability to coordinate movements, speak, remember, reason, or modulate behavior. Insight into the nature of an injury and its potential consequences can be gleaned from a knowledge of the causal agents and the nature, extent, and site of the damage. Differences in the effects of an injury are related to whether it is open (the result of a penetrating wound) or closed. Effects of traumatic head injury may also depend on the site of injury, including such factors as whether significant damage has occurred to the right versus the left hemisphere, the frontal versus the temporal lobes, or the brainstem versus the cortex. Frontal injury, for example, is more likely to be associated with impaired executive functions, whereas temporal lobe injury may have more profound effects on memory. Brainstem injuries often result in severe motor impairments, but cortical injury is more likely to affect higher intellectual and cognitive functions (Jennett & Teasdale, 1981; Luria, 1963). Brain damage following traumatic head injury implies structural or physiologic change in the nervous activity of the brain. Traumatic brain damage can be thought of as resulting from three separate mechanisms (North, 1984):

1. Primary damage includes macroscopic and microscopic structural lesions directly caused by the impact.

2. Secondary damage may result from raised intracranial pressure, brain swelling, infection, hemorrhage, infarction, and/or oxygen deprivation (hypoxia).
3. Nonneurologic alterations in physiology that affect brain function include metabolic changes such as hyperthermia (excessive fever), electrolyte disturbances (salt and water retention), damage to the hypothalamus or pituitary gland, and hyperventilation (increased respiration).

There are two major classes of traumatic head injury, *open* and *closed*. Open (penetrating) head injuries typically produce more discrete or focal lesions. Closed head injuries are more likely to cause generalized or diffuse cerebral involvement. It must be recognized, however, that features of both open and closed head injury may be seen in the same individual depending on the nature of the insult.

Open Head Injury

An open head injury results when the scalp and skull are penetrated. The agents commonly responsible for open cranial/cerebral injuries are bullets, rocks, shell fragments, knives, and blunt instruments (Bokay & Glasauer, 1980; Meirowsky, 1984). The primary brain damage in such injuries tends to be localized about the path of the penetrating object (Cooper, 1982). Primary damage may also occur from penetrating bone fragments in the case of skull fractures or shattered pieces of shells or bullets. With proper medical care, including surgical cleansing of the wounds and removal of the damaged tissue (debridement), the remainder of the brain usually remains spared and uncompromised. Exceptions include high-velocity missiles, commonly seen in wartime injuries, which may produce remote lesions as a result of significant displacement forces, and low-velocity projectiles such as bullets, which may not exit the skull and produce damage as they ricochet off the internal surfaces of the cranium (Levin, Benton, & Grossman, 1982).

In addition to the direct or primary damage, a penetrating brain injury may produce secondary damage as a result of raised intracranial pressure effects, swelling, bleeding from torn blood vessels (into the spaces around brain tissue or into brain tissue itself), and cranial and intracranial infection. Unlike closed head injuries, open head injuries rarely lead to coma, but the risk of epilepsy is much greater. Between 17 and 43% of all patients with open head injury develop seizures, as compared with 5% of closed head-injured individuals (Jennett, 1978; Levin et al., 1982).

Closed Head Injury

The mechanical forces present in closed head injury include the effects of both direct contact and inertial forces (Alexander, 1984; Pang, 1985). The force of impact is the primary cause of damage in static injuries wherein a relatively stationary victim sustains a blow to the head. The damage results from inward compression of the skull at the point of impact and rebound effects. The point of original impact is referred to as the *coup;* the cerebral area opposite the blow is the *contracoup*. The forces in such blows may literally bounce the brain, which is somewhat gelatinous in texture, off the inside of the skull at the point of impact and at the opposite side. As brain surfaces are pushed forcefully against the inner table of the skull, the brain sustains contusion or bruising. Areas of bruising are characterized by bleeding into tissue as a result of small tears in blood vessels, swelling, and crushing of nerve fibers. These focal cortical contusions caused by inertial impact against the irregularities of the skull generally result in damage to certain regions that are more predisposed by virtue of their position in the brain. These lesions most often occur to the undersurface and lateral surfaces of the frontal and temporal lobes (Alexander, 1984; Levin et al., 1985), the consequences of which are manifest in changes in modulation of behavior, affect, emotions, executive functions, memory, and attention (Lezak, 1983).

Strong inertial forces at play in incidents associated with high levels of acceleration and deceleration (e.g., whiplash injuries in motor vehicle accidents) result in another kind of injury. Twisting movement causes high-velocity rotation of the brain within the skull, putting strain on delicate nerve fibers and blood vessels. This can cause stretching, tearing, and shearing of these microscopic structures (Langfitt & Gennarelli, 1982). This kind of injury, termed *diffuse axonal injury* (DAI), can cause death and almost always results in widespread diffuse brain dysfunction. Coma results from a disruption of the nerve fibers in the brainstem reticular formation (Alexander, 1984). This diffuse injury to white matter (axons) is also thought to account for reduced speed of responding and information processing and in attention deficits.

Secondary Complications

Trauma to the head, whether from open or closed injury, can produce both primary (impact damage) and secondary complications. Primary injury is the direct result of the impact and reflects tissue disruption caused by mechanical tearing, the blow, or acceleration/deceleration effects. To a large extent, given the current level of medical knowledge, drugs and physiologic manipulations are ineffectual in reversing the effects of such direct and permanent tissue damage (North, 1984; Pang, 1985).

In addition to the primary damage, there are a wide variety of secondary complications that can result from head injury. These include:

raised intracranial pressure,
edema (brain swelling as a result of an increase in fluid content secondary to the trauma),

hypoxia (oxygen deprivation as a result of chest or airway injuries that affect the capability for blood oxygenation),

infarction (stroke-like effects in a focal area resulting from the death of tissue that has been deprived of regional blood supply),

hematomas (focal areas of bleeding or clotting within the skull secondary to tearing of blood vessels),

infection.

In addition, significant metabolic changes often occur and result in functional disturbances. These include hyperthermia (excessive fever), and disturbances of respiration and circulation. Pituitary disorders arising from damage to the hypothalamus and pituitary gland, electrolyte disturbances (salt and water retention), and/or hyperventilation may also develop (Friedman, 1984; Levin et al., 1982; Pang, 1985). Finally, multiple trauma can result in failure to maintain an airway (chest, neck, or focal injuries) or in orthopedic injuries that may lead to fat or air emboli and thus have neurologic effects. It is management of these potentially reversible or controllable effects that is the focus of emergency and acute medical management.

Given the wide variety of physiological damage that can be incorporated under the rubric of head injury, it is not unexpected that the resultant physical, cognitive, and psychoemotional changes that accompany these injuries are so variable. Information concerning the nature and extent of physiologic injury can be helpful in understanding and predicting the consequences of injury and potential outcome.

resilence

RECOVERY MECHANISMS

In addition to understanding the nature of brain trauma, it is valuable to have an appreciation of some of the mechanisms that may operate during healing and recovery. There is a period of time following the injury, termed spontaneous recovery, during which there are changes in the central nervous system. These can result from resolution and absorption of hematomas, decrease in swelling, normalization of blood flow, and return of electrolyte and neurochemical balance. This provides the clinician with an expected pattern of improvement that might be anticipated in the absence of treatment. As is discussed below, there are also neurostructural changes that are hypothesized to follow central nervous system damage. An understanding of these mechanisms provides possible explanations for why the implementation of cognitive rehabilitation might be effective in improving neurologic status.

Fundamental to most theories of neural recovery is the concept of *plasticity* of the central nervous system. Plasticity is a term that is used to refer to either or both neural and behavioral resilience, that is, the ability to

postulates — to assume to be true real, etc., especially as a basis for an argument.

reorganize after injury in a neurophysiologic/neuroanatomic sense or a behavioral/functional sense (Pirozzolo & Papanicolaou, 1986). Plasticity has been variably used to describe neuronal changes, chemical changes, and complex functional variations. The interrelationships between these areas are as yet unclear, and there is great confusion in the literature regarding issues of plasticity and recovery of function.

Much of the data in this area have been derived from laboratory animal models (e.g., Finger, 1978; Finger & Stein, 1982; Rosner, 1970). The work most related to cognitive rehabilitation is that which postulates reorganization capabilities in the mammalian central nervous system. The most commonly cited central nervous system mechanisms of recovery include *diaschisis, axonal growth, denervation supersensitivity, and substitution*. A brief description of each is provided below.

Diaschisis. Diaschisis is a term originally used in early studies by von Monakow (1914) to describe recovery following temporary disruption of functioning in areas adjacent to the primary damage. Brain trauma may result in such factors as edema, metabolic changes, intracranial pressure changes, and modification of blood flow, all of which can render otherwise intact brain regions temporarily dysfunctional. Following a reduction of these "shock" effects, the functions that were inhibited in the affected but undamaged brain tissue slowly reemerge. Diaschisis may be differentiated from the other mechanisms of recovery by the fact that it refers to the reestablishment of unimpaired neurologic systems.

Axonal Growth. Several studies have indicated that some forms of damage do not necessarily completely destroy neurons and that there may be regeneration of neural elements following injury (Finger & Stein, 1982; Stein, Finger, & Hart, 1983). Axonal sprouting, including growth from damaged axons as well as collateral sprouting from intact axons, is a frequently cited recovery mechanism. Although the notion of axonal growth is fairly well established, it is not known whether the process is always a beneficial one that results in the establishment of functional systems. Studies in young animals have shown that when brain tissue is damaged, there is a structural reorganization. Neural elements (dendrites, axons, axon terminals) can proliferate and support function normally mediated by the destroyed area (Kennard, 1942; Stein et al., 1983). Although these data are from young animals, it may be possible that adult mammals also have nascent neurons that can be incorporated into "rehabilitated systems."

Denervation Supersensitivity. In the peripheral nervous system, it has been documented that postsynaptic receptor sites not only proliferate but also become more sensitive to neurotransmitter agents in denervated neurons (Meier, Strauman, & Thompson, 1987). It is usually assumed that areas of the brain that are partially denervated by the lesion become hypersensitive to the remaining input, thus permitting a more rapid return

proliferate — to inc. rapidly.
nascent — coming into being; beginning to form or develop.

of function. Again, the role of this biologic mechanism in functional recovery is poorly understood.

Substitution. A much discussed recovery mechanism, substitution refers to the notion that existing intact brain structures can assume functions previously held by lesioned areas. Meier et al. (1987) suggest that redundancy or duplication of function may be a more reasonable explanation for recovery of functions such as language, visuospatial skills, and abstract thinking in which there is overlap of corresponding brain territory. In addition to substitution of function, which requires an active reorganization of brain–behavior relationships, it has been postulated that there may be preexisting redundant representation of certain structural systems (Rosner, 1970). In this latter case, following damage to one area, another previously designated neurosystem would be available to carry out the work of the damaged system.

 It does not necessarily follow that there is only one explanation for recovery of function. It may be that one of the above mechanisms applies early in the recovery process (e.g., diaschisis) and that another operates more fully in the later phases of recovery (e.g., substitution). In other words, one theory does not preclude the operation of another. Correlation with functional recovery, however, has not been very encouraging. Some researchers have proposed that mechanisms such as sprouting and denervation supersensitivity are "growth" rather than "healing" functions and may even be maladaptive under some circumstances (Finger, 1978). Possible examples of maladaptive outcomes of axonal and dendritic proliferation are seizures and increased spasticity (Stein et al., 1983).

An area receiving increasing attention in the animal literature is the possibility of using growth factors inherent in fetal brain tissue to selectively enhance or inhibit neuronal connections, such that a more controlled reorganization of function might be possible. Additionally, there is much experience in the Soviet Union with manipulation of acetylcholine levels in the brains of headtrauma patients. They have used a variety of methods to increase this critical neurotransmitter, asserting that significant behavioral improvements follow (Luria, 1963).

Some rehabilitation professionals postulate that targeted cognitive rehabilitation facilitates recovery via one or more of the above biologic changes in a functional direction. Unfortunately, to date, there have been no studies examining the correlation of central nervous system changes with the implementation of cognitive rehabilitation.

IMPLICATIONS FOR COGNITIVE REHABILITATION

There are two broad theories of how cognitive rehabilitation should be implemented, given the biologic recovery mechanisms hypothesized to exist

cortical

within the central nervous system. One school believes that rehabilitation is primarily useful in promoting spontaneous recovery. These individuals prefer to work with patients during the more acute phases of their recovery, when the operation of spontaneous recovery mechanisms is most intense. The second school believes that cognitive rehabilitation efforts stand alone in their efficacy and should be attempted regardless of the time post-injury. This view generally states that regardless of the natural healing processes, cognitive rehabilitation will facilitate a functional reorganization of brain ability.

It is the experience of the authors that both views hold merit. Certainly if magnitude and speed of recovery are greatest early on, this might logically be an important time to administer treatment, particularly in systems amenable to improvement. On the other hand, recent scientific findings suggest that significant improvements in neuropsychologic functioning can occur many years following injury as a result of cognitive rehabilitation (Sohlberg & Mateer, 1987). This evidence is particularly important as it runs counter to the belief, unfortunately shared by many professionals in this area, that once brain damage has stabilized, recovery of cognitive capacity is unlikely.

Viable - workable

THEORETICAL BASIS OF REHABILITATION

The renowned Russian neuropsychologist Alexander Luria provides perhaps some of the soundest theoretical principles supporting cognitive rehabilitation as a viable clinical procedure. Luria (1980) suggests the presence of functional cortical systems that account for the organization of higherlevel thought processes. Observable behaviors, according to Luria, are composed of many basic processes stemming from contributions of different levels and sites within the brain. These form constellations of action that produce functional systems, which in turn generate observable, measurable behavior. Disruption of these processes results in changes in behavior and ability.

Although a complete review of Luria's theories is far beyond the scope of this chapter, a brief summary is in order since his work has helped shape the state of cognitive rehabilitation. Luria distinguished three functional units of the brain that are hierarchically organized and functionally integrated. These include (1) the arousal unit (responsible for regulating cortical tone; (2) the sensory-input unit (responsible for receiving, analyzing, and storing information; and (3) the organizational and planning unit (responsible for the programming, regulation, and verification of activity). These three units are essential to the execution of any cognitive task. He further describes the hierarchical organization of each unit into three cortical zones (Luria, 1973): (1) primary areas, which receive and send impulses to and from the periphery; (2) secondary areas, which perform information processing; and

(3) tertiary areas, which receive input from two or more of the secondary areas and serve to integrate information.

Luria's conceptual framework of brain organization shifted the field of neuropsychology away from the task of isolating discrete functional centers toward understanding integrated brain function. The notion that the brain is organized as a dynamic, integrated system has remained popular and has been expanded in modern views of brain organization. For example, current models of brain organization utilizing computer intelligence have as their basis the notion of integrated functional systems.

Because many of the important adaptive functions that human organisms possess must be learned (e.g., speech, computation), Luria theorized that recovery of function can occur through new learned connections established through cognitive retraining exercises specifically targeted at the source of problems or the basic processes that have been disrupted. He argued for the importance of direct intervention in the functioning of the nervous system to facilitate the rate of recovery. Direct training would result in the reorganization of the multiple levels of brain integration.

Luria also proposed that the brain may be in a state of disinhibition following brain insult. Pharmacologic approaches, particularly administration of anticholinergics, to restore the brain to a level of disinhibition that would facilitate transmission of nerve impulses across synaptic clefts, coupled with cognitive rehabilitation training methods, formed the basis of Luria's approach to rehabilitation.

Luria's revolutionary ideas regarding rehabilitation following brain injury have remained central to current developments in cognitive rehabilitation. It is only in the past several years, however, that these heuristic concepts are being supported by objective research.

To summarize, although the evidence is far from conclusive, a number of possible recovery mechanisms have been suggested that might be facilitated through the implementation of cognitive rehabilitation. Luria's revolutionary work in the 1960s further describes a conceptual framework of brain organization with the power to explain how cognitive rehabilitation might result in improved cognitive functioning.

STAGES OF REHABILITATION

As mentioned earlier, the course of recovery from head injury is extremely variable among individuals and is related to such factors as age, site and extent of damage, and the length of time that an individual is amnesic. For example, Russell and Smith (1961) demonstrated a particularly strong relationship between rate of recovery and duration of posttraumatic amnesia, the time following the injury in which the patient is unable to remember information from one minute to the next. According to Lezak (1976), the best prognostic indicator for recovery is the initial rate of improvement; the faster the initial recovery speed, the greater is the ultimate return of function.

The usual course of recovery following the onset of a serious traumatic brain injury involves a period of unconsciousness followed by some duration of confusion, with gradual return of functions. The period of time for these phases, as well as the extent of recovery observed, varies greatly among individuals. It is impossible to outline a common course of recovery because of this great variability among the head-injured population.

Perhaps a more practical conceptualization of recovery is to examine the stages of rehabilitation. Five possible distinct periods can be identified:

- emergency care
- coma care
- inpatient rehabilitation
- outpatient rehabilitation
- community reintegration

Of course, not all patients require or have access to the entire spectrum of rehabilitation. Some patients, for example, never regain full consciousness and thus would not benefit from all of the services. However, there are a great number of individuals with severe to moderate head injuries for whom this continuum would be appropriate. A discussion of the full range of rehabilitation phases is useful in providing a context for current practices in cognitive rehabilitation.

Emergency Care

Brain injury often is caused by a traumatic event requiring emergency intervention at the site of the accident. The main goal of this intervention is to maintain an open airway and continued circulatory function. Adequate oxygen delivery to the essential organs—the brain, heart, kidneys, and liver—is the crucial concern. A patient will then be transported to a hospital and receive further medical intervention, which may include neurosurgical procedures such as debridgement, to clear the area in the brain of bone fragments or other debris, or evacuation of hematomas, to relieve pressure caused by bleeding around or into brain tissue. At this point, the goal is to keep the patient alive and to prevent as much permanent neurologic damage as possible.

Coma Care

Frequently, if there has been injury to brainstem mechanisms responsible for arousal, patients will be in a state of unconsciousness or coma. In this phase, although continuing efforts at medical stabilization comprise the bulk of treatment, sensory stimulation activities using auditory or tactile input may be attempted.

Inpatient Rehabilitation

Once the patient has regained some level of consciousness and is medically stable, he or she may be transferred to a rehabilitation unit in order to receive multidisciplinary rehabilitation services. This may include physical, occupational, speech/language, and recreational therapies, psychologic and neuropsychologic treatment, and social work services in addition to nursing and medical care. The goals of hospital-based inpatient rehabilitation typically include reestablishment of basic motor and sensory integration (head and neck control, postural reflexes, balance, gait, swallowing), reestablishment of basic self-care skills (feeding, dressing, grooming), and reestablishment of basic cognitive skills (orientation, attention, receptive and expressive communication).

ambulation — to move about; walk

Outpatient Rehabilitation

Often a patient is discharged from the hospital when ambulation and a reasonable degree of self-care ability have been achieved. There is no consistent formula, however, used to determine appropriate time of discharge; and unfortunately, reimbursement factors and hospital utilization review codes usually play the largest role in this decision. Many times, a patient will continue with multidisciplinary services such as speech/language therapy and physical therapy on a less intensive outpatient basis.

Community Reintegration

These first four rehabilitation stages are well established as legitimate processes in head injury rehabilitation. By both tradition and necessity, they are medically oriented. The fifth stage, community reintegration, is usually conducted in a nonmedical setting and has just recently been recognized as a vital part of the rehabilitation process. This phase includes postmedical, intensive day treatment or residential programs designed to assist patients with maximal reintegration into society. Often, vocational and independent-living issues become a focus in this rehabilitation phase. Such programs came into existence when it was recognized that many head-injured patients were being discharged to their families' homes unable to pursue productive work and unable to live independently. Much of the pioneer work in cognitive rehabilitation was carried out in the context of postacute community reentry programs, since patients are often in these programs for many months, which allows orderly administration of clinical trials and longitudinal follow-up.

The first postacute day treatment program grew out of a joint project between the New York University Institute of Rehabilitation Medicine and the Israeli Defense Ministry. The work of Yehuda Ben-Yishay and his colleagues at New York University (e.g., New York University Medical Center, 1980) with soldiers who had received head injuries in the Yom Kippur war in the Middle East during the 1970s resulted in a major breakthrough in cognitive rehabilitation. Through the development of a postacute, community-oriented therapy approach, it was demonstrated that the potential level of cognitive and social recovery was greater than previously thought. Fashioned after this original program, other centers dedicated to assisting brain-injured individuals to reintegrate into society at higher levels were established throughout the country. Today, there are over 1,000 postacute head injury facilities across the United States.

Executive—

SUMMARY

The definition of cognitive rehabilitation as used in this text includes the following concepts. (1) Cognitive rehabilitation can be conceived of as a set of therapy methods to retrain or alleviate deficits in Attention/Concentration, Visual Processing, Language, Memory, Reasoning/Problem Solving, and Executive Functions. (2) Therapy methods should be rationally derived and have theoretical foundations in the cognitive sciences. (3) Rehabilitation programs should also contain well-prescribed treatment goals defining the specific component to be remediated in the target cognitive process.

Physical, cognitive, and psychosocial impairments following head injury vary greatly with the nature and degree of trauma to the nervous system. The mechanisms involved in head trauma are multiple and diverse. Recovery mechanisms related to the healing and reorganization of the central nervous system include diaschisis, axonal growth, denervation supersensitivity, and structural substitution. Each may have implications for cognitive rehabilitation. It was suggested that cognitive rehabilitation may facilitate and encourage recovery. Luria's work proposes a reorganization of higher cortical functions given direct retraining.

The five possible stages in the rehabilitation process are emergency care, coma care, inpatient rehabilitation, outpatient rehabilitation, and community reintegration. The first four stages are fairly well established and accepted processes in the management of head injury. Community reentry programs have only recently been recognized as essential components for maximizing vocational and independent living circumstances of head injury patients.

STUDY QUESTIONS

1. Describe the important components that define cognitive rehabilitation as used in this text.
2. What factors present research obstacles to studies of treatment efficacy?
3. What are the implications of biologic recovery mechanisms for cognitive rehabilitation?
4. Describe Luria's model for recovery from brain trauma.
5. Why is community reintegration an important phase in the rehabilitation process?

REFERENCES

Alexander, M. P. (1984). Neurobehavioral consequences of closed head injury. *Neurology and Neurosurgery, 20:*1–8.

Bokay, L., & Glasauer, F. E. (1980). *Head injury.* Boston: Little, Brown.

Cooper, P. (1982). Post-traumatic intracranial mass lesions. In P. Cooper (Ed.), *Head injury* (pp. 185–233). Baltimore: Williams & Wilkins.

Finger, S. (Ed.). (1978). *Recovery from brain damage: Research and memory.* New York: Plenum.

Finger, S., & Stein, D. G. (1982). *Brain damage and recovery.* New York: Academic Press.

Friedman, A. H. (1984). Head Injuries: Initial evaluation and management. *Post-Graduate Medicine, 70:*219–222.

Gianutsos, R., & Gianutsos, J. (1979). Rehabilitating the verbal information processing of brain injured patients: A demonstration using single-case methodology, *Journal of Clinical Neuropsychology, 1:*117–133.

Goldstein, G., & Ruthven, L. (1983). *Rehabilitation of the brain-damaged adult.* New York: Plenum.

Jennett, B. (1978). Severity of brain damage. Altered consciousness and other indicators. In G. L. Odom (Ed.), *Central nervous system trauma research status report* (pp. 204–219). Bethesda, MD: National Institute of Health, National Institute of Neurological and Communicative Disorders and Stroke.

Jennett, B., & Teasdale, G. (1981). Management of head injuries. *Contemporary Neurology Series, 20:*258–260.

Kennard, M. A. (1942). Cortical reorganization of motor function: Studies on a series of monkeys of various ages from infancy to maturity. *Archives of Neurology and Psychiatry, 48:*227–240.

Langfitt, T. W., & Gennarelli, J. A. (1982). Can the outcome from head injury be improved? *Journal of Neurosurgery 56:* 19–25.

Levin, N., Benton, A. L., & Grossman, R. G. (1982). *Neurobehavioral consequences of closed head injury.* New York: Oxford University Press.

Levin, H. S., Kalisky, Z., Handel, S., Goldman, A., Eisenberg, H., Morrison, D., & von Lauter, A. (1985). Magnetic resonance imaging in relation to the sequelae and rehabilitation of diffuse closed head injury. Preliminary findings. *Seminar in Neurology* 5:221–231.

Lezak, M. D. (1976). Recovery of memory and learning functions following traumatic brain injury. *Cortex* 15:63–72.

Lezak, M. (1983). *Neuropsychological assessment*. New York: Oxford University Press.

Luria, A. R. (1963). *Restoration of function after brain injury*. New York: Basic Books.

Luria, A. R. (1973). *The working brain*. New York: Basic Books.

Luria, A. R. (1980). *Higher cortical functions in man*. New York: Basic Books.

Meier, M. J., Strauman, S., & Thompson, W. G. (1987). Individual differences in neuropsychological recovery: An overview. In M. Meier, A. Benton, & L. Diller (Eds.), *Neuropsychological rehabilitation* (pp. 71–110). New York: Guilford.

Meirowsky, A. M. (1984). *Penetrating cranicerebral trauma*. Springfield, IL: Charles C. Thomas.

National Head Injury Foundation (1985). *An educator's manual: What educators need to know about students with traumatic head injury*. Framingham, MA: Author.

New York University Medical Center. (1980). *Working approaches to remediation of cognitive deficits in brain damaged persons* (Rehabilitation Monograph No. 61). New York: Author.

North, B. (1984) *Jamieson's first notebook of head injury* (3rd ed.). London: Butterworths.

Pang, D. (1985). Pathophysiologic correlations of neurobehavioral syndromes following closed head injury. In M. Ylvisaker (Ed.), *Head injury rehabilitation: Children and adolescents* (pp. 3–71). San Diego: College Hill Press.

Pirozzolo, F. J., & Papanicolaou, A. C. (1986). Plasticity and recovery of function in the central nervous system. In J. Obrzut & G. Hynd (Eds.), *Child neuropsychology: Vol. I. Theory and research* (pp. 141–154). San Diego: Academic Press.

Rosner, B. S. (1970). Brain functions. *Annual Review of Psychology* 21:555–594.

Russell, W. R. (1974). Recovery after minor head injury. *Lancet ii:*1315.

Russell, W. R., & Smith, A. (1961). Post-traumatic amnesia in closed head injury. *Archives of neurology* 5:4–17.

Sohlberg, M. M., & Mateer, C. A. (1987). Effectiveness of an attention training program. *Journal of Clinical and Experimental Neuropsychology* 9(2):117–130.

Sohlberg, M. M., Sprunk, H., & Metzelaar, K. (1988). Efficacy of an external cuing system in an individual with severe frontal lobe injury. *Cognitive Rehabilitation,*

Stein, D. G., Finger, S., & Hart, T. (1983). Brain damage and recovery; problems and perspectives. *Behavioral and Neural Biology* 37:185–222.

von Monakow, C. (1914). *Die Lokalisation in Grosshirn und der Abbau der Funktion durch korticale Herde*. Wieisbaden: Bergmann. Translated and excerpted in K. H. Pribam (Ed), (1969). *Moodstates and mind*. London: Penguin

2
A Process-Specific Approach to Cognitive Rehabilitation

The increasing attention to cognitive rehabilitation has demanded the development of new hypotheses regarding the nature of cognitive recovery and the means to bring it about. One approach to treatment that is gaining increasing support is the Process-Specific Approach. It is discussed in detail in this chapter, along with other current approaches to the management of cognitive deficits. A model for designing a theoretically based cognitive rehabiliation program will also be presented, along with a discussion of the use of microcomputers in rehabilitation. Key topics include the process-specific approach to cognitive rehabilitation, theoretically motivated therapy, data-based treatment, treatment efficacy, cognitive rehabilitation software selection, and evaluation of treatment programs.

CURRENT THERAPY APPROACHES

Prigatano (1986) categorized the three approaches to cognitive retraining used today as (1) the use of compensation to get around a deficit; (2) the use of substitution to solve a problem that the brain is able to solve, but by alternative methods; and (3) attempts to retrain specifically impaired cognitive functions. He advocates a four-step process utilizing each of these training principles for facilitating cognitive recovery.

The first step in the process is to reduce the overall, generalized cognitive confusion that patients experience by systematically helping them improve their attentional skills. Secondly, group and individual counseling is used to enhance the patient's awareness of his or her strengths as well as deficits. Next, the patient is helped to recognize the need for compensatory behaviors. Finally, cognitive deficits are addressed in the broader context of how they affect interpersonal skills. Essentially, Prigatano's approach combines psychosocial and neuropsychologic interventions to alleviate the effects of impaired cognitive function.

18

amenable – responsible, answerable; able to be controlled; submissive.

Adamovich, Henderson, and Auerbach (1985) also divide cognitive retraining into a sequential, step-by-step process. These clinical researchers recommend the following three-stage treatment hierarchy: stimulation or arousal and alerting; followed by structured, goal-oriented programs or operative retraining; and finally, community-oriented training or teaching self-reliant functioning for individual cognitive deficits.

During the second, operative retraining phase of treatment, specific remediation areas would include perception and attending, discrimination, organization, recall, and higher-level thinking skills (convergent thinking, deductive reasoning, inductive reasoning, divergent thinking, and multi-process reasoning) The final phase is the carryover treatment phase in which home and community training, within and outside the hospital, provides opportunities for the practice of necessary skills.

Goldstein and Ruthven (1983) advocate behavioral therapy as a way to manage cognitive deficits. They encourage the use of behavioral assessments, including interviews and naturalistic observation, to supply the clinician with target behaviors that would be most amenable to treatment. Naturalistic observation involves observing and recording the frequency, duration, and circumstances under which a particular behavior occurs. This serves as a therapy baseline. Skills training, using single-subject designs and token-economy reinforcement systems, comprises the bulk of their rehabilitation methods. (Skills training refers to methods of training discrete behaviors related to the cognitive areas of memory, perceptual ability, language, and motor skills.) Behavioral methodologies (e.g., use of reinforcement strategies) provide a means of motivating the patient to continue participating in the program, and single-subject research designs in the form of training modules to increase the target behaviors provide an indication of whether or not the program is effective.

Trexler (1987) divides the current methodologies into what he terms *reductionist* versus *dynamic* approaches to neuropsychologic rehabilitation. Central to the reductionistic approach are the following three tenets:

1. The components of the neuropsychologic defect in question are diagnosed from an analysis of performance on a neuropsychologic test.
2. The ability to divide cortical functions into distinct entities is assumed.
3. Practice is used to "restore" deficits to some predetermined criteria.

In contrast, *dynamic approaches* to rehabilitation have the following characteristics:

Little emphasis is placed on the absolute level of performance on specific neuropsychologic measures.
There is no predetermined, prescribed sequence of therapy methods.

cortical entities.

Therapy is delivered in a reactive mode whereby the patient's individual cognitive and psychosocial responses determine how and what therapy will be administered. Thus, therapy plans may change on a minute-by-minute or day-by-day basis.

There is an emphasis on the therapist–patient relationship.

There is very little empirical research on this second approach, and outcome is solely based on an estimation of change and global adaptation in a variety of functional situations.

Based on the authors' survey of a sampling of hospitals and head injury clinics throughout the United States and Canada, it appears that clinicians tend to adhere to one of three basic approaches when treating their patients' cognitive deficits. These are the General Stimulation Approach, the Functional Adaptation Approach, and the Process-Specific Approach to cognitive rehabilitation.

The General Stimulation Approach to cognitive rehabilitation uses tasks that encourage cognitive processing at any level. The clinician administers commercially available cognitive retraining materials, such as cognitive rehabilitation workbooks or cognitive retraining microcomputer programs, without operating from any real theoretical orientation. For clinicians working outside facilities specifically designed for head injury rehabilitation, this is perhaps the most commonly used therapy approach. It assumes that any stimulation of cognitive processing will result in improved mental faculties.

A second general therapy orientation, the Functional Adaptation Approach, is usually based on the general philosophy of a particular head injury program. It assumes that cognitive function cannot be improved with specific retraining and argues that therapy should be carried out in a wholly functional context. Therapy within a clinical setting is held as inappropriate; rather, improved functioning is targeted within a particular naturalistic work or living situation. Patients are trained for specific avocational or vocational settings using such methods as work or living trials. Limited generalization of behavior to a different work or living setting would be expected. In general, the functional adaptation orientation produces individuals who can perform particular activities under the conditions in which they were taught. (The third method, the Process-Specific Approach, is discussed in detail later in this chapter.)

LIMITATIONS

The previous discussion suggests several problems. One involves the difference between cognitive rehabilitation and total management of head-injured individuals. If, as some advocate, cognitive rehabilitation cannot be im-

milieu— environment; social setting.

proved in the absence of other multidisciplinary treatments such as psychosocial, vocational, or occupational therapy, then these components need to be carefully defined and outlined within the cognitive rehabilitation framework. The authors have demonstrated that distinct cognitive processes can be independently improved (Sohlberg & Mateer, 1987). However, experience has shown that greater functional gains can be achieved when mechanisms to apply improved cognitive abilities to naturalistic settings are pursued. Disciplines such as occupational therapy and vocational rehabilitation often address functional application of cognition.

Cognitive rehabilitation practices need to be distinguished from an overall program description of head injury management such as those described in Chapter 13. Most current descriptions of cognitive rehabilitations are difficult to implement because of their vague references to the psychodynamic, social milieu, and functional training events intermixed with the specific cognitive rehabilitation techniques.

Perhaps the greatest shortcoming of current descriptions of cognitive rehabilitation approaches is the absence of a sound theoretical base. Neither the sequential step-by-step recipes for cognitive rehabilitation nor many of the independent treatment techniques targeting specific cognitive impairments have their foundation in research from the cognitive or educational sciences. The cognitive psychology literature is a rich souce describing how cognition operates in the normal individual. Similarly, information from the field of neurology/neuropsychology provides a needed data base for pathological characteristics of cognitive functioning within the damaged brain. Finally, educational psychology contains important resources concerning models of learning and methods of facilitating cognitive change. These distinct literature bases give us an excellent starting ground on which to develop cognitive retraining programs. Unfortunately, most of the theoretical basis that can be identified in current approaches to cognitive rehabilitation is restricted to neuropsychology assessment models. Neuropsychology models stress the psychometric–statistical methods of diagnosis of cognitive problems and have traditionally focused on localization of identified impairments. A broader view of developing treatments based on the general framework of what is known about brain–behavior relationships with the shift away from the restricted diagnostic frame of reference limited to analysis of localization of function allows a stronger, more comprehensive library of theoretical principles on which to base cognitive rehabilitation methods.

The Process-Specific Approach described in the remainder of this chapter attempts to address these limitations and pick up where many other treatments fall short. It is based on current research and a broad theoretical base. It offers a clear methodology that can be used by independent clinicians, and it describes a total program for both rehabilitation and management of brain-injured patients.

Facilitating— to make easy or easier.

management —
residual —

THE PROCESS-SPECIFIC APPROACH
TO COGNITIVE REHABILITATION

In the Process-Specific Approach to cognitive rehabilitation, treatment is oriented toward targeted remediation of specific cognitive areas. It assumes that these specific areas can be treated individually and that they can be directly retrained and remediated. It thus might be conceived of as a restorative model. It also advocates methods to assist individuals in compensating for residual deficits, recognizing that restoration of cognitive capacity to a functional level is not always possible. Unlike some other methods, however, these compensatory techniques or alternative methods for achieving a result without taxing the impaired cognitive process are theoretically motivated and process-specific. The essential strategy of this approach is the repeated administration of hierarchically organized treatment tasks that target distinct, theoretically motivated components of a cognitive process. Data are gathered on each performance of the task. When set criterion levels are reached, remediation of another cognitive process or an additional component of the current process is initiated.

There are six fundamental rehabilitation principles that comprise this therapy approach:

1. A *theoretically motivated* model defines each cognitive process area.
2. Therapy tasks are administered *repetitively*.
3. Goals and objectives are *hierarchically* organized.
4. Remediation involves *data-based* and directed treatment.
5. The use of *generalization probes* provides measurements of treatment success.
6. Ultimate measures of success must be *improvements in level of vocational ability and independent living*.

A discussion of each principle is provided in the next section, followed by the description of an initial efficacy study.

Perhaps the two biggest criticisms of this approach are (1) a fear that it is overly task-oriented and (2) a concern regarding the lack of empirical data supporting its efficacy. In reference to the former criticism, it is very important that clinicians not be excessively focused on the therapy exercises. Practice or drills are simply a means of attacking the deficient cognitive capacity; the exercises do not have any inherent value in and of themselves. Attention to task performance alone would be dangerous and is not what this therapy promotes. Instead, the clinician should focus on changes in overall neuropsychologic functioning that result from the administration of therapy tasks.

The cognitive process of memory may be the area in which the Process-Specific Approach has received the most pessimistic reports. It provides an example of the problems encountered when therapy becomes overly task-focused. A review of the memory literature (Glisky & Schacter, 1986) suggests that memory cannot be improved through practice or repetitive recall drills. It should be noted, however, that the drills used in the studies cited were not theoretically derived and exercised only one component of memory—retrieval (see Chapter 9). Subsequent studies using theoretically based memory exercises have shown a restorative capacity (Mateer & Sohlberg, 1988).

The latter criticism, the lack of empirical data to support the efficacy of this approach, has some foundation. However, this is true of all approaches in the very new field of cognitive rehabilitation. Initial studies on the Process-Specific Approach are encouraging (e.g., Sohlberg & Mateer, 1987).

empirical relying or based on experiment or experience,

Theoretical Model

A theoretical basis is important both to assure that treatment techniques are consistent with established scientific principles and to allow systematic delivery of rehabilitation. Under the Process-Specific Approach, a constellation of related tasks, all of which target the same component of a particular cognitive process, are systematically and repetitively administered. It thus differs from the General Stimulation Approach, in which sound treatment decisions are difficult to make because there is no overall working model.

The conceptualization of language as a cognitive process provides an example of the utility of having a theoretical model. Language can be divided into the following components: phonology (speech sounds), semantics (word meaning), syntax (grammar), and pragmatics (the use of language in conversation). This categorization is derived in part from neurological models of language functioning and has been accepted by scientists and clinicians for years. Analogous models for other cognitive processes are presented in this text. For example, theoretical models of attention, visual processing, and reasoning/problem solving have been developed that permit a conceptualization of the spectrum of mental activities that define these processes. Diagnostic and remediation techniques are then organized that selectively target the specific components that are identified in need of treatment.

Repetition

Repetition is perhaps the hallmark of the Process-Specific Approach to cognitive rehabilitation. This orientation is based, in part, on the Lurian concept described in the previous chapter, which states that direct retraining of cognitive processes can result in a reorganization of higher level thought processes. Because this is an ambitious (if not presumptuous) project, multiple trials providing stimulation and activation of the target process are required to achieve neurologic reorganization. The notion is that the repeated taxing of the same neurological system facilitates and guides the reorganization of function. Thus, the Process-Specific Approach requires implementation of repetitive exercises within a planned program that places demands on the patient to perform an impaired skill.

Hierarchically Organized Treatment Tasks

Initial neuropsychological testing allows determination of the brain processes that have been disrupted; treatment programs can then be designed that place demands on the brain to use the disrupted processes. Organization of the tasks in a hierarchical fashion enables them to be administered systematically. As soon as a patient has mastered a particular exercise or group of exercises, higher-level treatment tasks targeting the same cognitive component need to be available so that continued stimulation and activation of the objective cognitive process can occur.

Rehabilitation of visuomotor skills serves as an example. Let us say that a clinician has designed a program to improve a patient's visuomotor ability relative to constructional skills. At the initial level, therapy tasks may consist of two-dimensional, single-form construction exercises, such as block design assembly. Once a patient has met criterion levels for these activities, therapy may progress to single-form block assembly tasks requiring construction in three-dimensional space. A further increase in complexity might involve introduction of multiform tasks, using pieces of different sizes and shapes and alternate methods of connection. These tasks may culminate in a naturalistic activity such as the mechanical assembly of a bike or radio. Therapy designed to increase visuomotor skills would thus have progressed along a continuum of complexity. The neurologic systems utilized to complete visuomotor activities would have been repetitively taxed in order to facilitate a reorganization of this ability.

Data-Based and Directed Treatment

The need for treatment that is data-based is certainly not unique to the discipline of cognitive rehabilitation. Accountability issues related to progress in treatment are popular topics in all rehabilitation specialties. The Process-Specific Approach lends itself well to data-based planning because performance on most tasks can be described by empirical measurements of accuracy and speed. The data derived facilitate treatment decision making. For example, if scores on a cognitive task reach a plateau and no further progress is demonstrated, a clinician might try to develop a branch step that makes the task easier in order to move the patient beyond a particularly difficult spot. Ongoing evaluation of the utility and efficacy of a clinical treatment tool is also possible, given these data. Sound decision making about when to continue, modify, or terminate a particular treatment activity can be made.

Figure 2.1 provides an illustration of a data collection sheet used to gather objective performance information.

An adjunct rationale for collecting data on therapy performance concerns the motivation and level of investment that a patient has in his or her performance. Many patients can understand a performance graph. Use of such a visual aid can be very helpful in educating a patient about his or her progress. Similarly, goals can be set that the patient can try to exceed in subsequent therapy sessions.

Generalization Probes

How does the clinician know if therapy is effective? As described in the beginning of this chapter, the actual therapy tasks used within the cognitive

visuomotor —

Task:				
Date:				
% Correct:				
Time:				
Observations:				
Date:				
% Correct:				
Time:				
Observations:				
Date:				
% Correct:				
Time:				
Observations:				
Date:				
% Correct:				
Time:				
Observations:				
Date:				
% Correct:				
Time:				
Observations:				
Date:				
% Correct:				
Time:				
Observations:				

FIGURE 2.1 Generic data collection chart. Permits recording of accuracy and speed of performance variables, which can be compared across trials.

anecdotal- a short, entertaining
account of some event.

rehabilitation session provide a means to access the impaired cognitive process. The clinician is only interested in performance on the task insofar as it correlates to improved neuropsychologic functioning. One might expect to see improvement on tasks simply as a result of practice, given repetitive administration of the therapy exercises. In order to demonstrate improved cognitive functioning, gains on unpracticed measures of cognitive functioning must be noted. This is accomplished through periodic administration of neuropsychologic tests sensitive to the cognitive process being trained. Of course, the tests used must have little practice effect or must contain alternate forms for repeated administration.

A second, less objective but equally important, means of assessing whether treatment is resulting in improved cognitive functioning is to elicit anecdotal information from other staff or family members who observe the patient's performance in everyday environments. Functioning in real-world, practical tasks is an important indicator of level and changes in cognitive functioning. If no change in functional ability is evident, any therapeutically measured gains in neuropsychologic status need to be questioned.

Gordon (1987) describes therapy generalization as occurring on three levels:

Level 1. At the most fundamental level, it is expected that remediation results should generalize from one treatment session to another as well as to alternate forms of the same training materials.

Level 2. A higher level of generalization is evident when improvement is demonstrated on neuropsychologic tests that contain similar cognitive requirements but different task demands than those of therapy tasks.

Level 3. The highest level of generalization involves transfer of ability gained in the treatment sessions to functioning as it occurs in natural day-to-day living.

Untrained normative neuropsychologic measures provide objective data regarding whether cognitive processing is, indeed, improving with therapy. Observation of functioning in real-world tasks provides a qualitative functional indicator of progress. Attention to these two sources of information allows evaluation of all three important levels of generalization.

Case Studies

The case of a 30-year-old male 2 years after closed head injury secondary to a motor vehicle accident provides a good illustration. Following initial neuropsychologic testing, which included administration of the *Paced Auditory Serial Addition Task* (PASAT) (a sensitive test of attentional processing—see Chapter 6), cognitive rehabilitation began with Attention Process Training. The patient received 4 weeks of intensive training on a

elicit — to draw forth; to evoke a response

premorbid—

constellation of tasks that targeted sustained attention. This included serial numbers (backward subtraction exercises) and cancellation tasks. Following this period, the PASAT was readministered, with a gain of 1 standard deviation noted on all three trials of the test. This represented a significant decline from estimated premorbid levels of functioning but an improvement since the beginning of treatment. Reports from the occupational therapist regarding meal preparation included observations that the patient's attention ability remained poor. He could only pay attention to one task at a time and could not prepare more than a one-item meal.

Attention Process Training continued with the addition of a divided-attention component, using activities that targeted simultaneous processing of more than one stimulus. Following an additional 4 weeks of treatment, the PASAT was readministered and showed an additional improvement of 1 standard deviation across trials. This brought the patient's score to within the low-average range. Simultaneously, the occupational therapist reported that the patient was able to attend to two burners on the stove, and the quality of meal preparation had improved. Thus, both the neuropsychologic and naturalistic measures suggested that there was an improvement in attention ability. Of course, there is no sure way of knowing that a positive correlation existed between cognitive therapy and improvements on functional tasks, but attention to naturalistic uses of cognitive processes encourages the clinician to evaluate this important aspect of patient functioning.

Another example illustrates the utility of generalization probes. A 47-year-old male, 3 years after closed head injury secondary to an industrial accident, underwent 6 weeks of Visual Process Training. The patient was demonstrating steady, consistent gains on individual visual processing therapy tasks. However, administration of the Perceptual Speed Cluster from the Woodcock–Johnson Psycho-Educational Battery (Woodcock & Johnson, 1977) indicated no change in visual processing as measured by this test. Anecdotal reports from the spouse regarding visual processing with respect to household tasks also suggested no gains. Following an additional 3 weeks of training with no change noted in generalization probes, cognitive rehabilitation in the form of retraining of visual processing was discontinued, and a wholly functional, compensatory orientation to therapy began. The use of generalization probes allowed the decision to be made that recovery of visual perceptual ability was limited, and alternative, and more appropriate, therapy techniques could then be implemented. In select cases, the Process-Specific Approach may not be realistic, and a purely functional orientation may need to be set up. Generalization probes enable the clincan to make this decision.

usefulness,

Ultimate Measures of Success

This final principle of process-specific therapy is a reminder that the ultimate measure of success in therapy lies with improvements in living and work status rather than changes on test scores. It is important for the cognitive rehabilitation therapist to be aware of the vocational and living issues relevant to his or her patients, even if he or she is not the actual case manager. The cognitive therapist can provide other specialties with relevant information about cognitive strengths and weaknesses and any changes in cognitive status, so that maximum levels of independent living and vocational (or avocational) pursuits can be identified.

The above six therapy principles define the Process-Specific Approach to cognitive rehabilitation. Basically, this approach holds that cognitive processes such as Attention, Visual Processing, Memory, Executive Functions, and Problem Solving can be improved in many brain-injured individuals given repeated and targeted stimulation of specific theoretically derived components of the deficit cognitive process. The implementation of therapy that is data based and whose efficacy is measured via generalization probes allows the clinician to make treatment decisions that will ultimately result in maximum levels of cognitive functioning that can assist a patient in increasing his or her vocational and independent-living potential.

DESIGNING THEORETICALLY BASED COGNITIVE REHABILITATION PROGRAMS

Thus far, this chapter has reviewed the therapy principles involved in implementing the Process-Specific Approach to cognitive rehabilitation. What about the process that must occur before treatment implementation? What are the steps that are taken to design a sound, theoretically based cognitive program that applies the therapy principles? The first treatment principle of the Process-Specific Approach prescribes the use of a theoretical model. How have the models presented in this text been derived?

Although many sources have acknowledged the gap between theory and practice within the context of cognitive remediation, there is not much available information suggesting how one might correct this state of affairs. The individuals implementing cognitive retraining programs often are not equipped with the knowledge of brain–behavior relationships to enable them to develop theoretically motivated treatment programs. Similarly, those professionals armed with the needed background in cognitive functions frequently do not have experience in implementing behaviorally oriented therapy programs. Given such a discrepancy, how can we achieve an integration of theory and practice such that effective cognitive remediation programs grounded in established neuropsychologic principles will be available? What follows is a description of the process involved in designing theoretically based cognitive remediation programs such as those presented in this text. As our understanding of cognition, neurology, and mechanisms of recovery increases, clinical models will need to be updated. It is thus useful to have an appreciation of the development process.

Over the past five years, a number of cognitive retraining programs that are theoretically based have been developed at Good Samaritan Hospital's Center for Cognitive Rehabilitation. Our experience with these programs suggests that information must be collected from a range of scientific and clinical sources in order to generate rehabilitation programs that address the clinical manifestations of cognitive dysfunction seen in the brain-injured patient and that utilize sound pedagogy from the cognitive sciences. There are essentially three stages that should be acknowledged when attempting to design theoretically based cognitive rehabilitation programs (see Table 2.1). These include an *information collection phase,* a *program development phase,* and an *efficacy evaluation phase.*

There are basically four steps within the information-gathering phase, which requires a review of three distinct bodies of information as well as careful observation of the patient population. The first step is to gain an

TABLE 2.1 Stages for Designing Theoretically Based Cognitive Rehabilitation Programs

Stage	Step	Action	Goal
Information gathering	1	Review cognitive psychology literature	To understand nature of cognitive process in the normal brain
	2	Review neuropsychologic literature	To understand established scientific processes related to pathology in cognitive process area
	3	Examine current clinical remediation practice	Gain appreciation of which techniques have been successful and where shortcomings exist
	4	Observe cognitively impaired patients	To be aware of clinical manifestations of impaired cognitive process
Program development	5	Outline theoretical components of cognitive process areas	Develop theoretically based treatment model
	6	Design hierarchically organized treatment tasks for each component of theoretical model	Produce clinical remediation program
Efficacy evaluation	7	Run clinical trials	Assess efficacy and success of rehabilitation program

appreciation of the cognitive functioning in the normal individual by examining the cognitive psychology literature relevant to the particular cognitive process for which the remediation program is being designed. The next step also requires review of the literature, but it is directed at the neuropsychology/neurology field and has as its goal understanding the processes related to the pathology of a specific cognitive function. Examination of clinical rehabilitation models that are currently in use is the next logical step in gathering the information required to adequately design theoretically motivated cognitive rehabilitation programs. Completion of this third step may reveal certain techniques that have been established as efficacious and may also highlight limitations of current programs. The final information source to be tapped is the patient population itself. Careful observation of the clinical manifestations of cognitive impairment within the head-injured population will permit development of programs that target relevant areas of dysfunction.

The second phase, program development, consists of two steps that permit development of the actual rehabilitation treatment techniques. One of these (Step 5 in Table 2.1) outlines the theoretical components that comprise the cognitive area (utilizing the information gathered in the previous phase). Once the theoretical model has been established, hierarchically organized treatment tasks can be designed that tap each of the components in the theoretical model (Step 6). Following completion of this phase, a theoretically based clinical retraining program will be in place.

Finally, during the last phase, treatment efficacy is assessed. Clinical trials are run using the cognitive retraining program with the head-injury patients for whom it was designed. Based on the results of treatment efficacy studies, the program is modified appropriately, and further clinical trials are implemented to evaluate the effectiveness of changes.

The seven steps that comprise the three phases, information gathering, program development, and efficacy evaluation, provide an outline of the procedures necessary to produce effective cognitive rehabilitation programs based on established scientific and clinical principles. Certainly these procedures do not constitute a fast or easy process but, instead, require careful research and development that is both time consuming and dependent on availability of financial and investigatory resources. However, if we are to develop theoretically motivated cognitive retraining programs, this lengthy process needs to be followed.

MICROCOMPUTER USE IN COGNITIVE REHABILITATION

No chapter reviewing general procedures of cognitive rehabilitation would be complete without some discussion of the use of microcomputers in cognitive rehabilitation. Bracy (1985) conducted a study demonstrating that

73% of the centers surveyed that reported providing cognitive rehabilitation services used microcomputers in their clinical work with head-injured patients. Today, that number is presumably much greater. Computers have evolved from elaborate game machines to sophisticated instruments that deal with complex strategy and abstract thinking. Initially, their use was more restricted to developing reflexes and visuomotor coordination, whereas now they are used to facilitate concentration and problem solving as well.

Listed below are some of the advantages of microcomputer use in cognitive rehabilitation:

1. Consistent, often adjustable, rate of stimulus presentation.
2. Automatic collection and tabulation of performance data.
3. Efficient administration of tedious practice tasks.
4. Objective feedback.
5. Freeing of clinicians to observe and record valuable qualitative data that may be lost or forgotten in the course of administering even a simple task numerous times.

Microcomputer use fits well within the context of the Process-Specific Approach to cognitive rehabilitation. As the list above suggests, computers can help clinicians to deliver stimuli in a consistent, objective, and repetitive manner and to keep performance data. They allow data-based treatment with the use of hierarchically organized treatment tasks. Software programs can be selected that address certain components of specific cognitive processes.

Computers have proven most useful for working on Attention, Visual Processing, and Reasoning/Problem Solving. To date they have not been an effective means for rehabilitating memory. Most memory programs involve recall practice drills that try to increase the amount of information that the patient can remember. Studies have not shown such exercises to enhance memory (Glisky & Schacter, 1986). Similarly, certain aspects of language are not amenable to computerized retraining. Interactional therapy between the patient and clinician appears to be more effective for addressing impaired pragmatics or speech.

Although computers have advantages, an important caution is warranted regarding their use. Placing a patient in front of the computer will not automatically result in effective therapy. Quality therapy arises from careful planning and astute analysis of performance data. A selection of appropriate software programs is critical. It is important that the clinician know why a particular program is being used and how it fits into the treatment model. When evaluating a computer program for possible use within a therapy plan, a clinician will first review the program for its therapeutic merit. If it appears clinically sound, the therapist would then decide what type of cognitive process it addresses and determine where it fits within the theoreti-

astute

cal model used. Finally, the clinician would prepare a data collection sheet (if one did not come with the program). The computer program would then be ready to be included as one of the available therapy tasks. Considerations in selecting appropriate software necessarily involve evaluation of both clinical and administrative features. Below are eight important clinical considerations for choosing software:

1. Does the accompanying literature clearly define the objectives of the program?
2. Does the program address what it claims to address?
3. Is the reinforcement and feedback immediate, friendly, and age-appropriate?
4. Is the program interesting?
5. Are the instructions easy to follow?
6. Are appropriate and useful data collected and analyzed?
7. Where would this program fit within the treatment model that the clinician uses?
8. How much supervision is needed?

There are also six important questions to ask from an administrative standpoint regarding selection of computer software:

1. Is the program free of bugs and technological problems?
2. Are any types of extra equipment needed to run the program (e.g., game paddles, a special circuit board)?
3. Can screen advance be controlled?
4. Can the clinician add unique content to the disk so that additional stimuli will be available?
5. Are back-up disks available for a small fee?
6. Can software be returned after an initial review period?

Cognitive rehabilitation software can be obtained from a number of different software companies, some of which sell programs specifically designed for cognitive rehabilitation and some of which sell general educational software programs appropriate for cognitive rehabilitation. See the Appendix for a list.

As with all aspects of therapy, a certain amount of ingenuity and creativity is required to maximize potential therapy effects. There are a variety of ways to adapt computer hardware to meet the needs of particular handicaps. Whole books have been written about devices such as adaptive keyboards that accommodate particular physical handicaps. Similarly, there may be ways to modify the software to make it more usable. For example, a clinician might put stickers or marks on the screen to make a particular content more clear. Some disks allow addition to original stimuli and thus increase or decrease difficulty level. Competition might be used to motivate and facilitate more effortful participation, whereby a clinician simultaneously responds to information on the screen and "races" the patient when using a reaction time paradigm. Collection of data other than those provided by the computer may also make a program more suitable for a particular patient. In summary, effective use of computers requires the clinician to evaluate the individual patient and program and implement adaptations accordingly.

EVALUATING THERAPY PROGRAMS

A clinician needs to be critical when implementing any cognitive rehabilitation program. This chapter has described the process for designing a theoretically based cognitive rehabilitation program in addition to discussing issues related to treatment implementation. Diller and Gordon (1981) note that a remediation program should be as well planned as a good experiment. They provide a list of questions that are helpful for evaluating both commercially available and self-designed cognitive rehabilitation programs:

What cognitive deficit is being treated?
How is the deficit operationalized in measurable terms?
What are the stimuli that elicit the deficit, and how can they be manipulated to make them easier or harder?
What are the responses that serve as indicators of the deficit?
What is the content of the treatment? How is the program administered? How often? What standards are set for continuing, altering, or stopping the program?

SUMMARY

Currently there are a number of different approaches to cognitive rehabilitation. One common limitation is the close alliance of cognitive rehabilitation with particular treatment facilities, making it difficult to implement treatment procedures in an independent setting. Also, very few approaches to cognitive rehabilitation are theoretically based or related to established principles in the cognitive sciences.

The Process-Specific Approach offers an alternative, effective orientation to managing cognitive impairments. It consists of the following treatment principles: theoretically motivated models defining each cognitive process, repetition, hierarchically organized treatment tasks, data-based treatment, use of generalization probes, and ultimate measures of vocational and independent-living success. The basic assumption of this approach is the ability to improve distinct cognitive processes through targeted treatment.

The design of theoretically motivated cognitive rehabilitation is a three-step process involving information gathering, program development, and efficacy evaluation. Although this is a cumbersome process, it is important that therapy programs be developed that are theoretically sound.

Microcomputers offer an effective and convenient means of delivering therapy stimuli. Clinicians need to be judicious in selecting and using particular software programs. Programs should fit within a particular therapy plan and support specified therapy goals.

STUDY QUESTIONS

1. What are the primary limitations of many of the current approaches to cognitive rehabilitation?
2. What are the essential components of the Process-Specific Approach to cognitive rehabilitation that might distinguish it from other therapy orientations?
3. Why is repetition an important therapy principle within the Process-Specific Approach?
4. Describe the three phases involved in designing theoretically based cognitive rehabilitation programs.
5. What are some of the advantages of microcomputers in cognitive rehabilitation?
6. What should a clinician consider when selecting cognitive rehabilitation software?

REFERENCES

Adamovich, B., Henderson, J., & Auerbach, S. (1985). *Cognitive Rehabilitation of Closed Head Injured Patients: A Dynamic Approach*. San Diego: College Hill Press.

Bracy, O. (1985). Cognitive retraining through computers: Fact or fad? *Cognitive Rehabilitation* 3(2):10–23.

Diller, C., & Gordon, W. A. (1981). Rehabilitation and clinical neuropsychology. In S. Filskov & T. Boll (Eds.), *Handbook of Clinical Neuropsychology*. New York: John Wiley & Sons.

Glisky, E., & Schacter, D. (1986). Remediation of organic memory disorders: current status and future prospects. *Journal of Head Trauma Rehabilitation* 1(3):54–63.

Goldstein, G., & Ruthven, L. (1983). *Rehabilitation of the brain-damaged adult*. New York: Plenum.

Gordon, W. (1987). Methodological considerations in cognitive remediation. In M. Meier, A. Benton, & L. Diller (Eds.), *Neuropsychological rehabilitation.* New York: Guilford.

Mateer, C. A., & Sohlberg, M. M. (1988). Paradigm shift in memory rehabilitation. In N. Whitaker (Ed.), *Neuropsychological studies of nonfocal brain damage: Dementia and trauma* (pp. 202–225). New York: Springer-Verlag.

Prigatano, G. (1986). *Neuropsychological rehabilitation after brain injury.* Baltimore: Johns Hopkins University Press.

Sohlberg, M. M., & Mateer, C. A. (1987). Effectiveness of an attention training program. *Journal of Clinical and Experimental Neuropsychology* 9(2):117–130.

Trexler, L. (1987). Neuropsychological rehabilitation in the United States. In M. Meier, A. Benton, L. & Diller (Eds.), *Neuropsychological rehabilitation.* New York: Guilford.

Woodcock, R., & Johnson, B. (1977). *Woodcock–Johnson Psycho-Educational Battery.* Boston: Teaching Resources Corporation.

APPENDIX: SOFTWARE SOURCES

A. W. Pellar & Associates
Educational Materials
249 Goffle Road
Hawthorne, NJ 07507

American Micro Media
Box 306
Red Hood, NY 12571
(914) 756-2557

Berta-Max, Inc.
Micro School Programs
3547 Stone Way, North
Seattle, WA 98103
(206) 547-4056

Brain-Link Software
317 Montgomery
Ann Arbor, MI 48103

C. C. Publications, Inc.
P.O. Box 23699
Tigard, OR 97223

Charles Clark Co., Inc.
168 Express Drive, South
Brentwood, NY 11717

Clinical Software Resources
2850 Windemere
Birmingham, MI 48008

Cognitive Rehabilitation Series
Speech & Language Pathology
William Beaumont Hospital
3601 West 13 Mile Road
Royal Oak, MI 48072

College-Hill Press
Software Division
4284 41st Street
San Diego, CA 92105

Communication Skill Builders
3130 North Dodge Boulevard
Tucson, AZ 85733

Computer Learning Center
(Public Domain Software)
P.O. Box 45202
Tacoma, WA 98445

Computer Learning Materials, Inc.
P.O. Box 1325
Ann Arbor, MI 48106

DLM/Teaching Resources
P.O. Box 4000
Allen, TX 75002

Dormac, Inc.
P.O. Box 1699
Beaverton, OR 97075

Educational Audio Visual (EAV)
Pleasantville, NY 10570
(800) 431-2196

Educational Instructional Systems,
  Inc.
2225 Grant Road, Suite 3
Los Altos, CA 94022
(415) 969-5212

Follett Library Book, Co.
4506 Northwest Highway
Crystal Lake, IL 60014
(800) 435-6170

GAMCO
Box 310-P
Big Spring, TX 79720
(915) 267-6327

Hartley Courseware, Inc.
123 Bridge
Dimondale, MI 48821

J. L. Hammett, Co.
Box 545
Braintree, MA 02184
(800) 225-5467

K-12 Micro-Media
Box 17
Valley Cottage, NY 10989
(201) 391-7555

Laureate Learning Systems, Inc.
One Mill Street
Burlington, VT 85401 ·

Life Science Associates
One Fenimore Road
Bayport, NY 11705
(516) 472-2111

Lingguest Software, Inc.
3349 Beard Road
Napa, CA 94558

Lingui Systems, Inc.
1630 Fifth Avenue, Suite 806
Moline, IL 61265

Merit Computer Resource Center
3701 N. W. 50th
Oklahoma City, OK 73112

Microcomputer Implementation
4101 Somerset Lane
Kent, WA 98032

Opportunities for Learning
8950 Lurline Avenue
Chatsworth, CA 91311
(213) 341-2535

Parrot Software
190 Sandy Ridge Road
State College, PA 16801

Psychological Software Services
P.O. Box 29205
Indianapolis, IN 46229

Reston Publishing Co.
c/o Prentice Hall
Englewood Cliffs, NJ 07632

Scholastic
904 Sylvan Avenue
Englewood Cliffs, NJ 07632

Society for Visual Education (SVE)
Department VB
1345 Diversey Parkway
Chicago, IL 60614

Sunburst
39 Washington Avenue
Pleasantville, NY 10570
(800) 431-1934

Sunset Software
11750 Sunset Blvd., Suite 414
Los Angeles, CA 90049

The Micro Center
Box 6
Pleasantville, NY 10570
(914) 769-6002, (800) 431-2434

3
Issues Related to Documentation

This chapter covers several issues related to the documentation of treatment efficacy. Some of these issues arise from the newness of the field of cognitive rehabilitation. Because few standardized assessment and treatment protocols exist, each cognitive rehabilitation program that is implemented has the potential to make a significant clinical and scientific contribution. There is no usual and customary standard of care to treat cognitive impairments. Although it is an exciting proposition for today's clinicians to take part in creating a discipline, this also carries some responsibility. Each professional delivering cognitive rehabilitation services has the responsibility to document therapy outcomes systematically and to make informed clinical decisions regarding whether or not therapy is working. Documentation plays an important role in treatment, reimbursement, and credibility of the field.

Single-case experimental designs are well suited to the clinical and research functions that clinicians may encounter. Their advantages and limitations are described in this chapter in some detail. Other topics addressed include standardized classification systems, quantitative and qualitative analysis of performance data, trend and level changes, features of single-subject experimental designs, external validity, and overview of design types.

STANDARDIZED CLASSIFICATIONS

There are several standardized protocols for categorizing level of recovery that clinicians use to document improvement. The most common include the Glasgow Coma Scale (Jennett & Bond, 1975; Jennett, Snoak, Bond, & Brooks, 1981) used for acute patients in a coma, the Rancho Los Amigos Scale of Cognitive Level and Expected Behavior (Hagen & Malkmus, 1979), and the Glasgow Outcome Scale (Jennett et al., 1981) used for all levels of patients. Although these measures are useful for certain actuarial or epidemiologic studies, limitations in their use should be recognized.

The Glasgow Coma Scale (GCS) (Jennett & Bond, 1975) is designed to determine depth of coma and to monitor emergence from coma after closed head injury by rating the degree of eye opening, the highest verbal response, and the best motor response (see Table 3.1 and discussion of coma in Chapter 5). The GCS is only useful during the period the individual is in a comatose or semicomatose state. Although some actuarial predictions about long-term recovery for groups of individuals are provided by the GCS, individual recovery is best estimated by the patient's own performance levels over time.

The Disability Rating Scale (DRS) (Rappaport et al., 1982) incorporates the Glasgow Coma Scale as a measure of arousability, awareness, and responsiveness. It also rates cognitive ability for activities of daily living as well as employability on separate 4-point scales. Cognitive levels of independence are scaled along a 6-point continuum. There is an overall summed index represented in a total DRS score. One benefit of the scale is that it addresses a wide range of functioning from coma to community activity.

The Ranch Los Amigos Scale of Cognitive Level and Expected Behavior (Hagen & Malkmus, 1979) describes levels of cognitive and behavioral function that form a hierarchy of stages through which a head-injured person can progress as recovery occurs (see Table 3.2). The scale is used to identify a patient's highest level of cognitive functioning throughout the rehabilitation period. Although this scale reflects common trends in recov-

TABLE 3.1 Glasgow Coma Scale

Eyes	Open	Spontaneously	4
		To verbal command	3
		To pain	2
	No response		1
Best motor response	To verbal command	Obeys	6
	To painful stimulus	Localizes pain	5
		Flexion, withdrawal	4
		Flexion, abnormal (decerebrate rigidity)	3
		Extension (decerebrate rigidity)	2
		No response	1
Best verbal response		Oriented and converses	5
		Disoriented and converses	4
		Inappropriate words	3
		Incomprehensible sounds	2
		No response	1
Total			3–15

Note. From "Disability after severe head injury: Observations on the use of the Glasgow Outcome Scale" by B. Jennett, J. Snoak, M. Bond, and N. Brooks, 1981. *Journal of Neurology, Neurosurgery, and Psychiatry,* 44:285–293. Copyright 1981. Reprinted with permission.

TABLE 3.2 Rancho Los Amigos Scale of Cognitive Levels and Expected Behavior

Level I	Response	Unresponsive to all stimuli.
Level II	Generalized	Inconsistent, nonpurposeful, nonspecific reactions to stimuli; responds to pain, but response may be delayed
Level III	Localized response	Inconsistent reaction directly related to type of stimulus presented; responds to some commands; may respond to discomfort
Level IV	Confused, agitated response	Disoriented and unaware of present events with frequent bizarre and inappropriate behavior; attention span is short and ability to process information is impaired
Level V	Confused, inappropriate, nonagitated response	Nonpurposeful random or fragmented responses when task complexity exceeds abilities; patient appears alert and responds to simple commands; performs previously learned tasks but is unable to learn new ones
Level VI	Confused, appropriate response	Behavior is goal-directed; responses are appropriate to the situation with incorrect responses because of memory difficulties
Level VII	Automatic, appropriate response	Correct routine responses that are robot-like; appears oriented to setting, but insight, judgment, and problem solving are poor
Level VIII	Purposeful, appropriate response	Correct responding carryover of new learning; no required supervision, poor tolerance for stress, and some abstract reasoning difficulties

Note. From "Intervention strategies for language disorders secondary to head trauma" by C. Hagen and D. Malkmus, 1979. Atlanta: American Speech–Language–Hearing Association.

ery, it does little to clarify the status of the individual patient's cognitive processes at a particular time. For example, the scale assumes that abstract reasoning will be the last cognitive function to return. Although this is certainly a high-level thinking skill, depending on a patient's site and type of injury, abstract reasoning may be intact while attention and memory are poor. Over an extended cognitive rehabilitation program, changes in specific aspects of cognitive ability may not be reflected.

The Glasgow Outcome Scale (Jennett et al., 1981) has five categories (0–4), ranging from good recovery to persistent vegetative state. This scale has little of the heterogeneity in eventual cognitive, living, and vocational status that characterizes the head-injured population.

Cognitive status is best described by the level of functioning in each cognitive process area. The Good Samaritan Hospital's Cognitive Behavioral Rating Scale was developed specifically to delineate cognitive areas that may be impaired. The scale is broken down by cognitive processes and allows the clinician to look at each process separately. Functional tasks corresponding to the cognitive process are ranked, which increases the utility of the scale. (See the Appendix for sample portions of this scale.) Careful description of initial levels of functioning in attention/concentration, memory, visual processing, reasoning/problem solving, executive functions, and language will allow the clinician to assess treatment efficacy as intervention is applied to each deficit cognitive process.

DOCUMENTATION RELEVANT TO REIMBURSEMENT

Documentation of cognitive rehabilitation efforts is necessary for financial as well as clinical reasons. Cognitive rehabilitation comes under a number of different reimbursement schemes, and its coverage is less straightforward than that for other medical and rehabilitative procedures. As described in Chapter 1, it extends the service delivery continuum from medical care delivered in a hospital to community reentry services delivered in a nonmedical setting. Thus, payment may come from both medical care providers such as insurance companies and funding agencies that support vocational rehabilitation or independent-living skills training.

Depending on the agency providing payment, the clinician will need to document specific clinical information. If the Division for Vocational Rehabilitation in a particular state is paying for a cognitive rehabilitation program, it will want to know how cognitive rehabilitation relates to increased vocational potential. If a medical insurance company is the responsible reimbursement party, it will require information about how the impaired cognitive process is a direct result of the injury. The cognitive rehabilitation therapist thus needs to document more than treatment efficacy. He or she needs to be aware of the functional implications related to vocational potential, independent-living potential, and psychosocial adjustment as well as neuropsychologic functioning. These issues are examined in more detail in the last section of this book.

Sometimes there is pending litigation in a case where, for example, the patient is taking legal action to get compensation for an injury. In this situation, a clinician may be called on to provide information relevant to damage and recovery. Sometimes this involves ethical dilemmas for the clinician. Perhaps a patient stands to receive a larger settlement for greater impairments. This might reduce the incentive to improve with therapy. Clinicians need to be aware of such issues and should talk to the patient's attorney about the pending litigation, if appropriate. Discussion of and agreement about treatment goals is a necessary step prior to therapy implementation in such cases.

In addition to meeting the needs of third-party payers and professionals in the legal area, documentation is needed to demonstrate treatment efficacy, since cognitive rehabilitation is such a new field. Because there is no well-established system of reimbursement for cognitive rehabilitation services, many people are currently denied this therapy. If clinicians can provide empirical evidence supporting the efficacy of cognitive rehabilitation, reluctance to pay may be reduced. Attention to treatment outcomes, including neuropsychologic changes and improvement in vocational and independent-living ability, will begin to strengthen the belief that this is an area worthy of payment. If treatment outcomes are positive, state and private agencies will save money by paying the short-term rehabilitation costs rather than the long-term disability payments (Sohlberg & Brock, 1985).

ANALYZING PERFORMANCE DATA

Analyzing Performance on Therapy Tasks

The first level of patient performance that may be analyzed is the treatment data collected for performance on a particular therapy task. There are both quantitative and qualitative performance parameters that need to be examined for every therapy exercise. The specific assessment parameters will change, of course, depending on what the clinician is targeting. For example, one individual might perform a particular task in order to work on speed of information processing, whereas for another patient, the same task might be used to address visuospatial skills. In the former case, the clinician might be measuring rate of accurate responses, and in the latter case, information relevant to spatial ability, such the number of times an object was manipulated with correct spatial orientation would be analyzed. Thus, it is important for the clinician to determine a priori what it is he or she is targeting and then to set up a scoresheet to collect the relevant information. In the following section principles important to the collection and analysis of therapy performance data are discussed. This includes a discussion of the measurement of more quantitative as well as qualitative performance parameters.

Quantitative Parameters

Quantitative data are performance results that can be described using some sort of empirical index. Possible examples include the following:

- *Accuracy measures:* number of errors, percentage correct, number correct, etc.
- *Time:* speed of performance, rate of responding, latency of response, etc.
- *Cuing parameters:* amount and type of cuing utilized, number of self-corrects, etc.

Again, the type of data to be collected depends on the nature of the task and what exactly the clinician is interested in measuring. Careful recording of task conditions, as well as task performance, is essential when a clinician is delivering cognitive rehabilitation therapy.

Cuing is a particularly important part of the objective measurement process. Under the Process-Specific Approach to cognitive rehabilitation, the clinician attempts to activate the target deficit process repetitively via administration of specific cognitive tasks. Cuing will help achieve the level at which the task is appropriately exercising the cognitive mechanism and is neither too easy nor too hard.

It is important to quantify and standardize cuing so that trials may be compared with each other. For example, a patient working on Serial Numbers Exercises (backwards subtraction tasks targeting sustained attention) may at first have to write down the last number he or she said in order to hold onto it. This might be considered a branch step or a specific form of cuing. Gradually, as the patient's mental control ability improves, he or she may be able to retain the sequence and perform the mental arithmetic without the aid of paper and pen. The clinician then would want to compare trials within each specific cuing mode. Time and accuracy may not be as good initially under the more advanced, less cued condition; thus, it will be important for the clinician to document the presence of any particular cuing.

Qualitative Parameters

Qualitative data refer to the documentation of important clinical conditions and impressions. It is not possible to quantify all relevant aspects of clinical performance. Sample qualitative information that might be important to document include the following:

1. *Internal factors:* unusual degrees of fatigue, depression, distraction, anxiety, as well as positive states such as increased confidence.
2. *External factors:* excess noise, interruptions, uncomfortable room temperature, faulty materials (e.g., stopwatch did not engage or blip in computer disk), etc.
3. *Distinctive error patterns:* errors grouped at beginning or end of therapy task.

Qualitative data allow the clinician to go beyond the specific performance data and to examine why a certain performance profile was demonstrated. It is not enough to know that an error occurred; the clinician must examine *why* it occurred. The reasons may be very different for two individuals. Error patterns within a task can be very revealing and can provide valuable guidance for therapy planning.

There are three common error patterns that may be exhibited during task performance that can help the clinician diagnose problem areas: increasing errors over time, difficulty achieving ready-set, and inadequate comprehension of task instructions. The first pattern, increasing errors over time, is very common in head-injured persons, as it is often indicative of inadequate sustained attention. It may be expressed as a consistently increasing number of errors, frequency of mistakes, or latency of response. This profile suggests some type of fatigue factor, such as loss of the task directions over time or a specific problem in maintaining attention. Consideration of such an error pattern will allow the clinician to examine more closely the source of the problem.

The converse of this pattern is a greater number of errors at the beginning of a task or right after a task juncture. When a therapist sees this, he or she might become suspicious that a patient has a poor ability to achieve a "ready-set." Sometimes, following brain injury, individuals have difficulty picking up a new task efficiently, and it takes them a while to "catch on." Thus, more errors are seen in the beginning of a task or whenever the task parameters are altered. Recognition of this problem may lead the clinician to target mental flexibility and new learning skills. Alternatively, the clinician might want to spend more time explaining and demonstrating new tasks before administering the particular exercise.

The third error pattern is evident when a patient simply does not understand the directions or is completely unable to do the task. This might be suspected when there are many errors throughout the task. In this case, the clinician will want either to provide more instruction or to move back to an easier level.

Latency of response can also provide a distinctive error pattern. In paced tasks in which the stimuli are generated by a second party (e.g., the clinician or computer provides therapy stimuli) and the patient has no control of the rate of presentation, a slow latency response can result in a high number of errors. If analysis of errors reveals that responses are simply late in coming and that a correct response occurs after subsequent stimuli have been presented, the clinician might be advised to target speed of information processing or to slow down the rate of stimulus presentation.

It is important for a clinician to document and quantify task performance, but this is not sufficient. Attention to response patterns and analysis of errors can provide very valuable clinical information.

Analyzing Performance Over Time

There are two major methods of analyzing performance data, both of which allow the clinician to make informed treatment decisions. One involves simple visual inspection of treatment data, and the other involves statistical analyses.

Visual inspection requires that the data be graphically displayed. This has two advantages: various characteristics of the data can be readily examined by the clinician, and it is useful for many patients to see a visual plot of their performance. An easy clinical system is to use a generic graph to which the clinician can add scales appropriate for that task (see Figure 3.1). Usually, the data are plotted so that the ordinate (vertical or y-axis) contains treatment results (dependent variable) and the abscissa (horizontal or x-axis) represents time. Typical ordinate values include such labels as number correct, percentage correct, or number of errors. Typical abscissa values include sessions or dates. Every time a clinician administers a task, he or she can plot performance. Over time, patterns can be analyzed that will guide treatment decisions. The basic parameters that the clinician can examine include (1) stability of baseline, (2) changes in trend, and (3) changes in level.

Analysis of the initial baseline is important in order to establish what would happen without intervention. This allows the clinician to have a comparison against which to judge treatment efficacy. If baseline measures are extremely variable, it is more difficult to identify treatment effects. In terms of cognitive rehabilitation, the baseline may consist of several neuropsychologic measures that determine level of functioning in a particular cognitive process.

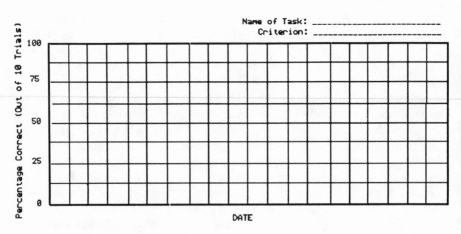

FIGURE 3.1 Generic graph for plotting performance on cognitive therapy tasks. Allows visualization of performance trends.

Changes in trend and level refer to the particular pattern that may be seen in the data. Trend involves the slope of changes over time. It is a systematic variation in the direction of the data. Level refers to the overall magnitude of performance. Often level changes will occur as the result of changes in cuing or alterations in the administration of the task. The clinician can analyze trend and level changes to get an idea of performance over time (see Figure 3.2).

There are a variety of statistical tests that may be applied to analyze data. Caution is warranted, however: statistical significance does not necessarily match clinical significance, and it is very important to have a good idea of what is occurring within the individual patient. A detailed description of statistical options is not provided in this text, since they are generally used for research rather than clinical purposes (with the exception of the Split-

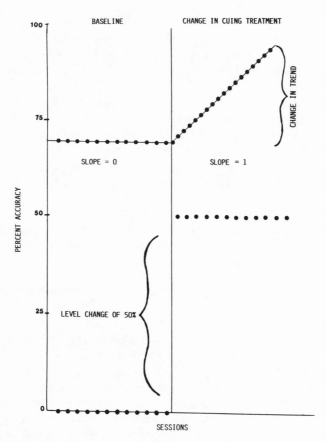

FIGURE 3.2 Illustration of trend and level changes. Trend changes show changes in rate of behavior, whereas level changes show variance in magnitude of behavior.

Middle Method; Kazdin, 1982a). Excellent reviews of these methods are provided elsewhere (e.g., Kazdin, 1976). Specific statistical analyses that may be used with single-case designs include conventional t and F tests, time series analyses, randomization tests, and the Split-Middle technique.

Single-subject or within-subject experimental designs provide an ideal method of documenting and possibly evaluating the efficacy of cognitive rehabilitation. These are discussed in the next section.

SINGLE-SUBJECT DESIGN

Group-oriented research designs hold a preeminent place in most areas of scientific inquiry. In group designs, there is usually an equivalent control group of subjects who do not receive intervention. Data are collected on treatment and no-treatment groups, and then statistical tests of significance are applied to see if any observed differences occurred by chance. The control group acts as a comparison and gives believability or internal validity to whether or not change can be attributed to the intervention. The researcher is interested in knowing if the variability between groups is bigger than the variability within groups. Although this is excellent for answering certain actuarial questions (e.g., What percentage of individuals treated using intervention X went back to employment?), it is not effective in examining behavior change in individuals over time, which is precisely what the cognitive rehabilitation specialist must strive to understand.

Wilson (1987) describes five limitations in the use of group studies to evaluate neuropsychologic rehabilitation:

1. Individual differences may be masked.
2. Group studies are usually carried out with homogeneous groups.
3. Statistical significance is emphasized more than clinical significance.
4. Group studies may take measurements at only one or two points in time.
5. Certain syndromes may be too rare to allow the forming of groups.

A major shortcoming of group designs is that they infer a functional relationship between treatment and behavior change by looking at group averages, which may not represent any one individual within the group. Individual differences can easily be masked in large designs. The second problem, the reliability or homogeneity, is particularly germane to the study of head injury. Most group studies are conducted using homogeneous groups. The head-injured population, however, varies greatly in cognitive parameters, which are difficult to control. If a group study demonstrated the efficacy of a perceptual skills training program, for example, it would be difficult to be confident whether other subjects would respond to treatment in the same way (Wilson, 1987).

Wilson (1987) also discusses the problem encountered when priority is placed on statistical significance over clinical significance. She uses bio-feedback therapy as an example of a therapy technique that might be shown to have statistically significant results but not result in any functional change. Conversely, clinical effects may occur in the absence of statistical significance. Ideally, both types of significance should be demonstrated.

A particularly large obstacle in group designs is the predominance of pre/posttest design formats, which only collect data at two times. In rehabilitation, therapists are interested in evaluating changes over time. The ability to identify patterns of change is essential for examining treatment effects and perhaps more importantly, for making timely changes in treatment programs.

Finally, in the field of head injury rehabilitation, rehabilitation specialists are continually presented with patients who present rather rare, exotic disorders (e.g., visual agnosias, capgras syndrome, cortical blindness). Studies on such cases would not be completed if groups of patients had to be identified (Wilson, 1987).

The distinguishing features of the single-subject design are that they are individually based and that the designs involve repeated measurement. Such characteristics are particularly well suited to examining rehabilitation outcomes. In single-case experimental studies, the performance of an individual is measured over time. Data are usually presented separately for each subject, although several individuals may be included in a single study. Internal validity—or the extent to which one can infer a functional relationship between intervention and response—comes through replication. Designs used to replicate treatment effects rely on intrasubject variability. Repeated measurements are taken as a function of sessions, trials, or time, which permits the assessment of treatment effects for each individual longitudinally.

Perhaps the main advantage of single-subject designs over group designs for cognitive rehabilitation purposes is that they allow the clinician/researcher to dissociate treatment effects from recovery factors that would occur in the absence of treatment. Single-subject experimental case studies begin by establishing a baseline that is used to predict the behavior of the independent variable if no intervention were to occur. Then treatment is introduced, and the examiner can look at the deviations from the predicted course of behavior.

McReynolds and Thompson (1986) summarized the following technical advantages of single-subject experimental designs:

1. *They are useful in identifying functional relationships.* Because they are experimental, single-subject designs permit examination of functional relationships between independent and dependent variables. Treatment is introduced while other variables are held constant, thereby allowing isola-

tion of the treatment in order to determine if it is responsible for changing the behavior.

2. *They allow exploration of intersubject variability.* These designs acknowledge that simply because individuals have a common problem (e.g., reduction in cognitive capacity), they are not necessarily homogeneous. Patients differ in both nature and degree of impairment, and they may vary in responsiveness to a treatment technique. In single-subject design, a functional relationship is first demonstrated between an independent variable (e.g., treatment) and a dependent variable (e.g., cognitive ability) in a single subject. Then, in order to establish generality, the procedure is replicated in other subjects.

3. *They allow exploration of intrasubject variability.* Single-subject designs also allow examination of variability within an individual. Since all of the designs require analysis of repeated measurements, the natural variability of the behaviors over time can be explored. The use of baseline measures additionally allows clinicians/researchers to examine behavior prior to treatment.

There are several practical and clinically relevant advantages to these designs. First of all, single-subject experimental designs produce objective data on the effects of clinical intervention that should be of interest to all cognitive rehabilitation specialists. Secondly, most of the designs are appropriate for a clinical setting. They are economical in terms of time needed to collect and analyze data. They also provide essential clinical evaluation tools, useful for a new field trying to pioneer effective treatment methods. The single-subject methodology allows evaluation of treatment efficacy and enables sound decisions to be made on when and how to modify a treatment program. Like case studies, which have traditionally held the most appeal for rehabilitation specialists, single-case designs are sensitive to the unique parameters surrounding the individual case. They preserve this individual focus but have the additional advantage of experimental control. (For a review of single-subject experimental methodology, see Kazdin, 1982a.)

The Multiple-Baseline Design is particularly useful because it closely approximates clinical format. The repeated measurements of specified behaviors required by this design are exactly those that should be part of properly documented cognitive rehabilitation. Clinicians can keep data on their client's performance (just as they should normally), and with a little added attention to trends and levels that exist in baseline and treatment conditions, treatment effects will have been demonstrated that are supported by scientific control. Although clinical and research needs may not always be exactly compatible (e.g., research may require an extended baseline), it is important to approach cognitive rehabilitation in a controlled, scientific manner in order to evaluate treatment efficacy.

Assessing Generality of Effect

External validity, or the extent to which one can generalize findings to other people or situations, is of great interest to both the scientific and clinical worlds. In group studies, it is evaluated through statistical analysis. Subject selection is based on random sampling techniques; thus, the subject sample is assumed to be a representative of the population from which it was drawn. In fact, however, it is difficult to form a truly representative group, and the populations studied are often not well defined. A statistically derived group average does not guarantee that the results are representative of even one individual within the study.

Generality in single-subject experimental studies is often thought to be problematic because inferences must be made from only one case. However, because the one subject is well described, there will be at least one individual with known characteristics for whom the study might be replicable.

Clinicians and clinical researchers need to know which individuals will benefit from treatment and under what conditions. Replication of treatment effects in single-subject designs addresses that issue. There are two types: direct replication and systematic replication. Direct replication establishes generality across the same subject type. The experiment is replicated across subjects and conditions that share all parameters that might be expected to be pertinent. External validity is demonstrated if similar treatment effects can be repeatedly demonstrated. The second approach, systematic replication, evaluates external validity by demonstrating treatment effects across different types of subjects, settings, or experimenters. Specific parameters such as subject age, therapist, or setting are systematically changed to see if treatment effects are still evident. The researcher can use these replications to establish the limits of external validity and demonstrate that treatment is effective despite changes in certain variables.

The experimental process can begin with treatment effects demonstrated in a single subject. This is followed by direct replication to establish treatment efficacy with similar individuals. Finally, the research process branches out to systematic replication, which allows examination of the effects of secondary characteristics.

There are certain threats to external validity or generalizability in single-subject designs of which clinicians need to be aware (Kazdin, 1977). Four of these threats are summarized below:

1. *Reactive effects of testing or observation.* For example, if a therapist is counting the frequency of a particular behavior, and the client is aware that he or she is being observed, there may be a corresponding increase or decrease in the frequency of the behavior that is independent of the treatment. One way to skirt this problem is to take covert or unobtrusive measures.

2. *Subject selection biases.* An interaction effect can occur between selection biases and the independent variable. In other words, a particular subject may be more responsive to treatment as a result of unique properties within that subject. A clinician/researcher can handle this potential threat by carefully describing the subject in a thorough manner.

3. *Reactive effects of experimental conditions.* Environment can present a threat to external validity if there are reactive effects of particular experimental arrangements. For example, the position of a chair in front of a computer monitor and the setting of the lights might be influential on a therapy task outcome. Again, careful description and documentation of treatment and research settings will reduce this problem.

4. *Multiple-treatment interference.* Multiple-treatment or sequence effects can occur when effects of prior treatment or other concurrent treatment interact with the target intervention and determine outcome. For instance, it may be that a particular treatment was successful only because the treatment session always followed an exercise class, which served to increase level of alertness. Careful control and documentation of possible variables are important for dealing with this potential threat to generality.

With these considerations in mind, we may now move on to describe actual single-subject designs.

Specific Design Methodology

There are five major types of single-subject experimental designs used in applied behavior analysis (Billingsley & Wolery, 1985; White, 1987). There are numerous extensions, modifications, and permutations of the designs, but these five provide a good sampling of the features of single-subject experimental studies. All of the single-subject designs share the following characteristics: (1) The dependent variable is measured repeatedly over time. (2) Believability of treatment results is established through replication.

Withdrawal Design

This is conceptually the simplest design and may also be referred to as the *sequential introduction, operant,* or *within-subject replication design.* It is the classic A–B–A or A–B–A–B design, where there is a successive alternation of A and B conditions. The A usually signifies the baseline conditions, and the B signifies the treatment conditions. Experimental control is demonstrated by a change in the level and trend of the data, dependent on the introduction or removal of the treatment. The more distinctive the change in data following change in treatment phases, the more believability is exhibited, and the more confident one can be that the effects seen are caused by the treatment.

The main advantages of this design are that only one behavior is required and that the replication of treatment effects provides solid evidence for demonstrating functional relationships. The major limitation is that the behavior must be reversible. That is, it must be possible for behavior changes to revert back to baseline levels when treatment is discontinued. Each condition must be independent of the other, so therapy that has lasting treatment effects will not be appropriate for this type of study. Interventions that have limited potential for carryover effects should be considered. Another limitation is that ethical problems may arise from the requirement that treatment be withdrawn. If treatment has been successful, it may not be clinically advisable to withdraw it. Finally, the withdrawal design is particularly susceptible to sequence effects described in the previous section.

The following hypothetical example illustrates this design. Suppose a clinician wished to examine the effects of particular type of cuing—such as the beep on a watch—to increase a memory-disordered patient's ability to remember to make entries in his or her memory notebook. The clinician could begin by charting the frequency of recording in the memory notebook without cuing. Once a clear, stable baseline was established, he or she could implement the watch-cuing procedure and continue charting. After a clear trend had been established with treatment, the watch could be removed to see if the frequency of memory notebook charting declined. If it was the cuing system that was maintaining the charting behavior, then there would presumably be a return toward baseline in this behavior. Of course, this design could only be used if the clinician felt that after being cued by the watch, the patient would not automatically adopt the behavior. In other words, this design would only be appropriate if it were predicted that there would be no long-lasting impact on the target behavior given the watch-cuing intervention (see Figure 3.3).

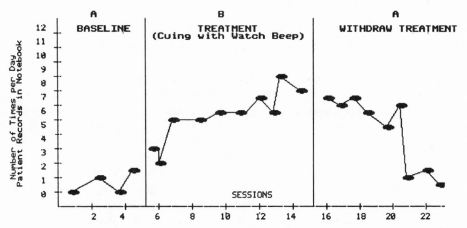

FIGURE 3.3 Sample of A–B–A treatment design showing effectiveness of cuing system for encouraging patient to write in memory notebook.

Multiple-Baseline Design

In this particular design, several behaviors or subjects are measured concurrently. It is a time-lag design that requires repeated measures of either (1) more than one behavior of a single subject, (2) one behavior in more than one setting, or (3) one behavior across several subjects. The behaviors that are selected for baselines should be independent of each other; they should not covary.

In a multiple-baseline design, treatment is introduced to each baseline at a different time, and any corresponding change in behaviors is noted. Control is established when there is a change only in the baseline to which the treatment is applied. All baselines are monitored from the first day to the conclusion of the experiment or program.

A study by Gianutsos and Gianutsos (1979) provides a clear example of the multiple-baseline-across-subjects design. Four brain-injured individuals participated in a series of 18 sessions. Two of them received treatment early (following six baseline sessions), and the other two began treatment later (following twelve sessions). Improvements were associated with the introduction of treatment (regardless of when it was initiated) (see Figure 3.4). Another example of a Multiple Baseline Design examining treatment efficacy for Attention Process Training is presented in Chapter 6.

The main advantage of the Multiple-Baseline Design is that it does not require the withdrawal of treatment. It also affords an opportunity to observe the effects of a single treatment across different behaviors, settings, or subjects. The primary limitation is that it requires measurement of multiple behaviors; thus, it is more logistically complicated. A larger number of observations and greater amount of time are required.

Changing Criterion Design

The Changing Criterion Design (Hartmann & Hall, 1976) may be considered a variation of the Multiple-Baseline Design but is distinctive enough to be described separately. It is a sort of Multiple-Baseline Design with a single behavior. Repeated measurements are taken on one behavior with the requirement of a stable baseline. Treatment is introduced in a stepwise fashion with the purpose of bringing the behavior to increasingly stricter criterion with each successive change in the criterion. The behavior must occur at a stable rate at each criterion level before the patient progresses to the next criterion. Experimental control is demonstrated by a consistent shift in the rate of the target behavior as each successive criterion is applied. For example, following a baseline measurement, a subject might initially be reinforced for achieving 50% accuracy on a computerized therapy task, then 70%, and then 100%. If performances closely approximate the criterion in each phase, experimental control is demonstrated.

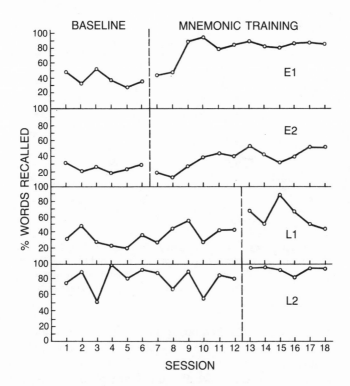

FIGURE 3.4 Sample of Multiple-Baseline, Across Subjects design. The time of intervention is staggered across subjects. Evaluates whether changes in performance are associated with the initiation of mnemonic training. From "Rehabilitating the verbal recall of brain injured patients by mnemonic training: An experimental demonstration using single-case methodology" by R. Gianutsos and J. Gianutsos, 1979. *Journal of Clinical Neuropsychology, 1*:117–135. Reprinted by permission.

The design is advantageous in that it does not require a withdrawal of treatment, and there is no need to measure multiple behaviors. It can be difficult to implement, however, because it is hard to judge both how large the change in criterion should be and how long the subject should remain at each criterion level. Figure 3.5 provides a schema of this design.

Multiple-Probe Technique

The Multiple-Probe Technique (Horner & Baer, 1978) is another distinct variation of the Multiple-Baseline Design, but it does not require continuous measurement of all baselines. To use the design, the behaviors (or subjects) to be treated are specified, and one-session probes or measures are taken in the rates of those behaviors at the beginning of the study. Continuous

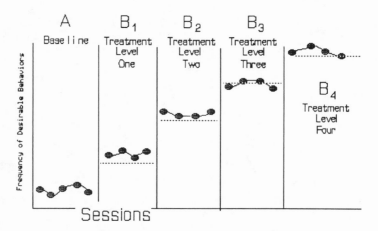

FIGURE 3.5 Stylized example of Changing Criterion Design. Dashed lines in the treatment phases indicate the level of performance required for reinforcement by the contingency in effect. The power of the design depends on how closely the performances "track" or "shift" with the changes in level of treatment.

baseline measurements are taken only on the behavior (or subject) that will first receive treatment. One-session probes on all behaviors are taken just before treatment is applied to any one of the baselines. A few days of continuous baseline measures are also taken just prior to treatment of the particular behavior on which intervention is being applied. The design is applicable to skills that are learned in a sequential manner, such that prerequisite behaviors are required in order to perform the composite skill. Experimental control is demonstrated in the same manner as in the Multiple-Baseline Design. If the behavior responds only as a function of treatment, a functional relationship may be inferred. Figure 3.6 shows a schema of this design.

Simultaneous Treatment Design

In the Simultaneous Treatment Design (Kazdin, 1982a,b), the relative power of two or more interventions may be assessed by altering their administration in a kind of split-session schedule. A baseline is taken for a behavior, followed by the introduction of two or more treatments at the same time (e.g., same day or same time unit being measured). Experimental control is demonstrated by a consistent difference in the data collected under one treatment compared to the other treatment.

The advantage of this design is that it can test varying levels of a treatment or be used to compare two or more treatments. The disadvantage is that it is difficult to implement and to analyze. Each treatment condition must be distinguishable, and carryover effects of treatment must not exist.

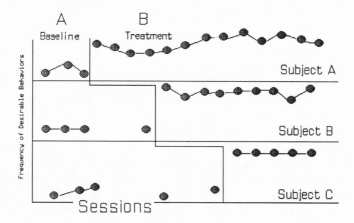

FIGURE 3.6 Stylized example of Multiple Probe (Across Subjects) Design.

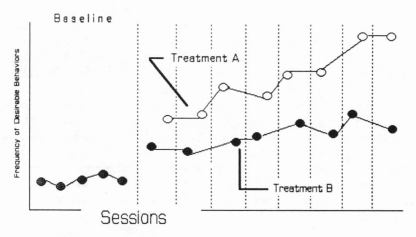

FIGURE 3.7 Stylized example of Simultaneous Treatment Design. Following a baseline, two treatments are randomly alternated within two-session blocks of time.

Gianutsos and Gianutsos (1985) describe a hypothetical example of this treatment design in the rehabilitation field in which two types of feedback were compared. Condition A used a graphic display and was implemented during part of a treatment session. Condition B provided feedback through a video game format and was used during the remainder of the treatment session. The clinician could examine possible differences in performance related to the feedback conditions. Figure 3.7 provides a schema of this design.

SUMMARY

Within-subject experimental designs are becoming increasingly popular in the evaluation of cognitive rehabilitation techniques. The technology of single-case experimental investigations is rapidly advancing. These designs are important to researchers and clinicians who seek information regarding individual patients' responses to treatment and who want to tease out effects of other recovery factors from the impact of rehabilitation.

Single-subject experimental designs provide powerful clinical and research tools for documenting the efficacy of cognitive rehabilitation. These designs require repeated measures over time. Their advantages include allowing examination of individual performance and of functional relationships between treatment and changes in behavior. The Multiple-Baseline Design is a particularly useful clinical tool because it can provide documentation of treatment efficacy and can be easily implemented within the clinical setting.

As discussed, analysis of performance data with a specific therapy task can be accomplished by examining both objective and subjective treatment data. Objective data include measurement of parameters related to accuracy, time, and cuing. Subjective data include documentation of possible internal and external factors that might be operating during task completion as well as analysis of error patterns. Collection of such information allows clinicians to make informed treatment decisions.

Examination of graphically displayed data provides information on variability of performance, trends in therapy performance, and changes in level of performance. Attention to these data is valuable in helping the clinician to determine when to maintain, modify, or discontinue treatment. Adequate documentation is also important for reimbursement purposes.

It is important for the clinician to examine the implications of cognitive status on vocational potential, independent-living skills, and psychosocial adjustment.

STUDY QUESTIONS

1. Why does documentation have particular importance, given the newness of cognitive rehabilitation?
2. How might the source of reimbursement for cognitive rehabilitation services affect documentation?
3. What are three common error patterns, and what do they suggest? Can you think of other possible error patterns?

4. How does collection of quantitative performance data (e.g., measurement of task accuracy) allow a clinician to make informed treatment decisions?
5. How can experimental designs provide demonstration of a functional relationship between a particular intervention and changes within a patient?
6. What advantages do single-subject designs offer the rehabilitation specialist over group designs?

REFERENCES

Billingsley, F., & Wolery, M. (1985). *Designs in applied behavior analysis*. Unpublished paper, Special Education Department, University of Washington, Seattle.

Gianutsos, R., & Gianutsos, J. (1979). Rehabilitating and verbal recall of brain injured patients by mnemonic training: An experimental demonstration using single-case methodology, *Journal of Clinical Neuropsychology* 1:117–135.

Gianutsos, R., & Gianutsos, J. (1987). Single-case experimental approaches to the assessment of interventions in rehabilitation psychology. In B. Kaplan (Ed.), *Rehabilitation psychology desk reference* (pp. 453–470). Rockville, IL: Aspen.

Hagen, C., Malkmus, D. (1979). Intervention strategies for language disorders secondary to head trauma. Paper presented at American Speech–Language–Hearing Association Convention, Short Course, Atlanta.

Hartmann, D. P., & Hall, R. V. (1976). The changing criterion design. *Journal of Applied Behavior Analysis* 9:527–532.

Horner, R. D., & Baer, D. M. (1978). Multiple-probe technique: A variation of the multiple baseline. *Journal of Applied Behavior Analysis* 11:189–196.

Jennett, B., & Bond, M. (1975). Assessment outcome after severe brain damage: Practical scale. *Lancet* 1:480–484.

Jennett, B., Snoak, J., Bond, M., & Brooks, N. (1981). Disability after severe head injury: Observations on the use of the Glasgow Outcome Scale. *Journal of Neurology, Neurosurgery, and Psychiatry* 44:285–293.

Kazdin, A. E. (1976). Statistical analyses for single-case experimental designs. In M. Hensen & D. N. Barlow (Eds.), *Single-case experimental designs: Strategies for studying behavior change* (pp. 265–316). New York: Pergamon.

Kazdin, A. E. (1977). Artifact, bias, and complexity of assessment: The ABC's of reliability. *Journal of Applied Behavior Analysis,* 10:141–150.

Kazdin, A. E. (1982a). *Single-case research designs: Methods for clinical and applied settings*. New York: Oxford University Press.

Kazdin, A. E. (1982b). Single-case experimental designs. In P. C. Kendall & J. N. Butcher (Eds.), *Handbook of research methods in clinical psychology* (pp. 461–490). New York: Wiley.

McReynolds, L. V., & Thompson, C. K. (1986). Flexibility of single-subject experimental designs: Part I: Review of the basics of single-subject design. *Journal of Speech and Hearing Disorders* 51:194–203.

Rappaport, M., Hall, K. M., Hopkins, K., & Belleza, T. (1982). Disability rating scale for severe head trauma: Coma to community. *Archives of Physical Medicine and Rehabilitation, 63*:118–123.

Sohlberg, M. M., & Brock, M. (1985). Taking the final step: The importance of post-medical cognitive rehabilitation. *Cognitive Rehabilitation 3*:10–14.

White, O. R. (1987). *A quick design overview.* Unpublished paper, Special Education Department, University of Washington, Seattle.

Wilson, B. (1987). Single-case experimental designs in neuropsychological rehabilitation. *Journal of Clinical and Experimental Neuropsychology, 9*(5), 527–544.

APPENDIX: SELECTED PORTIONS OF GOOD SAMARITAN HOSPITAL'S COGNITIVE BEHAVIOR RATING SCALE

Select the statement or statements which by your observation most accurately reflect the patient's level of functioning.

Attention/Concentration Rating Scale

Level 4

_____ The patient demonstrates the requisite attention skills to perform a familiar recreation activity at estimated premorbid levels.

_____ The patient demonstrates the requisite attention skills to perform a functional activity of daily living at estimated premorbid levels

_____ The patient performs standardized attention tests at a level compatible with estimated premorbid levels.

_____ The patient participates in an exercise program within physical limitations for 20–60 minutes without redirection.

_____ The patient exhibits the requisite attention skills to perform familiar tasks in work or home environments at estimated premorbid levels.

Level 3

_____ The patient participates in recreational activity (cards, computer) for 10–20 minutes without redirection.

_____ The patient participates in functional activities for daily living (cooking, woodworking, homemaking, dressing/grooming) for 10–20 minutes without redirection.

_____ The patient participates in a testing or treatment session for 10–20 minutes without redirection.

_____ The patient participates in an exercise program within physical limitations for 10–20 minutes without redirection.

_____ The patient maintains attention to tasks for 10–20 minutes without redirection as observed on nursing unit or in home environment (eating, dressing, socializing, phone conversations).

Level 2:

_____ The patient participates in recreational activity for 5–10 minutes without redirection.

_____ The patient participates in functional activities for daily living (dressing/ grooming, cooking, etc.) for 5–10 minutes without redirection.

_____ The patient participates in a testing or treatment session for 5–10 minutes without redirection.

_____ The patient participates in an exercise program within physical limitations for 5–10 minutes without redirection.

_____ The patient maintains attention to tasks for 5–10 minutes without redirection as observed on the nursing unit or home environment (eating, dressing, socializing, etc.).

Level 1:

_____ The patient cannot maintain attention on a specific task during recreational therapy with continual redirection.

_____ The patient cannot maintain attention on any functional activity for daily living (dressing, grooming, eating, etc.) with continual redirection.

_____ The patient cannot maintain attention in a testing or treatment session with continual redirection.

_____ The patient cannot participate in an exercise program with continual redirection.

_____ The patient cannot maintain attention to tasks surrounding nursing unit or home environment with continual redirection.

Memory Rating Scale

Level 4:

_____ The patient demonstrates the requisite memory skills, with or without spontaneous compensation, to perform activities of daily living independently at estimated premorbid levels.

_____ The patient demonstrates the requisite memory skills, with or without spontaneous compensation, to perform gross motor activities within physical limitations at estimated premorbid levels.

_____ The patient demonstrates the requisite memory skills, with or without spontaneous compensation, to perform tasks involving new learning at estimated premorbid levels.

_____ The patient demonstrates immediate recall of 5–9 items; is able to use schedules and appointment calendars to reliably arrive for appointments; able to recall events and conversations from the previous day with minimal reminders; reliably recalls 70% of abstract information after 30 minutes.

_____ The patient demonstrates the requisite memory skills, with or without spontaneous compensation, to perform recreational activities at estimated premorbid levels.

_____ The patient demonstrates the requisite memory skills, with or without spontaneous compensation, to manage their routine and daily medical needs at estimated premorbid levels.

Level 3:

_____ The patient demonstrates intermittent spontaneous compensation for memory problems, such as use of a memory book, writing notes to self, using rehearsal strategies, etc., in order to perform activities of daily living.

_____ The patient demonstrates intermittent spontaneous compensation for memory problems, such as writing down home assignments, using a daily memory book, etc., in order to complete physical therapy assignments or perform exercise program.

_____ The patient demonstrates intermittent spontaneous use of memory aids or memory strategies to enhance recall of information or to prepare for upcoming events.

_____ The patient demonstrates immediate recall of 5–7 items. The patient is able to retain repeatedly rehearsed information from session to session with occasional reminders; some information may be unreliably retained after 30 minutes.

_____ The patient demonstrates intermittent use of memory aids or strategies to recall information or times for routine and daily medical care.

_____ The patient demonstrates intermittent spontaneous use of memory aids or strategies while participating in recreational activities or community outings.

Level 2:

_____ The patient does not initiate compensation for memory impairments but can be instructed to use memory aids and strategies within a treatment session when performing activities of daily living such as dressing, grooming, and self-feeding.

_____ The patient does not initiate compensation for memory impairments but can be instructed to use memory aids and strategies within a treatment session when performing gross motor activities.

_____ The patient does not initiate compensation for memory impairments but can be instructed to use memory aids and strategies within a treatment session when performing structured retrospective or prospective memory tasks.

_____ The patient demonstrates immediate recall limited to 4 items; new learning requires repeated rehearsals; retrieval requires reminding or probing after an interference task or a 3-minute period of time; carry over from treatment session to session is limited, but progress is seen.

_____ The patient does not initiate compensation for memory impairments but can be instructed to use memory aids and strategies within a treatment session when performing familiar recreational activities or attending community outings.

_____ The patient does not initiate compensation for memory impairments but can be instructed to use very simple memory aids to improve awareness of daily routines.

Level 1:

_____ The patient is unable to perform activities of daily living which require memory skills with continual redirection from the therapist.

_____ The patient is unable to perform gross motor activities which require memory skills with continual redirection from the therapist.

_____ The patient is unable to perform novel communication tasks or demonstrate use of memory aids with continual redirection from the therapist.

_____ The patient is unable to retain/retrieve new learning after any interference task, even when supplied with maximum reminders and probes; carry over from session to session is not apparent.

_____ The patient is unable to perform recreational activities which require memory skills with continual redirection from therapist.

_____ The patient is unable to manage daily routine with continual redirection from the nursing staff.

Visual-Spatial Processing Rating Scale

Level 4:

_____ The patient demonstrates the requisite visuospatial processing skills (with or without spontaneous compensation) in order to perform activities of daily living independently at estimated premorbid levels.

_____ The patient demonstrates the requisite visuospatial processing skills (with or without spontaneous compensation) in order to perform exercise or mobility tasks independently at a level within physical limitations.

_____ The patient demonstrates the requisite visuospatial processing skills (with or without spontaneous compensation) in order to perform exercise or ability tasks independently at a level within physical limitations.

_____ The patient demonstrates the requisite visuospatial processing skills (with or without spontaneous compensation) in order to perform familiar recreational activities at estimated premorbid levels.

_____ The patient performs standardized visuospatial processing tests at estimated premorbid levels.

_____ The patient demonstrates the requisite visuospatial processing skills (with or without spontaneous compensation) in order to perform activities on the ward or in the home or work environments at premorbid levels.

Level 3:

_____ The patient demonstrates intermittent compensation for visuospatial problems, such as self–cuing, spontaneous use of environmental aids, etc., in order to perform activities of daily living. Supervision during activities of daily living is required.

_____ The patient demonstrates intermittent compensation for visuospatial problems during functional motor activities, but requires supervision from staff.

_____ The patient performs reading and writing tasks with intermittent cuing to compensate for visuospatial deficits.

_____ The patient performs recreational activities with intermittent cuing to compensate for visuospatial deficits. Supervision during activities is required.

_____ The patient can take standardized visuospatial processing tests; however, all scores are between the patient's estimated premorbid level.

_____ The patient demonstrates intermittent compensation for visuospatial deficits on the ward, at home, and in work environments in order to manage ongoing visuospatial impairments. Supervision during activities is required.

Level 2:

_____ The patient does not compensate for visuospatial impairments, but requires continual cuing to perform tasks such as dressing, grooming, and self-feeding.

_____ The patient is able to achieve body postures, ambulate, or propel wheelchair with continuous manual and verbal feedback on the visuospatial environment.

_____ The patient can perform reading and writing tasks with continuous cues to compensate for visual deficits.

_____ The patient can recognize basic shapes, match simple figures, and copy simple geometric forms (circle, square, and triangle).

_____ The patient can participate in simple visual games and activities with constant feedback and directions.

_____ The patient visually tracks people and objects. The patient is able to recognize familiar faces and objects. With constant feedback about visual environment, the patient can perform some tasks on the ward or in the home environment.

Level 1:

_____ The patient is unable to perform functional activities of daily living with verbal or physical directions due to spatial neglect, visuomotor impairment, lack of object recognition, and/or problems with body position in space.

_____ The patient is unable to perform motor activities including sitting on a mat, propelling wheelchair, or ambulation due to spatial neglect or problems orienting body in space.

_____ The patient is unable to discriminate or copy letters, numbers, or words due to visuospatial perceptions deficits and not due to language impairment.

_____ The patient is unable to perform simple visuospatial tasks including copying, matching, counting objects, or drawing.

_____ The patient is unable to play games requiring visuospatial skills (card games, pool, air hockey, Atari, computer), but may be able to play nonvisual games.

_____ The patient is unable to manage his/her daily routine at the hospital or in the home environment due to visuospatial deficits including spatial neglect, visuomotor impairment, lack of object recognition, and lack of awareness of body in space.

Reasoning/Executive Functions Rating Scale

Level 4:

_____ The patient demonstrates the requisite reasoning/executive function skills to perform activities of daily living independently at estimated premorbid levels.

_____ The patient demonstrates the requisite reasoning/executive function skills to perform gross motor activities within physical limitation at estimated premorbid levels.

_____ The patient demonstrates the requisite reasoning/executive function skills to perform tasks such as selection and execution of cognitive plans, time management, self-regulation, or solving concrete or abstract problems at estimated premorbid levels.

_____ The patient demonstrates the ability to initiate a plan of action necessary to attain a goal on command; problem-solving skills are equal to estimated premorbid abilities.

_____ The patient demonstrates the requisite reasoning/executive function skills to perform recreational activities at estimated premorbid levels.

_____ The patient demonstrates the requisite reasoning/executive function skills to manage their daily routine and medical needs at estimated premorbid levels.

Level 3:

_____ The patient requires supervision due to lack of consistency in self-monitoring of safety, physical limitations, and judgment while performing activities of daily living.

_____ The patient requires supervision due to lack of consistency in self-monitoring of safety, physical limitations, and judgment while performing gross motor activities.

_____ The patient exhibits intermittent impairments in one or more of these areas: selection and execution of cognitive plans, time management, self-regulation, or solving concrete or abstract problems.

_____ The patient can initiate a plan to attain a goal or command, but cannot generate alternative strategies if confronted with unexpected obstructions or novel circumstances.

_____ The patient requires intermittent supervision for tasks on the ward, in the home, and in work environments due to inconsistent self-monitoring of safety considerations and potential problems with making appropriate decisions.

_____ The patient demonstrates intermittent impairments in reasoning/executive function skills while participating in recreational activities and community outings due to inconsistent self-monitoring.

Level 2:

_____ The patient requires continual assistance for reasoning/executive function impairments when performing activities of daily living such as dressing, grooming, and self-feeding to avoid safety problems, to help with initiation, and to monitor performance.

_____ The patient requires continual assistance for reasoning/executive function impairments when performing gross motor activities to avoid safety problems, to help with initiation, and to monitor performance.

_____ The patient requires continual assistance to initiate tasks, to monitor time, to plan and organize, and to interrupt perseverative behavior.

_____ The patient recognizes appropriate goals and will initiate activities toward their attainment, but cannot modulate or maintain the purposeful direction of his/her efforts, perseverating on irrelevant aspects of a task.

_____ The patient needs constant supervision for safety on the ward, at home, or in the work environments, and help with initiation and monitoring of performance.

_____ The patient requires continual supervision when performing recreational activities and community outings due to concerns about safety, judgment, and initiation.

Level 1:

_____ The patient is unable to perform activities of daily living which require reasoning/executive function skills.

_____ The patient is unable to perform gross motor activities which require reasoning/executive function skills.

_____ The patient is unable to perform novel communication tasks or demonstrate use of reasoning/executive function skills.

_____ The patient is unable to recognize appropriate goals or to initiate or maintain any purposeful, goal–directed activity without prompting.

_____ The patient is unable to perform recreational activities which require reasoning/executive function skills.

_____ The patient is unable to manage daily routine and medical needs due to reasoning/executive function deficits.

4
Neuropsychologic Assessment

Neuropsychology, the branch of clinical psychology that focuses on relationships between brain function and behavior, has made contributions to cognitive rehabilitation in two important areas. The first involves research into the function of various regions of the brain. The second is the development of neuropsychologic assessment. More recently, efforts are being made to provide assistance and direction in the development and delivery of cognitive rehabilitation programs. This chapter deals with the nature and scope of neuropsychologic assessment, particularly as it pertains to rehabilitation.

The scope and purpose of the neuropsychologic examination have changed over the last decade. Early uses of the neuropsychologic examination were the detection and diagnosis of central nervous system abnormality, particularly of higher cortical function. The focus was on making reliable predictions about the location and nature of cerebral lesions. The application of neuropsychologic investigation to individuals with brain lesions in rehabilitation necessitates a paradigm shift in focus and purpose. In this shift, the neuropsychologic investigation has begun to focus on human behavioral and cognitive function in order to make meaningful predictions about the patient's future adaptation as well as to plan for rehabilitation efforts. The former focus on central nervous system structure (side and site of lesion) has in many rehabilitation centers given way to a focus on cognitive function, behavioral adaptation, and rehabilitation needs. Mere tabulations of deficits as defined by particular psychometric tests need to be replaced by descriptions of behavioral and cognitive strengths and weaknesses, statements about practical implications of the cognitive profile, and guidance in therapeutic intervention.

For rehabilitation professionals, the neuropsychologic assessment provides substantial, pertinent information about cognitive and behavioral functioning beyond that yielded by the traditional neurologic assessment. The classical neurologic signs of cerebral dysfunction include changes in motor and reflex function (weakness, paralysis, hypo-or hypertonic reflexes), discrete sensory deficits, alterations in basic arousal, and frank aphasic disorders of speech and language. In a rehabilitation setting, such deficits would have been well documented, and, in and of themselves, they suggest little about needs in the area of cognitive rehabilitation. In contrast, the neuropsychologic assessment should provide a comprehensive evaluation of the integrity of higher cortical functions, including intellect, problem-solving capability, capacity for memory and new learning, and other relevant capabilities. The advantages of the neuropsychologic assessment are that it makes use of standardized, objective tests that sample a wide range of cognitive functions. These instruments are capable of producing fine-grained, stable measurements and generating scores that permit reliable interest and retest comparisons.

HISTORICAL PERSPECTIVES

The field of neuropsychology has multiple roots. Its early experimental origins represented logical extension of experiments with nonhuman animals in an attempt to increase knowledge about fundamental brain–behavior relationships. In research settings, neuropsychologists used "experiments of nature" (e.g., strokes, focal seizure disorders, tumors) to study basic abilities associated with function of specific brain regions (e.g., see Kimura, 1967; Milner, 1967, 1975; Teuber, 1964). In psychiatric settings, neuropsychologists leaned on a growing tradition of psychometric assessment to help discriminate between patients with and without "organic" brain damage. In medical and clinical settings, neurologists and neuropsychologists sought to better diagnose and describe the ways in which central nervous system damage might be manifest cognitively and behaviorally (Geschwind, 1965, 1970; Luria, 1966). In rehabilitation settings, neuropsychologists are assisting in the development of tools not only to evaluate but to remediate cognitive deficits. Given the wide range of purposes for which neuropsychologic involvement may be valuable, it is not surprising that a variety of assessment approaches have developed. In this section, three approaches are presented: the Statistical–Psychometric Approach, the Theoretical–Clinical Approach, and the Process-Specific Approach.

The Statistical–Psychometric Approach

The diagnostically oriented neuropsychologic assessment approach developed, in part, to answer questions of neuropsychologists by medical specialties (e.g., "Is there evidence of an organic basis for behaviors observed?" "If so, where is the most likely site of brain dysfunction?" "What role do psychologic or functional variables play in the manifestation of symptoms?" "Is the condition progressive or stable?"). As a result, early neuropsychologic batteries have tended to focus on the likelihood of organicity, the degree and localization of organic involvment, and whether this involvement is static or dynamic in nature.

The Statistical-Psychometric Approach relies on statistical techniques for defining such constructs as "organic impairment" and "deficit." Diagnoses are assigned on an actuarial basis (Reitan, 1955). Tests are selected for use on the basis of statistical criteria. In such an approach, the most important variable in selecting a test for use may be its ability to discriminate on a more probable than not basis, brain-injured from non-brain-injured individuals. While "accuracy and prediction" with regard to questions about brain dysfunction have historically been the most valued criteria for a good neuropsychologic test (Filskov & Goldstein, 1974), a solely statistical approach to test selection has too often resulted in an a theoretical view of brain–behavior relationships. Assessment tools can become almost completely divorced from psychologic, cognitive, or behavioral knowledge and theory. Neuropsychologic tests designed, constructed, and validated for the purpose of predicting and even localizing brain damage may provide only a limited view or conceptualization of the deficits in cognitive, motor, behavioral, and/or other functions which are associated with the damage. It is likely to be deficits in these abilities and behaviors, however, that the rehabilitation specialists will need to address for the purposes of functional improvement.

The Theoretical–Clinical Approach

In a rehabilitation context, the confirmation of underlying brain pathology is not usually central to the evaluation. The critical questions are more likley to be qualitative and practical in nature (i.e., "To what extent has this individual recovered?" "Which functions continue to show impairment, and to what degree?" "What treatment approaches are likely to promote recovery and normalization?" "Can a process be retrained, or will accommodative strategies be necessary?" "How effective has the particular regimen of cognitive treatment been?"). To do justice to questions about brain–behavior relationships and intervention strategies as complex as these requires an adaptable, flexible assessment approach that incorporates both quantitative and qualitative features. The degree to which traditional psychometric tests, particularly those statistically selected on the basis of their ability to discriminate organicity, are able to measure these dimensions of dysfunction is often limited.

In the Theoretical–Clinical Approach, the analysis of each individual is a theoretically based, dynamic experiment designed to assess the behavioral effects associated with a particular pattern of brain disturbance. A. R. Luria, whose training was in neurology and psychiatry, developed an assessment approach in the Soviet Union, which developed out of a comprehensive and intensive case-study model (Luria, 1966). He viewed all cognitive functions as dependent on multiple brain areas, each acting as part of a dynamic system. The nature of breakdown in these systems was explored by means of sensitive, qualitative behavioral descriptions. The approach stresses exploration through hypothesis testing.

The theoretical–clinical approach to examination can be viewed as a series of experiments involving successive elimination of alternative diagnostic possibilities. Diagnoses move progressively from general hypotheses (i.e., the patient has suffered a brain injury) to increasingly specific hypotheses (i.e., the damage was primarily to the frontal system) by incorporating test results with history, appearance, and interview. Identification of specific deficits proceeds by setting up a general hypothesis and testing it in particular conditions. Lezak (1983) gives the following example (p. 101). If an examiner hypothesized that a patient's poor performance on a block design task was caused by general slowing, all other timed performances would be examined to see if the hypothesis held up. A finding that the patient was slow on all other timed performances would give strong support to the hypothesis but not rule out the potential contributions of other deficits to the low score. The neuropsychologist might, at that point, develop and test other hypotheses involving a constructional disorder, a perceptual disorder, or a deficit in fine motor coordination through the use of other test measures or observations. In this way, the underlying nature of the impairment is sought.

This approach has tremendous potential for guiding clinical analysis, diagnosis, and treatment (Luria, 1966, 1970, 1973). As an example, memory is known to depend on multiple contributions from different neuroanatomic regions, including frontal, temporal, and subcortical structures. The integrity of each of these contributions is evaluated through careful interview and creative probing of differnt kinds of memory subserved by each system. Dynamic assessment should seek to describe the way a particular neuropathology has influenced a complex functional system or systems. The assessment of subcomponents of a dynamic process such as memory does far more to provide an understanding of altered function, allow predictions, and provide support of theoretically based treatment approaches than does a global measure such as a memory quotient or a deficit score on a particular memory test that may merely confirm that a memory problem exists. Limitations of the theoretical–clinical approach are that evaluations may not be standard from one clinician to the next, from one patient to the next, or from one session to the next. Thus, for research purposes, when quantification is needed, or when careful longitudinal tracking is necessary, the approach has some drawbacks. It also requires an enormous amount of knowledge about cognitive, behavioral, and neurologic systems and is dependent on an extensive base of experience.

The Process-Specific Approach

The Process-Specific Approach (Kaplan, 1983) to neuropsychologic assessment might be considered to combine features of the Statistical–Psychometric and the Theoretical–Clinical approaches. The Process-Specific Approach holds that separate aspects of cognitive function can be differentially impacted through brain damage or disease. This is held to be true despite acknowledgment that cognitive systems work in concert. A process-specific analysis should have the following characteristics:

1. It must provide a systematic and comprehensive review of functional cognitive systems.
2. It must be structured according to current cognitive and neuropsychologic theory and seek to investigate major areas of cognitive function in terms of relevant components.
3. It must use available tests and clinical techniques that lend themselves to this process-analysis approach.

The core battery of tests in a Process-Specific Approach to assessment should examine the following major areas of cognitive function: an index of general intellect, executive function, attention and concentration, memory, language, perceptual and perceptual–motor function, and reasoning/problem solving. A comprehensive process-oriented assessment in each of these areas, with an eye to viewing both strengths and weaknesses, will yield valuable information about the level of functioning for the rehabilitation team. What an instrument measures and its degree of sensitivity to a specific cognitive function should be the primary criteria in test selection for use with this approach (Mapou, 1988). Although neuropsychologic function is viewed as a set of multidimensional and interactive capacities, the Process-Specific Approach attempts to reduce complex cognitive functions into theorietically and experimentally based components (Goodglass & Kaplan, 1979). How performance breaks down on a particular test and the nature of tests on which deficit performance is observed reveal what component parts of a cognitive ability are likely to have been impaired.

The comprehensive assessment of traumatic head injury provides a particularly challenging task. Because many functions are subject to disruption, many samples of different kinds of behavior must be taken (Lezak, 1983). The examiner must use a variety of formats and instruments in order to capture the full range of cognitive, motoric, behavioral, and social emotional functions (Luria, 1973). And, unless examination techniques are geared to elicit impairments that are common to the traumatically head-injured individual, serious and debilitating deficits may go unspecified (Eson & Bourke, 1980). Formal assessment following traumatic head injury should include measures of those functions most likely to be impaired. These include, in particular, attention/concentration, memory and new learning, speed of information processing, executive functions, and self-regulation.

THE NEUROPSYCHOLOGIC ASSESSMENT

The comprehensive assessment of cognitive and behavioral function involves far more than the administration of a standardized set of test instruments. Although the administration of an appropriate set of formal tests occupies a central position in the assessment process, diagnosis of neuropsychologic/cognitive disorders requires placing of the test data gathered in historical, current, and even future perspective. Then, on the basis of findings and interpretations, the neuropsychologist, together with the rehabilitation team, should propose a remedial program and attempt to predict its outcome. In carrying out these responsibilities, the following steps are necessary:

• establish the preinjury background
• review the pertinent medical history
• conduct the interview and make behavioral observations
• administer and score neuropsychologic tests
• draw conclusions describing the cognitive/behavioral profile
• formulate recommendations for a remedial plan
• attempt a prognosis

Information is compiled and normally conveyed in the form of a written report. It should normally contain the sections listed in Table 4.1.

Establishing the Preinjury Background

In establishing expectations for performance on neuropsychologic measures, it is important to establish and verify the extent of the formal

TABLE 4.1. Sections of a Typical Neuropsychologic Assessment Report

Relevant medical history
Relevant preinjury (and postinjury) educational and vocational history
A description of behavioral observations made at the time of evaluation
The results of formal assessment procedures
A summary of cognitive and behavioral strengths and weaknesses
A set of specific recommendations that follow from the evaluation process

education experience, strengths and weaknesses in different academic areas, prior need for any special educational services, and diagnosis of any previously identified learning disability or other developmental abnormality. To this end, it is important to request and review educational records. The nature and extent of postsecondary vocational training or educational experience should be explored. Information regarding previously held jobs and the nature of specific duties should also be gathered. Finally, interviews with family, friends, or co-workers are desirable in determining preinjury levels of independence, stability, judgment, leisure pursuits, and general personality style. All of these factors may influence the interpretation of neuropsychologic test results and their integration with the rehabilitation plan.

Review Relevant Medical History

Review of the medical history should include the data and nature of injury, medical procedures undertaken, and complications, and results of medical assessments, neuroradiologic findings (e.g., CT scan, magnetic resonance imaging [MRI]), or electrophysiologic responses (e.g., EEG, evoked response potentials). Also important is the history of previous injuries or significant illnesses, coexisting medical problems, and past and current drug and/or alcohol use. In addition, the current amount and dosages of various medications should be determined.

Conducting the Interview and Evaluating Behavioral Observations

In the interview, historical information can be confirmed, additional relevant details about background can be disclosed, and a listing of current concerns and problems can be elicited. By including family members, the examiner can also get a sense of qualitative change in the individual's abilities and deportment and information about the general course of recovery. Of greatest interest may be information from the family about the patient's preinjury personality, his or her interests, what motivates him or her, the former coping style, and his or her typical response to stress and frustration.

Often it is the behavioral observations made of an individual during the interview and assessment that provide the most critical information relevant to rehabilitation planning. Included in these behavioral observations should be statements about the affective presentation of the individual (Is the individual emotionally labile? Does the individual appear depressed or overly anxious in the testing situation?). The patient's capabilities for self-regulation and management in the test situation should be specifically documented (Does the individual reach for or grab testing materials inappropriately? Does he or she suddenly get up and walk over to the other side of the room when something catches his or her eye?). The patient's ability to communicate in terms of both understanding and expressing information is a critical variable relevant to rehabilitation planning (Do instructions need to be simplified or repeated? Does the individual have obvious problems with word finding or tangentiality when they attempt to respond to questions?). Notations about the patient's level of insight and judgment as to the severity and nature of his or her difficulties are also quite pertinent (Does the individual have any awareness of having difficulty on tasks or that the performances are filled with errors?). These kinds of observations can provide information about aspects of brain functioning and integrity that are difficult to measure by formal specific testing procedures; they can also provide an estimate of test validity and interpretability.

Administration and Scoring of Neuropsychologic Tests

Anyone can make up a test. A test becomes a useful instrument for appraisal only when one can be quite certain what it tests and what the range of response is for a group of people judged to be normal or in some respect abnormal. The more precise the data it provides and the more highly trained the examiner in use of the test, the more likely it will be that the expenditure of time required for the procedure will be profitable. Tests should be selected with a view to their psychometric characteristics, their construct validity, and their content validity (Are the size, sex ratio, and age distribution of control data on a test appropriate for the present application? Is the meaure adequately defined? Does it fit an acceptable theoretical construct for the process being addressed? Is the sample of behavior to be elicited large enough to draw conclusions? Is the test–retest reliability acceptable?) (Lezak, 1983).

In a rehabilitation setting, neuropsychologic assessment should aim to describe as fully as possible the underlying cognitive and behavioral capabilities of an individual. The uniqueness of each individual's injury and disability demands discriminating, flexible, and imaginative use of examination techniques. Creative selection and modification of testing procedures may be necessary and appropriate for comprehensive evaluation of an individual's capabilities. If test directions or response demands are inappropriate because of residual sensory, verbal, or motor impairment, formal instructions should be adapted with changes in format explicitly documented for the purposes of replication. Because fatigue is a common consequence following traumatic head injury, frequent rests or short evaluation sessions are recommended. Lezak (1983) suggests using a double scoring procedure with individuals in rehabilitation settings. Functional scores are obtained by following standardization rules, and the second score is a combination of standardized score plus raw score points for those items for which the client demonstrated knowledge on testing the limits. The disparity can provide some estimate of lost ability, the lower score suggesting current level of functioning. Testing the limits might include increasing the time available to complete tasks or providing cues that enhance test performance. When testing the limits, special attention should be paid to how the individual goes about solving problems and what kind of cues or what type of assistance is most beneficial in effecting improved performance (e.g., general verbal prompts, visual prompts, direct verbal instruction, demonstration, cues to check work, slow down, or work from top to bottom).

The section of the neuropsychologic report dealing with test results should provide a clear description of both the strengths and weaknesses across a broad range of cognitive capabilities. Included should be statements with regard to general intellectual function, attention and concentration, speed of information processing and motor responding, memory and new learning capability, communication and language functions, perceptual and perceptual–motor functions, and executive functions. Documentation of a deficit only provides one part of the picture. Equally important is a description of how the individual failed or succeeded and what that means about not only impaired but spared aspects of ability. Results of testing should be described in such a way that they are clear and provide information regarding theoretical as well as practical and functional implications. The evaluation process should provide a structured means for identifying current processing styles and determining optimal methods of instruction.

Drawing Conclusions

From a study of all the information gathered, the clinician makes a tentative identification of the scope of problems and a determination of their respective etiologies. It may be, for example, that problems with attention and executive function relate to a recent head injury but that a spelling disorder is of longstanding developmental nature. Or it may be that attentional memory and language problems are the direct result of a bullet wound in the left temporal region, but the overall level of functioning is further reduced by severe depression. Not only are levels of functioning in different cognitive and behavioral areas and etiologic variables important, it is also necessary to identify factors that may have predisposed the individual to deficits or that may maintain them. The *Summary* and *Conclusions* sections of a neuropsychologic report should relate the current cognitive profile to estimates of preinjury functioning. It may contain statements about the probability of extent and focus of injury based on the level and nature of neurobehavioral impairment. The *Conclusions* section should also contain implications for current and future life adjustment. Life adjustment depends on cognitive ability, the capacity for emotional experience and expression, and behaviors indicative of self-regulation and executive function.

Formulating Recommendations for a Remedial Plan

The *Recommendations* section of a neuropsychologic report should contain specific statements about treatment needs and suggestions regarding treatment approaches. If the evaluation has been conducted as a structured means for identifying current processing capability, it should immediately lead to the kind of process-specific approach to intervention discussed throughout this text. It should identify intact abilities that may be used to circumvent or compensate for lost functions or deficit skills. It should provide some information regarding the kinds of cues or modifications that are likely to enhance performance. It should suggest the most useful deficit process or processes to be initially addressed in the treatment plan. It should identify spared components of cognitive processes (i.e., procedural memory) on which alternative functional approaches to deal with cognitive impairment can be built.

In this way, the results an conclusions of the evaluation may be used to contribute to the various phases of treatment planning, including (Cohen & Mapou, 1988):

- development of an initial treatment plan
- problem solving during treatment
- monitoring the patient's treatment and progress
- disposition planning
- individual patient outcome evaluation
- program evaluation

Attempting a Prognosis

Given the problems as one sees them, the causes as one understands them, one's experience with this patient and with other patients over time, and the literature on recovery, the neuropsychologist predicts the future course of the deficits with and without further rehabilitation efforts or with different levels of remedial involvement. The prognosis should contain implications for current and future life adjustment in terms of independent living, ability to manage legal and financial affairs, and return to a former or an alternative vocation.

SPECIFIC EXAMPLES OF NEUROPSYCHOLOGIC ASSESSMENT BATTERIES

In the next sections, three specific examples of neuropsychologic test batteries will be reviewed. These include the Halstead–Reitan Battery (HRB), the Luria–Nebraska Neuropsychology Battery (LNNB), and the Process-Oriented Assessment used by the authors at the Center for Cognitive

Rehabilitation. It is important to note that this is by no means an exhaustive review of neuropsychologic tests in general. Such a review is well beyond the scope of this book; Lezak (1983), Walsh (1978), and Kolb and Wishaw (1980) provide useful and comprehensive coverage in this area. Recently there have also been a large number of authors who have advocated and described specialized approaches to assessment in the rehabilitation setting (Cohen & Mapou, 1988; Lezak, 1987).

Halstead–Reitan Battery

This instrument began as a battery of seven tests selected for their power to discriminate between patients with frontal lobe lesions and those with other lesions (Halstead, 1947; Reitan & Davidson, 1974). In that sense, it is a good example of the statistical–psychometric approach to assessment discussed earlier in this chapter. In its current form, the HRB (age 15 and above) consists of five tests:

1. *Category Test.* This test requires responding by pulling one of four levers to 208 predominantly visuospatial stimuli projected on a screen. The task is to figure out a principle presented in each of six sets of items. It requires abstracting ability, visuospatial analysis, learning, and the ability to benefit from feedback.
2. *Tactual Performance Test* (TPT). Blindfolded subjects put geometric pieces into a formboard first with the preferred hand, then the non-preferred, and finally with both hands. The Total Time score is the summed time to completion. Two additional scores, the Memory score and the Location score, are derived when the subject is asked to draw the formboard from memory.
3. *Speech Sounds Perception Test.* Sixty-four sets of four nonsense syllables are presented on tape and selected by subjects from a printed multiple choice form.
4. *Finger-Tapping Test.* In this text of manual dexterity, subjects use a tapping key with a device for recording the number of taps. The average score for each index finger is the average number of taps in 10 seconds.
5. *Seashore Rhythm Test.* Subjects discriminate between 30 like and unlike pairs of musical or rhythmic beats presented on a tape.

These five tests yield a total of seven scores, with the TPT yielding three. The HRB is generally supplemented by allied procedures, usually the Wechsler Adult Intelligence Scale, the Aphasia Screening Test, the Sensory Perceptual Examination, the Trail-Making Test, and a measure of lateral dominance (Barth & Macciocchi, 1985). Other authors have incorporated additional measures for use with special populations. Dodrill (1978), for example, incorporates the Stroop Test, the Wechsler Memory Scale (Logical Memory and Visual Reproduction subtests), and the Seashore Tonal Memory Test in his Neuropsychological Battery for Epilepsy (NBE).

In order to make gross diagnostic discrimination and assess the overall degree of brain dysfunction, Halstead used the proportion of individual subtest scores that exceeded "cutting scores" established in his study of frontal lobe patients to formulate an "Impairment Index" (Russell, 1984). These cutting scores determine the point at which a score falls into the range of scores associated with brain impairment. Over the years, the tests selected to make up the Impairment Index have changed on the basis of reliability and validity studies. Impairment ratings can range from 0.0 to 1.0. In general, an Impairment Index of 0.0 to 0.3 is indicative of normal functioning to mild cognitive impairment; 0.3 to 0.6 suggests mild-to-moderate dysfunction; 0.6 to 0.8 moderate to severe; and 0.8 to 1.0 indicates severe dysfunction (Barth & Macciocchi, 1985).

Predictions about the site of a lesion and its nature (diffuse or focal, static or changing) are based on statistically identified relationships between test scores (Boll, 1978; Reitan & Davidson, 1974). Test data are organized and reviewed in accordance with neuropsychologic tenets to permit inferential analysis of the following four types:

1. *Level of performance.* Standardized scores are compared to cognitive samples, a criterion group, or an absolute standard of expectation.
2. *Pattern of performance.* Relationships within subgroups of tests or subtests are analyzed to ascertain strength or deficit patterns.
3. *Review for presence of pathognomonic signs.* The presence of "hard" neurologic signs (e.g., asymmetric and abnormal strength, unilateral sensory loss, frank paraphrasic errors) and "soft" signs of CNS dysfunction (e.g., perseveration, spatial rotations) are interpreted within the context of the complete evaluation to determine their significance.
4. *Comparison of performance.* The sensory and motor efficiency between the left and right sides of the body are compared and used to make inferences about probable lateralization of damage and integrity of the hemispheres.

Although the HRB is widely used in this country, it is acknolwedged to have limitations. It takes a relatively long time to administer and is not suitable for the thorough examination of patients with sensory or motor handicaps, frequently seen in a rehabilitation setting. The original norms of the Halstead tests are not well founded (Boll, 1978), and "cutting scores" used to discriminate brain injury from normality are based on the performance of a young sample (mean age 28 years), although performance on most of the tests is known to fall off with age. From a rehabilitation perspective, the most serious limitations of the HRB are its limited sampling of cognitive functions in the areas of memory, attention, executive functions, and language and its largely a theoretical approach from a cognitive perspective. Most of the tests demand many different abilities, and poor performance on a test does not readily assist in therapeutic planning.

Luria–Nebraska Neuropsychologic Battery

Charles Golden and his associates developed the LNNB in an attempt to standardize Luria's (1966) clinical methods of evaluating brain-damaged patients. It drew heavily on Anne Lisse Christensen's collection of Luria's material (see Lezak, 1983). Although it purports to be built on the clinical–theoretical approach of Luria, it must, by virtue of its construction and scoring, be considered primarily to depend on the statistical–psychometric approach. The LNNB (Golden, Hammeke, & Purisch, 1980) consists of 269 items, which the authors contend represent approximately 700 procedures. Performance on each item is evaluated on a 3-point scale, from 0 for no impairment to 2 for severely impaired. The Battery includes 11 ability scales, two sensorimotor scales, a pathognomonic scale, and localization and factor scores. Each scale is purported to measure the intactness of respective primary, secondary, and tertiary functions in the major cognitive processing systems (Luria, 1966). Classification of dysfunction is determined by comparing systems (Luria, 1966). Classification of dysfunction is determined by comparing actual performance on the scales with the performance expected of a person with the same age and level of education.

Despite acknowledgment of its worthy intentions, the LNNB has been widely criticized. Neither the entire scale nor any subscale has been adequately shown to be a valid measure of any specific cognitive function (Adams, 1980; Delis & Kaplan, 1983). Score values were determined on the basis of how well scores separated control and neurologically impaired groups and, therefore, bear little relationship to the ways in which neurologic disorders are manifested. By imposing strict time limits on tests, it penalizes slow responders without providing a means for evaluating the quality of performance or distinguishing between failures caused by generalized slowing or by impairment of specific functions associated with an item (Lezak, 1983). Even more dangerous attributes of the LNNB have been highlighted by a number of authors who found that the tests either overestimated the degree of pathology in certain areas or failed to detect or mislocalized critical focal deficits. From a rehabilitation perspective, all of these criticisms would pose significant problems for practical decision making or treatment planning.

The Good Samaritan Hospital Process-Specific Neuropsychologic Assessment

At Good Samaritan Hospital, a process-specific approach to neuro-psychologic assessment has been adopted in which tests were selected for their ability to assess theoretically grounded aspects of cognitive function as discretely as possible. Interpretation of test scores is grounded in both the normative statistical base for each measure and an approach to testing that incorporates extensive observational information about how individuals go about completing tests and the nature of their successes and failures. In this way, it relies heavily on the methods developed and expounded on by Kaplan (1983). The assessment incorporates redundant measures of each cognitive function. This allows the examiner to look for consistency of performance in specific cognitive abilities and assess variations in perform-ance from a perspective of impaired component processes or noncognitive variables (anxiety, depression, etc.). The outcome is a comprehensive assess-ment of strengths and weaknesses in multiple components of different cognitive process areas.

The particular tests that are incorporated into this assessment approach are listed in Table 4.2. Tests were selected to fit the theoretically based models of cognitive processing discussed throughout the remainder of this book.

Intellectual Function. The Wechsler Adult Intelligence Scale and Shipley Institute of Living Scale are used to look at the general level of intellectual functioning. Although neither of these measures was designed as a measure of brain function per se, both provide some insights into the previous level of functioning. Such insights are based on scores for subtests involving vocabulary recognition and retrieval of old information of the type learned in school. Scores on these subtests tend to reflect educational background and to "hold" following injury to the brain. In addition, the breakdown between verbally based abilities (Verbal scale) and visuospatial/ visuomotor skills (Performance scale) may reflect lateralized or diffuse brain dysfunction. Finally, individual subtest performance may reveal relatively discrete cognitive deficits. The Digit Span, Arithmetic, and Digit Symbol subtests, for example, appear sensitive to deficits in attention, concentra-tion, and mental control.

Attention/Concentration. Multiple measures of concentration and attention sample performance on tasks designed to address vigilance (sus-tained attention), freedom from distractibility (selective attention), and attentional control (alternating and divided attention). A conceptual model incorporating these aspects of attention is described in Chapter 6.

TABLE 4.2. Cognitive Assessment Procedures
(Center for Cognitive Rehabilitation)

Intelligence
  Wechsler Adult Intelligence Scale—Revised (Wechsler, 1981)
  Shipley Institute of Living Scale (Zachary, 1986)

Attention/concentration
Sustained attention
  Seashore Rhythm Test (as used in Halstead–Reitan Neuropsychological Test
    Battery; Reitan, 1969)
  Corsi Block-Tapping Test (Milner, 1971)
Selective attention
  Stroop Test (Stroop, 1935; Golden, 1978)
Alternating attention
  Symbol Digit Modalities Test (Smith, 1973)
  Trailmaking A and B (Reitan, 1958, 1969)
Divided attention
  Test d2 (Hogrefe, 1962)
  Paced Auditory Serial Addition Test (Gronwall, 1977)
All levels of attention
  APT Test (as used in attention process training; see Chapter 6)

Memory/new learning
General memory scales
  Wechsler Memory Scale—Revised (Wechsler, 1945, 1987)
  Randt Memory Test (Randt & Brown, 1983)
Verbal learning measures
  California Verbal Learning Test (Delis, Kramer, Kaplan, & Ober, 1986)
  Learning Efficiency Test (Webster, 1981)
Nonverbal memory
  The Revised Visual Retention Test (4th ed.) (Benton, 1974)
  Test of Visual Perceptual Skills, Visual Memory and Visual Sequential Memory
    Subtests (Gardner, 1982)
  Rey Complex Figure Recall (Rey, 1941; Lezak, 1983)
Recognition memory
  Recognition Memory Test (Warrington, 1984)
Functional memory
  Rivermead Behavioral Memory Test (Wilson, Cockburn, & Baddeley, 1985)
  Prospective Memory Screening Test (Sohlberg & Mateer, 1987)

Executive functions
  Executive Function Behavioral Rating Scale (Sohlberg, 1987)
  Wisconsin Card-Sorting Test (Heaton, 1981)
  The Maze Test (Porteous, 1959)
  Rey Complex Figure Copy (Rey, 1964)

Divergent production
  Controlled Oral Word Association Test (Benton, Hamsher, Varney, & Spreen,
    1983)
  Design Fluency Test (Jones-Gotman & Milner, 1977)

TABLE 4.2. Continued

Visual processing

Featural perception and discrimination
    Form Discrimination (Benton et al., 1983)
    Judgment of Line Orientation (Benton et al., 1983)
    Test of Visual Perceptual Skills—Spatial Relations Subtest (Gardner, 1982)
Visual recognition
    Hooper Visual Organization Test (Hooper, 1983)
    Woodcock–Johnson Psychoeducational Battery—Visual Matching; Perceptual
        Speed Cluster (Woodcock & Johnson, 1977)
Spatial perception and judgment
    Visual Search Test (Kimura, 1984)
    Woodcock–Johnson Psychoeducational Battery—Spatial Relations; Perceptual
        Speed Cluster (Woodcock & Johnson, 1977)
Visuomotor skill
    Purdue Pegboard (Purdue Research Foundation, 1948)
    Three-Dimensional Block Construction (Benton et al., 1983)

Reasoning
    Differential Aptitude Tests—Abstract Reasoning Subtest (Bennett, Seashore, &
        Wesman, 1982)
    Shipley Test of Living Skills (Part II) (Zachary, 1986)
    Woodcock–Johnson Psychoeducational Battery (Woodcock & Johnson, 1977)
    Test of Nonverbal Intelligence (Brown, Sherbenou, & Johnson, 1982)

Communicative functions

Language
    Boston Diagnostic Aphasia Exam (Goodglass and Kaplan, 1972)
    Western Aphasia Battery (Kertesz, 1982)
    Boston Naming Test (Kaplan, Goodglass, & Weintraub, 1983)
    Test of Written Language (Hammill & Larsen, 1983)
    Detroit Test of Learning Aptitude (Hammill, 1985)
    Revised Token Test (McNeill & Prescott 1978)
    Woodcock–Johnson Test of Psychoeducational Ability-Verbal Ability Cluster
        (Woodcock & Johnson, 1977)
Speech motor function
    Assessment of Intelligibility of Dysarthric Speech (Yorkston & Beukelman, 1981)
    Apraxia Battery for Adults (Dabul, 1979)
Pragmatics
    Communication Performance Scale (Ehrlich & Sipes, 1988)

Academic function
    Key Math Test (Connolly, Nachtman, & Pritchett, 1976)
    Gates–MacGinitie Reading Test (MacGinitie, 1978)
    Woodcock Reading Mastery Tests (Woodcock, 1973)
    Speed of Reading Test (Williams, 1986)

Memory/New Learning. Given the enormous complexity of the memory system, evaluation in this area demands a broad range of assessment tools. They are chosen to incorporate immediate and delayed recall of verbal and nonverbal information, measures of learning (given the opportunity to hear or see information on multiple occasions), measures that require recognition as opposed to recall memory, and measures of functional memory.

Visual Processing. Assessment in the area of visual processing reflects the four-component model of this cognitive area presented in Chapter 8. The areas of featural perception and discrimination, visual recognition, spatial perception and judgment, and visuomotor skill are each thought to have separable underlying neurophysiological substrates.

Executive Functions. These measures all involve aspects of categorical reasoning, planning, organization, monitoring, and self-correction. All have been shown to be sensitive to frontal lobe pathology. It is well acknowledged that deficits in this area are extremely difficult to assess and may be best evaluated in more natural environmental settings. For this reason, we have incorporated an Executive Function Rating Scale (see Chapter 10).

Divergent Production. The two measures in this section both assess fluency and flexibility in the generation of information. The Controlled Oral Word Association Test requires rapid generation of words beginning with a certain letter; the Design Fluency Test requires generation of abstract designs. They have been shown to be sensitive to left and right frontal lobe impairment, respectively (Jones-Gotman & Milner, 1977).

Reasoning. These measures involve abstraction, sequential thinking, and problem solving.

Communication Functions—Language, Speech, and Pragmatics. Language is assessed through formal measures of expression and comprehension in auditory and visual modalities, with achievement- and aptitude-oriented measures of language supplementing traditional aphasia testing. The detailed assessment of aphasic speech and/or dysarthria is typically undertaken by a speech/language pathologist. Pragmatics is that component of communication that relates to how things are communicated in a social context rather than to what is said from a purely linguistical standpoint (see Chapter 9).

Academic Function. Multiple measures of functional mathematics, reading, and writing skills are rarely in themselves diagnostic in terms of brain dysfunction, but they will often provide practical information regarding ability to manage independently and to vocational options. They also provide support for selecting from among various treatment approaches that may require reading and/or writing skills (i.e., for independent memory book management).

We have found this approach to provide a comprehensive, multidimensional view of functioning within the major cognitive process areas. Not all tests would be used with all individuals. In an inpatient setting, testing typically takes place in brief but frequent sessions with tests selectively pulled from each of the major cognitive process areas. Within an outpatient or postacute rehabilitation program, all of the tests might be administered over several sessions to address each process area adequately from the standpoint of treatment planning. Implementation of treatment planning in each area based on the results of cognitive process assessment is the topic of the chapters in this text dealing with specific-process training (Chapters 5 to 11).

Cautions about Results of the Neuropsychologic Assessment

The recovery from brain injury is a dynamic process. Rehabilitation professionals, for the most part, will and should expect to see change. The changes are likely to be unpredictable in nature and course, although some broad general stages of recovery have been suggested (Rancho Los Amigos Scale, see Chapter 3). An evaluation done after 1 week on a rehabilitation unit may be completely out of date and no longer fairly represent the patient's ability a week later. For this reason, assessments on an acute rehabilitation unit are more productive and useful if they are short but frequent. Timely communication with the team by conference, chart note, report, or personal contact is critical.

For obvious reasons, a diagnostic work-up typically precedes remedial steps. Clinicians want to know with what they are dealing and to have a rationale for doing what they do about it. Nevertheless, there is no absolute division between assessment and therapy. Treatment itself can and indeed should be diagnostic, and appraisal should continue throughout the therapy process. Both assessment and treatment demand critical thinking on the part of clinicians, and in trying to piece together a coherent picture, they must gather all pertinent facts that might lead to a resolution of apparent contradictions.

It is likely that the rehabilitation specialist will recognize and appreciate a careful, comprehensive, and practically oriented neuropsychologic assessment. It may be, however, that a report does not seem to help with your treatment planning and fit with your own clinical impressions. The following is a list of possible limitations in a neuropsychologic assessment for the purposes of rehabilitation planning.

1. The assessment may have been too narrow. It may have failed to address or take into account a major cognitive process (i.e., attention).
2. It may have depended on too few measures of an individual cognitive process. Memory, for example, is a very complex, multidimensional capacity. One or two measures of memory are not likely to capture the consistency and extent of possible memory impairment or allow hypotheses about the possible reasons for memory failure to be addressed.
3. A reliance on global measures (such as an IQ or an Impairment Index) may be very misleading and sometimes mask profound disability in a particular area.
4. A failure to appreciate premorbid variables (a history of learning disability, educational limitations, language or cultural differences, or an above average to superior cognitive profile) is likely to lead to confusion and potential error with regard to the nature and degree of current difficulties.
5. In isolation, mild impairments in a number of different areas may look insignificant. Problems may result from an examiner's failure to appreciate the collective contribution of multiple, although subtle, deficits on adaptive functioning.
6. Brain injury may affect many aspects of behavior that are difficult to assess formally. A failure to appreciate the more intangible self-management and self-regulatory aspects of frontal lobe function may lead to overly optimistic estimates of adaptive capabilities.

A useful neuropsychologic report will replace jargon and overly general statements about levels of cognitive ability with a detailed description of the individual patient's specific cognitive profile and how that profile will interact with behavioral and environmental variables to affect functional capacity in a variety of real-life situations. It is not likely to be based on a fixed set of instruments but is oriented toward an in-depth understanding of cognitive processing capacity that will focus rehabilitation efforts in order to minimize the obstacles underlying functional problems. Frequent communication, dynamic interaction, and mutual respect among all rehabilitation professionals will provide a treatment team with the critical underpinnings for success.

SUMMARY

In recent years, the neuropsychologic assessment has become a critical part of the total evaluation of a person who has sustained a head injury. Neuropsychologic testing is a means of systematically probing complex cognitive and behavioral functions that, through decades of research, have been shown to correspond to specific aspects of brain function. An accurate and comprehensive picture of cognitive abilities also provides insights into the degree of impairment, probable effects of impairment on everyday functioning, and the ability to benefit from additional treatment.

Three broad approaches to neuropsychologic assessment include the statistical–psychometric approach, the theoretical–clinical approach, and the process-specific approach. Each approach has advantages and disadvantages and particular purposes for which it is most useful. Test selection and interpretation and the level of analysis applied to test results will vary depending on the specific questions that are being addressed.

Neuropsychologic test results must be interpreted in the context of relevant social, educational, and vocational history, pertinent medical hsitory, sensory and motor limitations, and behavioral and emotional status. Neuropsychologic assessment for the purpose of rehabilitation planning should go beyond a description of deficits to include overall patterns of cognitive and behavioral strengths and weaknesses and specific recommendations for therapeutic planning. An assessment battery useful in describing the integrity of component parts of different cognitive processes will provide the needed support and direction for developing and implementing a process-specific cognitive rehabilitation.

STUDY QUESTIONS

1. What are some limitations of test selection and battery development based on the Statistical–Psychometric Approach? What are the strengths?
2. Give an example of hypothesis testing with respect to an apparent inability to read.
3. List four major features of a Process-Specific Approach to neuropsychologic assessment.
4. What role does preinjury history play in the neuropsychologic assessment?
5. Describe two major test batteries and contrast them to a process-oriented, hypothesis-testing approach.

REFERENCES

Adams, K. M. (1980). In search of Luria's battery: A false start. *Journal of Consulting and Clinical Psychology* 48:511–516.

Barth, J. T., & Macciocchi, S. N. (1985). The Halstead–Reitan Neuropsychological Test Battery. In C. Newmark (Ed.), *Major psychological assessment techniques* (pp. 381–414). Boston: Allyn & Bacon.

Bennett, G., Seashore, N., & Wesman, A. G. (1982). *Differential Aptitude Tests.* New York: The Psychological Corporation, Harcourt Brace Jovanovich.

Benton, A. L. (1974). *The revised visual retention test.* New York: Psychological Corporation.

Benton, A. L., Hamsher, K. des. Varney, N. R., & Spreen, O. (1983). *Contributions to neuropsychological assessment.* New York: Oxford University PRess.

Boll, T. J. (1978). Diagnosing brain impairment. In B. B. Wolman (Ed.), *Clinical diagnosis of mental disorders* (pp. 601–675). New York: Plenum.

Brown, L., Sherbenou, R. J., & Johnson, S. K. (1982). *The Test of Nonverbal Intelligence.* Austin, TX: Pro-Ed Publishers.

Cohen, R. F., & Mapou, R. L. (1988). Neuropsychological assessment for treatment planning: A hypothesis testing approach. *Journal of Head Trauma Rehabilitation 3*:12–23.

Connolly, A. J., Nachtman, W., & Pritchett, E. M. (1976). *Key math-diagnostic arithmetic test.* Circle Pines, MD: American Guidance Service.

Dabul, B. (1979). *Apraxia Battery for Adults.* Tigard, OR: C. C. Publications.

Delis, D. C., & Kaplan, E. (1983). Hazards of a standardized neuropsychological test with low content validity: Comment on the Luria–Nebraska Neuropsychological Battery. *Journal of Consulting and Clinical Psychology 51*:386–398.

Delis, D. C., Kramer, J., Kaplan, E., & Ober, B. A. (1986). *The California Verbal Learning Test.* San Antonio: The Psychological Corporation.

Dodrill, C. B. (1978). A neuropsychological battery for epilepsy. *Epilepsia 19*:611–623.

Ehrlich, J., & Sipes, A. (1988). Group treatment of communication skills for head trauma patients. *Cognitive Rehabilitation 3*:32–37.

Eson, M. E., & Bourke, R. S. (1980). Assessment of information processing deficits after serious head injury. Paper presented at the eighth annual meeting of the International Neuropsychological Society, San Francisco.

Gardner, M. F. (1982). *Test of Visual-Perceptual Skills (Non-Motor).* Seattle: Special Child Publications.

Geschwind, N. (1965). Disconnexion syndromes in animals and man. *Brain 88*:237–294, 585–644.

Geschwind, N. (1970). The organization of language in the brain. *Science 170*:940–944

Golden, C. J. (1978). *Stroop Color and Word Test.* Chicago: Stoelting.

Golden, C., Hammeke, T. A., & Purisch, A. (1980). *Manual for the Luria Nebraska Neuropsychological Battery.* Los Angeles: Western Psychological Corporation.

Goodglass, H., & Kaplan, E. (1972). *Boston Diagnostic Aphasia Examination.* Philadelphia: Lea & Febiger.

Goodglass, H., & Kaplan, E. (1979). Assessment of cognitive deficit in the brain injured patient. In M. S. Gazzaniga (Ed.), *Handbook of behavioral neurobiology, Vol. 2, Neuropsychology* pp. 3–24. New York: Plenum.

Gronwall, D. M. (1977). A paced auditory serial addition task: A measure of recovery from concussion. *Perceptual and Motor skills 44*:367–373.

Halstead, W. C. (1947). *Brain and intelligence*. Chicago: University of Chicago Press.

Hammill, D. D. (1985). *Detroit Tests of Learning Aptitude (DTLA-2)*. Austin, TX: Pro-Ed.

Hammill, D. D., & Larsen, S. C. (1983). *Test of Written Language*. Austin, Tx: Pro-Ed.

Heaton, R. K. (1981). *A manual for the Wisconsin Card Sorting Test*. Odessa: Psychological Assessment Resources.

Hogrefe, C. J. (1962). *Test d2*. Gottingen: Verlag für Psychologie.

Hooper, A. E. (1983). *The Hooper Visual Organization Test Manual*. Los Angeles: Western Psychological Services.

Jones-Gotman, M., & Milner, B. (1977). Design fluency. The invention of nonsense drawings after focal cortical lesions. *Neuropsychologia 15:*653–674.

Kaplan, E. (1983). Achievement and process revisited. In S. Wepner & B. Kaplan (Eds.), *Toward a holistic development psychology*. Hillsdale, NJ: Erlbaum.

Kaplan, E., Goodglass, H., & Weintraub, S. (1983). *Boston Naming Test*. Philadelphia: Lea & Febiger.

Kertesz, A. (1982). *Western Aphasia Battery*. New York: Grune & Stratton.

Kimura, D. (1967). Functional asymmetry of the brain in dichotic listening. *Cortex 3:*163–178.

Kimura, D. (1984). *Neuropsychology test procedures*. London: D. K. Consultants.

Kolb, B., & Whishaw, I. Q. (1980). *Fundamentals of human neuropsychology*. San Francisco: W. H. Freeman.

Lezak, M. D. (1983). *Neuropsychological assessment*. New York: Oxford University Press.

Lezak, M. D. (1987). Making neuropsychological assessment relevant to head injury. In H. S. Levin, J. Grafman, & H. M. Eisenberg (Eds.), *Neurobehavioral recovery from head injury*. New York: Oxford University Press.

Luria, A. R. (1966). *Higher cortical functions in man* (B. Haigh, trans.). New York: Basic Books.

Luria, A. R. (1970). The functional organization of the brain. *Scientific American 222:*2–9.

Luria, A. R. (1973). *The working brain: An introduction to neuropsychology* (B. Hargh, trans.). New York: Basic Books.

MacGinitie, W. H. (1978). *Gates–MacGinitie Reading Tests*. Boston: Houghton Mifflin.

Mapou, R. L. (1988). Testing to detect brain damage: An alternative to what may no longer be useful. *Journal of Clinical and Experimental Neuropsychology 10:*271–278.

McNeill, M. R., & Prescott, T. E. (1978). *Revised Token Test*. Baltimore: University Park Press.

Milner, B. (1967). Brain mechanisms suggested by studies of the temporal lobes. In C. H. Millikan & F. L. Darley (Eds.), *Brain mechanisms underlying speech and language*. New York: Grune & Stratton.

Milner, B. (1971). Interhemispheric differences in the localization of psychological processes in man. *British Medical Bulletin 27:*272–277.

Milner, B. (1975). Psychological aspects of focal epilepsy and its neurological arrangement. In D. P. Purpura, J. K. Penry, & R. D. Walker (Eds.), *Advances in neurology, Vol. 8* (pp. 299–322). New York: Raven Press.

Porteuous, S. D. (1959). *The Maze Test and clinical psychology.* Palo Alto, CA: Pacific Books.

Purdue Research Foundation. (1948). *Examiner's manual for the Purdue Pegboard.* Chicago: Science Research Associates.

Reitan, H. M. (1958). Validity of the Trail Making Test as an indicator of organic brain damage. *Perceptual and Motor Skills* 8:271–276

Reitan, H. M. (1969). *Manual for the administration of neuropsychological test batteries for adults and children.* Tucson, AZ: Neuropsychology Laboratory.

Reitan, H. M., & Davison, L. A. (1974). *Clinical neuropsychology: Current status and applications.* New York: Hemisphere.

Rey, A. (1941). L'examen psychologique dans les cas d'encephalopathie traumatique. *Archives de Psychologie* 28:286–340.

Rey, A. (1964). *L'emamen clinique in psychologie.* Paris: Presses Universitaire de France.

Russell, E. W. (1984). Theory and development of pattern analysis methods related to the Halstead–Reitan Battery. In P. E. Logue & T. M. Shear (Eds.), *Clinical neuropsychology* (pp. 50–98). Springfield, IL: Charles C. Thomas.

Smith, A. (1973). *Symbol Digit Modalities Test.* Los Angeles: Western Psychological Services.

Sohlberg, M. M. (1987). *Executive Function Behavioral Rating Scale.* Puyallup, WA: Association for Neuropsychological Research and Development.

Sohlberg, M. M., & Mateer, C. A. (1987). *Prospective Memory Screening Test (PROMS).* Puyallup, WA: Association for Neuropsychological Research and Development.

Stroop, J. R. (1935). Studies of interference in serial verbal reactions. *Journal of Experimental Psychology* 18:643–662.

Teuber, H. L. (1964). The riddle of frontal lobe function in man. In J. M. Warren & K. Akert (Eds.), *The frontal granular cortex and behavior.* New York: McGraw-HIll.

Walsh, K. W. (1978). *Neuropsychology: A clinical approach.* Edinburgh: Churchill-Livingstone.

Warrington, E. k. (1984). *Recognition Memory Test.* Windsor: NFER–Nelson.

Webster, R. E. (1981). *Learning Efficiency Test.* Noveto, CA: Academic Therapy Publications.

Wechsler, D. (1945). A standardized memory scale for clinical use. *Journal of Psychology* 19:87–95.

Wechsler, D. (1981). *Wechsler Adult Intelligence Scale—Revised.* Cleveland: Psychological Corporation.

Williams, D. (1986). *Test of Reading Speed.* Pauyallup, WA: Association for Neuropsychological Research and Development.

Wilson, B., Cockburn, J., & Baddeley, A. (1985). *Rivermead Behavioral Memory Test.* Reading, England: Thomas Valley Test Company.

Woodcock, R. W. (1973). *Woodcock Reading Mastery Tests.* Circle Pines, MN: American Guidance Service.

Woodcock, R., & Johnson, M. B. (1977). *Woodcock–Johnson Psychoeducational Battery.* New York: Teaching Resources.

Yorkston, K. M., & Beukelman, D. R. (1981). *Assessment of intelligibility of dysarthric speech.* Tigard, OR: C. C. Publications.

Zachary, R. A. (1986). *Shipley Institute of Living Scale—Revised Manual.* Los Angeles: Western Psychological Services.

Part II
COGNITIVE PROCESS AREAS

5
Theory and Remediation of Orientation Deficits

The immediate effects of a sudden trauma to the brain often include loss of consciousness (LOC). The duration of LOC is highly variable, ranging from minutes to months. Contrary to the impression one gets from dramatic television shows, most individuals do not suddenly "wake up" from coma but rather emerge gradually. This period of emergence from coma is also highly variable and can be characterized by a variety of behavioral symptoms, including confusion, agitation, disorientation to time and place, diminished memory, and reduced capabilities for attending and appropriately responding to environmental cues. In this chapter, we discuss the salient features of the emergence and present approaches to rehabilitation that may be helpful. Topics to be covered include definitions of coma and posttraumatic amnesia states, relationship of the length of these states to patient outcome, distinguishing characteristics of confusion and disorientation, definitions and distinguishing characteristics of retrograde and anterograde memory loss, assessments of confusion and disorientation, including the Galveston Orientation and Amnesia Test (GOAT), the Good Samaritan Orientation Test, and informal tests to identify attentional deficits and aphasia, the structure and importance of orientation groups, external orientation aids and cuing levels, and rationale for orientation training.

COMA

Coma is a term applied to the condition in which the patient displays minimal, if any, organized or purposeful response to the external environment. In "deep" coma, the patient may demonstrate no discernable behavioral response to touch, pain, sound, or movement, although autonomic physiologic responses not under voluntary control such as blood pressure or heart rate are sometimes noted to change with sensory stimulation. In lighter stages of coma, there may be a response to external stimulation, but the response is generalized, that is, characterized by whole-body movement or motor responses not directed to or away from the stimulation. The level of stimulation necessary to produce a response may be very intense. In the past, terms such as *lethargy, stupor,* or *obtundation* have been used to describe individuals who could only be aroused by vigorous or continuous external stimulation (Plum & Posner, 1980). Coma is believed to result from lesions involving central portions of the brainstem between the third ventricle and the pons. It can result from head injury, intracranial tumor, vascular or inflammatory lesions, or from certain toxic and metabolic states.

The variable nature of responses during the period of coma and the lack of standardization in behavioral description led to the development, by Teasdale and Jennett (1974), of the Glasgow Coma Scale (Table 4.2). This systematic rating scale is of great practical value in assessing grades of impairment of consciousness. It focuses on three areas of possible response: (1) the level of stimulation required for eye opening, (2) the level of purposeful motor response, and (3) the level of verbal response.

It has been shown that the duration of coma has some predictive power in terms of the quality of long-term recovery. It is important to note, however, that long periods of coma may still be followed by relatively good recovery; and individuals may suffer very brief or no loss of consciousness and still have longstanding physical and/or cognitive sequelae.

POSTTRAUMATIC AMNESIA

Another time period that has been shown to correlate with the extent and quality of eventual recovery from head injury is a period that has been termed posttraumatic amnesia (PTA). This is the period following the comatose stage that is characterized chiefly by an inability to store or recall information on a day-to-day or even minute-to-minute basis. Table 5.1

TABLE 5.1 Relation Between Duration of Posttraumatic Amnesia (PTA) and Rating of Recovery According to the Glasgow Outcome Scale

PTA duration (days)	R	Severe disability (%)	Moderate disability (%)	Good recovery (%)
< 7	11	—	9	91
7–14	27	—	26	74
15–28	38	2	45	53
> 28	63	32	57	11

Note. From "Assessment of severity of head injury" by B. Jennett, 1976. *Journal of Neurology, Neurosurgery and Psychiatry,* 39:647–655. Copyright 1976 by British Medical Association. Reprinted by permission.

provides figures that support the relationship between the duration of PTA and eventual outcome. Levin, Benton, and Grossman (1982) have argued that this relationship is even stronger than that between outcomes and the duration of coma.

From a clinical perspective, the period that can be classified as PTA actually can be characterized by a number of behavioral and cognitive manifestations. These are described in the next two sections: *Confusion and Agitation* and *Disorientation*. Retrograde memory loss, loss of information or recalled experiences acquired prior to infury, and anterograde memory loss, loss of information or recall of experiences acquired after injury, are discussed in this chapter under the heading *Disorientation*. They are discussed again in Chapter 7 on a more comprehensive basis in reference to disorders of memory.

CONFUSION AND AGITATION

As patients begin emerging from coma, they generally become more responsive to external stimulation (including speech) and more purposeful in their movements and verbalizations. Early on, however, they may demonstrate marked *agitation*. This phase is often characterized by constant motion or activity involving arms, legs, and trunk. Patients may move their head around constantly, but they do not appear to focus on particular sights or sounds, at least not for more than a few seconds. They may speak, but speech is often completely irrelevant or meaningless beyond a few automatic social responses.

At somewhat higher levels of recovery, patients typically display less agitation and appear fully "awake," but they may be unable to maintain a coherent line of thought. They can attend or concentrate for very short periods but fail to maintain focus. Concentration is rapidly lost, and attention wanders or is taken by any other stimulus that is present (e.g., PA system announcements, someone walking by). They lose the content or focus of what they are saying and begin to ramble, sometimes maintaining loose association to the general theme, sometimes getting completely off topic.

The term *confusion* is most usefully applied only when referring to the kind of pervasive attentional deficits just discussed. It is almost always acute and reversible in patients with head injury (Strub, 1982), although more demanding levels of attentional capacity often remain impaired (see Chapter 6). In some very severely head-injured patients, confusional states may become fixed and chronic.

Neuroanatomic bases of confusion are not well understood, but dysfunction of the septal areas (medial posterior frontal) or frontal subcortical connections has been postulated. Toxic and metabolic disturbances (which are frequent following head injury) are hypothesized to be the most common causes of this awake–confused state (Cummings & Benson, 1983).

Important differential assessments should be undertaken in patients demonstrating confusion. It is necessary to discriminate among (1) an impaired level of wakefulness (characterized by depressed or fluctuating arousal), (2) severely impaired attentional capacity (characterized by full wakefulness but an inability to maintain attention), and (3) aphasia (characterized by expressive or receptive language deficits). Attentional and language deficits can usually be picked up through the use of simple language tests and interview, particularly with discussion of information in the "here and now." Simple tests, such as naming and yes–no questioning, are particularly useful in that they are likely to detect aphasia and indicate the appropriateness of other kinds of formal assessment. More open-ended measures such as picture description and general questioning are helpful in identifying impaired attention, as manifest by rambling conversation or incoherent lines of thought. Measures such as digit span (forward and backward) and other simple attentional tasks (e.g., saying the alphabet, counting backward, counting forward by 3's) can be useful in further evaluating the extent of basic attentional deficits.

DISORIENTATION

In the neurologic tradition, orientation is assessed in relation to a person's level of awareness in four spheres—person, place, time, and circumstance. In terms of brain function, appreciation of these different spheres of information may have very different neurologic substrates and thus may be differentially disrupted following disease or injury. Some aspects of disorientation may reflect retrograde memory loss; others, failures in new learning or anterograde memory loss.

Retrograde Memory Loss

Orientation to person can be considered part of autobiographic memory and includes explicit knowledge of one's name, age, marital status, number of children, address, home town, birth place, etc. This is all information that was acquired and stored prior to the onset of the injury. It thus should not need to be learned or acquired but simply retrieved; its loss represents a retrograde memory failure for autobiographic information.

Levin and colleagues (1985) conducted a study of retrograde memory failure for remote memories involving experiences in the decades prior to injury. Patients with moderate to severe head injuries were examined before and after resolution of PTA. Information for key events during various developmental periods (i.e., a patient's first date) was verified by interviewing a collateral source such as a relative. After clearing of PTA, patients could recall at least 80% of personally salient memories from each developmental period. When they were examined during PTA, however, the researchers found a temporal gradient in the autobiographic memory loss of patients such that a higher proportion of events were correctly recalled from early than from more recent developmental periods (see Figure 5.1). The investigators suggested that repeated reminiscence of early personal events incorporated these memories into a semantic structure that became relatively invulnerable to retrograde amnesia.

In our own experience, failure of orientation to basic autobiographic information almost always clears in the early stages of resolving PTA. When it does not, it is frequently associated with severe head injury involving widespread disruption of cortical structures. This is consistent with investigations of orientation in patients with dementia. Whereas minute-to-minute "forgetfulness" may be associated with subcortical dementias, disturbances of remote recall are almost always associated with extensive cortical involvement (Cummings & Benson, 1983). Most head-injured patients experience only a brief (minutes to seconds) permanent loss of memory for events just prior to a traumatic injury, with relatively normal access to memories up to the period of retrograde amnesia. Recovery of such memories may take some time, however, and despite apparent "con-

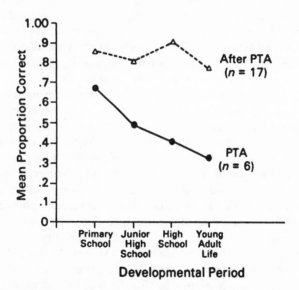

FIGURE 5.1 Mean proportion of correct recall of autobiographical information plotted as a function of developmental period for patients examined during PTA versus those tested after resolution of PTA. From Levin et al. (1985). Copyright 1985 by British Medical Association. Reprinted by permission.

solidation" of memory, islands of memory loss may remain. Some patients, in contrast, experience total loss of, or only very clouded access to, memories for events in their life preceding brain injury. Such patients often report experiencing profound loss of sense of self and are highly anxious.

Anterograde Memory Loss

Unlike orientation to person, orientation to date, place, and circumstances requires the capacity to take in, store, and recall new information presented after the injury. Head injury often severely disrupts this capability during the period of PTA. Of these, the patient's ability to recognize and remember that he or she is in a hospital often returns first, perhaps because of the ever-present environmental and situational cues.

Recalling which hospital they are in, the circumstances of their hospitalization, and that they had an accident often takes longer, perhaps because the information is not continually present. Indeed, many errors on questioning of orientation to place suggest possible misinterpretations of rehabilitation environments. Patients may report that they are in school, a military barracks, or a hotel.

Most difficult, and often last, to recover is consistent orientation to time. Orientation to time includes explicit awareness of year, month, date, season, and time of day. Unlike other aspects of orientation, time continually changes, and information about it must be constantly updated. It thus requires increased levels of awareness and more flexible, as well as efficient, new learning. Time orientation also incorporates features of sequence and order. The frontal lobes of the brain, which are often implicated in traumatic brain injury, are known to be critical for time tagging—identifying the relationship of one event to memory to another in time.

Confabulation is a term used to describe incorrect responses to orientation questions (but responses for which the patient might be quite confident). Confabulations can, at times, be bizarre, suggesting unreal or impossible activities. More often, however, the wrong responses reflect plausible but incorrect information (a recent day or date) or are a recital of personal activities that did occur at one time (an actual experienced event) but did not occur recently. Although confabulation is often seen in the period of posttraumatic amnesia characterized by severe anterograde memory loss and thus is generally associated with disturbed learning and memory, it is perhaps best correlated with the patient's ability to monitor his or her own responses and be self-corrective (Mercer, Wagner, Gardner, & Benson, 1977). Confabulation has also been specifically associated with frontal lobe dysfunction (Kapur & Coughlan, 1980; Shapiro, Alexander, Gardner, & Mercer, 1981; Stuss, Alexander, Lieberman, & Levine, 1978).

Disorientation and anterograde amnesia do not appear to reflect manifestations of a common underlying deficit. Correspondence was seen in only half the patients with minor head injuries studied by Sisler and Penner

(1975), and recovery of the two functions was not found to be coincident in patients studied by Gronwall and Wrightson (1980). Orientation is typically recovered first, but profound impairment in paragraph recall, associative learning, design recall and recognition, and memory for day-to-day events may remain severely disturbed.

APPROACHES TO ASSESSMENT OF ORIENTATION DEFICITS

In the lower-level patient, formal assessment of orientation must be preceded by preliminary observations to determine the appropriateness and validity of administering a formal orientation questionnaire. This process has two parts:

1. Determine the patient's overall level of arousal.
   —Observe the patient for any lessening in the normal level of wakefulness (lethargy, drowsiness, unresponsiveness).
   —Assess the patient's ability to focus and maintain attention for the duration of individual test items and over the time necessary to respond to a questionnaire.
2. Determine, at least in cursory fashion, the patient's expressive and receptive language capabilities.
   —Is the patient capable of single-word responses? Full-sentence responses? Are aphasic errors present?
   —If the patient cannot respond verbally, does he or she have a reliable yes/no response?
   —Assess the patient's comprehension for simple sentences.

Only if the patient can maintain alertness and arousal and has a reliable means of communication can formal testing of orientation proceed.

Although much of this information can be gathered informally at bedside, attempts have been made to standardize assessment of the low-level patient. The Neurobehavioral Cognitive Status Examination (NCSE) (Kiernan, Mueller, Langston, & Van Dyke, 1987) is a screening test that assesses cognition in a brief but quantitative fashion using independent tests to evaluate functioning within five major cognitive ability areas: language, constructions, memory, calculations, and reasoning. More important with reference to the current discussion, however, is that the examination also separately assesses level of consciousness, orientation, and attention.

The Galveston Orientation and Amnesia Test

Levin, O'Donnell, and Grossman (1979) developed a brief schedule of questions to measure directly amnesia and disorientation after head injury (Figure 5.2). Administration of the GOAT includes asking the person:

DIVISION OF NEUROSURGERY

THE UNIVERSITY OF TEXAS
MEDICAL BRANCH HOSPITALS
GALVESTON, TEXAS

Name _____

Date of Test └─┴─┴─┘
          mo day yr

Age _____ Sex   M   F

Day of the week s m t w th f s

Date of Birth └─┴─┴─┘
       mo day yr

Time   AM   PM

Diagnosis _____

Date of injury └─┴─┴─┘
           mo day yr

GALVESTON ORIENTATION & AMNESIA TEST (GOAT)

Harvey S. Levin, PhD., Vincent M. O'Donnell, M. A., & Robert G. Grossman, M.D.

INSTRUCTIONS: Error points (shown in parentheses after each question) are scored for *incorrect* answers and are entered in the two columns on the extreme right side of the test form. Enter the total error points accrued for the 10 items in the lower right hand corner of the test form. The GOAT score equals 100 minus the total error points. Recovery of orientation is depicted by plotting serial GOAT scores on at least a daily basis.

Error Points

1. What is your name? (2) _____ When were you born? (4) _____   └─┴─┘
     here do you live? (4) _____

2. Where are you now? (5) city _____ (5) hospital _____   └─┴─┘
     (unnecessary to state name of hospital)

3. On what date were you admitted to this hospital? (5) _____   └─┴─┘
     How did you get here? (5) _____

4. What is the first event you can remember *after* the injury? (5) _____   └─┴─┘
     Can you describe in detail (e.g., date, time, companions) the first event you can recall
     after injury? (5) _____

5. Can you describe the last event you recall *before* the accident? (5) _____   └─┴─┘
     _____ Can you describe in detail (e.g., date, time, companions) the first
     event you can recall *before* the injury? (5) _____

6. What time is it now? _____ 1 for each ½ hour removed from correct time to maximum   └─┴─┘
     of 5)

7. What day of the week is it? _____ 1 for each day removed from correct one)   └─┴─┘

8. What day of the month is it? _____ 1 for each day removed from correct date to   └─┴─┘
     maximum of 5)

9. What is the month? _____ 5 for each month removed from correct one to maximum   └─┴─┘
     of 15)

10. What is the year? _____ 10 for each year removed from correct one to maximum of   └─┴─┘
     30)

Total Error Points └─┴─┘

Total GOAT Score (100-total error points) └─┴─┘

(continued)

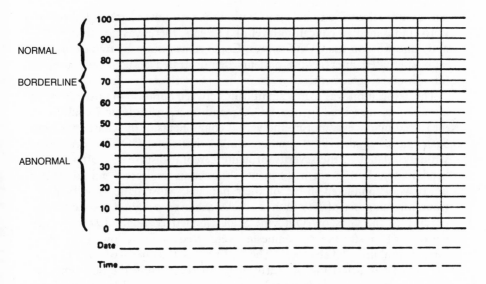

FIGURE 5.2 The Galveston Orientation and Amnesia Test: A practical scale to assess cognition after head injury. From Levin et al. (1979). Copyright 1979 by Williams & Wilkins. Reprinted by permission.

- his or her name, address, and birth date (Question 1)
- the city or town he or she is in and the type of facility (Question 2)
- the date of hospital admission (Question 3)
- events prior to the injury (Question 4)
- events after the injury (Question 5)

The first question probes for orientation to person, the second for possible geographic disorientation. The third was included because it was assumed that patients are inclined to obtain that information. Although the total GOAT score is interpreted as a global index of amnesia and disorientation, the questions do permit some separate estimates of posttraumatic anterograde and retrograde amnesia as conventionally defined.

After entering the error points for each question, the sum is deducted from 100, yielding the total GOAT score. It is advised that the GOAT be administered at least once a day. Based on a normative sample of 50 young adults who had recovered from mild closed head injury, the following cutoffs were determined: a score below the entire mild group (less than or equal to 65) is considered to be defective; the range from 66 to 75 is designated as borderline.

Error analysis by the authors revealed that the most frequent error responses were deviations from the correct day of the month, time of day, and date of admission to hospital. Within the restraints of an age limit of 50 years and a median education level of 11 years, there was no effect of age and education on the GOAT scores. Concurrent ratings by two examiners who alternated interviewing patients demonstrated a significant level of interobserver agreement.

The association was highly significant between duration of posttraumatic amnesia, as measured by the GOAT, and acute neurologic impairment, measured by the eye, motor, and verbal components of the Glasgow Coma Scale. Levin et al. (1979) thus concluded that serial GOAT scores were strongly related to the severity of acute cerebral disturbance after closed head injury. Long-term assessment of outcome at least 6 months after injury was completed in 32 of their patients. Most patients with posttraumatic amnesia of less than 2 weeks achieved a "good recovery" according to the Glasgow Outcome Scale (Jennett & Bond, 1975); longer periods of posttraumatic amnesia were frequently followed by prolonged disabilities (Table 5.2). The GOAT has thus been widely adopted for use in characterizing the early phase of recovery in the noncomatose patient and is particularly useful in patients who proceed from very brief periods of coma (e.g., 1 or 2 hours) to prolonged confusional states that fluctuate in the degree of disorientation, amnesia, and behavioral disturbance.

Rehabilitation staff at Good Samaritan Hospital in Puyallup, Washington, have developed an alternative orientation test. It is similar in construction to the GOAT but contains 20 items and is divided clearly into sections for personal information, orientation to place, orientation to time, and general information. One major addition is an alternate form that can be used with patients who do not have a verbal response but can reliably indicate yes and no (see Figure 5.3).

TABLE 5.2 Duration of Posttraumatic Amnesia on GOAT as a Predictor of Long-Term Outcome

Long-term outcome	Duration of PTA on GOAT						
	0–1 d	4–7 d	8–14 d	15 d–1 mo	1–2 mo	> 2 mo	Total
Good recovery	3	4	7	2	0	0	16
Moderate/severe disability	—	—	1	5	5	5	16

Note. From "The Galveston Orientation and Amnesia Test: A practical scale to assess cognition after head injury" by H. S. Levin, W. M. High, C. A. Meyers, A. Von Laufer, M. E. Hayden, and H. M. Eisenberg. 1979. Journal of Nervous and Mental Disease 167:675–684. Copyright 1979 by Williams & Wilkins. Reprinted by permission.

Directions: Administer this version of the Orientation Test to patients who cannot respond verbally more than yes/no and/or have a reliable way to indicate yes/no (e.g. pointing, writing, eye blink, thumbs up/ thumbs down, etc.). Vary the order in which correct and incorrect answers are presented for responses. Also vary the incorrect answer (i.e. use a variety of incorrect names instead of the same one each time).

PERSONAL INFORMATION: DATE

1. Is your name (first only) _____?
   (incorrect)
2. Is your name (first only) _____?
   (correct)
3. Are you _____ years old?
   (correct)...
4. Are you _____ years old?
   (incorrect)...
5. Do you live in _____?
   (city, correct)...........................
6. Do you live in _____?
   (city, incorrect).........................

ORIENTATION TO PLACE:

7. Is this place a school?..................................

8. Is this place a hospital?...............................

ORIENTATION TO TIME:

9. Is it the month of _____ now?
   (incorrect)...........................
10. Is it the month of _____ now?
    (correct).............................

                     PERCENT CORRECT

Good Samaritan Hospital
Orientation Test
(Yes/No Responses)

FIGURE 5.3 The Good Samaritan Hospital Orientation Test for yes/no response.

MANAGEMENT OF CONFUSION

Although there are no documented treatments for confusion and agitation, both pharmacologic and behavioral approaches have been proposed for their management. A review of pharmacologic treatments and issues in

TABLE 5.3 Guidelines for Home Management of the Chronically Confused Person

The following guidelines may be useful in providing a home environment which is well structured, predictable, and minimally threatening to the individual who is chronically confused:

Maintain the individual in familiar surroundings. Trips and visits to new places, while they may be entertaining for others, usually produce anxiety in confused persons.

Avoid ambiguity and do not present unnecessary choices or decisions. Use statements such as the following: "Now we must go to the store." "Now it is time to take a shower." "Brian is coming to visit after supper."

Mental tasks beyond the person's capacity produce anxiety. Avoid confronting the individual with tasks which stress areas of weakness. Therapies should be delivered routinely by the same therapist.

Try to maintain a daily routine that features well-established landmarks such as regular meals. Make life predictable. Avoid breaks in routine. Extend necessary changes in routine over time instead of abruptly making changes.

Fatigue will be poorly tolerated. Schedule visits to doctors after a period of sleep. Encourage very frequent periods of rest. Do not schedule several hours of unbroken activity.

Limit coffee and tea since stimulant effects may be amplified. Be alert for adverse side effects of other prescription and nonprescription medications.

Adequate lighting should be provided. Consider fluorescent fixtures in hallways, on stairs, and in bathrooms.

Limit confusion and confusing stimulation. Family gatherings may be overwhelming. Recreational activities may not be well tolerated, even if they involve previously favorite places or activities.

Be alert for indications of change in physical or mental status (prolonged agitation, escalated combativeness, changes in sleep or eating patterns).

It may help to have a radio tuned to a station playing familiar tunes. Television may contribute to the confusion of the environment.

Anticipate the possibility of the individual wandering off and getting lost. Sew labels into clothing to identify the person and who to call.

Schedule respite periods for primary caregivers.

Note: From "Management of the patient with chronic confusion" by D. Williams, 1987. Unpublished report. Good Samaritan Neuropsychological Services, Puyallup, WA. Reprinted by permission.

acute head injury rehabilitation can be found in a volume of the *Journal of Head Trauma Rehabilitation* (Cope, 1987). A list of behavioral and situational management approaches developed by Williams (1987) is provided in Table 5.3.

TREATMENT OF ORIENTATION DEFICITS

Rehabilitation approaches to orientation deficits usually focus on reacquainting patients in PTA with salient features of their environment (time, location, circumstance) and redirecting attention from internal states (e.g., pain) to external events. Both individual and group treatment approaches have been used to foster improved orientation.

Orientation Groups

Reality orientation groups were originally developed for use with geriatric patients (Brook, Degun, & Mather, 1975) but have been adapted for use with younger brain-injured patients. Goals typically extend beyond simple orientation and include increased attention, memory, cognitive functions (categorization or simple problem solving), and more appropriate social behavior. In order to benefit from such a group, patients must be able to demonstrate purposeful motor responses and some verbal communication. Patients with aphasia in addition to confusion and disorientation may find groups too frustrating.

John Corregan and his colleagues at Ohio State University (Corregan, Arnett, Houck, & Jackson, 1985) described an orientation group for brain-injured patients that was notable for its use of specific behavioral objects for each patient and inclusion of an extended (two-week) period for assessing criteria attainment. Specific information used during test sessions included:

1. Time: day, date, month, year, season, and daily schedule.
2. Locale: name and layout of the facility, location of various rehabilitation activities and the patient's room.
3. Identities: names and visual recognition of group members and the patient's therapists.
4. General facts: seasons, months, days of the week, current events, geography, money exchange, safe behavior, and other aspects of daily living.
5. Personal facts: family composition, premorbid history, and current circumstances of hospitalization.
6. Episodic information: events of the previous day or weekend.

Actual group process involved a variety of activities designed to elicit behaviors described in the group's objectives. Each day of the week is assigned a subset of behavioral objectives that must underlie the day's activities. For example, time orientation may be elicited every day, but episodic recall is only scheduled for Mondays, when weekend events are fresher. A schedule for a typical week is outlined in Table 5.4. The assigned objectives are minimums, allowing other tasks to be included in a day's activities. The distribution of objectives is periodically reviewed by the staff as part of ongoing evaluation.

The orientation groups typically meet daily for periods of an hour or less. It is often useful to have two staff members at each group—one leading

TABLE 5.4 Sample Schedule of Activities, Target Objectives, and Scoring Scale

Day	Activity	Objectives
Monday	Mark calendars	#1
	Group introductions	#3
	Recall weekend	#6, #4
	Present/recall current events	#4
Tuesday	Mark calendars	#1
	Therapists' identities	#3
	Test knowledge of schedule	#7, #4
Wednesday	Mark calendars	#1
	Elicit general fund of information	#3
	Elicit knowledge of facility and location	#2
Thursday	Mark calendars	#1
	Free recall tasks	#5, #4
	Sequential recall tasks	#5 #4
Friday	Mark calendars	#1
	Games	#4

Note. From "Reality Orientation for brain injured patients: Group treatment and monitoring of recovery" by J. D. Corregan, J. A. Arnett, L. J. Houck, and R. D. Jackson, 1985. *Archives of Physical Medicine and Rehabilitation* 66:626–630. Reprinted by permission.

while the other records patient performance. It is also helpful to maintain regular assignments in order to promote staff familiarity with the content of a particular day and individual patient goals. Table 5.5 lists objectives for patient performance in the reality orientation group.

External Orientation Aids

In addition to group approaches, a variety of external orientation aids can be provided in the environment. Labeled pictures of family members, friends, therapists, pets, cars, and home can be placed in the room, on the patient's lap tray, or in orientation/memory books. A large calendar with space for marking off days can be prominently displayed and brought to the patient's attention. Patients can begin to wear inexpensive watches even before they might spontaneously use them. Daily schedules should be posted in a central location and in a location that is physically and perceptually accessible to the patient. The patient's name can be prominently displayed outside his or her door, and hospital floor plans can be provided. Staff members can wear and direct attention to name tags.

TABLE 5.5 Objectives for Patient Performance in Reality Orientation Group

Patient is oriented to the day, date, and year 80% of the time over a 2-week period (time orientation aids such as calendars and clocks may be used)

Patient can correctly identify the name of the institution, city, state, and location of the group treatment room 100% of the time over a 2-week period

Patient can identify without aids other group members and therapists 80% of the time over a 2-week period

Patient is able to attend to group activities sufficiently to allow an appropriate response 75% of the time over a 2-week period

Patient is able to repeat five paired associations 100% of the time over a 2-week period

Patient correctly reports significant events of the previous day or weekend, with or without cues, 100% of the time over a 2-week period

Patient is able to use planning and scheduling aids to correctly report daily activities 100% of the time over a 2-week period

Note. From "Reality Orientation for brain injured patients: Group treatment and monitoring of recovery" by J. D. Corregan, J. A. Arnett, L. J. Houck, and R. D. Jackson, 1985. *Archives of Physical Medicine and Rehabilitation 66:626–630.* Reprinted by permission.

Individual Treatment

In most circumstances, orientation will also be addressed within individual treatment sessions. The most challenging part of these individual interventions is to obtain consistent data. Although a general stimulation approach may be useful, a systematic approach to facilitation and documentation of orientation data is far preferable. It is often valuable for each staff member to go through the orientation questionnaire, keeping data on daily performance, so that reports of inconsistencies in orientation may be revealed in staff conference. Following use of a formal orientation questionnaire, provision of cues necessary to get correct orientation responses should be considered. Levels of cuing might be conceptualized and recorded as follows:

Maximal cues: Therapist provides an immediate model of correct answer.

Therapist directs attention to an external orientation aid (e.g., calendar, watch, or orientation/memory book).

Moderate cues: Therapist provides multiple-choice format (e.g., "Were you born in January or April?").

Therapist provides yes/no question format (e.g., "Do you live in Detroit?").

General cues (see Table 5.6).

Partial cues (see Table 5.6).

Minimal cues: Patient spontaneously initiates referencing of external memory aids.

TABLE 5.6 Examples of General and Partial Cues for Orientation Questions

General cues	Partial cues
Personal information:	
Your birthday is in the summer	You were born in 1960. How old are you?
Identify persons in environment:	
I help people learn to talk again	My name starts with "B"
Place:	
You are in a hospital	The name of this town begins with "P"
Time:	
This season is cold	It's the day after Wednesday
Current events:	
Something happened in sports yesterday	The President's name begins with "R"

Thoughts on Training of Orientation

It has not yet been demonstrated that orientation training is instrumental in the resolution of disorientation, confusion, and memory loss. Indeed, since such training is quite new and the recovery of many patients has been observed, it is clearly not routinely necessary in such resolution. Even without empirical support for treatment efficacy, careful monitoring of orientation status is invaluable. The duration of PTA has been shown to be useful as one predictor of outcome, and self-report of internal states is known to be unreliable. Changing status during the period of PTA can indicate improved functioning even in the absence of formal neuropsychologic testing. Improvement in group performance can be used to justify continued hospital stay to families, the rehabilitation team, and external review bodies. In addition, persistent lack of improvement provides useful information in decisions about discharge. Finally, decline in performance may be the first objective evidence of a deteriorating medical condition such as slowly developing hydrocephalus, hypoxia from pulmonary insufficiency, or an adverse drug reaction. For these reasons, orientation and anterograde memory function should be carefully monitored.

The orientation group plays an important role in such monitoring. Standardized tests, such as the GOAT, for assessing PTA do not capture the multiple dimensions of impaired consciousness during this period of recovery. Patients may be able to answer accurately frequently repeated orientation questions before general confusion actually resolves and comprehensive episodic recall returns. Qualitative descriptions, such as the Rancho Scale (Table 4.1), do not provide discrete measurement of within-stage variability. Regular observation and measurement on a daily basis in an orientation group can provide a large sampling of behavior that minimizes biases caused by daily inconsistencies or highly structured one-on-one treatment tasks. To date, there is relatively little information about the limits of learning and memory during posttraumatic amnesia. Clearly, much additional research is needed regarding both the nature of cognitive ability during this phase of recovery and ways to positively affect it.

SUMMARY

Following gradual resolution of coma, patients who have sustained head trauma often move into a stage of disturbed consciousness, which has been termed posttraumatic amnesia or PTA. The persistence of PTA varies with the type and severity of neurologic injury. Cognitive and behavioral features during this period may include lethargy, confusion, incoherence of thought, severe attentional impairments, motor agitation, disorientation for past and current information, and a profound disturbance in new learning capacity. Differential assessment of these features can be helpful in identifying the underlying nature and degree of neurobehavioral disturbance and brain dysfunction.

Formal assessment procedures provide objective assessment of changing cognitive function during PTA. Improvements or declines in function during PTA and the overall duration of the period may provide early indicators of changing neurologic status as well as predictive information about the rate of short-term recovery.

Treatment approaches during this period have included environmental management strategies, orientation group activities, use of external orientation aids, and individual interaction in which cues for correct responses to orientation questions are gradually reduced. The efficacy of these approaches has yet to be proven. For this reason, careful documentation and systematic investigation are badly needed.

STUDY QUESTIONS

1. Describe the nature of the relationships among coma duration, length of PTA, and functional outcome.
2. Identify major distinguishing features of confusion and disorientation.
3. List several of the necessary behavioral and cognitive prerequisites for valid testing of orientation.
4. Describe the GOAT.

5. List three possible goals and three important principles for running orientation groups.
6. Give examples of five types of external orientation aids.

REFERENCES

Brook, P., Degun, G., & Mather, M. (1975). Reality orientation, a therapy for psychogeriatric patients: A controlled study. *British Journal of Psychiatry* 127:42–45

Cope, N. (Ed.) (1987). Psychopharmacology, *The Journal of Head Trauma Rehabilitation 2* (Part 4).

Corregan, J. D., Arnett, J. A., Houck, L. J., & Jackson, R. D. (1985). Reality orientation for brain injured patients: Group treatment and monitoring of recovery. *Archives of Physical Medicine and Rehabilitation 66:626–630.*

Cummings, J. L., & Benson, D. F. (1983). *Dementia: A clinical approach* (pp. 15–34). Boston: Butterworths.

Gronwall, D., & Wrightson, P. (1980). Duration of post-traumatic amnesia after mild head injury. *Journal of Clinical Neuropsychology 2:51–60.*

Jennett, B. (1976). Assessment of severity of head injury. *Journal of Neurology, Neurosurgery and Psychiatry 39:647–655.*

Jennett, B., & Bond, M. (1975). Assessment of outcome after severe brain damage. *Lancet i:480–487.*

Kapur, N., & Coughlan, A. K. (1980). Confabulation and frontal lobe dysfunction. *Journal of Neurology, Neurosurgery and Psychiatry 43:461–463.*

Kiernan, R. J., Mueller, J., Langston, J. W., & Van Dyke, C. (1987). The Neurobehavioral Cognitive Status Examination: A brief but differentiated approach to cognitive assessment. *Annals of Internal Medicine 107:481–485.*

Levin, H. S., O'Donnell, V. M., & Grossman, R. G. (1979). The Galveston Orientation and Amnesia Test: A practical scale to assess cognition after head injury. *Journal of Nervous and Mental Disease 167:675–684.*

Levin, H. S., Benton, A. L., & Grossman, R. G. (1982). *Neurobehavioral consequences of closed head injury.* New York: Oxford University Press.

Levin, H. S., High, W. M., Meyers, C. A., Von Laufer, A., Hayden, M. E., & Eisenberg, H. M. (1985). Improvement of remote memory after closed head injury. *Journal of Neurology, Neurosurgery and Psychiatry 48:556–563.*

Mercer, B., Wagner, W., Gardner, H., & Benson, D. F. (1977). A study of confabulation. *Archives of Neurology 34:429–433.*

Plum, F., & Posner, J. B. (1980). *Stupor and coma* (3rd ed.). Philadelphia: F. A. Davis.

Shapiro, B. E., Alexander, M. P, Gardner, H., & Mercer, B. (1981). Mechanisms of confabulation. *Neurology 31:1070–1076.*

Sisler, G., & Penner, H. (1975). Amnesia following severe head injury. *Canadian Psychiatric Association Journal 20:333–336.*

Strub, R. L. (1982). Acute confusional state. In D. F. Benson, & D. Blumer (Eds.), *Psychiatric aspects of neurologic disease, Vol. 2* (pp. 1–21). Grune & Stratton.

Stuss, D. T., Alexander, M. P., Lieberman, A., & Levine, H. (1978). An extraordinary form of confabulation. *Neurology 28:*1166–1172.

Teasdale, G., & Jennett, W. B. (1974). Assessment of coma and impaired consciousness. *Lancet ii:*81.

Williams, D. (1987). *Management of the patient with chronic confusion.* Unpublished report, Good Samaritan Neuropsychological Services, Puyallup, WA.

6
Theory and Remediation of Attention Disorders

Deficits in attention and concentration often go unrecognized or are misdiagnosed in the assessment of cognitive function following brain injury, yet such deficits are frequent. Concentration problems, together with poor memory, are reported to be among the most common postconcussional symptoms (Binder, 1986). Disruption of the physiological systems critical to the regulation of attention may occur as the result of seemingly minor, as well as severe, neurologic damage. Although their severity nearly always lessens over the course of recovery, significant deficits in attention and concentration are often present many months, or even years, post-injury. It has been posited that they are an underlying factor in many apparent failures of memory and contribute substantially to difficulty with reintegration into independent living and vocational settings. An understanding of attentional deficits is critical for the rehabilitation specialist, not only because of their frequency but because they are amenable to treatment (Sohlberg & Mateer, 1987).

This chapter begins by reviewing literature on the frequency of attention deficits and the current limitations in assessment. It then examines theories that have been proposed to explain the various aspects of attention and proposes approaches to the treatment of attentional deficits. Finally, it considers questions of efficacy and implications for the clinician. Topics to be covered include a review of attention theories (including selectivity models, working memory, conscious vs. unconscious processing, controlled vs. automatic processing, and vigilance); information-processing speed; sustained, selective, and divided attention; attentional control, a clinical model of attention, and attention training tasks and their efficacy.

INCIDENCE OF ATTENTION/CONCENTRATION PROBLEMS: INTROSPECTIVE STUDIES

Several studies support the conclusion that deficits in concentration and attention represent frequent and troublesome problems following traumatic brain injury. Caveness (1969) reported that 41% of veterans who had

110

received head injuries during the Korean War complained of difficulty concentrating 5 years later, as compared to only 14% of noninjured veterans. Since that time, a large number of prospective studies have reported increased incidence of concentration problems in head-injured subjects (see Gronwall, 1987, for review). Data from these studies suggest that although self-report of attention problems usually decreases in the months following injury (Lidvall, Linderoth, & Norlin, 1974; Rutherford, Merrett, & McDonald, 1977, 1979; Wrightson & Gronwall, 1981; McKinlay, Brooks, & Bond, 1983), a significant proportion of head-injured patients, particularly those with more severe injuries, still report problems two years posttrauma.

Mateer, Sohlberg, and Crinean (1987) surveyed a large sample of head-injured individuals and control subjects to assess the perceived incidence of various types of "forgetting" experiences. Both groups reported that problems related to tasks with significant attentional demands were experienced most frequently; the head-injured subjects reported significantly more frequent failures in this area. These results are consistent with other studies in that when concentration and memory problems are reported separately, concentration problems usually predominate (Lidvall et al., 1974; McLean, Dikmen, Temkin, Wyler, & Gale, 1984).

PROBLEMS IN THE ASSESSMENT AND MANAGEMENT OF ATTENTION DEFICITS

Despite the high incidence of attention disorders following traumatic brain injury, clinical treatment of these disorders has been hampered by a number of factors. The underlying bases and nature of attention deficits are still by no means clear. Although the phrase *paying attention* has definite connotations, it actually confuses and combines several different behaviors. To illustrate, statements like the following are frequently made by head-injured individuals: "I start watching a TV show and then just kind of drift off"; "I can't cook or drive or talk with someone while the radio is on. Any distraction upsets me"; and "I can't listen to a lecture and take notes at the same time."

These problems are respectively described in much of the cognitive and experimental literature as disorders of (1) sustained attention, (2) selective attention, and (3) divided attention. Clinical treatment must begin with accurate assessment of each of these. However, many of the standard psychometric batteries only cursorily examine attention. The most frequently used attentional measures include the Digit Span and Mental Control subtests of the Wechsler Memory Scale (Wechsler, 1945). In the Digit Span subtest, the maximum number of digits that can be repeated forward and backward is determined. The Mental Control subtests assess accuracy and rate for counting backwards, reciting the alphabet, and counting forward by

3's. Other commonly used measures that can be helpful in the elucidation of attention deficits include the Arithmetic and Digit Symbol subtests of the Wechsler Adult Intelligence Scale—Revised (Wechsler, 1981). These latter measures of mental calculation and of rapid visual–motor integration and tracking appear to sample certain aspects of attentional capacity.

Unfortunately, all of these measures are contaminated by requirements for sometimes complicated verbal, mathematical, or motoric requirements in addition to the attentional features. Furthermore, they are not theoretically based in any particular model of attention or even a component of such a model. Finally, they may not be sufficiently demanding of attentional capacity to reveal impairments.

Table 6.1 lists a number of different assessment tools that are currently used clinically to sample attentional capacity. They are roughly divided into (1) tests that primarily assess immediate or working memory, (2) tests in which performance on essentially simple information processing is timed, (3) tests in which information provided per time unit is controlled or "paced," and (4) tests that incorporate information processing in the face of high- or low-level distraction. These tests are very different in their requirements and, as a group, fit no consistent conceptual model, causing problems for the clinician who must pick and choose among them.

These problems derive, in large part, from the lack of a comprehensive theoretical formulation regarding the nature of attentional processes. Despite a large body of literature on attentional capability in normal subjects, many theories of attention are strongly tied to specific experimental tasks or paradigms. These theories say little about functional aspects of attention or

TABLE 6.1. Currently Available Tools to Assess Attention

Tests of immediate or working memory
    WAIS-R Digit Span Subtest (forward and backward)
    WAIS-R Arithmetic Subtest
    Seashore Rhythm Test
    Corsi Block-Tapping Test
Timed tests of information processing
    WAIS-R Digit Symbol Subtest
    d2 Test
    Trail-Making Tests
    Symbol Digit Modalities Test (SDMT)
Paced measures of information processing
    Paced Auditory Serial Addition Test (PASAT)
    Attentional Capacity Test (ACT)
Distractibility Measures
    Stroop Test
    Goldman–Fristoe–Woodcock Test of Auditory Discrimination

how the tasks relate to a model of attention that fits "normal" behavior. There is increasing movement toward a componential theory of attention and some move toward agreement as to what those components should be. Yet the literature continues to reflect an often bewildering array of terminology, which is applied inconsistently across studies and theories. In the remaining sections of this chapter, we review relevant aspects of the attention literature for the clinician who needs to develop a framework for conceptualizing attentional deficits in patient populations.

A BRIEF REVIEW OF ATTENTIONAL THEORIES

Experimental psychologists have been exploring the nature of normal attentional processes for decades, yet agreement on mechanisms of attention is far from universal. Most theoretical interpretations equate attention with information-processing capacity, that is, the amount of information that can be attended and responded to in a finite period of time (e.g., Broadbent, 1982; Craik & Levy, 1976; Kahneman, 1973; Shiffrin, 1975).

Broadbent (1958) first introduced the notion of *selectivity* in information processing, such that attention was viewed as a means by which target stimuli received priority over nontarget stimuli. That is, attention was considered to be the process by which one selectively responded to a specific event and inhibited responses to simultaneous events. Theorists differ on the stage or level of information processing at which attention operates. Under the rubric of selectivity models, there appear to be two classes of attention theory. The first class (the early selection theories) holds that differential processing of target and nontarget stimuli operates at the perceptual level. Target stimuli are processed more fully because there is *perceptual* suppression or nontarget stimuli (Broadbent, 1958; Treisman, 1969). According to this theory, brain mechanisms act to limit the amount of sensory input that an individual must process. The second class (late selection theories) proposes that a special attentional capacity within the organism allows for preferential processing of target stimuli over concurrent nontarget stimuli. All perceptual information enters the system, but only that which is selected by the special attention mechanism reaches higher processing centers (Shiffrin & Schneider, 1977). Thus, early selection theories propose that certain stimuli are never processed because of perceptual suppression; late selection theories propose that the unimportant information enters the system but simply is not chosen for further processing.

A shortcoming of both selectivity models is that they stop at the level of signal detection or target selection. The theoretical construct of *working memory,* as described by Baddeley and Hitch (1974) and Baddeley (1981), does begin to address function at higher levels of information processing. The "central executive," one component of Baddeley's model, is hypothesized to provide for temporary storage of information. The capacity for such temporary storage allows for division of attention during information processing. Modeled as a controller of memory, the central executive allows information to be held in short-term storage while attention is temporarily shifted to other stimuli. This model thus incorporates additional levels of information processing.

Distinctions have also been made between conscious and unconscious processing (Posner, 1980) and between controlled and automatic processing (Shiffrin & Schneider, 1977). These notions relate to the degree of awareness or effort required in the manipulation of attention. Van Zomeren (1981) contributed a differentiation between what he termed Focused Attention Deficits (FADs), in which automatic response tendencies conflict with the responses demanded in a task, and Divided Attention Deficits (DADs), in which poor performance results from speed limitations on unconsciously controlled processing.

Finally, there is the notion of *vigilance,* or the capacity to sustain behavior over time. Mirsky, Primac, Marson, Rosvold, & Stevens (1960) popularized this component of attention through use of continuous performance tasks, essentially simple tasks but ones for which attention needed to be maintained over long periods. The interactions between these various theories of attention and the associated terminology often leave the novice reader very confused.

Recent research reflects a number of trends. On the one hand, there is an attempt to examine simpler processes and simpler responses as a way of breaking down attention tasks into component parts. On the other hand, there is a tendency to posit ever higher and more complex levels of control over basic perceptual or information-processing mechanisms. There is little doubt that intensive investigation and controversy in this area will continue. In the following section, we attempt to relate specific aspects of attentional theory to what is known about the traumatically head-injured individual. In particular, we address the notions of information-processing speed, sustained attention, selective attention, divided attention, and attentional control.

Information-Processing Speed

Because of the prevalence of reports of "mental slowing" after head injury, reaction time measures have been used in many investigations. There is overwhelming evidence that head injury tends to produce an increase in reaction time (RT) (Hicks & Birren, 1970; Gronwall & Wrightson, 1974; Van Zomeren, 1981). In some cases of diffuse injury, such slowing can be one of the most conspicuous neurobehavioral symptoms. Studies have demonstrated that decrements in reaction time cannot be explained as simply the results of sensory or motor impairments. Theoretical explanations have suggested that the slowdown occurs particularly in the cognitive stages of stimulus encoding and response selection. This conclusion is based on studies that suggest that *choice reaction time* (where the subject must make one of a number of responses, depending on which of a number of stimuli are presented) is more sensitive to the effects of head injury than *simple reaction time* (where the subject has only to respond to one stimulus with one response). Simple RT appears to be equally prolonged after head injuries of all grades of severity and shows maximal degree of recovery within one year. Choice RT, in contrast, is more impaired with injuries of greater severity and continues to show recovery more than two years after injury (see Van Zomeren, 1981, for review).

Research with head-injured individuals suggests that the speed at which they can respond is decreased in direct proportion to the amount of information that must be processed before the response can be made. Many of the investigations in this area have derived from Broadbent's (1971) model of the human brain as a limited capacity processor. Measures such as the Paced Auditory Serial Addition Test (PASAT) (Gronwall, 1977) and the Attentional Capacities Test (ACT) (Weber, 1986) are based on the concept that attentional deficits will be manifest when the amount of information to be processed per available time exceeds the capacity of the system. (These measures are discussed again under the section on *Divided Attention.*)

Reaction time represents a behavioral measure of information-processing capacity, which may be reflected in any of the different areas of attention (sustained, selective, divided). It has been considered a measure of "tonic alertness" (Posner, 1975) or "cortical tone" (Luria, 1973).

Sustained Attention

Sustained attention refers to two aspects of performance relating to time. The first involves the *duration of time* over which a given level of performance can be maintained; the second, the *consistency* of performance over that period. Periods of poor performance, alternating with normal or near-normal performance, may imply lapses of attention. *Vigilance performance,* that is, the ability to respond rapidly to target stimuli (usually infrequent signals) presented over an extended time period, is a common measure of choice in the experimental assessment of sustained attention (Mirsky et al., 1960).

Head-injured patients do not seem to be particularly impaired, at least in the postacute stage, in their ability to maintain performance over time. The accuracy of their signal detection is often reduced, and their reaction times to signals are longer, but they are able to maintain task performance as long as control groups. This has been demonstrated with a variety of tasks, including continuous reaction time tasks such as the Continuous Performance Test (Greber & Perret, 1985) and vigilance tasks.

In a vigilance experiment by Brouwer and Van Wolffelaar (1985), EEG recordings showed that short periods of lowered alertness were no more frequent in concussed patients than in control subjects. Although problems with sustained attention are rarely reported with the mildly head-injured individual, more severely head-injured patients have frequently been reported to show such attention deficits in clinical settings (Jennett & Bond, 1975).

The concept of *lapses of attention* has been used anecdotally to explain poor performance on cognitive tests. Although few specific studies documenting lapses of attention in head-injured patients have been published, some indirect evidence suggests that such lapses are not the rule in individuals with mild or moderate concussion (Newcombe, 1982). Newcombe did, however, describe such lapses in more severely impaired patients.

Tasks that require crossing out certain visually presented targets in a complex array of stimuli (visual cancellation) appear to sample the same kind of sustained attention that is required by vigilance tasks. They are frequently used in clinical settings. Gentilini et al. (1985) compared a group of mild head-injury cases one month after trauma with controls on a cancellation task. They were required to mark from a matrix of 130 digits those that corresponded to 1, 2, or 3 digits at the top of each matrix. The score, the number of digits correctly marked in 45 seconds, was lower for the head-injured group than for the controls.

The Test d2 (Brickenkamp, 1962) is a cancellation task with somewhat more demanding attentional components. To be crossed out on a page are all the letter "d's" with two marks (two above, two below, or one above and one below). This requires more flexible and somewhat divided attention capabilities, as two different features must be attended to for each target. In a study in our own hospital, Text d2 performance was commonly depressed in patients with moderate to severe head injury. Although the task is also demanding on motoric requirements and visual discrimination, scores on the test were found to be significantly correlated with staff ratings of attention.

These authors' clinical experience suggests that whereas performance on simple cancellation or vigilance tasks usually recovers following mild closed head injury, the system for sustained attention often breaks down when the cognitive demands of the task or the amount of information to be attended to increases.

Selective Attention

Mention was made earlier of the notion of selectivity as a natural byproduct of the brain's limited processing capacity (Broadbent, 1958); Treisman, 1969). The term "selective attention" is also used when referring to the ability to focus on relevant stimuli in the presence of distracting stimuli and to select information for conscious processing. Within cognitive psychology, there have been two widely held views of selective attention. Some authors have argued that interference resulting from attention limitations is severe only when stimuli occur within the same modality or cognitive domain (e.g., two similar visual targets) but that different stimuli or tasks (e.g., a visual target and an auditory target) can be undertaken by simultaneous processing mechanisms (Allport, 1980). Other authors have favored the idea of a single-channel or limited-capacity processor, at least for the set of operations defined as conscious (Broadbent, 1958; Posner, 1978).

To confuse the matter further, several experimenters use the term *focused attention* when they are interested in the subject's ability to withstand distraction. Van Zomeren and Brouwer (1987) used this term to describe how well a subject can focus on relatively weak information in the presence of strong distraction. By "weak" and "strong" in this context, they are not referring to the physical intensity of stimulus but to association strength between stimuli and responses. As an example, the most common response to seeing a word is to read it, not to count the number of letters in it.

Within the context of head-injury research, the measure of selective attention or distractibility most commonly used has been the Stroop Test (Stroop, 1935). The Stroop Test measures the speed at which an individual can read a set of color names that are printed in letters of a conflicting color (e.g., the word "red" printed in blue ink). The time of reading the printed words is then compared with the speed at which the names of the *color of ink* in which the words are printed can be given. Even for control subjects, there is always a greater time on task when the colors to be identified conflict with the printed words. This difference has been taken to demonstrate a failure in selective attention and is assumed to be caused by an interference of the automatic reading response with the color-naming response required by the task. Studies have shown that although head-injured subjects are slower on all conditions of this task, they had no specific difficulty in focusing on the color dimension of the ambiguous stimuli, suggesting that there is only a mild effect of the "response conflict" or distractibility condition (Van Zomeren, 1981; McLean, Temkin, Dikmen, & Wyler, 1983). A limitation is that most of these studies involved chronic patients and/or mild cases of concussion.

Another task designed to assess selective attention after head injury (Van Zomeren, 1981) involved visual reaction time. Subjects watched eight lights in a semicircular array, four of which were stimulus lights. As soon as a stimulus light was turned on, subjects were to turn it off by pressing the light. In the second condition, they were to perform exactly the same task, but now most of the stimuli were accompanied by an irrelevant light, which they were instructed to ignore. This resulted in a strong response interference. The two lights were physically identical, and the author suggested that the subject's first impulse may have been to move his or her hand to the distractor. The distraction caused a large increase in RT in both groups but had a much stronger effect on the patient group. The author suggested that the distraction effect observed might indicate a specific deficit in response inhibition, particularly apparent in the first few months after severe concussion.

Research on selective attention or distractibility after head injury thus presents a somewhat inconsistent picture. Results of the Stroop Test, although limited, suggest normal focusing of attention in head-injury patients. On the other hand, reaction time experiments revealed that severely concussed patients need significantly more time to overcome distraction, particularly during the early stage of recovery. However, equivocal the literature, the frequent anecdotal reports by head-injury patients that they are distrubed by background noise and our own observations of patients in clinical settings suggest that this is an important area to consider.

Divided Attention

Slowness in elementary psychological operations is an important factor in complex tasks, particularly when time pressure is involved. One category in which slow information processing may be particularly limiting includes the so-called *divided-attention tasks*. In these tasks, either more than one kind of activity must be done simultaneously or multiple stimuli must be processed. A frequently cited example is the Paced Auditory Serial Addition Task (PASAT) (Gronwall & Sampson, 1974; Gronwall, 1977). This task requires the subject to add pairs of digits presented at a predetermined rate; after each digit, the subject is to give the sum of that digit and the immediately preceding digit. Since 60 digits are presented on each trial, this task incorporates demands on sustained as well as on divided attention. In two groups of head-injured patients with differing severity of injury (as defined by PTA duration), PASAT performance was shown to be impaired relative to controls within 24 hours of injury (Gronwall, 1977). Performance of both groups improved significantly one month later but remained relatively impaired in the patient group with PTA longer than 24 hours. It was postulated that head injury produces a slowing in the rate of information processing. This, in turn, may have other effects. Performance on this test has been shown to be related to reports of postconcussional complaints (Gronwall & Wrightson, 1974) and to performance in a practical occupational therapy program (Gronwall, 1976).

Although it has made a valuable contribution to clinical practice, the PASAT has been criticized on the basis that it requires mathematical skill (indeed, it correlates significantly with adding ability [Weber, 1986]) and requires a rapid motor response. The Attentional Capacity Test developed by Weber (1986) places similar demands on information-processing capacity but removes requirements for adding and for rapid verbal response.

Subjects listen to taped stimuli and count the number of targets presented in a series. The targets become increasingly complex (e.g., moving from simply counting 8's on a tape to counting the number of 8's followed by 5), but response requirements, saying a single number at the end of the tape, remain the same. The effect is that as the test proceeds, a greater amount of information must be processed in the same period of time. Weber has demonstrated not only that performance of individuals with head injury is significantly impaired relative to controls on this test but that test performance is significantly correlated with therapists' ratings of attentional capacity in clinical settings (Weber, 1986, 1988).

Reduced capacity for divided attention and complex information processing undoubtedly results in significant impairment in daily life. In many common activities, we are required to divide our attention among several subtasks such as listening to the radio while making dinner or driving while talking to a passenger. Our clinical experience is that situations in which a great deal of relevant information must be presented quickly or simultaneously are very frustrating and fatiguing for the head-injured patient. Assessment protocols must thus incorporate measures that adequately tap these higher levels of attentional capacity.

Attentional Control

Control strategies or executive functions (as used by Luria, 1966; Lezak, 1982; see Chapter 7 of this volume) refer to the planning, programming, regulation, and verification of goal-directed behavior. A related mechanism postulated by some attentional theorists is that of supervisory strategies that direct information processing according to task requirements. The work of three sets of researchers is particularly germane. Shiffrin and Schneider, in 1977, presented a model of information processing in which "automatic processing" played an important role. This automatic processing was done with minimal conscious control and was postulated as a basis for many overlearned or preprogrammed behaviors. The authors postulated a strategy through which it could be controlled. The "central executive" proposed by Baddeley and Hitch (1974) and Baddeley (1981) can also be included here; it was described as a controller of memory critical to dividing attention during information processing.

In a similar vein, Shallice (1982) proposed an information-processing model in which a so-called "Supervisory Attentional System" (SAS) supervises the running of highly specialized routine programs. These routines or schemes are activated by any mental activity, but the question of which schema to run is determined by the SAS and by "contention scheduling." Contention scheduling quickly selects schemes based on the strongest perceptual triggers; in a sense, it controls which stimuli will be selectively attended to. For example, in the Stroop Test (Stroop, 1935), the most automatic response favored by contention scheduling would be reading of the color word. The SAS is responsible for controlled processing and the selection of alternative strategies—in this case, to the less automatic or preferred strategy, naming the color of ink. With effort, the SAS can overcome contention scheduling and allow the individual to "concentrate" on the color of the words. As indicated earlier, the results of the Stroop Test do not necessarily suggest increased distractibility or deficits in contention scheduling in head-injured patients. However, this test requires only one reset. If there were sudden or repeated changes in schemata that would require flexibility of scheduling, the demands on the supervisory system would be much greater, and deficits might be revealed.

In many conditions of everyday life, there is a need to shift the focus of one's attention quickly and efficiently away from one stimulus to another and back again. Observations in patient populations suggest that such shifting is difficult for the traumatically brain-injured individual.

TOWARD A CLINICAL MODEL OF ATTENTION

Although a rich literature on normal attentional capacity and attentional theory exists and there is a growing body of research regarding attentional abilities in head-injured patients, it is difficult to identify ways in which any of these theories might directly lead to treatment strategies. Many of the theories stop at the level of signal detection or target selection. Additional processing is often left unaddressed. The theoretical constructs of *working memory* and *attentional control devices* begin to address a more comprehensive view of attention, yet most of the attention literature is very task dependent, and none of the current models adequately addresses the complex clinical phenomena related to attention deficits. The few treatment programs that do exist either lack a theoretical foundation or address only very restricted components of attention.

The clinical model of attention and associated treatment recommendations outlined in the remainder of this chapter is one we developed based on the experimental attention literature, clinical observation, and patients' subjective complaints. It considers attention as a multidimensional cognitive capacity critical to memory, new learning, and all other aspects of cognition. There are five levels of attention addressed in the treatment model: focused attention, sustained attention, selective attention, alternating attention, and divided attention. Descriptions of each level as used in this model are provided below. They were developed on the basis on both conceptual clarity and clinical utility. To some extent, however, definitions may differ from those provided in the nonclinical experimental literature.

Focused Attention

This is the ability to respond discretely to specific visual, auditory, or tactile stimuli. Although almost all patients recover this level of attention, it is often disrupted in the early stages of emergence from coma. The patient may initially be responsive only to internal stimuli (pain, temperature, etc.) and only gradually start responding to specific external events or stimuli.

Sustained Attention

This refers to the ability to maintain a consistent behavioral response during continuous and repetitive activity. It incorporates the notion of vigilance. Disruption of this level of attention is implied in the patient who can only focus on a task or maintain responses for a brief period (i.e., seconds to minutes) or who fluctuates dramatically in performance over even brief periods (i.e., variable attention or attentional lapses). It also incorporates the notion of mental control or working memory on tasks that involve manipulating information and holding it in mind.

Selective Attention

This level of attention refers to the ability to maintain a behavioral or cognitive set in the face of distracting or competing stimuli. It thus incorporates the notion of "freedom from distractibility." Individuals with deficits at this level are easily drawn off task by extraneous, irrelevant stimuli. These can include both external sights, sounds, or activities (the "cocktail party effect") and internal distractions (worry, rumination, or focus on personally important thoughts). Examples of problems at this level include an inability to perform therapy tasks in a stimulating environment (e.g., an open treatment area) or to prepare a meal with the children playing in the background.

Alternating Attention

This level of attention refers to the capacity for mental flexibility that allows individuals to shift their focus of attention and move between tasks having different cognitive requirements, thus controlling which information will be selectively attended to. Problems at this level are evident in the patient who has difficulty changing treatment tasks once a "set" has been established and who needs extra cuing to pick up and initiate new task requirements. Real-life demands for this level of attentional control are frequent. Consider the student who must shift between listening to a lecture and taking notes, or the secretary who must continuously move between answering the phone, typing, and responding to inquiries.

Divided Attention

This level involves the ability to respond simultaneously to multiple tasks or multiple task demands. Two or more behavioral responses may be required, or two or more kinds of stimuli may need to be monitored. This level of attentional capacity is required whenever multiple simultaneous demands must be managed. Performance under such conditions (i.e., driving a car while listening to the radio or holding a conversation during meal preparation) may actually reflect either rapid and continuous alternating attention or dependence on more unconscious automatic processing for at least one of the tasks. Modeling this level as a separate component of attention draws attention to its importance in the rehabilitation context and provides a foundation for retraining.

Given this five-component model of attention, a set of specific exercises was developed or selected. In the following sections, sample treatment tasks are presented. Many of those that were specifically developed in the context of this model are included in the commercially available set of materials called Attention Process Training or APT (Sohlberg & Mateer, 1987). Sources of other materials are referenced in the text. Clinicians are encouraged to use existing tasks or to develop new ones based on their relevance to the clinical model described.

TRAINING ATTENTIONAL PROCESSES

Sustained Attention Treatment Activities

These tasks require consistent responding to either aurally or visually presented information. Visually based exercises include a variety of cancellation tasks in which the patient scans an array of targets and crosses some out. Simple levels of the task might include crossing out one or two target letters or numbers. Auditory stimulation is often preferred; the transient nature of auditory stimuli puts greater demands on the attentional system. The APT materials include a set of 16 audio cassette tapes. Patients respond to targets by pushing a buzzer. At higher levels of sustained attention training, there are greater and greater demands on mental control and information processing.

A sample hierarchy of tasks might include the following:

1. Push the buzzer every time you hear the number 4 (e.g., 6, 4*, 1, 4*, 4*, 2, 7).
2. Push the buzzer every time you hear an "h" or a "b" (e.g., b*, j, a, h*, b*, o).
3. Push the buzzer every time you hear one number that comes just after the number before it (e.g., 4, 7, 6, 7*, 8*, 2, 5, 6*).
4. Push the buzzer every time you hear one number that is 2 less than the number before it (e.g., 3, 6, 4*, 1, 7, 5*, 3*, 2).
5. Push the buzzer every time you hear two months in a row, such that

the second month comes just before the first one on the calendar (e.g., December, November*, October*, March, June, May*, October, September*).

Data in the form of accuracy scores, number of omissions, and number of false positives are gathered on each training trial. In addition, notations are made about any notable error patterns. These might include delayed responding to targets, losing track of task requirements, missing only targets that immediately follow another target, difficulty establishing set (errors at beginning) or difficulty maintaining task performance over time (increasing errors toward the end of the trial). Individuals are moved to increasingly more demanding tasks when criterion (usually 95% accuracy) is maintained over at least three consecutive trials.

Other tasks include the Serial Numbers activities in APT. These are exercises in counting backwards by 2's, 3's, 4's, or 5's. The complexity of serial number counting can be increased by adding additional mathematical operations, for example, adding 2, then subtracting 1, or subtracting 4, then adding 2, consecutively, as numbers go up or down. These mental exercises involving control of mathematical operations appear to tap, and thus exercise, attentional capacities.

An example of data collection for a sustained attention training program is given in Figure 6.1. Various exercises are selected and repeated on a daily basis until criteria are met.

Selective Attention Training

Training at this level involves the incorporation of distracting or irrelevant information during task performance. For visual cancellation tasks, plastic overlays with distracting designs have been found to be useful. In the auditory modality, the same attention tape stimuli are used, but the targets are now embedded in a background of distracting noise. This may be in the form of a news broadcast, a sports commentary, cafeteria noise, or conversation. Although the APT tapes to be used for selective attention training have prerecorded background stimuli, use of novel or individually adapted distraction is encouraged. The patient with social interests might be most distracted by a tape of lunchtime conversation between staff members; another may be most distracted by a football game; yet another may be vulnerable to music or to the sound of children playing. Tapes can easily be made and used in conjunction with these tasks. Making such tapes is preferable to just turning on a TV or radio because the stimuli are better controlled and repeated data trials will be more comparable. Some patients are more disrupted by internal than external distraction, that is, worry, rumination, or preoccupation with personal concerns or agendas. With these patients, focus on reducing these intrusions may be primary. Tech-

ATTENTION TAPE SCORESHEET

NAME _B.K._

TAPE/Exercise

Date _12/1/87_	TOTAL
# of errors: TH TH III	13
# of false alarms: III	3
Observations (error patterns):	

Date _12/2/87_	TOTAL
# of errors: TH TH II	12
# of false alarms: III	3
Observations (error patterns):	

Date _12/3/87_	TOTAL
# of errors: TH TH I	11
# of false alarms: II	2
Observations (error patterns): _more errors at the end of the tape._	

Date _12/4/87_	TOTAL
# of errors: TH IIII	9
# of false alarms: I	1
Observations (error patterns):	

Date _12/7/87_	TOTAL
# of errors: TH TH III	13
# of false alarms: IIII	4
Observations (error patterns): _(Problem with Selective Attention)_	

*_The phone rang during this session._
Very Distractable / A lot of noise.

TAPE/Exercise

Date _12/8/87_	TOTAL
# of errors: TH IIII	9
# of false alarms: II	2
Observations (error patterns):	

Date _12/9/87_	TOTAL
# of errors: TH III	8
# of false alarms:	0
Observations (error patterns): _more errors at the end of the tape. (Problem with Sustained Attention)_	

Date _12/10/87_	TOTAL
# of errors: TH II	7
# of false alarms: I	1
Observations (error patterns):	

Date _12/11/87_	TOTAL
# of errors: TH I	6
# of false alarms: I	1
Observations (error patterns):	

Date _12/14/87_	TOTAL
# of errors: IIII	4
# of false alarms:	0
Observations (error patterns): _Good Effort!_	

FIGURE 6.1. Attention Process Training (APT). Example of completed scoresheet for Attention Tape exercise. This therapy task addresses sustained attention. Copyright © 1986 McKay Moore Sohlberg and Catherine A. Mateer.

niques such as writing things down and then setting the paper aside before beginning a task may be helpful.

There are a wide variety of other exercises including computer programs that appear to fit within this clinical model. In particular, the *Visual Reaction Stimulus Discrimination 1* and *Auditory Reaction Stimulus Discrimination*, published by Psychological Software Services, provide tasks that require inhibition of responses during target reaction tasks. Clinicians can incorporate the notion of distraction into many different kinds of exercises. Consider, for example, utilizing a pegboard exercise task at the same time a noise tape is played (visuo–motor task with distractor).

Alternating Attention Training

Training of attentional deficits at this level requires flexible redirection and reallocation of attention. Effective tasks have requirements of repeated changes in task demands. Examples of tasks on the APT include the following:

1. *Odd–Even Number Cancellation* (Sohlberg & Mateer, 1987). The patient first crosses out odd numbers on a sheet and then, when the therapist says "change," draws a slash mark and crosses out even numbers, and then goes back to crossing out odd numbers following the next instruction to "change." If this task is too difficult, an easier version might include writing "O" or "E" for odd and even at the beginning of each line. Response demands would then be somewhat more predictable and structured, and constant cues for task demands would be available. Task difficulty increases as the time between instructions to change decreases. An example of a patient's response on this task is given in Figure 6.2.

2. *Add/Subtract Calculation* (Sohlberg & Mateer, 1987). The patient first adds numbers presented in pairs and then, following instruction to "change," subtracts the numbers. Task difficulty can be manipulated as above.

3. *Stroop-like Activities.* (a) *High–Mid–Low* (Sohlberg & Mateer, 1987): In this task, the words "high, mid, and low" are typed in high, mid, and low positions on a line. Instructions to change response set involves switching from reading words to identifying their position on the line. (b) *Big–Little Task* (Sohlberg & Mateer, 1987): In the Big–Little task, the words "big" and "little" are written in big and little letters. The following is an example.

Targets: *BIG, little, LITTLE, big, BIG, LITTLE, big, little, big.*

Targets read as words: big, little, little, big, big, little, big, little, big.

Targets read as size: big, little, big, little, big, big, little, little, little.

Divided Attention Training

Training in this area involves the use of tasks in which multiple kinds of information must be attended to simultaneously, or it involves the simultaneous use of two or more tasks. Examples include the following:

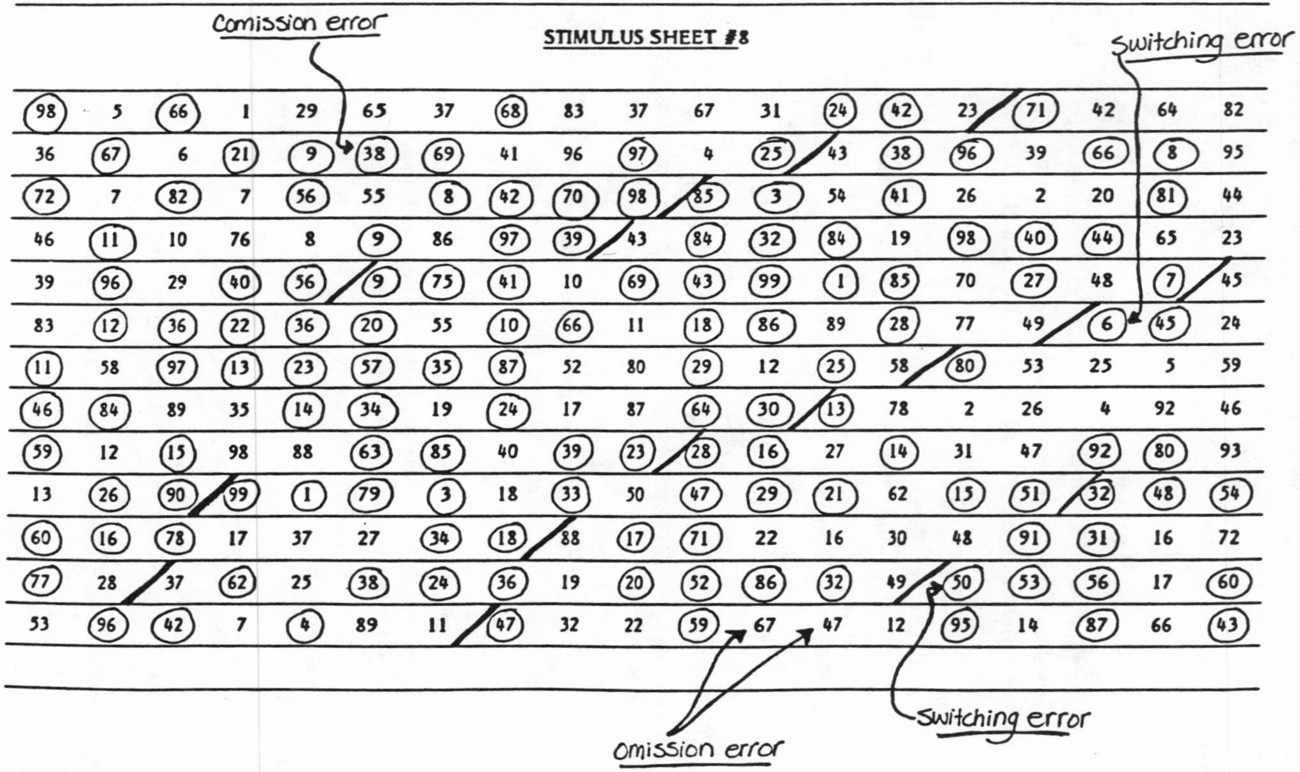

STIMULUS SHEET #8

98	5	66	1	29	65	37	68	83	37	67	31	24	42	23	71	42	64	82
36	67	6	21	9	38	69	41	96	97	4	25	43	38	96	39	66	8	95
72	7	82	7	56	55	8	42	70	98	85	3	54	41	26	2	20	81	44
46	11	10	76	8	9	86	97	39	43	84	32	84	19	98	40	44	65	23
39	96	29	40	56	9	75	41	10	69	43	99	1	85	70	27	48	7	45
83	12	36	22	36	20	55	10	66	11	18	86	89	28	77	49	6	45	24
11	58	97	13	23	57	35	87	52	80	29	12	25	58	80	53	25	5	59
46	84	89	35	14	34	19	24	17	87	64	30	13	78	2	26	4	92	46
59	12	15	98	88	63	85	40	39	23	28	16	27	14	31	47	92	80	93
13	26	90	99	1	79	3	18	33	50	47	29	21	62	15	51	32	48	54
60	16	78	17	37	27	34	18	88	17	71	22	16	30	48	91	31	16	72
77	28	37	62	25	38	24	36	19	20	52	86	32	49	50	53	56	17	60
53	96	42	7	4	89	11	47	32	22	59	67	47	12	95	14	87	66	43

FIGURE 6.2. Attention Process Training (APT). Example of completed scoresheet for Odd/Even Subtraction exercise, which targets alternating attention. Copyright © 1986 McKay Moore Sohlberg and Catherine A. Mateer.

1. *Card Sort Task* (Sohlberg & Mateer, 1987). In this task, playing cards must be sorted by suit (as in solitaire), but cards must be selectively turned over if their name contains a particular target letter (i.e., if the target letter is "e," then 1's, 3's, 5's, 7's, 8's, 9's, and queens all must be turned over as they are sorted by suit). Data are taken in terms of both errors and time to complete. An example of one patient's performance over time on this task is given in Figure 6.3.

2. *Dual Task Performance*. These combined tasks consist of simultaneous performance on two previously practiced and stablized tasks. For example, with the computer program *REACT* (Gianutsos & Klitzner, 1981), the patient is asked to listen to a sustained-attention training tape and respond to targets by pushing a buzzer while watching a computer screen for a given target.

In this section, we have given examples of particular kinds of activities. The possibility of creating others is endless. The most critical characteristic in selecting activities is that they be addressed to a specific component of attention as defined by the model. A listing of sample treatment tasks at different levels is given in Table 6.2.

EFFICACY OF ATTENTION TRAINING

In this section, we provide some information regarding an efficacy study using these kinds of attention-training procedures. This study is described in some detail. It offers both a model of a clinical efficacy study as well as an example of the application of an experimental paradigm to a clinical setting as described in Chapter 4.

Therapy was conducted using tasks and treatment materials as outlined in Attention Process Training (Sohlberg & Mateer, 1986). A multiple baseline across cognitive areas (Hensen & Barlow, 1976) was used to assess the effectiveness of the APT program in four brain-injured subjects. Previous research (Gianutsos, 1981; Gianutsos & Gianutsos, 1979) has established the practicality of using the single-case design to study the retraining of cognitive processes in individuals.

The subject were participants at the Good Samaritan Hospital Center for Cognitive Rehabilitation, a multidisciplinary postacute day treatment brain injury rehabilitation program. They were randomly selected from a consecutive series of admissions to the program. Subjects varied widely in both nature of injury and time post-onset. The study examined the relationship between the implementation of APT and changes in attentional skills as measured by the Paced Auditory Serial Addition Task (PASAT) (Gronwall, 1977), a neuropsychological test sensitive to attention deficits. Changes in attention, as measured by the PASAT, were plotted over time (during a

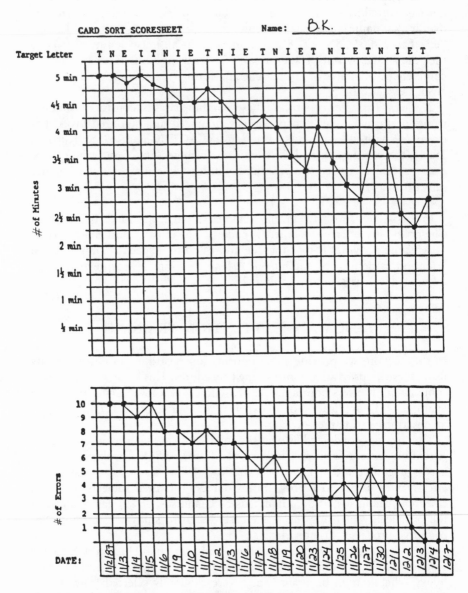

FIGURE 6.3. Attention Process Training (APT). Example of completed scoresheet for Card Sort exercise, which addresses divided attention. Copyright © 1986 McKay Moore Sohlberg and Catherine A. Mateer.

TABLE 6.2. Treatment Tasks Used in Attention-Training

Focused attention

REACT (reaction time computer programs published by Life Science Associates)
Attention Tape 1 (detection of auditorially presented number targets; developed
by Sohlberg and Mateer, 1986)

Sustained attention

Attention Tapes 2–8 (auditorially presented strings of stimuli with response
requirements of increasing difficulty; Sohlberg and Mateer, 1986)
Serial Numbers (number manipulation exercises; Sohlberg and Mateer, 1986)
Timesense (time estimation computer program published by Soft Tools)

Selective attention

Attention Tapes 9–16 (auditorially presented strings of stimuli recorded with
background noise; Sohlberg and Mateer, 1986)
Visual Reaction Stimulus Discrimination 1 (computer program requiring inhibi-
tion of responses; published by Psychological Software Services)
Auditory Reaction Stimulus Discrimination (computer program requiring inhibi-
tion of responses; published by Psychological Software Services)
Pegboard Exercises Using Noise Tape (visuomotor task with distractor)
Construx with Distractor Tape (visuomotor task with distractor)

Alternating attention

Addition/Subtraction Flexibility, Before/After, Odd/Even Number Flexibility,
(Sohlberg & Mateer, 1986)
Simultaneous Sequencing Exercises (Sohlberg & Mateer, 1986)
Set-Dependent Activity I and II (Sohlberg & Mateer, 1986)

Divided attention

Simultaneous Multiple Attention (computer program by Soft Tools)
Multilevel Card Sort (Sohlberg & Mateer, 1986)
React Plus Attention Tape (dual task, one requiring response to auditory informa-
tion and another requiring response to visual information)

Note: Materials referenced to Sohlberg and Mateer (1986) are available as part of Attention
Process Training.

pretreatment baseline period, during training, and after training). A multiple-baseline design (as described in Chapter 4) was utilized. Performance on
a task involving visual processing was measured at the same repeated
intervals. The measure used to assess visual processing abilities was the
Spatial Relations Subtest (SR) from the Woodcock–Johnson Psychoeducational Battery (Woodcock & Johnson, 1977). This is a test that
requires the subject to identify which of two discrete figures, if turned,
would fit together to form a whole target figure. The task thus requires
spatial perception and mental rotation.

Scores on both the PASAT and the SR test were obtained at regular
intervals over the course of 30 weeks. Once subjects met individually
determined criterion levels for the specific treatment tasks in each of the five
levels of the attention-training model (APT), remediation of visual process-

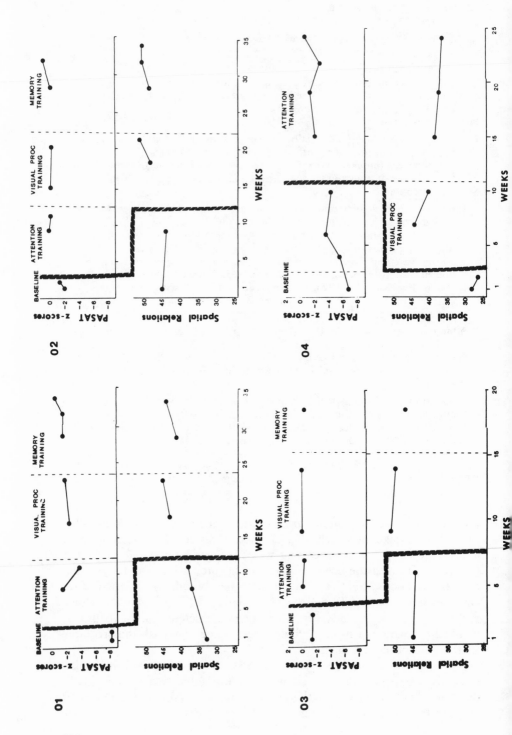

130

ing skills was initiated. One subject (04) received training in visual processing prior to attention training, to compare treatment-order effects.

Research findings for each of the four subjects are displayed in a form that reflects performance on the two tasks across time and treatments. Data for each subject (01, 02, 03, and 04) are represented in Figure 6.4. The ordinate on the upper section of the graph represents PASAT scores used to measure changes in attention ability. The ordinate on the lower section of the graph represents raw scores on the SR used to measure changes in visual processing. The abscissa on both graphs corresponds to both weeks of treatment (lower scale) and the treatment phase (upper scale). Scores to the left of the heavy striped line represent the pretreatment baseline measures.

Two subjects who presented with mild to moderate attention deficits (02 and 03), indicated by PASAT scores within two standard deviations of the mean, demonstrated an increase in attention skills as reflected in PASAT scores within normal limits. Two subjects with severe attention impairment (01 and 04), whose PASAT scores were greater than 3 standard deviations below the mean, achieved scores within the mildly impaired range following attention training. Improvements in attention to all cases remained above baseline levels following cessation of specific attention training for at least 8 months. These results demonstrate the potential for improvement of attention deficits in brain-injured persons given specific attention training. They also support the general effectiveness of the APT training model.

Results in this study further support the use of a process-specific approach to cognitive rehabilitation. The data suggest that although there may be some impact on attention skills following any focused cognitive treatment (e.g., visual processing), more significant improvement is made following specific attention training. In Subject 04, gains in attention are evidenced during the baseline condition, during which there was visual processing training but no specific remediation of attention. However, these gains appear to level off, and more dramatic increases are seen following specific attention training. In Subjects 02 and 03, analogous results were found relative to visual processing ability. Visual-processing-based SR scores remained stable during the period of attention training despite improved PASAT scores and increased only after the initiation of visual process training. This double dissociation provides powerful support for independent improvements in specific cognitive areas with process-specific training. The clinical implication is that therapy directed toward the remediation of underlying deficit processes should be encouraged.

←——————————————

FIGURE 6.4. Results of attention training in Subjects 01–04, using a multiple base-line across cognitive areas (attention, visual processing, and memory).

The authors' research with APT also points to the importance of addressing attention as a potential factor underlying memory problems. The preliminary data gathered on individuals who have completed APT strongly support the notion that increased attention ability often results in improved memory. Outcome data for five subjects who completed APT and subsequently demonstrated significant improvement in memory ability as measured by the Five Items Subtest (Acquisition and Delayed Recall scores) from the Randt Memory Test (Randt & Brown, 1983) are presented in the next chapter, which specifically discusses memory rehabilitation (see Table 7.1). Each subject improved at least 1 standard deviation on both recall measurements even though they had received no formal memory training. Attention skills, as measured by Trial 1 of the PASAT, also improved at least 1 standard deviation. Each of the subjects was initially found to have severe attentional deficits as measured by the PASAT.

These results have important implications for the treatment of memory disorders because they imply that memory problems, if related to attention disorders, may be treatable. Current clinical literature has suggested that memory rehabilitation is not a viable option; however, it may be that we have not been utilizing the appropriate treatment methodology. It appears that some individuals have attentionally based memory problems that may be identified through an appropriate combination of neuropsychologic measures, behavioral observations, and interview and may be treated with a cognitive rehabilitation program specifically targeted toward remediation of attention deficits, such as APT.

SUMMARY

There is little doubt that the physiologic and cognitive substrates of attention are frequently disrupted by traumatic head injury. The cognitive psychology literature describes some of the basic theories underlying attentional processing, but little has been done to relate these theories to attentional problems manifested in head-injured patients. There are a number of limitations with current assessment and treatment tools. A five-level model of attention addressing Focused, Sustained, Selective, Alternating, and Divided Attention has been shown to have utility in conceptualizing attentional deficits from a clinical perspective. The efficacy of attention training has been demonstrated in a series of single-case studies. Appropriate attention training appears instrumental not only in improving scores on untrained attention tests but in improving capacity at the initial stages of information processing for memory, with resultant increases in memory function. For the individual with primary attentional deficits or memory impairment secondary to attentional problems, systematic attention training appears to be effective and beneficial.

STUDY QUESTIONS

1. When concentration and memory problems are reported separately in introspective studies, which predominate?
2. Describe early and late selection models and tell how they are different.
3. Describe the central executive in Baddeley's model of working memory.
4. Explain the difference between *choice* and *simple* reaction time.
5. List and define the five levels in the proposed clinical model of attention.
6. Make up five new selective- and five new alternating-attention tasks.

REFERENCES

Allport, D. A. (1980). Attention and performance. In G. Claxton (Ed.), *Cognitive psychology: New directions*. London: Routledge and Kegar Paul.

Baddeley, A. D. (1981). The concept of working memory: A view of its current state and probable future development. *Cognition 10*:17–23.

Baddeley, A. D., & Hitch, G. J. (1974). Working memory. In G. A. Bower (Ed.), *The psychology of learning and motivation, vol. 8* (pp. 47–85). New York: Academic Press.

Binder, L. M. (1986). Persisting symptoms after mild head injury: A review of post concussive syndrome. *Journal of Clinical and Experimental Neuropsychology 8*:323–346.

Brickenkamp, R. (1962). *Test d2*. Gotingen: Verlag fur Psycholople, Dr. C. J. Hogrefe.

Broadbent, D. E. (1958). *Perception and communication*. London: Pergamon.

Broadbent, D. E. (1971). *Decision and stress*. London: Academic Press.

Broadbent, D. E. (1982). Task combination and the selective intake of information. *Acta Psychologica 50*:253–290.

Brouwer, W. H., & van Wolffelaar, P. C. (1985). Sustained attention and sustained effort after closed head injury: Detection and 0.10 H2 heart rate variability in a low event rate vigilance task. *Cortex 21*:111–119.

Caveness, W. F. (1969). Post traumatic sequelae. In A. E. Walker, W. F. Caveness, & M. Critchley (Eds.), *The late effects of head injury* (pp. 209–219). Springfield, IL: Charles C. Thomas.

Craik, F. I., & Levy, B. A. (1976). The concept of primary memory. In W. K. Estes (Ed.), *Handbook of learning and cognitive processes* (pp. 133–176). Hillsdale, NJ: Lawrence Erlbaum Associates.

Gentilini, M., Nichelli, P., Schoenhuber, R., Bortolotti, P., Tonelli, L., Falasca, A., & Merli, G. (1985). Neuropsychological evaluation of mild head injury. *Journal of Neurology, Neurosurgery, and Psychiatry 48*:137–140.

Gianutsos, R. (1981). Training the short- and long-term verbal recall of a post encephalitic amnesic. *Journal of Clinical Neuropsychology 3*:143–153.

Gianutsos, R., & Gianutsos, J. (1979). Rehabilitating the verbal recall of brain injured patients by mnemonic training: An experimental demonstration using single-case methodology. *Journal of Clinical Neuropsychology 1*:117–135.

Gianutsos, R. & Klitzner, C (1981). *Computer programs for cognitive rehabilitation.* Bayport, NY: Life Science Associates.

Greber, R., & Perret, E. (1985). *Attention and short-term memory disorders after brain stem lesions.* Paper presented at the EBBS Workshop on Clinical Neuropsychology, Zurich.

Gronwall, D. (1976). Performance changes during recovery from closed head injury. *Proceedings of the Australian Association of Neurology 13:*143–147.

Gronwall, D. (1977) Paced Auditory Serial Addition Task: A measure of recovery from concussion. *Perceptual Motor Skills 44:*367–373.

Gronwall, D. (1987). Advances in the assessment of attention and information processing after head injury. In H. S. Levin, J. Grafman, & H. M. Eisenberg (Eds.), *Neurobehavioral recovery from head Injury* (pp. 355–371). New York: Oxford University Press.

Gronwall, D. M., & Sampson, H. (1974). *The psychological effects of concussion.* Auckland: Auckland University Press.

Gronwall, D., & Wrightson, P. (1974). Delayed recovery of intellectual function after minor head injury. *Lancet ii:*95–97.

Hersen, M., & Barlow, D. H. (1976). *Single case experimental designs: Strategies for studying behavior change.* New York: Pergamon.

Hicks, L., & Birren, J. E. (1970). Aging, brain damage, and psychomotor slowing. *Psychological Bulletin 74:*377–396.

Jennett, B., & Bond, M. (1975). Assessment of outcome after severe brain damage. *Lancet i:*480–487.

Kahneman, D. (1973). *Attention and effort.* Englewood Cliffs, NJ: Prentice-Hall.

Lezak, M. D. (1982). The problems of assessing executive functions. *International Journal of Psychology 17:*281–297.

Lidvall, H. F., Linderoth, B., & Norlin, B. (1974). Causes of the postconcussional syndrome. *Acta Neurologica Scandinavica 50* (Supplement 56).

Luria, A. R. (1966). *Higher cortical functions in man.* New York: Basic Books.

Luria, A. R. (1973). *The working brain.* New York: Basic Books.

Mateer, C. A., Sohlberg, M. M., & Crinean, J. (1987). Focus on clinical research: Perceptions of memory function in individuals with closed head injury. *Journal of Head Trauma Rehabilitation 2:*74–84.

McKinlay, W. W., Brooks, D. N., & Bond, M. R. (1983). Post-concussional symptoms, financial compensation and outcome of severe blunt head injury. *Journal of Neurology, Neurosurgery and Psychiatry 46:*1084–1091.

McLean, A., Temkin, N. R., Dikmen, S., & Wyler, A. R. (1983). The behavioral sequelae of head injury. *Journal of Clinical Neuropsychology 5:*361–376.

McLean, A., Dikmen, S., Temkin, N., Wyler, A. R., & Gale, J. L. (1984). Psychosocial functioning at 1 month after head injury. *Neurosurgery 14:*393–399.

Mirsky, A. F., Primac, D. W., Marson, C. A., Rosvold, H. E., & Stevens, J. R. (1960). A comparison of the psychological test performance of patients with focal and nonfocal epilepsy. *Experimental Neurology 2:*75–89.

Newcombe, F. (1982). The psychological consequences of closed head injury: Assessment and rehabilitation. *Injury 14:*111–136.

Posner, M. I. (1975). The psychobiology of attention, In M. S. Gaszzaniga & C. Blakemoer (Eds.), *Handbook of psychobiology* (pp. 441–180). New York: Academic Press.

Posner, M. I. (1978). *Chronometric explorations of mind.* Hillsdale, NJ: Lawrence Erlbaum Associates.

Posner, M. I. (1980). Orienting of attention. *Journal of Experimental Psychology* 32:3–26.

Randt, C. T., & Brown, E. R. (1983). *Randt memory test.* Bayport, NY: Life Science Associates.

Rutherford, W. H., Merrett, J. D., & McDonald, J. R. (1977). Sequelae of concussion caused by minor head injuries. *Lancet i:*1–4.

Rutherford, W. H., Merrett, J. D., and McDonald, J. R. (1979). Symptoms at one year from minor head injuries. *Injury 10:*225–230.

Shallice, T. (1982). Specific impairments in planning. In D. E. Broadbent & L. Weiskrantz (Eds.), *The neuropsychology of cognitive function* (pp. 199–209). London: The Royal Society.

Shiffrin, R. M. (1975). The focus and role of attention in memory systems. In P. M. A. Rabbitt & S. Dornic (Eds.), *Attention and performance, Vol. V* (pp. 158–193). London: Academic Press.

Shiffrin, R. M., & Schneider, W. (1977). Controlled and automatic human information processing II: Perceptual learning, automatic attending and a general theory. *Psychological Review 84:*90–190.

Sohlberg, M. M., & Mateer, C. A. (1986). *Attention process training (APT).* Puyallup, WA: Association for Neuropsychological Research and Development.

Sohlberg, M. M., & Mateer, C. A. (1987). Effectiveness of an attention training program. *Journal of Clinical and Experimental Neuropsychology 9:*117–130.

Stroop, J. R. (1935). Studies of interference in serial verbal reactions. *Journal of Experimental Psychology 18:*643–662.

Treisman, A. (1969). Strategies and models of selective attention. *Psychological Review 76:*282–299.

Van Zomeren, A. H. (1981). *Reaction time and attention after closed head injury.* Lisse: Swets Publishing Service.

Van Zomeren, A. H., & Brouwer, W. H. (1987). Head injury and concepts of attention. In H. S. Levin, J. Grafman, & H. M. Eisenberg (Eds.), *Neurobehavioral Recovery From Head Injury* (pp. 398–415). New York: Oxford University Press.

Weber, A. M. (1986). *Measuring attentional capacity.* Ph.D. Dissertation, University of Victoria, Victoria, Canada

Weber, A. M. (1988). Attentional Capacity Test. Paper presented at the International Neuropsychology Society Meeting, New Orleans, LA.

Wechsler, D. (1945). A standardized memory scale for clinical use. *Journal of Psychology 19:*87–95.

Wechsler, D. (1981) *Wechsler Adult Intelligence Scale—Revised.* Cleveland: Psychological Corporation.

Woodcock, R., & Johnson, B. (1977). *Woodcock–Johnson Psychoeducational Battery.* Boston: Teaching Resources Corporation.

Wrightson, P., & Gronwall, D. (1981). Time off work and symptoms after minor head injury. *Injury 12:*445–454.

7

A Three-Pronged Approach
to Memory Rehabilitation

Memory must be considered one of the most pervasive aspects of our mental life. Memory function reflects our experience of the past and allows us at each moment to adapt ourselves to the present and look forward to the future. It is critical to the acquisition and utilization of new information. It is involved with every aspect of how we think, what we do, and how we behave. In this chapter, we review some basic information about how memory does and does not function and about the known neurologic substrates for memory function. Based on that review, we propose a three-pronged approach to the rehabilitation of individuals with memory disorders. Topics covered include the classical temporally based model of memory, memory as an information-processing system, etiologies of memory impairment, clinically relevant factors, learning without awareness, memory rehabilitation (restoration and compensation), external and internal memory aids, and prospective memory process training.

THEORETICAL BASES OF MEMORY

Many disciplines have contributed to our knowledge about memory function. In the last decade, for example, neurology and neuropsychology have contributed much rich information about the organization of multiple memory systems within the brain. Memory is no longer considered a unitary cognitive function; it is well accepted that "amnesia is not amnesia" and that memory function can break down in a myriad of ways. Diagnostically differentiable amnesic syndromes that follow separate disease processes or disrupt different neuroanatomic substrates have begun to emerge.

Cognitive psychologists have begun to extend the study of memory to situations outside the laboratory. From work with aging individuals, children, and neurologic populations, new insights and theories about memory function have emerged. Greater and greater interest has developed in assessing memory function in naturalistic every-day environments. The result has been more complex yet more realistic models of normal memory functioning.

This research is a crucial aspect of developing more targeted and appropriate rehabilitative treatment approaches. It is gradually being reflected in the sensitivity and sophistication of neuropsychologic assessment of memory. However, although knowledge of memory function is growing rapidly, research that might have very rich implications for treatment or assessment is often not reflected in the neuropsychologic or rehabilitative literature. The clinician working with individuals who demonstrate memory disorders is still often without practical tools and approaches. Researchers and clinicians in rehabilitation need to gain as strong a background in memory theory as possible in order to develop innovative treatment approaches.

THE CLASSICAL TEMPORALLY BASED MODEL OF MEMORY

The traditionally hypothesized model of memory is a temporally based storage model with three stages: sensory memory, short-term memory, and long-term memory (Walker, 1976; Squire, 1975). In the *sensory memory* stage, a significant amount of information remains available to the individual immediately after presentation of a stimulus. These transient memories for visual input (iconic memory) or auditory input (echoic memory) are generally held to be a consequence of the "persistence effect" that typically follows any brief, moderately intense stimulus (Neisser, 1967). The persistence effect is a rapidly fading visual image or auditory echo of the stimulus. In that form, the information is very susceptible to disturbance by subsequent stimulation. The impact of sensory memory on other aspects of memory has been widely disputed (see Coltheart, 1980, for a review).

Short-term memory usually refers to maintenance of information presented a brief period before recall or recognition. Usually there is no intervening stimulus to distract the subject from the presented material. No permanent storage is postulated. There may or may not be overt rehearsal or active review of the information before recall. Recall of word lists or paragraphs immediately after their presentation is often used as a clinical measure of short-term verbal memory. When there is some requirement to analyze or mentally manipulate the material, the notion of *working memory* (described later in this chapter) is often introduced. The rate of information decay is usually considered in the range of seconds to minutes. The capacity of the short-term memory store is limited (usually 7 ± 2 bits of information). Short-term memory is also distinguished by the fact that encoding is likely to be phonologically based rather than semantically based.

Long-term memory implies storage and subsequent retrieval through recall or recognition of information "some time" after the initial presentation. It does incorporate a period of delay or a degree of distraction that would force refocusing of attention on other information before recall or recognition is requested. It is sometimes used interchangeably with the terms *postdistraction* or *delayed memory*. Different authors vary quite a bit in the time frame discussed. Long-term memory is often measured after intervals of minutes to hours or even days, but actual retention of memory is hypothesized to be permanent. The capacity of long-term storage is felt to be unlimited or at least unknown. Encoding style is usually seen as semantically based.

Limitations of the Model

The model of short- versus long-term memory was originally based in experimental paradigms. It gained some credibility and ascendancy as a theory when, in the 1950s, H.M., a patient who was rendered amnesic following bilateral temporal lobe insults, demonstrated preserved short-term/immediate-memory skills but failed to demonstrate any retention of information after even minor distraction or periods of delay (Scoville & Milner, 1957). This finding resulted in the expansion of the short-term/long-term memory theory to include neuroanatomically separate structural as well as functional storage systems, with transfer between them mediated by a process of "consolidation."

Although this rather simplistic dual model was appealing, it has not held up well under continued scrutiny and investigation. The defining characteristics of the two systems (rate of information decay, capacity of the store, and type of preferred encoding) are not consistently experimentally discriminable. Consequently, there is a lack of consensus not only about how to define short- and long-term memory but also about the theoretical status of distinction. Wickelgren (1973) provides an excellent discussion of the kinds of evidence that do and do not support such a distinction.

From a clinical perspective, a distinction between short- and long-term memory may produce some useful information about the nature of memory breakdown. An individual who has a great deal of difficulty with immediate or short-term paragraph recall but retains that information well over a 30-minute interval may have a problem with the initial intake, registration, or analysis of information. The clinician might want to consider exploring an attentional deficit or a language-processing deficit. If, however, the individual has adequate short-term memory but loses considerable information rapidly over time, difficulties may lie with retrieval or with organization of recall. An assessment that focuses very heavily on this short-term/long-term memory distinction may effectively diagnose the existence of a memory deficit, but it often fails to direct the clinician toward appropriate or reasonable treatment techniques. Thus, not only are there underlying theoretical problems with the short-term/long-term memory distinction, but there are also significant limitations in its implication for rehabilitation.

MEMORY AS AN INFORMATION-PROCESSING SYSTEM

A more dynamic and multidimensional approach to memory views it as an information-processing system, conceptualized according to levels of processing rather than as a store-based mechanism (Cermak, 1982; Craik & Lockhart, 1972). Although there is some variation from author to author, most models involve components of attention, encoding, storage, consolidation, and retrieval (Squire & Butters, 1984; Posner, 1984; Huppert & Piercy, 1982; McDowell, 1984).

Attention (Chapter 6) incorporates a multiplicity of notions, including, at the most fundamental level, alertness and arousal, and at higher levels, focusing of perceptual systems (preparedness), sustaining concentration (vigilance), being more or less vulnerable to interference (distractibility), and being able to allocate attentional resources efficiently (divided attention). Particularly pertinent concepts include that of working memory proposed by Baddeley and Hitch (1974) (see Chapter 5). This concept incorporates the capacity to hold information in a temporary store while mental operations are performed. Attentional capacity is a logical component of any memory model since it is this capacity that allows information to have access to the system to begin with.

The concept of *encoding* is that the level of analysis performed by an individual on material to be remembered affects the likelihood of its being recalled or recognized later. As an extreme example, an English speaker will more easily recall a sentence spoken in English than one in French, presumably because he is better able to analyze and make sense of it. Craik and Lockhart's (1972) influential work proposed that "deeply" (semantically) encoded information is better retrieved that "shallowly" (phonologically) encoded information. For example, subjects have been shown to better recall words about which they were asked meaning-based questions ("Is it a kind of jungle animal?") than those about which they were asked questions relating to the sound ("Does it rhyme with dog?"). Other studies suggest that memory can be facilitated not only by cuing to features of the stimuli at the time of presentation but by organizing ("chunking" or categorizing) information and by active repetition or rehearsal (Craik & Watkins, 1973).

Storage refers to the transfer of a transient memory to a form or location in the brain for permanent storage or access. This may be facilitated by *consolidation*, a theoretical construct that provides for integration of new memories within the individual's existing cognitive/linguistic schema or framework. Finally, *retrieval* implies search for or activation of memory traces and consistent monitoring of the accuracy and appropriateness of memories pulled from storage.

An information-processing model of memory such as the one just described provides a useful framework from which to evaluate possible breakdown in memory function after neurological damage or disease. It views memory as a dynamic, multistage cognitive activity rather than as a more passive, storage-based phenomena.

DISORDERS OF MEMORY

Although the degree and nature of memory deficits differ among individuals, several patterns of impairment are commonly seen in the traumatic brain-injured population. Immediately following brain injury or with gradual recovery from coma, patients may not be able to retain any information from one moment to the next. This early, severe disruption of memory is termed "posttraumatic amnesia." Its persistence is often indicative of a more severe brain injury. Patients who are in this state may exhibit such behaviors as repetitious question-asking in which the same questions are posed over and over. Often this state is associated with confusion and disorientation to place, time, and circumstances. In almost all cases, patients with traumatic brain injury recover consistent orientation. Many are left, however, with residual impairments in learning and retaining new information. (These phenomena are discussed in Chapter 5.)

Transient Memory Disruption

It is important to keep in mind a distinction between factors that transiently disrupt memory and factors that may result in more persistent memory disruption. Transient memory disturbance involves a period of time or a particular state during which an individual has a severe deficit in the ability to take in, encode, store, or retrieve information. As the name implies, it is a reversible state, following which the memory recovers or substantially improves.

The posttraumatic amnesia state is just one of many forms of transient memory disruption. A variety of toxic and metabolic conditions and vitamin deficiencies may also result in reversible memory disruption. Examples include hypoglycemia and vitamin B_1, B_6, or B_{12} deficiency—conditions that occur with certain disease states and under situations of neglect or poverty. A variety of pharmacologic agents including the major anesthetics, the benzodiazepines, scopolamine, or other cholinergic antagonists will disrupt active memory storage for a period of time. Acute alcohol intoxication and focal transient ischemic attacks (i.e., temporary restriction of blood flow to discrete brain areas) involving memory structures may also result in transient amnesias. During temporal lobe or generalized seizures, and in the postictal state, there is commonly a loss of memory for events. In patients undergoing electroconvulsive therapy (ECT), there is usually memory loss for the period just prior to, during, and following ECT administration. During a wide variety of psychoemotional states, including depression, there can also be a transient disruption of memory capacity that is reversible with recovery to a more normal emotional state.

In transient amnesia, memories are not typically regained for the periods during which memory systems were dysfunctional, but individuals can recover the ability to store new memories when the condition reverses. Memory assessment must always include an awareness of the potential reversibility of memory loss if it is related to such factors.

Permanent Memory Disruption

There are a variety of other conditions that give rise to more persistent, pervasive, or progressive kinds of memory disruption. Many individuals who have survived head trauma have a primary memory deficit, that is, a significant restriction in their ability to store new information. Others may experience memory problems as the result of attentional deficits or information-processing limitations that presumably affect earlier stages of the memory system. Variable kinds of memory deficit following head trauma probably reflect variable extent and focus of lesions.

Chronic alcohol abuse that develops into a Korsakoff syndrome is associated with destruction of the mammillary bodies and dorsomedial nucleus of the thalamus. Severe chronic amnesia results. Many hypoxic or anoxic conditions seem to have rather specific influence on at least the most debilitating affects on memory structures. Different parts of the brain vary in the degree to which they are dependent on or "hungry for" oxygen, and certain structures are very vulnerable to even small decreases in oxygen. The hippocampus, with its high metabolic rate, has a high oxygen demand; if there is a disruption in available oxygen, the hippocampus is more likely to be damaged than other parts of the brain (see Butters & Cermak, 1980, for a review).

In a variety of infectious diseases, the virus tends to attack particular structures within the brain. In the case of herpes simplex encephalitis, for example, mesial temporal lobe structures including the hippocampus and mammillary bodies and the orbital structures of the frontal lobes are particularly vulnerable (Lishman, 1978). Pervasive, chronic amnesic disturbance may follow such infections. Many of the degenerative diseases (Alzheimer disease, Pick disease) affect multiple brain systems and have memory impairment as a cardinal feature. Cortically based dementias may have somewhat different memory manifestations than subcortical dementias, however, so that a good working knowledge of current dementia research is critical to accurate diagnosis (Cummings & Benson, 1983). With certain conditions have including a variety of dementias, changes in the underlying metabolic system may result in memory improvement. Any time there is bilateral temporal lobe damage as a result of disease, lesions, surgical intervention, or any combination thereof, there is a strong likelihood that primary memory systems will be disrupted. Even with persistent or chronic memory disruption, serial evaluation over time is critical to establish improvement in, stability, or progression of memory system impairment.

Neuroanatomic Correlates

There are many known neuroanatomic correlates of memory. These are illustrated in Figure 7.1. The hippocampus and hippocampal gyri, bilateral structures deep in the temporal lobes, are critical for the registration and storage of new memories. The lateral temporal cortical structures appear to be important in immediate and short-term recall. The thalamus, particularly the dorsomedial nuclei, seems to be critical in the encoding and integration of new information. The roles of the amygdala and of the mammillary bodies in memory are acknowledged though not fully understood. Increasingly, researchers are recognizing the very important role of the frontal

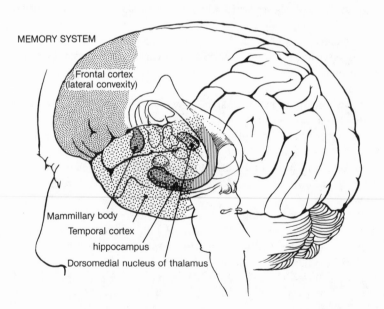

FIGURE 7.1. The major neuroanatomic structures involved in memory and new learning, including the lateral temporal cortex, the hippocampus, the dorsomedial nucleus of thalamus and the frontal lobe. Copyright 1988 by Biomedical Illustrations, Inc.

lobes in allocating attention, organizing memories, and timetagging—the ability to retrieve the temporal order of information from memory (see Squire & Cohen, 1984, for discussion of neurological substrates of amnesia in humans).

Various systems and structures in the brain are thus involved in different aspects of memory. The type of memory loss that results from brain trauma will depend on the nature of the pathology and the degree and locus of injury.

Clinically Relevant Factors in Patients with Memory Impairment

A variety of factors with regard to memory impairment are important from a clinical perspective. Although many seem somewhat obvious, they are critical to keep in mind throughout the interview and assessment process.

Degree of Deficit—A Continuum from Mild to Profound

In addition to different kinds of memory loss, there are certainly different degrees of memory loss, on a continuum from very mild to very severe. The term "global amnesia" typically refers to profound difficulty in learning and remembering nearly all kinds of new information. The less severely impaired individual may learn or store new information inefficiently or unreliably, and the amount of information they can hold onto may be limited. Two patients, one with a pervasive severe amnesia and the other a less severe memory limitation, may require treatment programs that are quite different in scope. However, they may not necessarily score very differently on any single memory test. A single measure of memory obtained on any one day will provide insufficient information to diagnose even the existence of a memory problem, much less its nature and degree. Multiple measures of memory, and an assessment of the reliability of those measures within and across situations, are important.

Memory Interacts with Other Cognitive Functions

The integrity of other cognitive functions is an important variable in assessing memory and developing memory treatment programs. Although this text presents a Process-Specific Approach and discusses separately the processes of attention, memory, language, and reasoning, none of these cognitive abilities or processes functions in isolation. The brain operates in an integrated way. Whenever you are working on "memory," you are also involving many other cognitive skills. Memory deficits can occur in the context of normal or near-normal functioning in other cognitive areas. There are individuals with average or above-average intelligence, adequate attentional capacity, functional problem-solving skills, and intact executive functions who have a very specific, selective deficit in the ability to record or store new memory. More commonly, however, the memory deficit is accompanied by deficits in one or more of the other cognitive areas, including orientation, initiation, attention, language function, reading ability, and/or visuoperceptual functions. In developing treatment tasks or putting together compensatory strategies, one must make sure that the other aspects of cognition are going to be able to support the kind of rehabilitation program being implemented.

Verbal versus Nonverbal Memory Impairments

The notion of material specificity in memory impairment, most frequently modeled as a verbal/nonverbal or verbal/figural distinction, is a common feature of many tests for memory. It implies that memory for verbally based information (letters, words, names, paragraphs) is encoded and stored separately from information that is not easily verbally labeled (abstract designs, figures, melodies, faces, spatial position). This verbal/nonverbal dichotomy was identified through the experimental work on memory conducted by Brenda Milner and her colleagues at the Montreal Neurological Institute. They noted that following left temporal lobectomy, patients had difficulty with memory for words or letters but not designs, whereas patients who underwent right temporal lobectomy had the opposite pattern of memory impairment (Milner, 1970). It is important to recognize that this research was conducted with patients who had very discrete lesions involving the anterior temporal lobe and underlying amygdala and hippocampus. Although statistically significant deficits could be documented in the patients with specially designed psychometric tests, the deficits were typically not severe, and the degree to which they were manifest in everyday life was not clear.

Test results may indicate a selective memory impairment in clinical patients with other etiologies, but all such results must be interpreted with caution. It is often the case that performance on measures of verbal and nonverbal memory reflects differences in the patient's underlying capacity for the analysis of verbal versus nonverbal information. The patient with measured verbal memory deficits often has a pervasive problem with language comprehension or production; conversely, patients who demonstrate poor performance on nonverbal memory tests often have perceptual, spatial, or constructional impairments. The problem may originate in analysis and encoding processes.

On the other hand, it is important not to conclude too much on the basis of the test "design." Just because an experimenter sits down and attempts to make a "nonverbal memory test" does not mean that an individual patient or subject cannot or does not in some way verbalize the task. Care should be taken in making presumptions about how patients are encoding, processing, or analyzing information that is presented to them. We must also acknowledge that it is very hard to rank tasks in terms of level of difficulty. It is impossible to conclude that remembering a particular paragraph is exactly as difficult as remembering a particular set of designs. Although such comparisons are interesting and useful in some diagnostic situations, the clinician should be cautious about focusing too strongly on apparent verbal/ nonverbal dissociations. Many, if not most, patients with head trauma will have diffuse disruption of bilateral memory systems and additional cognitive impairments. Finally, from a rehabilitation perspective, although training procedures based on using "intact" memory modalities (e.g., using imagery techniques in patients with apparently preserved nonverbal but not verbal memory) have been investigated (Jones, 1974), there are few, if any, studies that have shown such an approach to have functional utility.

Retrograde Memory Loss

Retrograde memory loss refers to the loss of memory for events prior to an insult or injury. We currently do not have adequate ways of measuring the extent of retrograde memory loss. Autobiographic or remote memory impairment is tested experimentally using rather ingenious procedures, such as recognition of old television program titles, but any such procedure should be used with caution in clinical situations. Clinical experience certainly suggests that there is a great deal of variability in the integrity of long-term retrograde memory. Most individuals with head trauma have relatively normal access to old memories up until a relatively brief period of minutes or hours prior to an accident. If they do not have good recall for longer periods prior to injury (weeks or months), they tend to have islands of spared recall and to piece a history together from what others tell them. For some amnesic patients, however, access to autobiographic memory may be very clouded. We have seen individuals who do not remember anything about their attendance at school, their marriage, or children; one patient actually went to the courthouse to look up the documents because he did not believe he was married. Following a severe cardiac arrest and anoxia, one patient could not remember his career of 30 years. These kinds of losses are not only devastating cognitive impairments; they also have tremendous emotional effects. Progress and treatment are often enormously affected by the patient's response to loss of history and sense of prior self.

Memory Disruption Related to Specific Stages of Information Processing

The model of normal memory presented earlier in this chapter included the stages of attention, encoding, storage, and retrieval. In this section, we discuss how certain kinds of neurologic impairment seem to differentially disrupt these specific stages of information processing.

Memory Problems Secondary to Attention Deficits

Functional Impairment. As discussed in Chapter 5, some individuals do have difficulty with focused, sustained, selective, alternating, and divided attention. These problems prohibit the effective registration of information for further information processing or subsequent recall.

Probable Lesion Site. Decreased vigilance, alertness, and arousal are usually related to deep brainstem dysfunction or to diffuse bilateral depression of subcortical mechanisms. Problems with higher levels of attention including selective attention mechanisms and attentional control (alternating and/or divided attention) are more likely to reflect disruption of higher-level thalamic structures (which are modeled as having attentional gating functions) or frontal lobe structures (modeled as controllers of attentional focus).

Memory Problems Secondary to Encoding Deficits

Functional Impairment. Impaired language, impaired ability to integrate semantic information, or impaired perceptual abilities may or may not reflect memory problems. For patients who have lateralized damage to language systems or visual processing systems, memory failures may reflect decreased ability to adequately encode the stimuli. If a patient did not understand the story that was told or was confused about the words in a list, memory for that information would naturally be reduced. The patient might remember adequately if the information were correctly interpreted (encoded). Similarly, a patient with perceptual deficits may have difficulty reproducing or even recognizing visually presented designs but may not have a memory deficit *per se.*

Individuals who have damage to diencephalic structures, including dorsomedial thalamus and frontal lobe systems (e.g., Korsakoff patients), also have an impaired ability to analyze information. Their understanding, organization, and categorization of material to be remembered is reduced, and attempts at subsequent recall of information are diminished. Once such patients do appropriately understand, categorize, and organize the information (with the assistance of extra cues, extra structuring, or extra time), they often target or "lose memories" at a normal rate.

Treatment. A patient with primary language-processing problems should receive language treatment focusing on the ability to process the information to be recalled as part of any memory treatment approach. Patients with executive function problems related to frontal lobe deficits may benefit from executive function training (see Chapter 10).

Memory Problems Related to Storage

Functional Impairment. Some memory problems are related to limited or dysfunctional storage—an impaired capacity to keep or put things in memory. Such problems are modeled as a disorder of the processes that ordinarily operate after the period of encoding or elaboration. Patients with storage impairments often have normal immediate and short-term memory. They may analyze information appropriately but be unable to maintain it in storage. Their long-term memory is seriously impaired. Retention deteriorates progressively over time after exposure. This form of amnesia is associated with an abnormally rapid rate of forgetting.

Probable Lesion Sight. Patients who most often have this sort of problem are those patients with hippocampal injury following bilateral damage to mesial temporal lobes (anoxic patients, herpes encephalitic patients, patients receiving ECT, etc.).

Memory Problems Secondary to Retrieval Deficits

Functional Impairment. The ability to "pull" information from memory is sometimes impaired while earlier stages of processing are spared. In such cases, the information is stored somewhere in the patient's nervous system but cannot be retrieved. Such patients may have intact *recognition* abilities (a recognition paradigm only requires that information be identified). These patients can retrieve information with the help of cues but have difficulty independently activating the memory traces.

Probable Lesion Site. The biologic bases of retrieval mechanisms and the primary sites of injury that would affect retrieval are not well understood. Many patients benefit from cues and prompts. Patients with depression have been noted to have particular difficulty in this area.

In the context of head trauma, rehabilitation specialists will most often be dealing with diffuse, nonfocal cerebral injuries. Patients are likely to have difficulty with more than one of these aspects of information processing for memory. Treatment paradigms must take this into account.

Learning without Awareness

A new concept in the field of memory research, with great potential relevance to rehabilitation, is the notion of "learning without awareness." This concept has grown out of observations that there are certain "memories" that appear to be stored in the nervous system for which we may not have conscious, explicit knowledge or awareness. All individuals, including even most severely amnesic patients studied, demonstrate some learning without apparent awareness. The next section addresses four components of this emerging concept. They are: *procedural versus declarative memory, semantic versus episodic memory, priming effects,* and *feelings of knowing* (see Cohen, 1984, for a review of issues related to preserved learning capacity and learning without awareness).

Procedural versus Declarative Memory

Procedural memory refers to the ability to learn rule-based or automatic behavioral sequences, such as motor skills, conditioned responses, performance on certain kinds of rule-based puzzles, perceptual motor tasks, and the ability to carry out sequences for running or operating things. Procedural learning may occur even though the individual does not remember having done it and cannot talk about it.

As an example, H.M., a severe amnesic with bilateral temporal lobe involvement, has not been able to store new verbal or figural information for many decades (Cohen, 1984). He does not remember facts or people that he has met, but when he repeatedly performed certain kinds of activities, he showed some evidence of benefiting from the experience. When brought into a room to do a particular kind of motor task (e.g., pursuit rotor task) on a daily basis, he would not remember seeing the room or doing the task before. But over the course of three or four sessions, he would start correctly performing the task, and his performance would consistently improve. He would still deny that he had done it before, and he had no conscious recollection of ever doing it, but he improved.

In many similar experimental paradigms, investigators have demonstrated that individuals, even severely amnesic individuals, are able to acquire this kind of rule-based memory. This capacity can be made use of in training strategies. It is one of the fundamental features that we have incorporated into our work with retraining of compensatory memory systems.

In contrast, the *declarative* system is one that implies conscious awareness and the ability to explicitly report something. This kind of memory may be most consistently disturbed in brain-injured patients and may not be the kind of memory that is most amenable to treatment.

Semantic versus Episodic Memory

Semantic memory refers to knowledge of word meanings, classes of information, ideas—the kinds of things you learned and you know, but you have no idea when you learned them or who taught them to you. Many of our patients do begin to demonstrate some semantic learning with repetition. When severely amnesic patients are seen for 7 or 8 hours over the course of a neuropsychologic evaluation, one may not get the sense that they would remember anything; but over the course of a week or 2 weeks of treatment, they often demonstrate the ability to find their way about a new clinic setting, to remember the names of therapists, etc. What they often really lose are memories for personally experienced events. That is, they cannot place events in time and in space. They may have little sense of what happened an hour ago—where thet were, whom they were with, or what happened. These recollections of time- and place-specific experiences have been termed *episodic* memory. One focus of the memory training programs we discuss is the development of ways to utilize preserved semantic or procedural memory to help people supplant the loss of episodic memory or recreate memories of an episodic nature. This is largely done through the use of compensatory external memory aids.

Priming Effects

Priming effects refer to the observation that cues (partial bits of information) can prompt an accurate recall without the individual's even being aware of, or remembering, that the information was presented before. For example, if you give someone a list of words that includes the word "chair" and then, after a few minutes, present a word-completion task prompted by the stimulus "ch_ _ _," they are more likely to say "chair" than they are to say "chain" or some other word that could fit the frame, even though they may have no recollection of having seen the word before. These priming effects work not only with normal individuals but also with amnesic patients, if not always so successfully. The underlying theory is that something in the nervous system has been altered by previous exposure to information (primed), and the information can be pulled out with appropriate cues or prompts. The challenge is to capitalize on this preserved capacity in amnesic patients to achieve functional goals. A treatment approach using the phenomenon of priming developed by Schacter (Glisky & Schacter, 1986) is discussed in a later section of this chapter.

Feelings of Knowing

In addition to remembering things and knowing things, we have a sense of what we know. If someone asks, "What is the name of the movie you saw last week?" you might not immediately remember its name, but you "know" that if it were told to you, you would recognize it. We have metacognitive information about what we know, a sense of security about what we could recall or recognize, and some knowledge about what we do and do not know.

Researchers are starting to investigate these concepts in patients with neurologically based memory impairment (Shimamura & Squire, 1986). Patients with frontal lobe lesions have been shown to be poor at judging the accuracy of what they know and the likelihood that they will recognize the correct answer if it is given. Their capacity to judge whether a memory is valid or not has been shown to be impaired. Some patients are absolutely secure that they know something but are wrong; other patients do not trust their memory at all and do not have any sense that their information is accurate but are often correct if you push them to respond. This kind of research is now in its infancy but has the potential to assist patients with memory impairment.

MEMORY ASSESSMENT

Psychometric assessment of memory may be improving. Tests are becoming more sensitive not only to the existence of but also to the nature of memory impairment. Researchers and clinicians remain far from satisfied, however, with the current ability to assess the comprehensive nature of memory. Most test batteries still strongly focus on memory within very specific contexts through the recall or recognition of information (see Chapter 2). Many other aspects of behavior that involve memory performance are never addressed.

The implications of memory test results for functional capacities are largely unknown. Clinicians often have patients who score very low on memory tests yet function quite well according to family reports. They get meals prepared, care for children, and go to work. There are also those patients who do very well on memory tests but who report much difficulty managing on a day-to-day basis. We must examine our testing procedures to try to resolve these inconsistencies.

Clinicians all too rarely get answers to such realistic questions as: Is the memory problem really affecting the patient or the family? How and when do you notice memory impairments? What would be the most important thing that could be changed? What kind of information, if remembered, would be most useful? If rehabilitation specialists are going to try to develop useful, cost-effective treatments, greater sensitivity to the prioritization of needs will be valuable.

Memory assessment needs to include the following:

1. Measures of immediate memory span (verbal and spatial).
2. Multiple measures of attention, including sustained, selective, and alternating attention.
3. Measures of new learning in which the individual has the opportunity to be exposed repeatedly to information. Such measures describe the ability of the patient to benefit from repeated presentation and more truly reflect learning capacity.

4. Traditional and recognition tests as well as recall tests. Recall tests will continue to play a role, but recognition tests need to be increasingly incorporated into assessment, so that retrieval problems can be differentiated from other levels of impairment.

Clinicians need to become more sophisticated and more thoughtful about assessing autobiographical information, doing more extensive interviewing about what people remember of past information about their daily lives. (The notion of prospective memory and its assessment is explored in a later part of this chapter.) In general, memory assessment needs to become more comprehensive, more functionally based, and, at the same time, more attuned to the new and important theoretical notions of memory function and dysfunction. These notions have tremendous implications for memory treatment.

REHABILITATION OF MEMORY IMPAIRMENTS

Reduced memory capacity may be the complaint most frequently voiced by individuals who have suffered a head injury. Recent literature indicates that 70% of persons with traumatic brain injury continue to experience significant memory difficulties at 1 year post-injury (Brooks, 1983). Since memory is a primary cognitive process critical for successful functioning in even the most basic aspects of everyday living, memory impairment is often one of the most debilitating deficits following traumatic brain injury. Decreased performance in memory can affect all aspects of the rehabilitation process and can have devastating effects on a person's educational or vocational goals as well as on independent living status. In the remainder of this chapter, we briefly review traditional approaches to memory retraining, provide a rationale for a more ecologically valid approach to the treatment of memory disorders, and describe a three-pronged approach to memory rehabilitation.

Traditional Approaches to Memory Rehabilitation

Although there is some literature—often of a popular nature—on enhancing memory skills in normal individuals, limited research is available on the remediation of memory disorders. Clinically, two broad approaches have been utilized. They are restoration and compensation.

Restoration

Restoration involves use of exercises, repetitive practice, or drills that have restoration of memory as their goal. Commonly included in this approach are list-learning tasks or paragraph recall tasks. Despite the face value of such activities, published studies have repeatedly documented their failures in either enhancing scores on untrained memory tasks or, more importantly, impacting functional memory outside the clinic (Godfrey & Knight, 1985; Prigatano et al., 1984; Schacter, Rich, & Stampp, 1985). For example, Prigatano and colleagues (1984) reported minimal improvement on logical memory and visual reproduction subtests following 625 hours of cognitive rehabilitation training.

Despite the lack of evidence that this muscle-building approach has any generalizable effects on memory enhancement, repetitive drilling is the approach taken in almost all of the published computer programs for so-called "memory retraining." A review of the commercial memory programs reveals a long list of software packages requiring patients to practice remembering letters, digits, words, pictures, shapes, and stories. The stimuli utilized in the programs do not have any inherent practical value; the notion is that they will build memory power through a practice effect. Although such programs are in widespread use, they rarely, if ever, are evaluated for effectiveness; and within the authors' own clinics, no memory-oriented computer program has been found useful in improving memory.

Based on these negative research findings, many scientists and clinicians have concluded that a damaged memory cannot be restored or improved. It must be understood, however, that all of the negative research findings were gathered from studies of memory rehabilitation within the context of repetitive practice or drills. All training focused on retrospective memory and addressed only this level of the memory process system. Thus, although it can be said that this particular form of memory rehabilitation is not effective, this does not necessarily mean that memory cannot be retrained. Later in the chapter, some promising alternative techniques are presented.

Compensatory Techniques

The second approach commonly used in memory rehabilitation involves training of strategies or techniques for memory compensation. Compensation refers to the process of circumventing difficulties that arise as a result of memory impairment without necessarily producing an improvement in memory capacity. There are two traditional types of training techniques. One is the teaching of external memory aids, and the other is training the use of internal memory aids. A third, more recent technique, the method of vanishing cues (Glisky & Schacter, 1986), will also be reviewed.

External memory aids may be subdivided into the following three types:

1. *Multicomponent organizational devices.* This category refers to devices such as electronic memories, memory notebook systems, and computers that allow an individual to organize, store, and retrieve relatively significant amounts of information.

2. *Simple prospective memory devices.* These are tools that will remind a memory-disordered person to perform a particular activity at a specified future time. Alarms, calendars, buzzers, and watches all fall within this category.

3. *Environmental modification.* Any restructuring or alteration of the environment to decrease the impact of a memory deficit on everyday life would be included within this group of external memory aids. Posted reminders on a mirror, labeled shelves, alphabetized cupboards, or specially structured work environments would all be examples of environmental modification.

Clinicians often report difficulty in using external aids with this population. Because these patients have difficulty with new learning, the teaching of new strategies and techniques is often unsuccessful. Later in this chapter, we describe a system that has been effective for teaching the use of an external memory aid.

A second type of compensatory technique involves use of *internal memory aids.* There are internal mnemonic strategies that can be used to compensate for memory failure. Such strategies may focus on enhancing organization of information to be recalled, rehearsing information to be remembered, or training specific mnemonic devices such as peg words or visual imagery. Several studies have suggested that recall performance in memory-disordered patients can be improved through training in such internal mnemonic learning schemes (Cermak, 1975; Crovitz, 1979; Gianutsos & Gianutsos, 1979; Gasparrini & Satz, 1979; Wilson, 1981, 1982). None of these studies, however, has shown that use of these strategies generalizes to naturalistic settings.

The utility of internal memory aids for this population should be suspect. These techniques place heavy demands on patients' already deficient cognitive systems; they are thus ineffectual for many persons with significantly compromised intellectual functions (Baddeley, 1982; Butters & Cermak, 1980; Schacter et al., 1985). They also presume to impose an approach to analyzing information or developing associations that cannot be explicitly observed or measured. Finally, it is very hard to imagine ways in which internally generated strategies such as imagery techniques or verbal associations could begin to be utilized to remember the myriad of facts, events, people, activities, or future intended actions important to daily life. In the authors' experience, attempts to utilize such procedures have been useful only for acquisition of very specific, small bodies of information (e.g., a medication schedule). Similarly, Glisky and Schacter (1986) noted that the training of internal memory strategies does not result in adequate maintenance of strategies beyond the training period or satisfactory generalization of techniques to other tasks and situations beyond the clinical or laboratory setting.

A more recent compensatory memory rehabilitation technique developed by Glisky, Schacter, and Tulving (1986) is termed the method of vanishing cues. It makes use of the demonstrated priming effects that exist in severely memory-disturbed patients. Priming effects refer to a type of preserved learning in which there is a facilitative effect of an exposure to an item on subsequent processing of that same item. Thus, if a patient is shown a certain picture or word, he or she will be more likely to choose that item in a recall task over another word that was not viewed. Glisky and Schacter have used the priming effect within the context of teaching amnesic patients new information. Their method involved the systematic reduction of letter fragments of to-be-learned words across trials. Although learning was slow and strongly dependent on first-letter cues, all patients acquired a substantial amount of vocabulary and eventually were able to produce the target words in the absence of fragment cues. Further, they retained their vocabulary over a 6-week interval and showed some transfer of the knowledge they had acquired. Since vocabulary involved terms applicable to the operation of a computer, the authors suggested that this method would help memory-impaired patients to be able eventually to use a microcomputer as a prosthetic device.

The method of vanishing cues is restricted to teaching domain-specific knowledge or information limited to a particular procedure or topic. The technique is thus a compensatory strategy; there is no expectation that there will be an increase in memory function for any knowledge domain other than the one targeted.

The Need for a Paradigm Shift in Memory Rehabilitation

Current research on memory rehabilitation suggests minimal gains in memory as measured by neuropsychologic tests and no gains in memory function as measured by extralaboratory assessments following much of the traditional memory treatment. Although this might suggest a grim future for memory rehabilitation efforts, there are, in fact, several possible explanations, including (1) the narrow focus on retrospective memory and retrieval in rehabilitation programs; (2) the tendency to draw prematurely negative conclusions from the research to date, which is based on experience with drills and practice alone; and (3) the lack of ecologic validity in current conceptualizations of memory assessment and treatment.

Taken together, these suggest the need for a paradigm shift in our memory rehabilitation efforts. There is a need to shift away from the traditional, restricted conceptualization of memory and to recognize the comprehensive, multicomponent model of information processing. There is a need to test other types of training and assessment formats. Medical professionals do not assume that diseases such as cancer are incurable; instead, they acknowledge current limitations and continue to research other options.

Cognitive rehabilitation specialists need to follow suit. Results from studies at Good Samaritan Hospital's Center for Cognitive Rehabilitation suggest that memory problems are amenable to treatment given careful matching between the type of treatment and the presenting symptoms.

Finally, research is needed on ecologic validity. Much is known about cognitive and experimental variables related to memory that operate within controlled experimental designs (Neisser, 1982). Results from such studies, however, lack the scope and functional context necessary to apply experimentally derived principles to the evaluation or rehabilitation of memory in persons with acquired neurologic damage. Theories of memory are often so closely bound to particular laboratory paradigms that they limit practical application. Current memory assessment and treatment techniques rarely, if ever, reflect information derived from studies of everyday memory. For instance, prospective memory is rarely addressed in clinical treatment programs, although it has been shown to be requisite for successful functioning in the everyday world (Kreutzer, Leonard, & Flavell, 1975; Meacham & Dumitru, 1976; Wilkins & Baddeley, 1978; Meacham & Leiman, 1982; Harris & Wilkins, 1984).

A Three-Pronged Model for Memory Rehabilitation

The relationship between the site of a focal lesion and the type of memory disruption was discussed earlier in this chapter. Although most traumatically brain-injured patients do not have focal or easily identifiable lesions, the notion that there are different types of memory problems requiring different treatment approaches still holds true. It is important to match a memory rehabilitation program with a specific constellation of sequelae. The first step toward an appropriate marriage between disorder and treatment is a comprehensive memory assessment. A thorough evaluation of memory is crucial in order to understand the nature of the memory problem. Unfortunately, the most widely used assessment procedures—the Wechsler Memory Scale (Wechsler, 1945), the Auditory Verbal Learning Test (AVLT), the Selective Reminding Test (Buschke & Fuld, 1974), and the Randt Memory Test (Randt, Brown, & Osborne, 1980)—focus only on recall ability. Evaluations of prospective memory ability and attentional processing are also essential for understanding the nature of the memory impairment. It is further important to analyze *why* an individual fails on a particular memory test and to examine the underlying factors potentially responsible for a memory failure. Examination of results on other diagnostic tests sensitive to attention would be critical for sorting out the nature of the impairment.

To address the different constellations of memory problems, the current authors have developed a three-pronged approach to memory rehabilitation that has proven very effective in enhancing memory function in persons who have sustained traumatic brain injury (Mateer & Sohlberg, 1988). The memory model consists of three distinct treatment programs, including (1) Attention Process Training (APT) (Sohlberg & Mateer, 1987); (2) Prospective Memory Process Training (PROMPT) (Sohlberg & Mateer, 1986); and (3) Memory Notebook Training (M. M. Sohlberg & C. A. Mateer, unpublished data). Each of the three treatment programs is described with accompanying supportive experimental and clinical data.

ATTENTION PROCESS TRAINING

As mentioned earlier, deficits that initially present as memory impairments are often found to reflect underlying impairments in attention (Sohlberg & Mateer, 1987). Thus, it is important for clinicians examining memory to be aware of the potential contribution of decreased functioning in attentional processing. Preliminary data strongly suggest that attention training results in improved memory among some patients.

The importance of addressing attention as a potential factor underlying memory problems has been sorely ignored. The preliminary data gathered on individuals who have completed APT as outlined in Chapter 5 strongly support the notion that increased attention ability for select patients results in improved memory. Table 7.1 provides data for five subjects who completed APT and subsequently demonstrated significant improvement in memory ability as measured by the Five Items Subtest (Acquisition and Delayed Recall scores) from the Randt Memory Test. Each subject improved at least one standard deviation. Each of these subjects initially presented with severe attentional deficits as measured by the Paced Auditory Serial Addition Task (Gronwall, 1977).

It appears that there are some individuals who have attentionally based memory problems, which may be identified through the use of neuro-

TABLE 7.1 Memory Improvement Following Attention Process Training

Subject	Length of time post-injury at initiation of treatment	PASAT z-score, trial 1		Randt Memory Test, Five items subtest, scaled score			
				Acquisition		Delayed recall	
		Pre	Post	Pre	Post	Pre	Post
01	24 months	−3.6	−1.6	7	10	7	11
02	52 months	−2.5	0.4	4	8	4	9
03	28 months	−3.3	−1.4	7	10	4	9
04	30 months	−5.0	−1.0	5	8	7	10
05	33 months	−1.0	0.4	8	10	7	11

psychologic measures sensitive to attention in conjunction with behavioral observations and interview. Assessment may be followed by a cognitive rehabilitation program specifically targeted toward remediation of attention deficits such as APT, which is described in Chapter 5.

PROSPECTIVE MEMORY PROCESS TRAINING

As discussed in the initial portion of this chapter, clinical models of memory have traditionally been tied to the classical structure model, which viewed memory as a dual time-based system (Walker, 1976; Squire, 1975). There was a tendency to look at memory solely as a dichotomous storage system of long- versus short-term memory. Again, the clinical emphasis was heavily weighted on retrospective memory with the length of delay on recall tasks operating as the variable parameter used to assess and treat memory. Subsequently, new hypotheses were formed, and memory was conceptualized according to levels of processing rather than to a store-based mechanism with components of attention, encoding, storage, or retrieval (Butters & Cermak, 1980; Cermak, 1982; Craik & Lockhart, 1972). We know that to successfully remember an item, there must be a mechanism or series of steps for adequately getting the information into the brain as well as for recalling it.

Unlike most treatment models, PROMPT (Sohlberg & Mateer, 1986; Sohlberg, 1986) addresses the different levels of processing in memory. For those patients who present with a primary memory deficit (as opposed to an attentionally based problem) and who exhibit difficulty with the encoding/recall of information, PROMPT offers an effective means of management.

To document better the functional importance of prospective memory, Mateer, Sohlberg, and Crinean (1987) conducted a study surveying over 300 brain-injured and normal subjects. The subjects received a questionnaire describing various types of forgetting experiences, which they ranked on a frequency-of-occurrence scale. The results suggested that both brain-injured- and non-brain-injured individuals perceived themselves as experiencing significantly more forgetting experiences related to prospective memory than to other types of memory (Figure 7.2). A factor analysis of survey responses yielded four separate Memory factors, which were labeled Attention/Prospective Memory, Anterograde Memory, Retrograde Memory, and Historical/Overlearned Memory. Mean reports of frequency of memory failure are plotted for the four Memory factors and three subject groups (head injury with coma, head injury without coma, and controls) in Figure 7.2. Almost half of the total variance (47%) in responses was accounted for by frequency ratings on items that loaded on the Attention/Prospective Memory factor. In every subject group, the mean frequency rating for forgetting related to Attention and Prospective Memory was higher than that for any of the other three factors.

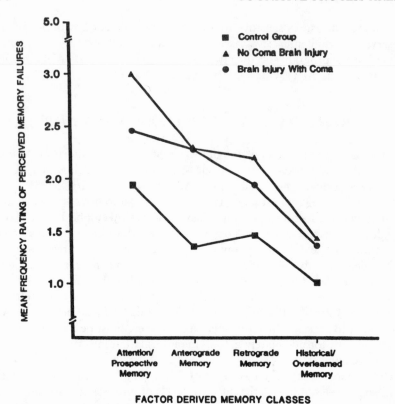

FIGURE 7.2. Mean frequency of different classes of forgetting experience as perceived by control (non-brain-injured) subjects, head-injured subjects who reported coma greater than 24 hours, and head-injured subjects without coma. The classes of memory disorder were derived though a factor analysis of questionnaire data. All groups reported that the most frequent kind of memory failure involved experiences dependent on attentional skills or prospective memory (Mateer et al., 1987).

The Prospective Memory Screening (PROMS) (Sohlberg, Mateer, & Geyer, 1985) was developed to try to quantify patients' prospective memory ability. This assessment tool provides structured opportunities for the patient to demonstrate the ability to carry out assigned tasks at a specified future time. It assesses several parameters. One is the time dimension. Sometimes patients' breakdown in prospective memory tasks relates to the duration of time between the presentation of prospective memory tasks and the target time in which the task is supposed to be initiated. Thus, the individual has more difficulty retaining the task as the time from presentation increases. To identify and quantify this type of problem, the PROMS includes measurements of prospective memory at 60 seconds, 2 minutes, 10 minutes, 20 minutes, and 24 hours. The other parameter examined is the type of cuing employed. One sort of prospective memory task involves associative cuing such that when one action occurs (e.g., a timer goes off), then an individual must remember to carry out a certain task (e.g., turn down the oven). Another type of cuing requires that a person keep track of the time. For instance, a person might need to watch the clock in order to leave the house on time to make an appointment. The PROMS takes measurements using both associative cues and time cues at 1 minute, 2 minutes, 10 minutes, and 20 minutes. The 24-hour measurement uses a time cue only. Such an assessment can provide an index of this important type of memory function. If this ability appears to be deficit, the clinican may initiate PROMPT.

The overall goal of PROMPT is to extend systematically the amount of time an individual is able to remember to carry out specified tasks. The subject is provided with a target task and a target time for initiating the task. It may be that the act of continually updating memory traces, as the target time approaches, exercises the encoding mechanism as well as the retrieval mechanism.

Treatment may be carried out in either a single- or dual-treatment paradigm. In the dual-task format, the patient is performing a simultaneous distractor task during the waiting period. There is a heavier load on memory than in the single-task paradigm, since the patient must hold onto the prospective memory task as well as engage in a cognitive task. Time is usually extended by 2-minute intervals following five consecutive correct responses. Table 7.2 is an example of a data collection chart that includes sample data.

Initial results from PROMPT are very encouraging (see Table 7.3). Following training, three closed-head-injury subjects were able to complete prospective memory tasks 15 minutes from task presentation using the single-task paradigm (the maximum time limit to which treatment was extended). Simultaneous improvements were noted on the standard score (memory index) of the Randt Memory Test. (Length of training time for PROMPT varied from 4 to 12 weeks. Individuals were given prospective memory tasks at least three times a day, four days each week.)

Compared to traditional treatments, prospective memory tasks more closely approximate naturalistic or real-life demands on memory. A more ecologically valid approach to memory rehabilitation is essential if clinicians are to have an impact on vocational and independent living status. Initial results in this area suggest that prospective memory training could offer a new frontier in memory rehabilitation research.

TRAINING USE OF A COMPENSATORY NOTEBOOK SYSTEM

It is important to recognize that for patients with more severe memory impairments, memory may improve on being given PROMPT, but the residual disability is often too great to allow for successful, independent

TABLE 7.2 Prospective Memory Data Collection Sheet

Date	Duration	Type of task remembered	Distractor task[a]	Correct task initiated (+/−)	Task initiated at target (+/−)	Comments
3/13	5 min	Clap hands	Math worksheet	−	+	Couldn't recall task
3/14	5 min	Close door	Math worksheet	−	+	Did wrong task
3/15	5 min	Stand up	Math worksheet	+	−	1 min early
3/16	5 min	Touch Nose	Math worksheet	+	+	Hesitated
3/17	5 min	Snap fingers	Math worksheet	+	+	Great!
3/20	5 min	Stomp feet	Math worksheet	+	+	
3/21	5 min	Open curtain	Math worksheet	+	+	
3/22	5 min	Clap	Math	+	+	Met goal
3/23	7 min	Open desk drawer	Math	−	−	
5/2	9 min	(1) Clap hands (2) Say name	Computer cognitive task	+	+	
5/3	9 min	(1) Shut door (2) See TV Show	Computer cognitive task	+	+	

[a]Distractions mean another task was assigned simultaneously.

TABLE 7.3. Memory Improvement Following Prospective Memory Process Training (PROMPT)

Subject	Number of months post-onset	Initial length of prospective memory ability (minutes)	Length of prospective memory ability following PROMPT (min) (15 max)	Randt Memory Test Memory Index Pre-PROMPT	Randt Memory Test Memory Index Post-PROMPT
01	15	0.5	15	33	65
02	36	3.0	15	79	86
03	17	0.5	15	40	73

functioning in the everyday world. There is a need for compensatory techniques that can minimize the barriers to independent living and vocational success that are so common with severe memory impairment.

One kind of external memory aid that is frequently suggested for patients with memory disorder is the memory notebook. Often, however, these aids are given with minimal instruction or training in their use and are unsystematic in their design. A commonly reported experience of clinicians is that memory notebooks are rejected by patients or used only a short time outside the clinical setting. To date, there is little research on the effectiveness of such aids.

In consideration of these problems, the authors developed theoretically based, systematic, formal training procedures to teach the use of a memory notebook (M. M. Sohlberg & C. A. Mateer, unpublished work). The theoretical foundation for these procedures comes in part from the learning theory literature and in part from studies of preserved learning in amnesics.

To be successful, memory notebooks must be designed to meet the specific needs of the patient. A first step in this process is a needs assessment; the clinician must determine what an individual will require in his or her particular living and/or work setting. Based on the information gleaned from the needs assessment, different sections in the notebook are designed to meet different needs (see Table 7.4). For example, some patients will require an *orientation section* with pertinent autobiographical information, whereas others may not have difficulty with this type of information.

TABLE 7.4. List of Possible Notebook Sections

Orientation:	Narrative autobiographic information concerning personal data and/or information surrounding the brain injury
Memory Log:	Contains forms for charting hourly information about what patient has done; diary of daily information
Calendar	Calendars with dates and times, which would allow a patient to schedule appointments and dates
Things to do:	Contains forms for recording errands and intended future actions; includes place to mark due date and completion date
Transportation:	Contains maps and/or bus information to frequented places such as work, schools, store, bank, etc.
Feelings log:	Contains forms to chart feelings relative to specific incidences or times
Names:	Contains forms to record names and identifying information of new people
Today at work:	Various forms have been adapted for specific vocations and settings that allow individuals to record the necessary information to perform their job duties

Almost every notebook will contain a *calendar section* to allow recording of future dates and appointments, a *memory log section* to record hourly events that occur, and a *things-to-do section* to provide a place to record future intended actions.

Learning Theory

It is hypothesized that spontaneous and functional use of a memory notebook is predicated on appropriate, systematic training procedures. Researchers in learning theory (Liberty, Haring, & White, 1980: White & Haring, 1980; White, 1984) identify three phases of learning critical for mastering new skills that may be applied to memory notebook training: acquisition, application, and adaptation. Efficiency building is an essential learning parameter that must also be incorporated within each of these learning phases. The authors note that each phase imposes somewhat different demands on a learner and requires adjustment in instructional strategies if continued progress toward mastery is to be realized.

Acquisition refers to that stage of learning in which the patient is learning *how* to perform a certain skill. In the case of memory notebook use, the patient needs to become familiar with the purpose and use of each different section in the notebook. This familiarization training is achieved through repetitive administration of questions regarding notebook contents and use specific to that patient's individual notebook. (See Table 7.5 for an example of the training questions and corresponding data.)

The second stage, application, refers to learning *when* and *where* to utilize a new skill. It is not enough simply to know how to perform a task; in order to be successful, a person must be able to apply that skill to the appropriate situation. Role play provides an excellent training format to facilitate application of appropriate notebook use. The clinician can administer role-play events in person or can simulate telephone situations by telephoning the patient from a nearby telephone. The patient is given feedback regarding performance, and these variables are then scored on a data collection chart. (See Table 7.6 for an example of the Application scoresheet.)

The third phase of learning is termed adaptation. In this stage, an individual demonstrates the ability to adapt and modify skill use to accommodate novel situations. Because it is not possible to role play every situation in which a patient might encounter the need to utilize a memory notebook, it is important that the adaptation phase of learning be adequately addressed. This is best accomplished by training in naturalistic settings. The clinician accompanies the patient out into the community or to settings within the medical facility such as the gift shop or cafeteria and scores performance on notebook use (see Table 7.7).

The above three training phases constitute a sequence of instruction that would establish basic skills necessary for memory notebook use. Each level of instruction must also incorporate efficiency building. Efficiency building is the instructional process that ensures that a patient will actually use this skill.

Efficiency aims, or performance criteria, that will allow a patient to maintain and use this skill must be established for each instructional phase in order for the clinician to determine when the patient can move onto the next level (see Table 7.8). For the purpose of memory notebook use, efficiency aims are accuracy and consistency criteria that result in skill maintenance and use. The values were determined by examination of data from past individuals who had successfully learned to use the memory notebook system.

To summarize, teaching a new skill to an individual with compromised new learning ability requires careful planning of instruction. The outcome of instruction needs to be skill acquisition with enough fluency or efficiency to allow appropriate skill application in different environments (i.e., spontaneous, independent use of the memory notebook across settings).

Training Methodologies

Training methodologies for memory notebook use are derived from research on how individuals with severe impairments can best learn. Areas of preserved learning and memory in severely amnesic patients may include perceptual motor skills, memory for overlearned information, and responsivity to repetition priming effects (e.g., Cohen, 1984; Warrington, 1982). One type of preserved learning that has been much discussed is procedural memory (Cohen & Squire, 1980; Fisk & Schreider, 1984). This ability to learn procedures or motor sequences, even in the absence of conscious awareness of learning, is frequently spared in even severely amnesic patients. The training procedures outlined in this section depend heavily on intact procedural memory. Establishment of instructional sequences, including repeated administration of questions and answers regarding notebook use and contents (acquisition phase), repetitive role play allowing practice with the mechanics of notebook use (application), and community training allowing further notebook practice in naturalistic environments (adaptation), all utilize the spared procedural memory that has been documented in this population.

The techniques described in this chapter have been used successfully to teach a compensatory memory system to four globally amnestic patients. Following a 6- to 8-month daily outpatient program, all of the patients continue to use the compensatory systems to support independent living, and all are gainfully employed, yet none of them improved substantially on formal measures of recall performance.

TABLE 7.5. Acquisition Chart for Learning Notebook Use

	Dates																		
	3/2	3/2	3/2	3/3	3/3	3/3	3/4	3/4	3/5	3/5	3/5	3/6	3/6	3/6	3/9	3/10	3/11	3/12	3/13
Name the five sections in your notebook (Orientation, Memory Log, Calendar, Things to Do, Transportation)	–	– 1/5	– 2/5	– 3/5	– 3/5	– 3/5	– 4/5	– 4/5	– 4/5	+	+	+	+	+	+	– 4/5	+	+	+
What is the Orientation section for? (tells information about myself and my injury)	–	+	–	–	–	–	–	–	+	+	+	+	+	+	+	+	+	+	+
What is the Memory Log section for? (to keep track of what I do each hour)	–	–	+	–	–	–	+	+	+	+	+	+	+	+	+	+	+	+	+
What is the Calendar section for? (to plan scheduled events and appointments)	–	+	+	–	–	+	+	+	+	+	+	+	+	+	+	+	+	+	+
What is the Things to Do section for? (to keep track of errands)	–	–	+	–	–	–	+	+	+	+	+	+	+	+	+	+	+	+	+
What is the Transportation section for? (it has maps and bus information so I can get to school, work, bank, store, etc.)	–	–	+	+	+	+	+	+	+	+	+	+	+	+	+	+	+	+	+

	0	10	30	40	30	30	70	60	90	80	90	100	100	80	100	100	100
When do you write in your Memory Log? (every time I finish one activity and start a new one)	−	−	−	−	−	−	+	+	+	−	+	+	+	−	+	+	+
When should you look at your Calendar and Things to Do sections? (in the morning, at lunchtime, and at dinnertime)	−	−	−	−	−	−	−	+	+	+	−	+	+	+	+	+	+
Where should you record information about appointments, meetings, or events with particular days and times? (in the Calendar section)	−	+	+	−	+	+	+	+	+	+	+	+	+	+	+	+	+
What should you do when you finish something on your Things to Do list? (cross it off—draw a line through it)	−	+	+	+	+	+	+	+	+	+	+	+	+	+	+	+	+
Total correct (%)	0	10	30	40	30	30	70	60	90	80	90	100	100	80	100	100	100

TABLE 7.6. Application Chart (Role Play)

Date	Role-play situation	Number of notebook sections required	Spontaneously wrote in proper sections (+/−)	Wrote appropriate information (+/−)	Comments
2/24	Invitation to dinner (phone from neighbor's office)	2 (Memory Log plus Calendar)	−	−	Needed maximal cuing for what and where to write
2/24	Reminder of meeting (phone)	2 (Memory Log plus Calendar)	−	−	Needed maximum cuing for what and where to write
2/25	Reminder to bring sack lunch (phone)	2 (Memory Log plus Things to Do)	− (got one out of two sections)	+	+ Wrote spontaneously in Memory Log; needed minimal cuing to write in Things to Do. +Wrote appropriate information in each
2/25	Invitation to bowling (in person)	2 (Memory Log plus Calendar)	+	+	No cuing
2/26	Reminder of relative's birthday (in person)	2 (Memory Log plus Calendar)	+	−	Identified appropriate sections but did not write complete information in calendar
	Continue 2 section exercises twice daily until criterion of 2 consecutive error-free days is met				
2/26	Invitation to potluck (phone)	3 (Calendar, Memory Log, Things to Do)	− (got two out of three)	+	Needed minimal cuing to write potluck item on Things to Do list
2/27	Instructions regarding new work schedule	3 (Calendar, Memory Log, Things to Do)	+	+	

TABLE 7.7 Adaptation Chart (Community Training)

Date	Situation	Score[a]	Comments
4/07	Buying item at hospital gift shop	1	Needed cuing to write in Memory Log and Things to Do
4/07	Buying candy bar for therapist	2	One reminder to use Memory Log section
4/08	Phone call at home with request to bring picture to therapy	2	Cued on the phone to write in Things to Do section
4/08	Buying item in hospital cafeteria	3	Wrote item in Things to Do but forgot to write place of purchase
4/09	Buying item in vending machine	3	
4/09	One-stop errand at neighboring therapist's office	3	Minimal cuing to write more complete information in Memory Log
4/10	Bring message to receptionist	4	Hurray!
	Patient moves to outpatient therapy.		
4/28	Obtain travel brochure from local agency	2	Reminder to write in Things to Do before leaving clinic
4/28	Obtain business card from any local business	3	Reminder to write *where* he was going

[a]Scoring: 4, spontaneously and accurately recorded information in appropriate sections; 3, needed cuing for what to write in each section but identified appropriate sections; 2, needed minimal cuing for what sections should be utilized; 1, needed maximum cuing for both what and where to write.

TABLE 7.8. Memory Book Training Phases and Efficiency Goals

Training phase	Description
Acquisition	Learn names, purpose, and use of each notebook section via question/answer format
Efficiency goal	100% accuracy on questions for five consecutive days
Application	Learn appropriate methods for recording in notebook via role-play situations
Efficiency goal	100% accuracy of response to three role-play situations with no cuing on two consecutive days
Adaptation	Demonstrate appropriate notebook use in naturalistic settings via community training
Efficiency goal	Receive a score of 4 for two situations on two consecutive days

An important feature of the memory notebook training system is its emphasis on prospective memory. The system gives patients a way to keep track of and carry out future tasks. The ability to carry out needed or intended activity can make the crucial difference in allowing independent living or vocation.

Case Study
The following case study illustrates the implementation of the memory notebook teaching sequence. F.S., a 19-year-old male with a 10th-grade education, sustained a severe injury in a logging accident. He underwent evacuation of a right subdural and right epidural hematoma in the first 6 days post-injury. He was in a coma for 4 weeks. Initial deficits included disorientation, left hemiplegia, left hemianopsia, severe visual–spatial processing deficits, severe attention deficits, and profound memory impairment. He received 5 months of inpatient and 6 months of outpatient rehabilitation. He was admitted to a postacute rehabilitation program 1 year after his injury.

At the time of program entry, F.S.'s intellectual function was in the borderline range (WAIS-R: Verbal IQ 87, Performance IQ 66, Full-Scale IQ 76) (Table 7.9). Severe deficits were seen on the delayed recall of the Wechsler Memory Scale paragraphs and designs. Frequent confusion was noted across all tasks.

TABLE 7.9. Neuropsychological Test Scores for F.S.

	Program entry	Program discharge
WAIS-R		
Verbal IQ	87	87
Performance IQ	66	71
Full-Scale IQ	76	78
Wechsler Memory Scale		
Paragraph Recall, Immediate	5.75	4.50
Delay	2.25	4.25
Retention	37%	95%
Figural Reproduction, immediate	8	9
Delay	2	4.5
Retention	25%	50%
Rey Auditory Verbal Learning Test		
Trials I–Trial V (learning curve)	7, 7, 7, 10, 8	6, 6, 9, 8, 8
Trial VI–V (3.02 + 1.51) (loss after distraction)	6	1
Recognition (max = 15)	9	7
False Positives	7	5
Trailmaking Test		
Trails A	101 sec/1 error	93.1 sec/0 errors
Trails B	360 sec/3 errors	184.3 sec/1 error

On the Rey Auditory Verbal Learning Test, he demonstrated almost no learning curve over five repetitions of the 15-word list. His recognition of the words was also severely impaired, with frequent false-positive responses noted. He was dependent on his family for all aspects of independent living, including medications, schedules, meal planning and preparation, shopping, money management, and transportation. He required 24-hour supervision. Because of the severity of F.S.'s memory impairment, use of a compensatory memory book system had been instituted while he was an inpatient. Although he consistently carried the book with him, he did not make entries in the daily memory log or calendar section without maximal assistance from therapists. The book was not functional for independent living or community or vocational needs.

The acquisition phase of training focused on having F.S. demonstrate explicit, declarative knowledge about the purpose and use of new sections in this book, in addition to the daily log that was already present. These included a Calendar section, a Things-to-Do section, and a Transportation section (containing maps of the surrounding community and one bus route). A series of 10 questions regarding these notebook sections was developed, and they were asked in different order twice each day. If he was incorrect or unable to answer a question, the correct answer was immediately provided and he was asked to repeat it. It took F.S. 17 program days to achieve 100% accuracy in his responses to the questions on both administrations of the questionnaire (morning and afternoon) for five consecutive days. Throughout this period, he was prompted to make entries in the hourly log section of his book after each therapy session and to refer to his calendar section in order to determine his therapy schedule. Each day's log was reviewed in the cognitive group the following morning.

At this point, the application stage of training was begun. This involved two components. First, a record was kept of whether or not he wrote in his hourly log at the end of each session and the level of cuing needed for him to do so. Minimal cuing referred to such indirect reminders as, "We are switching therapy activities now," or "I'll bet you want to remember this later." Moderate cuing was defined as direct reminders such as, "What should you do to remember this?" Recording of cues as part of the data base allowed systematic fadding of cues over time. It took an additional 23 days of training for him to write in his hourly log after 90% of the hours spent in a day treatment program (7 of 8 possible log entries per day) for 3 consecutive days. An additional 32 days were required before he wrote in his log at least three times in the evening and at least four times each weekend day. In the second aspect of application training, role-play situations were introduced. These were hypothetical situations that mimicked potentially real events for which the memory notebook would be necessary. They covered all sections of the memory notebook and consisted of such activities as calling him from another room to schedule an evening event, requesting him to bring something to a particular treatment hour the next day, or scheduling a treatment hour the next day in an unusual location. He required

38 treatment days before appropriately using the book without cuing for all three role-play situations presented on each of two consecutive days.

The adaptation phase of training began approximately 10 weeks after program entry. At least five situations requiring notebook use in community-based settings were structured every day. Hospital settings were initially utilized until F.S. achieved independence in the community. The clinician would give F.S. a community talk and record data on his performance in using the memory book. Accuracy of notebook memory book use and level of cuing were scored on each item. Many of these situations involved his transitional living setting. In the last month of his program, he was trained in the use of a similar but separate book, which was used in a sheltered employment setting where he worked (electronic assembly). A total of 6 months of intensive training was required for F.S. to achieve independent use of the system.

On discharge, F.S. was living in an apartment with 1 hour of assistance in the early evening and help with some weekly shopping. He prepared his own meals, had a regular recreation program, and got himself to and from work each day. Production increased at work (so that he became eligible for transition to paid employment training).

Psychometric scores on discharge (Table 7.9) revealed mild to moderate gains in attention and delayed recall after distraction, but profound limitations in memory and new learning persisted. Despite this, he was living with only minimal daily assistance and functioning in a sheltered work environment. Memory book usage continues to be consistent and is felt to be critical to his adaptive skills.

SUMMARY

In the past, researchers and clinicians have been too narrow in their view of memory. This has placed unfortunate limitations on the rehabilitation of memory disorders in patients with brain damage and has necessitated a paradigm shift in memory rehabilitation away from the unitary focus on retrospective memory or recall towards a more comprehensive view of memory. Memory is increasingly viewed as a complex information-processing system with multiple components.

There are many neuroanatomic correlates of memory impairment; disruption of different neurological systems results in different patterns of memory loss. Clinically relevant factors in the clinical management of memory disorders include attention to the nature and degree of loss and the degree of associated cognitive impairment.

Consideration of prospective memory, or the ability to remember future intentions, has led to the development of memory-training techniques such as PROMPT that are able to enhance memory function in some individuals with primary memory deficits. Devices such as memory notebooks, which provide a means for carrying out prospective memory tasks, have permitted some memory-disordered patients to live independently and pursue gainful employment. These approaches are hypothesized to build on aspects of memory, such as procedural memory, that reflect learning without awareness and are often preserved in the amnesic patient. Similarly, the recognition of attention as an important aspect of memory has led to the development of training procedures *(APT)* that can restore memory functions in patients with attentionally based memory problems.

A comprehensive evaluation, including examination of attentional processing and prospective memory ability, allows clinicians to match the appropriate treatment procedures with the existing disorder. This chapter has argued for a more ecologically valid view of memory and outlined a three-pronged approach to memory rehabilitation that includes Attention Process Training (APT), Prospective Memory Process Training (PROMPT), and Memory Notebook Training. In persons who exhibit memory impairment as a result of a primary deficit in attention, the first training program would be most appropriate. For persons with severe, more primary memory involvement, a combination of the latter two approaches would be advisable. There may be individuals who benefit from all three approaches. Fundamental consideration must be given to the type of memory disorders exhibited. Today's diagnostic and treatment tools must continue to be expanded.

This essential paradigm shift in memory rehabilitation offers optimistic, yet realistic, hope to persons experiencing memory impairment as a result of diffuse brain damage.

STUDY QUESTIONS

1. List the supposed defining characteristics of short- and long-term memory and describe problems with this distinction.
2. List the major components of information-processing theories of memory.
3. How do transient and permanent amnesias conceptually differ?
4. Discuss some of the problems with conceptualization of verbal versus nonverbal memory.
5. How would a patient with diencephalic damage (e.g., a patient with Korsakoff's syndrome) differ in terms of memory pattern from a patient who had suffered bilateral temporal lobe injury (e.g., an anoxic patient)?
6. Describe procedural memory.
7. Contrast semantic versus episodic memory.

8. Describe traditional approaches to memory rehabilitation. What are some of the problems with past approaches to memory retraining?
9. Why might professionals be quick to say that memory is not amenable to treatment?
10. How does PROMPT incorporate a more comprehensive view of memory as an information-processing system?
11. Describe the three training phases for teaching use of a memory notebook. How might they be applied to teaching the use of other external memory aids?

REFERENCES

Baddeley, A. D. (1982). Amnesia: Minimal model and an interpretation. In L. S. Cermak (Ed.), *Human memory and amnesia* (pp. 305–330). Hillsdale, NJ: Lawrence Erlbaum Associates.

Baddeley, A. D., & Hitch, G. J. (1974). Working memory. In G. A. Bower (Ed.), *The psychology of learning and motivation, Vol. 8.* New York: Academic Press.

Brooks, N. (1983). Disorders of memory. In M. Rosenthal, E. R. Griffith, M. R. Bond, & J. D. Miller (Eds.), *Rehabilitation of the Head Injured Adult.* Philadelphia: F. A. Davis.

Buschke, H., & Fuld, P. A. (1974). Evaluations storage, retention, and retrieval in disordered memory and learning. *Neurology* 11:1019–1025.

Butters, N., & Cermak, L. S. (1980). *Alcoholic Korsakoff's syndrome: An information processing approach to amnesics.* New York: Academic Press.

Cermak, L. S. (1975). Imagery as an aid to retrieval for Korsakoff patients. *Cortex* 11:163–169.

Cermak, L. S. (Ed.). (1982). *Human memory and amnesia.* Hillsdale, NJ: Lawrence Erlbaum Associates.

Cohen, N. (1984). Preserved learning capacity in amnesia: Evidence for multiple memory systems. In L. R. Squire & N. Butters (Eds.), *Neuropsychology of memory* (pp. 83–103). New York: Guilford Press.

Cohen, N., & Squire, L. (1980). Preserved learning and retention of pattern-analyzing skill in amnesia: Dissociation of knowing how and of knowing that. *Science* 210:201–120.

Coltheart, M. (1980). Ironic memory and visible persistence. *Perception and Psychophysics* 27:183–228.

Craik, F., & Lockhart, R. (1972). Levels of processing: A framework for memory research. *Journal of Verbal Learning and Verbal Behavior* 11:671–684.

Craik, F. I. M., & Watkins, M. H. (1973). The role of rehearsal in short-term memory. *Journal of Verbal Learning and Verbal Behavior* 12:599–607.

Crovitz, H. F. (1979). Memory retraining in brain-damaged patients: The airplane list. *Cortex 15:* 131–134.

Cummings, J. L., & Benson, D. F. (1983). *Dementia: A clinical approach.* Boston: Butterworths.

Fisk, A., & Shrieder, L. (1984). Memory as a function of attention level of processing and automatization. *Journal of Experimental Psychology: Learning, Memory and Cognition* 10:181–197.

Gasparrini, B., & Satz, P. (1979). A treatment for memory problems in left hemisphere CVA patients. *Journal of Clinical Neuropsychology* 91:66–73.

Gianutsos, R., & Gianutsos, J. (1979). Rehabilitating the verbal recall of brain-injured patients by mnemonic training: An experimental demonstration using single-case methodology. *Journal of Clinical Neuropsychology* 2:117–135.

Glisky, E. L., & Schacter, D. L. (1986). Remediation of organic memory disorders: Current status and future prospects. *Journal of Head Trauma Rehabilitation 1:* 54–63.

Glisky, E. L., Schacter, D. L., & Tulving, E. (1986). Learning and retention of computer-related vocabulary in memory-impaired patients: Method of vanishing cues. *Journal of Clinical and Experimental Neurospsychology 8:* 292–312.

Godfrey, H., & Knight, R. (1985). Cognitive rehabilitation of memory functioning in amnesic alcoholics. *Journal of Consulting and Clinical Psychology 43:555–557.*

Gronwall, D. (1977). Paced auditory serial addition task: A measure of recovery from concussion. *Perceptual and Motor Skills 44:367–373.*

Harris, J. E., & Wilkins, A. J. (1984). Remembering to do things: A forgotten topic. In J. E. Harris & P. E. Morris (Eds.), *Everyday memory actions and absent-mindedness.* London: Academic Press.

Huppert, F., & Piercy, M. (1982). In search of the functional locus of amnesic syndromes. In L. Cermak (Ed.), *Human memory and amnesia.* Hillsdale, NJ: Lawrence Erlbaum Associates.

Jones, M. (1974). Imagery as a mnemonic and after left temporal lobectomy: Contrast between material specific and generalized memory disorders. *Neuropsycholoqia 12:21–30.*

Kreutzer, M., Leonard, C., & Flavell, J. (1975). An interview study of children's knowledge about memory. *Monographs of the Society for Research in Child Development 40* (1, Serial No. 159).

Liberty, K., Haring, H., & White, O. (1980). Rules for data-based strategy decisions in instructional programs: Current research and instructional implications. In W. Sailor, B. Wilcox, & L. Brown (Eds.), *Methods of instruction for severely handicapped students.* Baltimore: Paul H. Brookes.

Lishman, W. (1978) *Organic psychiatry.* Oxford: Blackwell Scientific Publications.

Mateer, C. A., & Sohlberg, M. M. (1988). A paradigm shift in memory rehabilitation. In H. A. Whitaker (Ed.), *Neuropsychological studies of non-focal brain damage: Dementia and trauma,* (pp. 202–225). New York: Springer.

Mateer, C. A., Sohlberg, M. M., & Crinean, J. (1987). Perceptions of memory function in individual with closed head injury. *Journal of Head Injury Rehabilitation, 3:74–84.*

McDowell, J. (1984). Processing capacity and recall in amnesics and control subjects. In: L. R. Squire and N. Butters (Eds.), *Neuropsychology of memory* (pp. 63–66). New York: Guilford Press.

Meacham, J., & Dumitru, J. (1976). Prospective remembering and external retrieval cases. *J. S. A. S. Catalog of Selected Documents in Psychology 5:65* (MS No. 1284).

Meacham, J. A., & Leiman, B. (1982). Remembering to perform future actions. In V. Neisser (Ed.), *Memory observed, remembering in national contexts* (pp. 327–336). San Francisco: W. H. Freeman.

Milner, B. (1970). Memory and the medial temporal regions of the brain. In K. H. Pribram & D. E. Broadbent (Eds.), *Biological bases of memory* (29–50). New York: Academic Press.

Neisser, U. (1967). *Cognitive psychology*. New York: Appleton-Century-Crofts.

Neisser, U. (1982). Memory: What are the important questions? In V. Neisser (Ed.), *Memory Observed* (pp. 3–19). San Francisco: W. H. Freeman.

Posner, M. (1984). Selective attention and storage of information. In J. Lynch, J. McGaugh, & N. Weinberger (Eds.), *Neurobiology of learning and memory*. New York: Guilford Press.

Prigatano, G., Fordyce, D., Zeiner, H., Roueche, J., Pepping, M., & Wood, B. (1984). Neuropsychological rehabilitation after closed head injury in young adults. *Journal of Neurology, Neurosurgery, and Neuropsychiatry* 47:505–513.

Randt, C. T., Brown, E. R., & Osborne, D. J., Jr. (1980). A memory test for longitudinal measurement of mild to moderate deficits (rev.). Unpublished manuscript, Department of Neurology, New York University Medical Center, New York.

Schacter, D., Rich, S., & Stampp, A. (1985). Remediation of memory disorders: Experimental evaluation of the spaced-retrieval technique. *Journal of Clinical and Experimental Neuropsychology* 7:79–96.

Scoville, W. B., & Milner, B. (1957). Loss of recent memory after bilateral hippocampal lesion. *Journal of Neurology, Neurosurgery, and Psychiatry* 20:11–21.

Shimamura, A., & Squire, L. (1986). Memory and metamemory in amnesic syndromes. *Journal of Experimental Psychology* 12:452–460.

Sohlberg, M. M. (1986). Rehabilitation of memory disorders. Presented at the Western Regional Conference of the American Speech Language and Hearing Association, Seattle.

Sohlberg, M. M., & Mateer, C. A. (1986). *Prospective memory process training (PROMPT)*. Puyallup, WA: Association for Neuropsychological Research and Development.

Sohlberg, M. M., & Mateer, C. A. (1987). Effectiveness of an attention training program. *Journal of Clinical and Experimental Neuropsychology* 9(2):117–130.

Sohlberg, M. M., Mateer, C. A., & Geyer, S. (1985). *Prospective memory survey*. Puyallup, WA: Association for Neuropsychological Research and Development.

Squire, L. R. (1975). Short-term memory as a biological entity. In L. D. Deutch & J. A. Deutch (Eds.), *Short-term memory* (pp. 2–40). New York: Academic Press.

Squire, L. R., & Butters, N. (Eds.). (1984). *Neuropsychology of memory*. Hillsdale, NJ: Lawrence Erlbaum Associates.

Squire, L. R., & Cohen, N. J. (1984). Human memory and amnesia. In G. Lynch, J. L. McGaugh, & N. M. Weinberger (Eds.), *Neurobiology of learning and memory* (pp. 3–64). New York: Guilford Press.

Walker, K. (1976) Memory. In *Clinical methods—the history of the physical and laboratory examination*. Boston: Butterworth.

Warrington, E. K. (1982). The double dissociation of short and long-term memory deficits. In L. Cermak (Ed.), *Human memory and amnesia*. Hillsdale, NJ: Lawrence Erlbaum Associates.

Wechsler, D. (1945). A standardized memory scale for clinical use. *Journal of Psychology 19:*87–95.

White, O. (1984). Performance based decisions: When and what to change. In R. West & K. Young (Eds.), *Precision teaching: Instructional decision making, curriculum, and management and research.* Provo, UT: Utah State University, Department of Special Education.

White, O., & Haring, N. (1980). *Exceptional teaching* (2nd ed.). Columbus, OH: Charles Merrill.

Wickelgren, W. A. (1973). The long and the short of memory. *Psychological Bulletin 80:*425–438.

Wilkins, A., and Baddeley, A. (1978). Remembering to recall in everyday life: An approach to absent-mindedness. In M. Gruneberg, P. Morris, & R. Sykes (Eds.), *Practical aspects of memory.* London: Academic Press.

Wilson, B. (1981). Teaching a patient to remember people's names after removal of a left temporal tumor. *Behavioral Psychotherapy 9:*338–344.

Wilson, B, (1982). Success and failure in memory training following a cerebral vascular accident. *Cortex 18:*581–594.

8
Theory and Remediation
of Visual Processing Disorders

The degree to which we depend on visual and visuospatial processing in our daily lives is staggering. Visuoperceptual function is essential for effectiveness and safety in activities of daily living and in many work environments. Accurate visual perception is critical to academically related functions such as reading, checking work, and completing clerical tasks. Spatial skills are essential for finding one's way around in public places and operating motor vehicles. Yet the clinical approach to assessment and treatment in this area is often disjointed or incomplete. The evaluation and rehabilitation of visual and visuospatial function have suffered from a lack of theoretical foundation.

This chapter attempts to pull together a model of visual and spatial perception that would lend itself to systematic and comprehensive ways of assessing and remediating visually based impairments. Topics covered include peripheral and brainstem mechanisms (acuity, binocularity, eye movement), upper brainstem and midbrain mechanisms (a second visual system sensitive to location and movement), occipital lobe mechanisms (visual discrimination), temporal lobe mechanisms (object recognition), parietal lobe mechanisms (spatial awareness and visuomotor integration), and efficacy of visual process training.

THE NEED FOR A MULTIDIMENSIONAL MODEL

Researchers involved in investigations of visual system function have struggled to specify successive stages of information processing from early sensory processing to the integration of information and the assignment of meaning. Neurophysiologic studies of the visual system provide evidence for multichanneling of different categories of visual information (e.g., location, movement, orientation, shape, and color) at early stages of sensory processing. Distributed networks support the analysis of this visual and spatial

176

information through at least three major circuits: tectal (upper brainstem), occipitotemporal, and occipitoparietofrontal (Cowey, 1979; Pandya Yeterion, 1984; Ungerleider & Mishkin, 1982). At this time, however, attempts to specify neuropsychologic deficits in these terms are rare. Clinicians are constrained by the absence of a "plausible, theoretical framework for analyzing visual and spatial performance" (Newcombe, 1987).

There is a tendency to think about just two primary brain areas for visual processing, the peripheral sensory organ (eyes) and the occipital cortex. There are, however, multiple representations of visual information at many different sites within the central nervous system.

The frequency and nature of visual processing problems after head injury are still largely unknown. Patient reports suggest a range of changes including double vision, blurry vision, light sensitivity, and difficulty judging distances. Formal testing often reveals visual spatial confusion, slow visual/motor integration, and/or unilateral neglect. Many therapists are frustrated by a limited knowledge of what their patients are "seeing." Patients may move their head in peculiar ways, squint, report a variety of distortions, misrecognize objects, or make errors in reaching for targets. Over the course of acute recovery, there is usually some apparent resolution, but there is limited information about residual visual processing problems.

A serious complication in determining the incidence and nature of visual processing deficits is that individuals with visuoperceptual impairments often demonstrate only a limited awareness or acknowledgment of these deficits (Brain, 1941). Unlike motor and language deficits, which are often quite obvious, perceptual deficits may go undetected not only because they are not obvious to an observer but because patients are often unable to appreciate or to describe the difficulty they may be having.

There are a variety of perspectives from which to view visual processing. Neurologic and ophthalmologic approaches tend to focus on the integrity of peripheral and brainstem mechanisms. Neuropsychologic approaches, for the most part, address more central, cognitively based processes, but rarely from a strong neurologic systems perspective. (The most notable exception is Luria's [1973] brilliant discussion of the disturbances of visual analysis and synthesis that arise with lesions in different parts of the occipital regions of the brain.) Educational and even many rehabilitation-oriented approaches tend to ignore the brain or treat it as a kind of black box that cannot be understood; instead, they focus on psychologically oriented assessment of different hypothesized visual processing capabilities. Although each of these disciplines has contributed to the understanding and treatment of visuospatial processes, there is really no comprehensive or formalized model of normal visual processing currently available to the clinician. Too often, information about visual function in the clinical literature is restricted to a listing of interesting and perhaps diagnostically useful pathologic phenomena such as prosopagnosia (impaired recognition of familiar faces), left neglect, and constructional apraxia. Assessment tools are usually very task oriented and have limited theoretical underpinning. Tasks that purport to measure visual closure, visual sequential memory, or visual discrimination often have only minimal face and construct validity, and performance may not be related to other measures that purport to assess the same function. Many of the tasks used are multidimensional; it is hard to sort out which of the components are really contributing to disrupted performance.

What is needed is a framework in which to view these particular deficits and a sense of the normal multidimensional cognitive substrate of visual processing. A model that meets these requirements is outlined in the next section.

A PHYSIOLOGICALLY BASED MODEL OF VISUAL PROCESSING

The components of the basic model are derived from neurophysiology and neuropsychology and incorporate functions of five major parts of the brain:

- *Peripheral and brainstem mehcnisms.* These functions support visual acuity and ocular motor function.
- *Upper brainstem and midbrain mechanisms (including superior colliculi).* These nuclei support a "second visual system" that supplies information about the location and movement of visual stimuli.
- *Occipital lobe mechanisms.* These mechanisms support visual discrimination, color vision, and the appreication of visual detail.
- *Temporal lobe functions.* These mechanisms support a system of object recognition.
- *Parietal lobe mechanisms.* These mechanisms support both appreciation of spatial information and the integration of visuomotor responses and assist in supporting visual attention to the full range of visual space.

In the following sections, the functions attributable to each of these areas are described, followed by recommended assessment and treatment procedures for each area.

Peripheral and Brainstem Mechanisms

As mentioned above, peripheral mechanisms are responsible, in large part, for what might be thought of as acuity or clarity of vision. To better understand these mechanisms, some brief descriptions and definitions are in order. The major structures of the eye from outside to inside are the cornea, iris, pupil, lens, retina, and optic nerve (Figure 8.1). Light entering the eye passes through the cornea (a protective covering), then through the pupil or opening in the iris, and on through the lens and a body of fluid behind it to the retina. The amount of light let into the eye is controlled by the pupil, its size being controlled by the dilator and constrictor muscles of the iris. Through changes in the curvature of the lens, which is regulated by muscles in the eye, light rays are focused on the retina, where they stimulate the rods and cones, the sensory receptors. Cones are concerned with color vision, rods with vision in dim light. Sensory impulses are then conveyed via the optic nerve to the brain. Movements of the eyeball, which determine the direction from which light enters the eye, are produced by six muscles (extraocular eye muscles) under the control of three cranial nerves.

Damage to this system (structural, mechanical, or neurologic) can result in an abnormal pupillary response to changes in light in one or both eyes, less efficient lens accommodation or refraction, impaired function of primary sensory receptor cells (rods and cones), and/or damage to the integrity of the optic nerve and tract. Impaired-acuity following head trauma may result when increased intracranial pressure causes damage to the optic tract, including the retina. Direct trauma to the eye can obviously result in injury to delicate eye structures and muscles and to the neural input that controls this stem. Damage to a particular part of the retina can result from direct

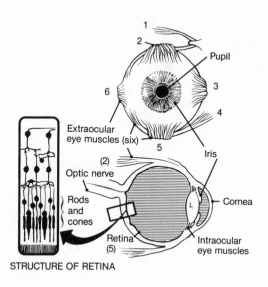

FIGURE 8.1. Major structures of the eye. Copyright © 1988 Biomedical Illustrations, Inc.

trauma or from small emboli of fat or air in the vascular bed that supplies air and nutrients to the retina. A small area of retinal destruction may result in a scotoma or island-like blind gap in the visual field.

Assessment of acuity is usually done by an ophthalmologist or an optometrist. Acuity can be tested with eye charts and should be determined for stimuli at both near point (16 inches or less) and far point (20 feet or more). Because many therapeutic activities are conducted at close range with the nonambulatory brain-injured patient, assessment of near-point acuity is particularly important Gianutsos & Matheson, 1987). Increasingly, sophisticated behavioral procedures as well as techniques involving the use of electrical brain activity in the form of evoked responses to different light patterns are being developed for the assessment of acuity in patients and in young children who are unable to respond behaviorally to traditional assessment techniques.

Injury to the cranial nerves involved in vision is frequent following traumatic brain injury. Optic nerve injury can result in blindness of various types. Injury to the oculomotor nerve (III) results in ptosis (drooping) of the eyelid, deviation of the eyeball outward, dilation of the pupil, and double vision. Damage to the trochlear nerve (IV) results in rotation of the eyeball upward and outward, to the abducens (VI) deviation of the eye outward; both of these can result in double vision. Although neurologic assessment is necessary for accurate diagnosis, the clinician can observe during treatment activities whether the eyes move smoothly and whether they move in all directions. Appropriate interpretation of test and treatment activities requires the clinician to note whether the patient can sustain fixation on a stationary and on moving targets and whether the eyes appear to converge on a near stimulus.

Binocularity, the coordinated use of both eyes, is a common problem for the head injured, yet it is too infrequently evaluated or treated. The effects of disturbance in binocularity functions include double vision (sometimes experienced as blurring or eye strain), which may be exacerbated by close work. Stereoscopic assessment devices test for functions such as vertical and lateral phoria (alignment of the eyes), diplopia (double vision), fusion capability, stereopsis (the ability to perceive depth based on binocular cues), and suppression (the tendency for one macula not to function when the other is working). Accommodative range, the ability to adjust focus between near and far, has frequently been found in head injury, but may not be part of a stereoscopic assessment.

The rehabilitation specialist must begin to address the possibility of visual imperception, impaired binocularity, and/or oculomotor dysfunction in their patients more seriously. Gianutsos, Ramsey, and Perlin, (1988) reported that 48% of patients in a postacute rehabilitation setting benefited from the services of a rehabilitation optometrist. Possible treatments following detailed optometric assessment included new glasses to correct refractive errors, the use of different glasses for near and distant viewing in patients with accommodative insufficiency, patching or occlusion of one eye (especially for reading), prism lenses, and fusion training. This will undoubtedly be an area of increasing interest and study.

Upper Brainstem and Midbrain Mechanisms

Most visual information passes from the optic nerve via visual pathways to thalamic nuclei (lateral geniculate) and then via the optic radiations to cortical visual processing areas in the occipital lobe. Some information, however, passes into an alternative or "second" visual system mediated through the upper brainstem and midbrain structures, most notably the superior colliculus (or tectum) (Figure 8.2). This latter colliculat system has been shown to be involved in noticing, locating, and shifting gaze to visual stimuli but not in recognizing or identifying them (Holmes, 1938; Schneider, 1969; Goldberg & Robinson, 1978). Monkeys with almost total destruction of the striate cortex (traditional primary visual cortex in the occipital lobe, the destruction of which causes cortical blindness) can often still avoid obstacles and pick up small objects. Such an animal may appear normal in many respects, but testing reveals an inability to recognize the

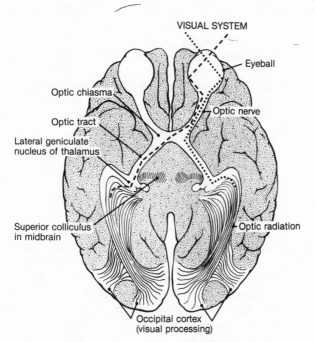

FIGURE 8.2. Major structures along the visual pathways including cortical and subcortical (thalamic) structures as well as deep midbrain (superior colliculus) nuclei. Copyright © 1988 by Biomedical Illustrations, Inc.

same objects that it can clearly detect and locate and an inability to discriminate between similar objects. Human patients with restricted occipital lobe damage have been shown to reach accurately for stimuli presented in the "blind" areas of their visual fields and can even discriminate between shapes and orientations of simple stimuli despite the fact that they cannot consciously "see." They do not have any subjective awareness of the operation of this system, yet perform far better than chance in a forced-choice paradigm. This phenomenon has been termed "blindsight" (Weiskrantz, Warrington, Sanders, & Marshall, 1974; Weiskrantz, 1980). The acuity of this "blindsight" may actually respond to training (Weiskrantz et al., 1974; Zihl, 1980). It also has been reported to be sensitive to the perception of motion (Zihl, von Cramon, & Mai, 1983; Pizzamigalio, Antonucci, & Francia, 1984).

In other cases, selective destruction of these upper brainstem structures results in disturbed visual orienting, visual tracking, and localization of objects in the visual fields. Progressive supranuclear palsy (PSP), a condition that includes damage to the colliculi, results in poor performance on tasks requiring visual scanning and search (Kimura, Barnet, & Burkhart, 1981). Paralysis of upward gaze, commonly associated with collicular lesions, should alert the therapist to the possibility of more subtle disorders of oculomotor function, visual attention, and visual orientation. Ratcliff (1987) describes a "treatment" strategy whereby a patient with PSP, who complained that the picture got "confused" when she watched television, obtained some relief when he had her substitute a small, portable set placed on the floor (below eye level) for a larger console model. This change presumably decreased requirements for the number and size of visual saccades (movements) and avoided the necessity of upward gaze.

Awareness of this "second visual system," which can locate objects and shift visual gaze, can provide greater appreciation of some potentially paradoxical behavior in patients. It decreases the possibility that the cortically blind patient who cannot identify patterns or experience the sensation of seeing but who avoids obstacles and reaches for things accurately will be seen as "inconsistent" or malingering. In terms of therapeutic implications, it is conceivable that residual vision or "blindsight" may be exploited to compensate in part for visual field defects. Zihl and von Cramon (1979, 1982), for example, showed that a scotoma could be made to shrink by appropriate training. Patients with pronounced hemianopsia might be taught to respond to potentially intact movement perception in their impaired fields as a means of compensation. In a similar fashion, patients whose visual function is presumably intact (based on measured levels of acuity and visual discrimination), but who voice a variety of concerns about their visual perceptual functioning, may receive more appropriate assessment.

Occipital Lobe Mechanisms

The primary visual cortex (also known as the striate cortex) is described as being involved in the analysis of visual stimuli. Different groups of neurons in this area are tuned to respond to different properties of visual stimuli (e.g., color, orientation). They are often particularly responsive to edges (sharp demarcations in intensity) that are presented at a particular orientation or angle and are moving in a particular direction. These neuronal networks are conceptualized as specialized visual analyzers responsible for sensing particular properties of stimuli they are equipped to recognize (Cowey, 1979). Discrete cortical lesions occasionally result in a selective impairment in analyzing one aspect of visual stimuli. Reports of isolated impairments of color discrimination (Meadows, 1974, for example) have appeared. The most obvious impairments following extensive occipital lesions are impairments in pattern perception and form discrimination for objects or visual stimuli in the contralateral field. If the lesions are bilateral, the patient with such cortical blindness may demonstrate severe perceptual losses and may not have any awareness of seeing. Focal occipital lesions are relatively rare. This region of the brain is not commonly involved in cerebral vascular accidents, at least not major CVAs, and is an area that appears relatively protected from common traumas to the head.

Assessment of occipital lobe mechanisms will be highly dependent on the degree of visual disruption. In general, however, it should focus on the patient's ability to analyze visual detail and to perceive form and color. Theoretically useful measures might include Benton's Judgment of Line Orientation Test (Figure 8.3), which involves matching a line at one orientation to the one in an array of lines that is at the same orientation (Benton, Hamsher, Varney, & Spreen, 1983); Benton's Visual Form Discrimination Test (Benton et al., 1983), which involves matching of multiple geometric shapes; and the Visual Discrimination subtest of the Test of Visual Perceptual Skills (TVPS) (Gardner, 1982). All of these tests require that the patient match identical visual patterns. The Form Constancy, Visual Figure Ground, and Visual Closure subtests of the TVPS (Figure 8.4) also require pattern matching but in somewhat more visually complicated contexts that require more precise analysis of visual detail. Measures of facial discrimination and matching such as the Facial Recognition Test are also appropriate (Benton et al., 1983) (Figure 8.5). The emphasis should be on facial matching and facial discrimination as opposed to facial recognition. All of these measures focus on the identification of discrete visual features, and all use abstract, nonrepresentational stimuli—aspects that intuitively force a major involvement of occipital lobe feature and pattern detection mechanisms. Color discrimination can be tested informally with paint samples or color plates.

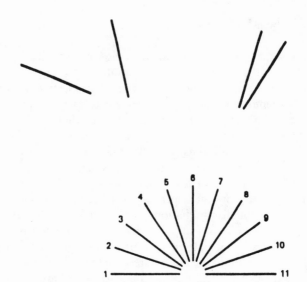

FIGURE 8.3. Judgment of Line Orientation (Benton et al., 1983). Angles at the top are matched with one of the numbered lines below. Copyright © 1983 by Oxford University Press. Reprinted by permission.

Treatments of cortical blindness or more discrete aspects of occipital lobe dysfunction are as yet poorly conceptualized. Training and compensation for major visual field deficits have already been discussed in the context of upper brainstem and midbrain functions. Direct treatment approaches might incorporate workbook activities or computer programs that exercise visual discrimination, form matching, or line orientation, tasks that emphasize attention to visual detail and minimize the use of meaningful material. The use of nonrepresentational material tends to force analysis of pattern.

Case Study
M.V. was a 35-year-old woman who suffered a right occipital–parietal infarct and anoxic encephalopathy secondary to stab wounds to her neck and chest. She was comatose for 10 days following the incident. She had completed 13.5 years of education and worked as a cab driver, cashier, and waitress. She was admitted to the CCR postacute program 11 months after her injury.

In addition to severe attention and memory problems, she demonstrated profound visual processing deficits. Initial drawings of a man and a clock could not be identified, and gross spatial distortions and absent parts were noted. At discharge 6 months later, her drawings of a man and a clock were recognizable and properly oriented. Her recognition of untrained single-syllable words increased from 20% to 95%. Recognition of numbers she herself had written increased from 40% to 100% (after a 24-hour delay). Scores on the Hooper Test of Visual Organization and Benton's Form Discrimination improved more

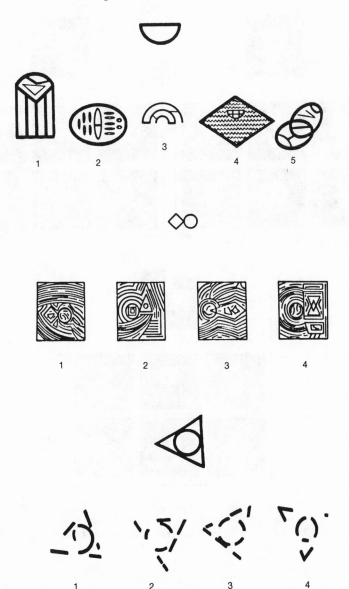

FIGURE 8.4. Selected items from subtests of the Test of Visual Perceptual Skills (TVPS) by Gardner (1982). (A) Visual Discrimination, (B) Visual Figure Ground, and (C) Visual Closure. In each case, the target shape above must be identified in one of the figures below. Copyright © 1982 by Special Child Publications. Reprinted by permission.

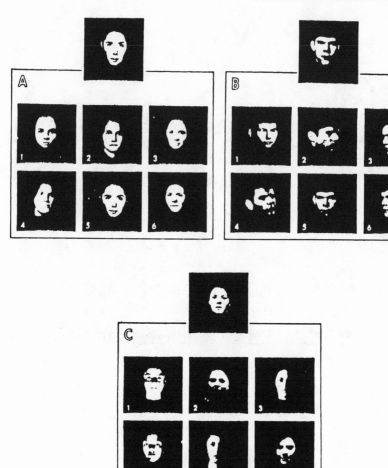

FIGURE 8.5. Facial Matching Test (Benton et al., 1983). Faces are matched from frontal views (A), side views or angled perspectives (B), and in partial shadow (C). Copyright © 1983 by Oxford University Press. Reprinted by permission.

than one standard deviation. Reading and writing skills and community orientation improved sufficiently to allow safe independent living and use of public transportation, although tasks requiring analysis of visual detail and precise visuomotor functioning remained severely compromised. Figure 8.6 illustrates her drawings of a man before and after visual training. The latter, although still simplified, does indicate greater appreciation of spatial relationships.

FIGURE 8.6 On the left is the human figure drawing of a patient who demonstrated severe visual impairments at the time of program entry 18 months following an episode of anoxia and parieto-occipital infarct. On the right is a re-attempt at human figure drawing, after 10 weeks of targeted visual process training.

Visual Processing beyond Occipital Lobe

Neurophysiologic studies have shown that the analysis of visual information does not stop at the visual cortex. There are two distinct anatomic pathways that represent the cortical continuation of the visual processing system (Figure 8.7). One pathway leads into the temporal lobe and is responsible for object recognition and identification. The other leads into the parietal lobe and subserves spatial aspects of vision and visually guided movement (Ungerleider & Mishkin, 1982; Mishkin, & Appenzeller, 1987). These anatomically and functionally dissociable systems have been demonstrated in both monkeys and man. Monkeys with a temporal lobe lesion cannot discriminate objects but readily learn a spatial task (e.g., going to a food well in a particular location). Monkeys with parietal lesions show just the opposite pattern (Pohl, 1973). In the following two sections, we discuss how these two systems function in humans and how they might be assessed and treated.

Temporal Lobe Mechanisms

The temporal lobe system allows recognition of stimuli through a representational network organized by experience and conceptual proximity. Essential here is the notion that individuals are able to recognize familiar visual input (colors, objects, people, places, etc.) if they have previous

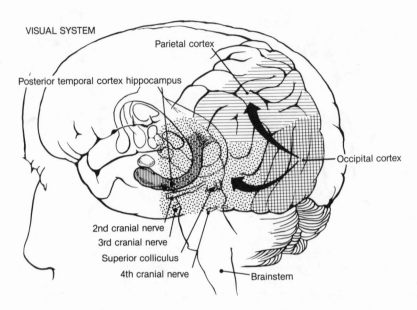

FIGURE 8.7   Included in this figure are cranial nerve roots and midbrain structures (superior colliculi) involved in vision. Also illustrated are the three major cortical regions involved in visual processing with pathways extending from the primary occipital cortex (involved with feature detection) to the parietal region (full field scan and visuomotor control and the posterior temporal region (object recognition). Copyright © 1988 by Biomedical Illustrations, Inc.

experience with them and if the stimulus is a good exemplar or good "representation." The best known and most striking clinical manifestation of a disruption of this object recognition mechanism is seen in patients with *visual agnosia*. In the classic case, an individual with visual agnosia can describe the *features* of an object (size, shape, color, texture) and can discriminate it from other objects or stimuli but cannot tell what it is or even how it may be used. A patient with this disorder looked at and described an object as being made of "some kind of white cloth material with five long, slender pockets." He could even draw a reasonable facsimile of it. Although he did not visually recognize it as a glove, he could readily name it when he handled it for just a moment. Tactile inputs had access to a representational memory system, whereas visual inputs did not. This patient could also write but not read even what he himself had written (alexia without agraphia).

Patients with striking and relatively pure visual agnosias are quite rare (see Rubens, 1979, for review), but similar disorders of lesser severity are more commonly seen. Such deficits may be picked up on tasks that require the recognition of stimuli that are in some way degraded or incomplete and thus provide more limited information to the object recognition system. Examples include black-and-white line drawings in which portions of the lines are omitted or photographs of objects that depict only partial information or are taken from unusual perspectives. For some patients with disruption of this system, the lines are perceived clearly, but the information provided by the intact occipital visual analyzers is insufficient to enable recognition. A considerable body of research has utilized visual closure tasks in this regard (Lansdell, 1968; Mooney, 1960).

There may be other special categories of stimulus recognition that are dependent on this system, specifically the recognition of faces and the recognition of written language. Although facial matching and discrimination can presumably be done with (albeit complex) visual pattern analyzers, the recognition of familiar faces (family or community members, famous celebrities or politicians) depends on some access to stored visual memory based on one's experience of the face. Face recognition, a predominantly nonverbal task, has been shown to be impaired in patients with right temporal and temporo—parietal lesions (Benton van Allen, 1968; Hamsher, Levin, & Benton, 1979) and with right temporal lobe electrical stimulation (Mateer, 1983). The term *prosopagnosia* refers to an impairment in the recognition of familiar faces, sometimes even one's own face in a mirror or photograph.

Conversely, word and letter recognition, but not discrimination, has been reported in alexic syndromes (impaired ability to read) following left posterior temporo-occipital lesions. Impaired ability to read may be associated with impaired ability to write (alexia and agraphia) or with spared ability to write (alexia without agraphia). In the latter case, a patient may demonstrate the ability to write but then be unable to read what has just been written. There are many varieties and postulated mechanisms of alexia, only some of which have a strong visual processing basis. Other reasons for reading failure are postulated to be more linguistic in nature (i.e., surface vs. deep dyslexia associated with phonologic and semantic aspects of words, respectively; see Heilman & Volenstein, 1985, for review).

Different pathologic conditions thus reflect the specialized nonverbal and verbal functions of the visual recognition system in the posterior temporal (and perhaps posterior occipital) lobes. Cortical zones involved in visual processing in the left hemisphere retain their intimate connections with speech and language (letter recognition); cortical zones involved in the right hemisphere retain their intimate connection with spatial and gestalt-oriented processing (face and object recognition). The access to memory systems is postulated to function through temporal lobe interactions with underlying limbic and hippocampal systems (Mishkin & Appenzeller, 1987).

Assessment

The temporal lobe system can be assessed through tests that sample recognition skills. At the lowest level, patients can just be asked to name real objects. A hierarchical approach might then dictate moving to photographs, line drawings, and finally perceptually degraded or distorted stimuli. Examples of tests that utilize degraded stimuli include the Street Completion Test (Street, 1931), the Mooney Visual Closure Test (Mooney & Ferguson, 1951), the Gollin Incomplete Figures Test (Gollin, 1960), the Cognition of Figural Units (CFU) subtest of the Structure of Intellect, Learning Abilities Test, and the Poppelreuter Overlapping Figures Test (Poppelreuter, 1917). Examples of the latter two tests are given in Figures 8.8 and 8.9. Another test we often use to assess function of this area is the Hooper Visual Organization Test (Hooper, 1958) (Figure 8.10). In this test, line drawings of objects are made less recognizable by cutting them up and depicting the pieces scattered about the page. All of these tests use stimuli that can be labeled but that are degraded in various ways.

Assessment of face memory or recognition can be done with the Recognition Memory Test by Warrington (1984). Recognition of written material can be done through letter and word recognition tasks of standard aphasia batteries. Another important aspect of recognition is the efficiency and speed with which an individual can recognize information. To get at this ability, one might use the Visual Matching or Perceptual Speed Cluster subtests of the Woodcock–Johnson Psychoeducational Battery (Woodcock & Johnson, 1977) or a number of other tests that sample rapid word, symbol, or number recognition.

Also of value in assessing the visual recognition system are visual perceptual tasks involving rapid computer displays. Levin, Meerson, and Tonkonogii (1969) showed that on discrimination tasks requiring accurate perception of the size of angles, line length, and degree of curvature, head-injured patients showed elevated thresholds compared to normal subjects only when stimulus exposure was limited to less than 0.5 seconds. Hannay, Levin, and Kay (1982) also demonstrated that tachistoscopic thresholds for letter recognition were elevated in head injury. The computer program *Speeded Reading of Word Lists* (SRWL) by Gianutsos and Klitzner (1981) is useful for recognition testing. This program involves reading of words rapidly presented in tachistoscopic displays. *FAST READ* (Gianutsos, Cochran, & Blouin, 1984) is another computer-based reading task that involves rapid presentation. (Since these approaches depend heavily on accurate central vision, patients with focal hemiimperception or neglect often show consistent patterns of misreading involving the beginnings or ends of words. This would not, however, constitute a recognition disorder in the sense that is meant here.)

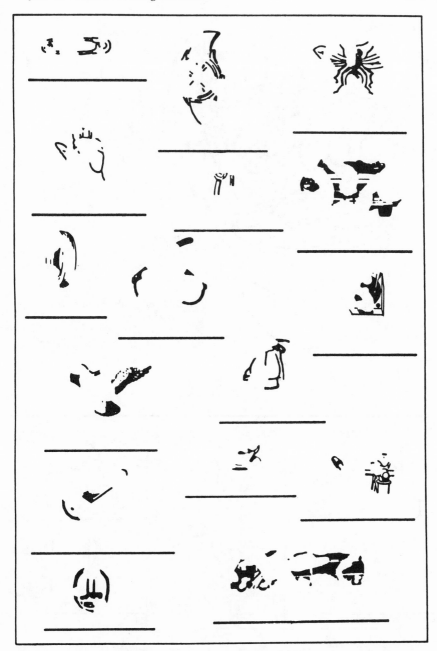

FIGURE 8.8. Cognition of Figural Units (CFU), a visual closure subtest of the Structure of Intellect Learning Abilities Test (SOI-LA) (Meeker et al., 1985). Copyright © 1975 by Mary Meeker. Reprinted by permission of the publisher, Western Psychological Services, 12031 Wilshire Boulevard, Los Angeles, CA 90025.

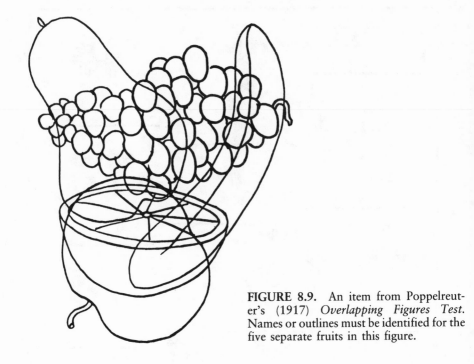

FIGURE 8.9. An item from Poppelreuter's (1917) *Overlapping Figures Test*. Names or outlines must be identified for the five separate fruits in this figure.

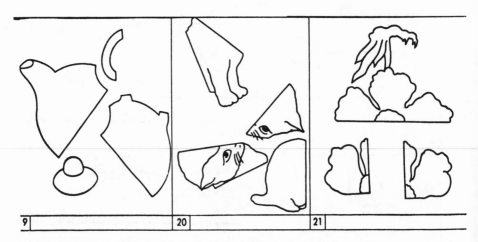

FIGURE 8.10. The Hooper Visual Organization Test (VOT) (Hooper, 1958) requires object recognition given cut up and scattered line drawings of the objects. Copyright © 1983 by Western Psychological Services. Original edition © 1958 by H. Elston Hooper. Reprinted by permission of the publisher, Western Psychological Services, 12031 Wilshire Boulevard, Los Angeles, CA 90025.

Treatment

Treatment activities in the area of visual recognition might include visual closure tasks for pictures or words. Grids can be laid over stimuli to confuse and degrade the critical visual information. A variety of speeded recognition tasks can be used; computer programs are very useful, in that they can precisely limit the processing time available. Both speeded number-matching and rapid word-reading computer tasks can be effective in improving recognition of numbers and words.

Parietal Lobe Mechanisms

The parietal lobe, as you will recall from earlier in this chapter, contains the second of the two pathways that extend the visual system from the occipital lobe. The parietal lobe system can be thought of as having two major interrelated functions. The first, spatial perception and appreciation, allows the individual to be responsive to the full range of visual space and to appreciate spatial relationships. The second, visuomotor integration, supports the coordination of motor response with visual feedback.

Spatial Perception and Appreciation

Unilateral Neglect. Patients with impairments in their ability to respond to visual information most commonly demonstrate neglect of one side of visual space. Visual neglect is a recognizable clinical syndrome characterized by a failure to respond to objects or situations in the space contralateral to a cerebral lesion. Patients with severe neglect often collide with objects, ignore food on one side of the plate, and, in general, attend to only one side of their bodies. They often have difficulty in reading, writing, and drawing. It may also be demonstrated in testing situations as a tendency to make more errors of omission on the contralateral (opposite) side of space than on the ipsilateral (same side) (Chedru & LeBlanc, 1972). Neglect of left space following right brain damage is much more common than is neglect of right space following left damage (see Heilman & Volenstein, 1985, for review). Disorders of neglect have been shown to be one of the major disruptive factors impeding functional recovery and rehabilitation success (Denes, Semerza, Stoppa, & Lis, 1982).

Most but not all patients with severe unilateral neglect will have a hemianopsia, a demonstrable visual field defect resulting from disruption of the visual pathways (optic radiations) that does not allow information from one field of visual space to reach primary cortical areas. Although unilateral neglect and hemianopsia are often found together (probably because of the proximity of the optic radiations to the parietal lobe mechanisms involved in the redirection of visual attention and their common blood supply), they are not identical. Neglect is known to result from damage to many different parts of the brain including the frontal lobe and a variety of subcortical structures in addition to the parietal lobe (Heilman, 1979).

Unilateral neglect should be assessed independently of the visual fields. Omission or inaccuracy of elements on one side of visual space is often picked up in simple drawing and copying tasks, cancellation tasks, visual search tasks, reading tasks, line bisection tasks, or a response bias in multiple choice tasks that use a horizontal array. Figure 8.11 is an example of a visual search task; the time needed to locate objects and the positions of objects matched (i.e., in which of the four quadrants the matching object is located) are recorded. Computer programs such as REACT (Reaction Time Measure of Visual Field) and SEARCH, both by Gianutsos and Klitzner

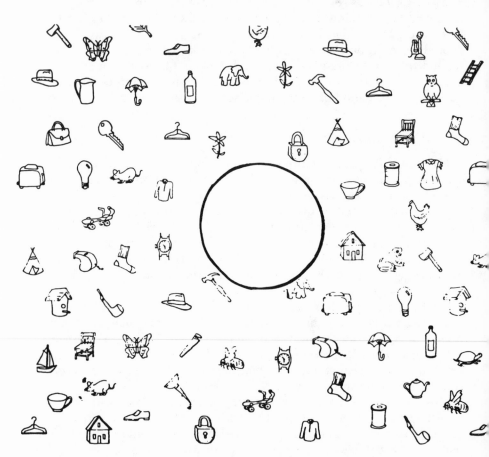

FIGURE 8.11. This Visual Search Task developed by Kimura et al. (1977) assesses object search and identification by allowing the examiner to indicate the speed of search and preference for locating items (target items for matching are put in the central circle). Reprinted by permission.

(1981), can provide valuable data regarding the ability to respond to and find stimuli in different parts of visual space. The computerized search task displays an array of nonsense shapes, in the center of which is a target shape. The task is to find its match in one location in the visual display. Different test locations are sampled in a random fashion, and the response time for each location is automatically measured and displayed as part of the results.

Although the preceding tasks may provide useful information about the presence of unilateral visual neglect, they do not necessarily predict or correlate with the degree to which patients will encounter difficulty in everyday life. The Behavioral Inattention Test (BIT) (Wilson, Cockburn, & Halligan, 1987) was developed and standardized for the purpose of providing an objective behavioral test of everyday skills relevant to visual neglect. The BIT has nine subtests that reflect aspects of daily life: picture scanning, telephone dialing, menu reading, article reading, telling and setting the time, coin sorting, address and sentence coping, map navigation, and card sorting. Six conventional subtests (the crossing, letter cancellation, star cancellation, figure and shape copying, line bisection, and representational drawing) are also included. Results of the BIT should provide a comprehensive picture of a patient's performance as a number of wide-ranging visually mediated and contextualized ("real-life") tasks. It is standardized on stroke patients and non–brain-damaged control subjects.

Based on the hypothesis that patients with unilateral visual neglect fail to scan the environment properly, several rehabilitation approaches have focused on teaching this skill. The most impressive and well-controlled efforts have been those of Joseph Weinberg and Leonard Diller (Weinberg et al., 1977, 1979). Their 1977 report used 25 experimental and 32 control subjects, all with right brain damage secondary to cerebral vascular accident. They used three types of tasks in their test battery: (1) basic academic measures requiring simple reading (words and paragraphs), copying of their home address, and written arithmetic; (2) measures requiring cancellation of letters on a printed page; and (3) related visual tasks requiring counting and matching of faces, double simultaneous stimulation trials, and subtests of the WAIS-R (Digit Symbol, Object Assembly, Picture Completion; Wechsler, 1981). The Digit Symbol subtest requires rapid visual scanning and a fine motor response on a symbol-matching task; Object Assembly involves putting pieces of a puzzle together to construct a recognizable figure; Picture Completion involves identification of the missing feature on a line drawing of on object or figure.

Weinberg's treatment program was designed to train compenstion for failures in spontaneous contralateral scan by (1) presenting compelling tasks that would encourage leftward head turning, so that the left side targets would be viewed in the right visual field, (2) providing a left-sided target as an anchoring point, (3) decreasing density of stimuli, and (4) pacing the patient's tracking pattern to slow down pathological right scanning, often manifest as an impulsive drift to the right. The description of their sequence of training materials is presented in Table 8.1.

Experimental subjects received 20 sessions of specific training over 4 weeks; controls received standard rehabilitation. Experimental subjects performed more accurately on posttraining tests than did control subjects. Reading was used as the training task because it is a functional activity that

TABLE 8.1 Description of Training Materials for Left Side Neglect

Sequence of Cuing	Stimulus materials[a]		Task demand
1 (a) A vertical anchoring line on left side (b) Beginning and end of line sequentially numbered	1. The Treasury Secretary 2. is not now a member of 3. the National Security 4. Council but is occasion- 5. ally invited to participate 6. in its deliberations.	-1 -2 -3 -4 -5 -6	Patient is asked to look at the anchoring line, and the number at the beginning and end of lines. He uses the vertical line to find the beginning of the paragraph, and the numbers not to skip lines. Patient also asked to copy the paragraph
2 (a) A vertical anchoring line (b) Beginning of line sequentially numbered	1. A growth of 6% in the 2. nation's output of goods 3. and services next year 4. would be higher than what 5. is now being forecast by 6. most economists. In the 7. third		Patient uses only anchoring line and number at the beginning of paragraph
3 A vertical anchoring line	Among the subjects discussed in the series of meetings, most of them an hour long, were foreign policy, the international economic situation, government reor-		Patient uses only the anchoring line
4 No cues provided	At meetings with the Senate Foreign Relations and House International Relations and House International Relations Committees, Mr. Carter said that he would cooperate and consult closely		Patient reads without any lines

[a]The stimuli materials range from paragraphs consisting of single letters, numbers, letters and numbers, nonsense syllables, words and paragraphs.

From Winberg et al. (1977). Reprinted by permission.

depends, in our society, on anchoring in the left side of space, the over-learned starting point. Without this anchor, patients become lost. Weinberg and his colleagues stress the utility of this technique, not only in making the person more aware of his or her problem but also in providing a reasonable solution.

Failure to Appreciate Spatial Relationships. Patients with spatial disorders fail to perceive the spatial aspects of visual experience. They may perceive individual components of stimuli but cannot integrate them into a coherent spatial framework (Benton, 1979). Spatial disorders are often most obvious on tasks such as drawing or constructing, which require some manipulation of elements, yet they can reflect disrupted internal spatial representations or mental operations as well. Patients with right parietal lesions, for example, were shown to be selectively impaired on a task that did not involve drawing but that required mental rotation of visual stimuli (Ratcliff, 1979). Spatial deficits must be recognized as potentially involving internal schemas or memories, because impairments are often seen on tasks in which the patient is asked to draw a map of a familiar environment, such as his or her house (McFie et al., 1950) or town square (Bisiach & Luzzatti, 1978).

Aspects of spatial ability should be assessed in the absence of requirements for motor control. Tests that sample this capacity include measures of mental spatial rotation. The Spatial Relation subtest of the Woodcock–Johnson Psychoeducational Battery requires that the patient judge which two forms in an array could be rotated so that they would form a larger target figure. It requires holding an image in mind and mentally turning it in space. Other examples include the Cognition of Figural Systems (CFS) and the Cognition of Figural Transformations (CFT) subtests of the SOI-LA (Meeker, Meeker, & Royd, 1985). The former test (CFS) requires that the patients imagine themselves viewing a shape from another angle (Figure 8.12); the latter task (CFT) requires that the shape be mentally rotated to exactly match another shape (Figure 8.13).

Treatment of deficits in this area might include exercises that allow practice of spatial analysis and visuomotor skills. The task hierarchy for spatial rotation tasks might initially incorporate cutout shapes that can actually be turned to make the spatial rotation more concrete and observable. Once the patients understand the concept of rotation in different spatial planes, the treatment exercises can focus on more internal analysis.

Visuomotor Integration

The second aspect of parietal lobe function to be addressed is that of visuomotor integration. By virtue of its location at the intersection of occipital lobe visual system and the Rolandic motor and tactile functions,

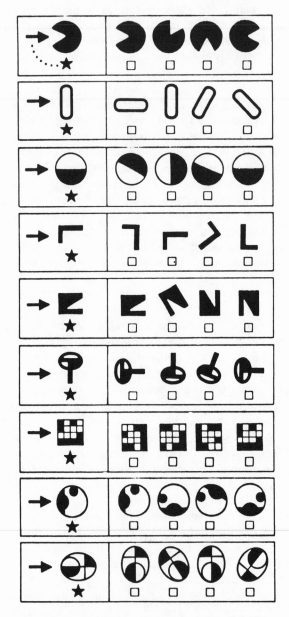

FIGURE 8.12. The Cognition of Figural Systems (CFS) of the Structure of Intellect Learning Abilities Test (SOI-LA), (Meeker et al., 1985) requires that the subject imagine he or she is viewing the figure would look from that perspective. Copyright © 1975 by Mary Meeker. Reprinted by permission of the publisher, Western Psychological Services, 12031 Wilshire Boulevard, Los Angeles, CA 90025.

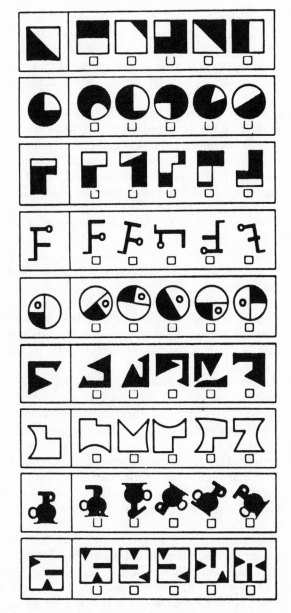

FIGURE 8.13. The Cognition of Figural Transformations (CFT) of the Structure of Intellect Learning Abilities Test (SOI-LA), (Meeker et al., 1985) requires that the figure on the left be mentally rotated until it exactly matches one or more of the figures on the right. Copyright © 1975 by Mary Meeker. Reprinted by permission of the publisher, Western Psychological Services, 12031 Wilshire Boulevard, Los Angeles, CA 90025.

the parietal lobes subserve visually guided movement. The first and simplest component of this function might be thought of as visually guided reaching. Neurons that are involved in the direction of attention to contralateral visual stimuli and the coordination of eye and hand movement have been identified in this posterior parietal region (Mountcastle, 1975; Lynch, 1980).

The cortical control of visually guided reaching is complex (Humphrey, 1979). Disruption of this system results in inaccurate reaching, pointing, and grasping and has been described in the clinical literature as a syndrome of visual disorientation. Patients with a classical "visual disorientation syndrome" following a bilateral parietal lesion will misreach for objects anywhere in the visual field, including those on which they are fixating. They may extend the hand far beyond the object and bring it in with a sweep of the arm rather than reaching out to grasp an object directly. Patients with such deficits may be seriously disabled, feeling their way about almost as though they were blind. Yet they may be able to identify and describe objects, name their colors, etc. despite their inability to locate them. Stimuli that can be located by another sensory modality (e.g., a sound or a tactile sensation) can be reached or pointed to accurately, indicating that the disorder is not one of reaching *per se* but of visually localizing. Patients with unilateral posterior parietal lobe damage will have difficulty with visual localization only in the half field contralateral to the lesion (Ratcliff & Davies-Johnson, 1972).

More complex levels of visuomotor integration are needed for drawing, constructing, and assembling. When these are impaired, the term "constructional apraxia" is often used (Benton, 1973; Warrington, 1965). Although constructional apraxia often is mentioned after damage to either hemisphere, the effects are different. Following left parietal lesion, patients demonstrate limb apraxia (impaired movement selection and sequencing). This can result in impaired motor performance. Following right parietal lesions, patients demonstrate impaired spatial appreciation and impaired integration of visual input with what might otherwise be quite adequate motor output.

Measures of visuomotor integration include a wide variety of standardized tasks including the Block Design and Assembly subtests of the WAIS-R (Wechsler, 1981), the Visual Motor Gestalt Test (Bender, 1946), the Rey Complex Figure Copy Test (Rey, 1941; Osterrith, 1944), and many others. Careful analysis of both the behavior of the patient during the task (qualitative analysis) and the final figure (qualitative and quantitative analysis) should be done to determine whether errors are more spatial or more praxic in nature. Supplementary tests of an apraxia without a visual referent (e.g., saluting, waving) and of spatial abilities without a motor component (e.g., mental rotation) will be helpful in the differential diagnosis. Another test that is hierarchically organized and has the virtue of two test forms is the

Three-Dimensional Block Construction Test of Benton et al. (1983). A figure depicting two levels of difficulty on this Block Construction Test is given in Figure 8.14.

Treatment tasks are usually implemented in a hierarchy, moving from simple reaching, pointing, and grasping to two-dimensional copying, drawing, and design reproduction tasks to three-dimensional constructional tasks. Training in a design reproduction task using various shapes, colors, and sizes of blocks (e.g., parquetry blocks) might move from assembling pieces on top of the design to assembling pieces on a drawing that illustrates the outlines of the pieces to putting pieces in a simple frame of the figure (providing the major outline only) to final independent construction. The therapist might also want to consider systematically varying the number of overall pieces, the number of differently shaped pieces, the complexity of the design, and the total number of pieces available from which to choose. In order to assess generalization at the lowest level, task generalization, the therapist might gather performance data on 10 designs in terms of accuracy,

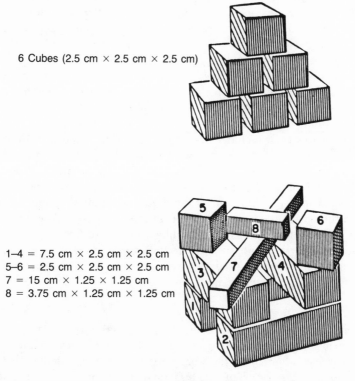

6 Cubes (2.5 cm × 2.5 cm × 2.5 cm)

1–4 = 7.5 cm × 2.5 cm × 2.5 cm
5–6 = 2.5 cm × 2.5 cm × 2.5 cm
7 = 15 cm × 1.25 × 1.25 cm
8 = 3.75 cm × 1.25 cm × 1.25 cm

FIGURE 8.14. Examples of a two-dimensional six-cube figure and a three-dimensional, 8-block figure to be reconstructed from a photo. Items preselected from the Three-Dimensional Block Construction Test by Benton et al. (1983). Copyright © 1983 by Oxford University Press. Reprinted by permission.

need for assistance, and time for completion. The therapist might then select five of the designs for training purposes. When criterion is reached, performance on the five untrained designs would be assessed to see if training affected performance on at least a different set of designs. Generalization should, of course, also be checked on untrained visuomotor tasks that presumably require the same skills.

At the highest levels of construction, there are greater and greater demands not only on visuomotor integration but on the executive functions of planning, organizing, sequencing, and self-monitoring. Thus, constructional problems sometimes reflect frontal lobe deficits as well.

EFFICACY OF VISUAL PROCESS TRAINING

At the Center for Cognitive Rehabilitation, several studies have addressed the efficacy of visual process training using the models, techniques, and procedures described in this chapter. A series of single-subject multiple-baseline designs were conducted in four patients. All were males ranging in age from 25 to 30 years. All were injured at least 1.5 years prior to program entry. Three tests of visual processing were used as independent measures. They were readministered at regular intervals prior to, during, and after visual process training. In three of the cases, attention training preceded visual process training, and in these cases, the effect of gains in attention could be assessed on visual processing measures. In one patient, visual process training was initiated first.

The measures used included the Spatial Relations subtest of the Woodcock–Johnson Psychoeducational Battery (Woodcock & Johnson, 1977). It requires mental spatial rotation, a function we have modeled as depending on the parietal lobes. The Hooper Visual Organization Test (Hooper, 1958) was selected to assess function of the object recognition system (temporal lobe), although some mental rotation may be required. A Block Design subtest was developed to assess two-dimensional visuomotor construction, modeled as a parietal and, in part, frontal lobe function. The Visual Form Discrimination Test was used to assess attention to and appreciation of visual detail, a task probably most dependent on occipital lobe mechanisms.

Case 01
J.B. (Figure 8.15) was a 29-year-old man who had sustained a severe brainstem contusion in a motor vehicle accident and was in coma for 6 weeks following the injury. He was admitted to the Center for Cognitive Rehabilitation from a nursing home a year and a half after his injury. Prior to his accident, he had been a supervisor for a periodicals distribution company. Following a 2-week baseline period, he received 5 weeks of attention training and 8 weeks of visual process training. In the 7 weeks prior to visual process training, scores on the Spatial Relations Test and on Visual Form Discrimination remained stable

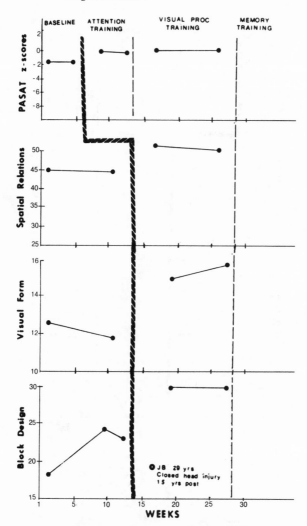

FIGURE 8.15. Efficacy of visual process training in Patient J.B. (Case 01). Graphs indicate results of a single-subject multiple-base-line design. The PASAT scores on the top serve as an independent measure of attention. Visual–spatial tasks include SR (Spatial Relations subtest of the Woodcock–Johnson Psychoeducational Battery), the Hooper Visual Organization Test (Hooper, 1958), Block Design (WAIS-R) (Wechsler, 1981), and Form Discrimination (Benton et al., 1983). The horizontal axis represents weeks. Training of processes was phased as indicated at the top. All points to the left of the broken line indicate baseline performance for the test measured.

despite improved attention as measured by the PASAT, the independent measure of attention. Block Design constructions improved but leveled off. With visual process training, improvements to levels well above base line were seen on all three tasks. J.B. returned to work, although not in a supervisory role, and to independent living.

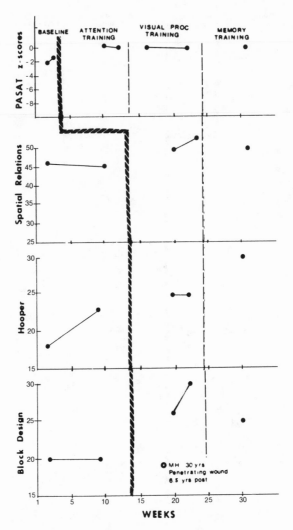

FIGURE 8.16. Efficacy of visual process training in Patient M.H. (Case 02). See Figure 8.15 for definitions.

Case 02

M.H. (Figure 8.16), 30-years-old, was admitted 6½ years after sustaining a severe bilateral frontal lobe injury following a penetrating head wound. A former diesel mechanic, he was hospitalized for 1½ years after his injury, and subsequently was unsuccessful in two sheltered workshops. Following a 2-week baseline period, he received 10 weeks of attention training and 12 weeks of visual process training. Scores on the Hooper Test of Visual Organization improved without training in the baseline phase prior to visual process training, while scores on the Spatial Relations and Block Design tests were stable. With specific visual process training, improvements were seen on all scores but were most dramatic on the Block Design test. We postulate that executive functions, important to monitoring and carrying out purposeful goal-directed activity, were most responsible for the improvement on this task. Severe disruption of frontal lobe function was seen in many other aspects of cognitive performance in this individual. Regardless of the underlying nature of improved processing or compensatory skills, it is striking that gains of this degree were seen 6½ years post-injury.

Case 03

D.T. (Figure 8.17), a 30-year-old man, was seen for treatment 2 years postsubarachnoid hemorrhage. Previously the owner of an auto mechanic shop, he was unemployed and about to be transferred to a psychiatric facility from a relative's home because of his unmanageable behavior. Following a 2-week no-treatment baseline period, this individual received 10 weeks of attention training and 13 weeks of visual process training. Scores on visual processing tests tended to show a gradual improvement during the base-line phase and throughout visual process training. Judging from the dramatic gains in attention (top graph, PASAT performance), it may be that improved scores in visual process training reflect increasingly consistent and effective attentional skills. He returned to independent living and work in a supervised food preparation position.

Case 04

J.A. (Figure 8.18), a 25-year-old man, was seen 4½ years after he sustained a closed head injury with right parietal contusion in an auto–pedestrian accident. He had been comatose for 2 weeks following the injury. He received visual process training prior to attention training in an effort to assess the effect of treatment order on outcomes. He made excellent gains on the Spatial Relations test, the Hooper Test of Visual Organization, and the Visual Form Discrimination Test over the course of visual process training. Following cessation of visual process training, gains generally stabilized at levels well above base line. This man returned to work in an electronics assembly position and lives independently.

Results of these case studies suggested significant gains on tests that sampled visual processing skills following the initiation of visual process training, according to the model outlined in this chapter. They suggest that the training was specific in some cases, whereas in others it may have been more a reflection of improved attentional capacities. It is difficult to sort out the degree to which improvement reflects the motoric and/or spatial components (parietal mechanisms) as opposed to organizational and planning components (more frontally based functions). Improvement was generally seen on some but not all measures, suggesting that different tasks are sampling different aspects of visual processing, and that some processes may

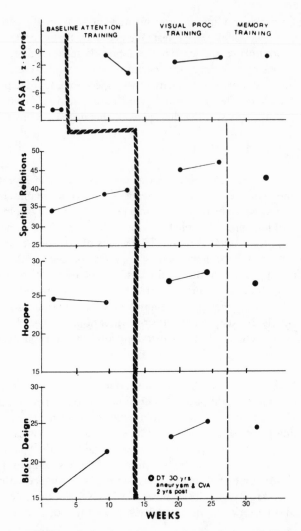

FIGURE 8.17. Efficacy of visual process training in Patient D.T. (Case 03). See Figure 8.15 for definitions.

be more amenable to intervention in a particular patient than others. Not all test performances improved the same way in all patients. Multiple measures of visual function should always be used, as no single measure of visual processing will necessarily reflect changes. Improvements were seen well after the period of spontaneous recovery in all cases and appeared to help patients function in more independent work and living environments.

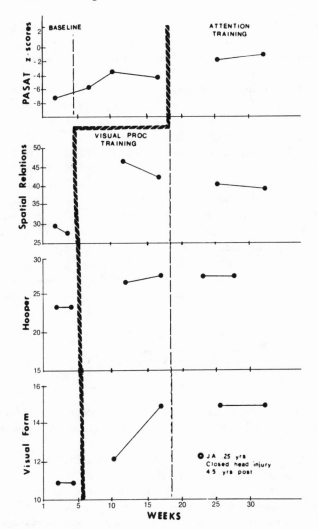

FIGURE 8.18. Efficacy of visual process training in Patient J.A. (Case 04). See Figure 8.15 for definitions.

SUMMARY

The visual system is extremely complex and widely distributed in the brain. A greater understanding of the different structures involved, and how they support different aspects of visual processing, can help clinicians bring some order to the assessment and treatment of visual processing impairments. The chapter divides the system into four major areas. *Peripheral and brain-*

stem mechanisms are critical to visual acuity, coordination of the eyes, and eye movement. *Upper brainstem and midbrain mechanisms* operate as a "second visual system" that can provide information to the nervous system about the location (but not the form) of information in visual space and can direct movement of the head and eyes toward external visual stimuli. This system is responsible for "blindsight" following occipital lesions and is not accessible to conscious awareness. *Occipital lobe mechanisms* support detailed visual discrimination through specialized feature detectors. *Temporal lobe mechanisms* provide for object recognition based on experience. *Parietal lobe mechanisms* are critical for awareness of and attention to information for spatial analysis and visual motor integration. *Frontal lobe mechanisms* become critical when the complexity of construction demands higher-level executive and planning skills. Suggestions for assessment and treatment based on this model were provided, and a series of single-case studies addressing the efficacy of visual process training were discussed. As the complexity and diversity of the visual processing system are better understood, clinicians will become increasingly able to develop appropriate approaches to the clinical management of impairments in visual processing.

STUDY QUESTIONS

1. List several problems with current assessment tools for visual processing.
2. List several possible reasons for decreased acuity in a head-injured patient.
3. How might it be that someone with total occipital lobe destruction could avoid obstacles yet declare he or she could not see?
4. List several test features that might discriminate visual processing tests sensitive to occipital versus temporal cortex lesions.
5. Try to think of several nonmotor exercises that might stress visual spatial analysis.
6. Discuss the possible differential effects of cognitive, perceptual, and motor impairment on a three-dimensional construction task.

REFERENCES

Bender, L. (1946). *Instructions for use of Visual Motor Gestalt Test.* New York: American Orthopsychiatric Association.

Benton, A. L. (1973). Visuoconstruction disability in ptients with cerebral disease: Its relationship to side of lesion and aphasic disorder. *Documenta Ophthalmologica 33*:67–76.

Benton, A. L. (1979). Visuoperceptive, visuospatial and visuoconstructive disorders. In K. M. Heilman & E. Valenstein (Eds.), *Clinical neuropsychology* (pp. 186–232). New York: Oxford University Press.

Benton, A. L., van Allen, M. W. (1968). Impairment of facial recognition in patients with cerebral disease. *Cortex 4:*344–358.

Benton, A. L., Hamsher, K., Varney, N. R., & Spreen, O. (1983). *Contributions to neuropsychological assessment: A clinical manual.* New York: Oxford University Press.

Bisiach, E., & Luzzatti, C. (1978). Unilateral neglect of representational space. *Cortex, 14:*129–133.

Brain, W. R. (1941). Visual disorientation with special reference to lesions of the right cerebral hemisphere. *Brain 64:*244–272.

Chedru, F., & LeBlanc, M. (1972). Application of a visual searching test to the study of unilateral inattention. *International Journal of Mental Health 1:*55–64.

Cowey, A. (1979). Cortical maps and visual perception. The Grindley Memorial Lecture. *Quarterly Journal of Experimental Psychology 31:*1–17.

Denes, G., Semerza, C., Stoppa, E., & Lis, A. (1982). Unilateral spatial neglect and recovery from hemiplegia—a follow-up study, *Brain 105:*543–552.

Gardner, M. F. (1982). *Test of Visual Perceptual Skills.* Seattle: Special Child Publications.

Gianutsos, R., & Klitzner, C. (1981). *Computer programs for cognitive rehabilitation.* Bayport, NY: Life Science Associates.

Gianutsos, R., & Matheson, P. (1987). The rehabilitation of visual perceptual disorders attributable to brain injury. In N. J. Meier, A. L. Benton, & L. Diller (Eds.), *Neuropsychological rehabilitation* (pp. 203–241). Edinburgh: Churchill Livingstone.

Gianutsos, R., Cochran, E. E., & Blouin, M. (1984). *Computer programs for cognitive rehabilitation, Vol. III.* Bayport, NY: Life Science Associates.

Gianutsos, R., Ramsey, G., & Perlin, R. R. (1988). Rehabilitative optometric services for survivors of acquired brain injury. *Archieves of Physical Medicine and Rehabilitation, 69:*573–578.

Goldberg, M. E., & Robinson, D. L. (1978). Visual system: Superior colliculus. In R. B. Masterton (Ed.), *Handbook of behavioral neurology, Vol. 1: Sensory integration* (pp. 119–164). New York: Plenum.

Gollin, E. S. (1960). Developmental studies of visual recognition of incomplete objects. *Perceptual and Motor Skills 11:*289–298.

Hamsher, K., Levin, H. S., & Benton, A. L. (1979). Facial recognition in patients with focal brain lesions. *Archives of Neurology, 36:*837–839.

Hannay, H. J., Levin, H. S., & Kay, M. (1982). Tachistoscopic visual perception after closed head injury. *Journal of Clinicical Neuropsychology, 4:*117–129.

Heilman, K. M. (1979). Neglect and related disorders. In K. M. Heilman & Evalenstein (Eds.), *Clinical neuropsychology.* New York: Oxford University Press.

Heilman, K. M., & Volenstein, E. (1985). *Clinical neuropsychology.* New York: Oxford University Press.

Holmes, G. (1938). The cerebral integration of the ocular movements. *British Medical Journal, 2:*107–112.

Hooper, H. E. (1958). *The Hooper Visual Organization Test. Manual.* Los Angeles: Western Psychological Services.

Humphrey, D. R. (1979). On the cortical control of visually directed reaching: Contributions by non-precentral motor areas. In R. B. Talbot & D. R. Humphrey (Eds.), *Posture and movement*. New York: Raven Press.

Kimura, D. (1977). *Neuropsychology Test Procedures*. London: DK Consultants.

Kimura, D., Barnet, H.J.M., & Burkhart, G. (1981). The psychological test pattern in progressive supranuclear palsy. *Neuropsychologia, 19*:301–306.

Lansdell, H. (1968). Effect of extent of temporal lobe ablations on two lateralized deficits. *Physiology and Behavior 3*:271–273.

Levin, G. Z., Meerson, Y. A., & Tonkonogii, I. M. (1969). Visual perception of the elements of form in focal cerebrovascular lesions. *Zhurnal Neuropatologii i Paikhiatrii 69*:1794–1799 (English summary).

Luria, A. R. (1973). *The working brain* (Chapter 3). London: Allen Lane, Penguin.

Lynch, J. C. (1980). The functional organization of posterior parietal cortex. *Behavioral and Brain Sciences 3*:485–534.

Mateer, C. A. (1983). Functional organization of the right nondominant cortex: Evidence from electrical stimulation. *Canadian Journal of Psychology 37*:36–58.

McFic, J., Piercy, M. F., Zangwill, O. L. (1950). Visual-spatial agnosia associated with lesions of the right cerebral hemisphere. *Brain, 73*:167–190.

Meadows, J. C. (1974). Disturbed perception of colours associated with localized cerebral lesions. *Brain 97*:615–632.

Meeker, M., Meeker, R., & Roid, G. H. (1985). *Structure of Intellect Learning Abilities Test (SOI-LA)*. Los Angeles: Western Psychological Services.

Mishkin, M., & Appenzeller, T. (1987). The anatomy of memory. *Scientific American 256*:80–89.

Mooney, C. M. (1960). Recognition of ambiguous and unambiguous visual configurations with short and longer exposures. *British Journal of Psychology 51*:119–125.

Mooney, C. M., & Ferguson, G. A. (1951). A new closure test. *Canadian Journal of Psychology 5*:129–133.

Mountcastle, V. B. (1975). The view from within: Pathways to the study of perception. *Johns Hopkins Medical Journal 136*:109–135.

Newcombe, F. (1987). Psychometric and behavioral evidence: Scope, limitations, and ecological validity. In H. S. Levin, J. Gratman, & H. M. Eisenberg (Eds.), *Neurobehavioral recovery from closed head injury* (pp. 129–145). New York: Oxford University Press.

Osterrith, P. A. (1944). Le test de copie d'une figure complexe. *Archives de Psychologie 30*:206–356.

Pandya, D. N., & Yeterian, E. H. (1984). Proposed neural circuitry for spatial memory in the primate brain. *Neuropsycholosia 22*:109–122.

Pizzamiglio, L., Antonucci, G., & Francia, A. (1984). Response of the cortically blind hemifields to a moving scene. *Cortex 20*:89–99.

Pohl, W. (1973). Dissociation of spatial discrimination deficits following frontal and parietal lesions in monkeys. *Journal of Comparative and Physiological Psychology 82*:227–239.

Poppelreuter, W. (1917). Die psychischen Schadigungen durch Kopfschuss im Kriege 1914/16. Leipzig: Verlag von Leopold Voss.

Ratcliff, G. (1979). Spatial thought, mental rotation and the right central hemisphere. *Neuropsychologia, 17*:49–54.

Ratcliff, G. (1987). Perception and complex visual process. In M. Meier, A. Benton, & L. Diller (Eds.), *Neuropsychological rehabilitation* (pp. 242–259). New York: Guilford.

Ratcliff, G., & Davies-Johnson, G.A.B. (1972). Defective visual localization in focal brain wounds. *Brain 95:46–60.*

Rey, A. (1941). L'examen psychologique dans les cas d'encephalopathie traumatique. *Archives de Psychologie 38:286–340.*

Rubens, A. B. (1979) Agnosia. In K. M. Heilman & E. Valenstein (Eds.), *Clinical neuropsychology* (pp. 233–267). New York: Oxford University Press.

Schneider, G. E. (1969). Two visual systems. *Science 163:895–902.*

Street, R. F. (1931). *A gestalt completion test. Contributions to education No. 481.* New York: Columbia University.

Ungerleider, L., & Mishkin, M. (1982). Two cortical visual systems. In D. J. Ingle, R.J.W. Mansfield, & M. S. Goodale (Eds.), *The analysis of visual behavior.* Cambridge, MA: MIT Press.

Warrington, E. K. (1965). Constructional apraxia. In P. J. Vinker & G. W. Breyn (Eds.), *Handbook of clinical neurology, Vol. 4* (pp. 67–83). Amsterdam: North Holland.

Warrington, E. K. (1984). *Recognition Memory Test.* Berkshire, UK: NFER-Nelson.

Wechsler, D. (1981). *Wechsler Adult Intelligence Scale—Revised.* Cleveland: The Psychological Corporation.

Weinberg, J., Diller, L., Gordon, W. A., Gerstman, L. J., Lieberman, A., Lakin, P., Hodges, G., & Ezrachi, O. (1977). Visual scanning training effect on reading-related tasks in acquired right brain damage. *Archives of Physical Medicine and Rehabilitation 58:479–486.*

Weinberg, J., Diller, L., Gordon, W. A., Gerstman, L. J., Lieberman, A., Lakin, P., Hodges, G., & Esrachi, O. (1979). Training sensory awareness and spatial organization in people with right brain damage. *Archives of Physical Medicine and Rehabilitation 60:491–496.*

Weiskrantz, L. (1980). Varieties of residual experience. *Quarterly Journal of Experimental Psychology 32:365–386.*

Weiskrantz, L., Warrington, E. K., Sanders, M. D., & Marshall, J. (1974). visual capacity in the hemicropic field following a restricted occipital ablation. *Brain 97:709–728.*

Wilson, B., Cockburn, J., & Halligan, P. (1987). *Behavioral Inattention Test.* Titchfield, UK: Thames Valley Test Company.

Woodcock, R. W., & Johnson, M. B. (1977). *Woodcock–Johnson Psychoeducational Battery.* Boston: Teaching Resources Corportion.

Zihl, J. (1980). "Blindsight": Improvements of visually guided eye movements be systematic practice in patients with cerebral blindness. *Neuropsychologia 18:71–77.*

Zihl, J., & von Cramon, D. (1979). Restitution of visual function in patients with cerebral blindness. *Journal of Neurology, Neurosurgery, and Psychiatry 42:312–322.*

Zihl, J., & von Cramon, D. (1982). Restitution of visual fields in patients with damage to the geniculostriate pathway. *Human Neurobiology 1:5–8.*

Zihl, J., von Cramon, D., & Mai, N. (1983). Selective disturbance of movement vision after bilateral brain damage. *Brain 106:313–340.*

9

The Remediation of Language Impairments Associated with Head Injury

Rehabilitation professionals recognize that certain components of language and speech are correlated with and mediated by specific neurological structures. Damage to particular areas in the brain produces predictable deviant speech and language symptomatology. For example, damage to the posterior left frontal lobe region results in a nonfluent aphasia, whereas pathology in the left parietotemporal region surrounding the posterior Sylvian fissure region produces a fluent aphasia with additional impairment in the comprehension of language. There are many different types of impairments that result from lesions within the brain.

Patients with more focal damage to the speech areas, particularly those with open or penetrating head wounds or those who sustain a left cerebral vascular accident, are more likely to demonstrate overt speech and language disturbances than those with diffuse axonal injuries resulting from head trauma. The classic aphasias, dysarthrias, and apraxias diagnosed in head-trauma patients are not different from those produced in patients with differing neurogenic etiologies. A variety of textbooks and research studies devoted to descriptions of the nature of these impairments and the associated remediation techniques are available (e.g., Chapey, 1981; Davis, 1983; Darley, Aronson, & Brown, 1975).

Therefore, this chapter focuses primarily on less understood and often overlooked communication problems so prevalent in the head-injury population, particularly poor pragmatics or deficient use of language in a social context. A review of pragmatics is provided, as well as a discussion of current assessment and treatment techniques. Topics include anomic aphasia, confused language, higher-level language deficits, pragmatics, illocutionary/prelocutionary acts, observational protocols, and group therapy process.

Speech/language pathologists who specialize in neurogenic speech and language disorders are trained in techniques to manage language and motor speech symptoms and are usually the preferred professionals for addressing this area. Professionals targeting the language and speech sequelae following head injury should demonstrate a comprehensive understanding of the communication problems that can result from damage to nonlinguistic processes as well.

THE INCIDENCE OF APHASIA IN CLOSED HEAD INJURY

The reported incidence of aphasia in closed head injury varies greatly. Heilman, Safran, and Geschwind (1971) reported that only 13 of the 750 post-head-injury patients admitted to a city hospital for a 10-month period exhibited aphasia. A similar study (Constantinovici, Arseni, Iliesciu, Debrota, & Gorgea, 1970) found aphasia in only 34 closed-head-injury cases out of 1,544. In contrast, investigations by Levin, Grossman, and Kelly (1976) and Thompson (1975) reported that nearly half of the patients they studied (50 and 26 patients, respectively) had aphasic disturbances. Sarno (1980) found that 32% of patients admitted to a rehabilitation hospital with closed head injury over a 7-year period had frank aphasic disturbance. It is difficult to compare available studies because of the differences in subject-selection criteria and measures and definitions used to evaluate the presence of aphasia.

In general, it might be said that aphasia can be a sequela of closed head injury, but it is not nearly as prevalent as disturbances in other cognitive areas such as memory and attention.

More interesting and relevant than the frequency of aphasia are the types of aphasic disturbances that follow head injury. A review of the literature suggests that the most common is anomic aphasia, characterized by impairment in visual naming and word association processes (Heilman et al., 1971; Sarno, 1980; Thompson, 1975).

Sarno identified a subgroup of closed-head-injury patients whom she labeled as having subclinical aphasia. These were patients who were without signs of aphasia in their conversational speech but who exhibited linguistic disturbances on evaluation. Sarno reminds clinicians of the importance of understanding and treating the subclinical as well as clinical manifestations of verbal impairment. In order to accomplish this, however, it is important to distinguish linguistic deficits of an aphasic nature from those that might be manifestations of other cognitive problems.

COGNITIVE VERSUS LINGUISTIC IMPAIRMENT

Confusion produces a disorientation with regard to language as well as to time, place, and person. Both Halpern, Darley, and Brown (1973) and Groher (1977) contend that there is a dichotomy between confused language skills and disorders that deserve the term aphasia. Halpern and colleagues described patients' language capabilities after closed head trauma as confused. Groher's research suggested that patients initially suffered a reduction of both memory and language skills and that after 4 months, expressive and receptive language abilities improved (they became less aphasic), although language remained confused.

Aphasia is considered a reduced capacity to interpret and formulate language symbols, whereas confused language skills involve faulty short-term memory, mistaken reasoning, inappropriate behavior, poor understanding of the environment, and disorientation. Groher's theory that closed-head-injured patients initially manifest both aphasia and confused language skills and then gradually become less aphasic while still remaining confused may account for some of the variability found in the literature. Weinstein and Keller (1963) also support the theory that patients initially demonstrate more aphasic disorders, which gradually resolve to a more confused language profile. The nature of language impairments depends on when the subject was evaluated. Many studies do not control for time post-trauma.

PRAGMATICS

The term "pragmatics" refers to a system of rules that clarify the use of language in terms of situational or social context. For example, language may be used to command, placate, query, impress, threaten, or establish rapport with the listener. Some communication specialists view pragmatics as a distinct component of language, along with syntax and semantics (e.g., Bloom & Lahey, 1978). Others view pragmatics as an umbrella function under which lie all other aspects of language behavior including phonology, syntax, and semantics (Bates, 1979). Irrespective of definition or theoretical orientation, the issue of how language is used in naturalistic situations has received increasing attention (Milton, Prutting, & Binder, 1984; Prutting & Kirchner, 1983).

Holland (1977) notes that most patients with certain classic types of aphasia communicate better than they talk. The converse might be said of individuals who have sustained head injury; this population often appears to talk better than they communicate. The combination of relatively spared verbal skills with decreased cognitive abilities and compromised psychosocial functioning frequently leaves head trauma patients with a poor ability to use language effectively in interpersonal situations. Prigatano (1986) describes three nonaphasic language disturbances observed following significant craniocerebral trauma: problems of talkativeness, tangential verbalizations, and peculiar phraseology. He notes that these disturbances greatly compromise a patient's ability to communicate effectively in both social and vocational settings and may result in significant social isolation or unemployment. Pragmatic deficits are perhaps the most pervasive communication problem in adults with acquired brain injury. There has, however, been very little research in this area.

Patients with focal right hemisphere damage may be particularly prone to a variety of specific pragmatic deficits. Interpretation and expression of prosody are examples of right hemisphere function (Ross, 1983). Prosody refers to the distribution of stress and melodic contour of speech. Modulation of prosody can be used to impart affective tone, introduce subtle grades of meaning, and vary emphasis in spoken language. Recognition of faces and both the production and appreciation of facial expression are other abilities that depend more on the right hemisphere than the left. Recognition of faces has been proposed to have an important role in species-specific communication in complex social networks. Facial expressions convey mood and emotional state of an individual, and these set the stage for important dynamics of a communication setting (Ekman, Hager, & Friesman, 1981; Strauss & Moscovitch, 1981). Finally, inappropriate reactions to humor, misinterpretation of metaphors, and difficulty producing and perceiving the emotional tone of linguistic utterances may all be seen in patients with right hemisphere damage (Buck & Duffy, 1980; Wapner, Hamby, & Garner, 1981; Tompkins & Mateer, 1985).

In this text, pragmatic behaviors refer to those behaviors that, if used inappropriately or in some cases if absent, would penalize the speaker in a conversational exchange. Milton, Prutting, and Binder describe pragmatics as that component of communication that transcends language in terms of its isolated word and grammatical structures. This crucial aspect of interaction, the ability to manage one's communication, needs to be an important part of every language assessment and, if appropriate, should be addressed in a treatment program.

ASSESSING COMMUNICATIVE FUNCTION

Groher (1977) found that the Porch Index of Communicative Ability (Porch, 1967) appeared to offer a good indication of aphasic characteristics but did not provide information about the presence of high-level language deficits or pragmatic problems. Halpern et al. (1973) arrived at a similar conclusion after using the Minnesota Test for the Differential Diagnosis of Aphasia (Schuell, 1965). These and other researchers found that aphasia batteries do not measure cognitive factors or pragmatic skills. Some researchers encourage the testing of "higher language functions" as a means of delineating the nature of verbal impairment after closed head injury. Such researchers warn clinicians that the administration of an aphasia battery is not sufficient for diagnosing and describing potential language impairments associated with closed head injury (e.g., Thompson, 1975; Sarno, 1980; Levin et al., 1976). Typical measures of high-level language include tests sensitive to abstract language—such as descriptions of thematic pictures, synonyms, antonyms, metaphors—and assessments of verbal power and speed such as word fluency.

A comprehensive evaluation of communication function in the head-injured population needs to consider the following three areas:

- speech/language abilities
- cognitive capacity
- pragmatic functions

The assessment of cognitive processes is discussed throughout the text. In this section, three different observational protocols for evaluating pragmatic skills are presented.

In the child language literature, speech/language pathologists are encouraged to assess pragmatics by taking transcriptions of communication behavior and analyzing various pragmatic components. For example, Lund and Duchan (1983) organized pragmatics into four areas, each of which describes one aspect of context and how this affects language production. The areas are:

- situational context (physical setting, the speech event frames, and the topic);
- intentional context (communicative intent, the agenda);
- listener context (physical perspective, background knowledge, and role relationships);
- linguistic context (syntax, semantics).

The authors suggest utilizing elicitation procedures with children to obtain naturalistic samples of those specific areas in which the clinician is interested in measuring and performing pragmatic analysis of the recorded conversation. Although the analysis of recorded interaction samples is an effective method for evaluating the details of interaction, it is not always a clinically feasible task because of the heavy time demands of these analyses. More efficient means for the identification of pragmatic impairments are required. One such method is the use of observational protocols discussed in the remainder of this chapter.

It should be noted that pragmatics is a very young area of speech/ language pathology, and assessment and treatment instruments are not yet well established. However, the protocols presented here offer promise for use with the head-injured population.

Regardless of the specific tool used, the following ingredients need to be present for assessment of communication ability:

1. The clinician must observe the head-injured individual in a natural communication situation in which he or she is conversing with a discourse partner.
2. The clinician needs to have a list or taxonomy of pragmatic behaviors from which to judge performance.
3. A method for translating information gleaned through observation into treatment goals and objectives should be established.

The Pragmatic Protocol

The Pragmatic Protocol (Prutting & Kirchner, 1983) is designed to help clinicians understand how an individual uses language. It presents a taxonomy of 32 pragmatic behaviors in four categories (derived from the research of Austin, 1962; Searle, 1969). These are:

1. The *utterance act,* which includes verbal, nonverbal, and paralinguistic behaviors related to how the message is presented.
2. The *propositional act,* which refers to the linguistic meaning of the sentence.
3. The *perlocutionary act,* which relates to the effects of the speaker on the listener.
4. The *illocutionary act,* which refers to the speaker's intention.

These last two areas regulate the discourse between speaker and listener and contain 15 pragmatic items. Appendix A provides a more complete listing of the components of the Pragmatic Protocol.

The clinician's task is to observe the client in a conversation and to judge the appropriateness or inappropriateness of each pragmatic behavior (whether or not the behavior would be socially punishing to the client). The Pragmatic Protocol is used for screening purposes to identify problem areas. A more in-depth analysis of various behaviors may be performed when designing treatment programs.

The utility of this protocol is supported by some research. In a study of five head-injured adults and five normal adults matched for age, sex, and education level, Milton et al. (1984) found that the head-injured adults differed from the control group primarily in illocutionary and perlocutionary behaviors. The authors suggested that communication breakdown occurs most frequently in the head-injured person's ability to regulate discourse. The types of behaviors that were observed to be the most problematic included prosody (e.g., intonation, stress, timing), topic selection (e.g., restricted range of topics), topic maintenance (e.g., topic change occurred following minimal speaking turns); turn-taking initiation, turn-taking pause time, and turn-taking contingency (e.g., awkward phrasing of new information added to the ongoing exchange); and quantity/conciseness (e.g., redundant information or excess detail). The authors concluded that the Pragmatic Protocol was useful in identifying strengths and weaknesses in conversational competence in head-injured adults and that it provided a focus for treatment.

The Interaction Checklist for Augmentative Communication

The Interaction Checklist for Augmentative Communication (INCH) (Bolton & Dashiell, 1984) is an observational protocol that assesses pragmatic ability. Although designed for individuals who use augmentative communication systems such as communication boards, it provides a taxonomy of pragmatic behaviors that could easily be adapted to the head-injured population. It provides another conceptualization of pragmatic skills and an alternative assessment format. (See Appendix C for a sample INCH protocol.)

The INCH is organized according to three components: strategies, modes, and contexts. *Strategies* refer to those skills a person uses in a communication exchange. There are four types, including initiation, facilitation, regulation, and termination. In each context observed, the clinician judges the different strategies as present, emerging, absent, or not applicable for each of the five modes. *Modes* are the means by which messages are transmitted. The five types are linguistic, paralinguistic, kinesic, proxemic, and chronemic. *Contexts* describe the particular communication partners and situations, including familiar–trained, familiar–untrained, unfamiliar–trained, and unfamiliar–untrained (the first word in the pair refers to the interpersonal relationship between the sender and receiver, and the second word refers to the level of competence the receiver has with users of augmentative communication systems).

Because this tool was specifically designed for augmented communicators, it contains some important features not present in the Pragmatic Protocol that may be useful in an evaluation of pragmatic behaviors in closed-head-injured adults. The breakdown of context classes is especially useful, since context can have a dramatic effect on interaction. The detailed description of strategies may help the clinician to specify exactly what the client is doing and to formulate appropriate therapy goals and objectives. For example, there are six different repair behaviors listed under the facilitation strategy section; thus, on examination of a completed checklist, one could determine not only whether or not the individual appropriately repairs communication breakdowns but also exactly how he or she manages the repairs and sets appropriate intervention goals.

The INCH is lacking in some areas, however, It does not, for example, consider the effect of interaction on the listener. The list of pragmatic behaviors is incomplete, and components such as lexical selection and intelligibility are not addressed. Thus, the organization and layout of the INCH provides a good assessment format, with Prutting and Kirchner's Pragmatic Protocol offering a more exhaustive list of pragmatic behaviors.

Communication Performance Scale

The Communication Performance Scale (Ehrlich & Sipes, 1985) was adapted from the Pragmatic Protocol described earlier (see Appendix B). It contains 13 pragmatic behaviors, each of which is rated on an interval scale from 1 to 5, and includes those behaviors most commonly disrupted in head-injured patients. The scale was intended to assist in the clinical judgment of clients' progress following communication intervention and to provide empirical documentation of change. Clinical implementation of the scale is described in the section discussing treatment of pragmatic deficits; it allows the clinician to rate 13 selected pragmatic skills.

TREATMENT OF PRAGMATIC DEFICITS

If the assessment of pragmatics is in its infancy, the treatment of pragmatic deficits must be in an embryonic stage. However, it is important for clinicians to adopt the pioneer spirit and to implement trial remediation programs. The inability to communicate effectively may be the barrier that prevents an individual from being hired for a job or from fully reintegrating into society. This section reviews two treatment approaches currently being developed.

Group Model of Intervention

Ehrlich and Sipes (1985) present a model of group intervention designed to increase the pragmatic abilities of head trauma patients. A communication group comprised of therapists and head-injured clients provides the therapy setting. Therapists assist patients in identifying appropriate group communication goals. Patients receive feedback on the effectiveness of observed communication, including positive social reinforcement and feedback regarding problem behaviors. A modular format is utilized to address the following four behaviors.

1. *Nonverbal communication:* vocal inflection, facial expression, eye gaze, body posture, and gestures.
2. *Communication in context:* topic maintenance, initiation, and response during conversation; awareness of social context.
3. *Message repair:* awareness of communication breakdown, consideration of listener needs, and clarification strategies.

4. Cohesiveness of narrative: sequencing of information and comprehension; production of temporal and spatial concepts.

Therapists introduce each module by describing and demonstrating the target behaviors to be learned. Role play (initially between the therapists and then between clients) is used to illustrate appropriate and inappropriate behaviors. These role plays are videotaped and reviewed by the group. Patients are helped to look at specific behaviors that increase communication success or failure. Ways to modify communication behavior are also discussed. The authors suggest the following procedural outline:

- *Introduction of the module.* The therapist defines target behaviors and provides videotaped role-play samples modeling appropriate and inappropriate behaviors.
- *Client role-play exercises.* The clients perform role plays of assigned social situations, which are videotaped. The group reviews the role play and discusses relevant aspects of communication, including ways to modify and improve observed communication behaviors.

The authors evaluated the success of the above intervention program by weekly assessments using the Communication Performance Scale. Comparison of pre- and posttreatment rating scales for six patients indicated improvement significant at the .001 level. As shown in Figure 9.1, the greatest change was evident in topic maintenance, initiation, syntax, cohesiveness, and repair. Less significant improvements were observed in intelligibility, listening, and lexical selection. Little or no change was evident for body posture, interruptions, prosody, facial expression, and variety of language use. The authors concluded that the group format provides a successful therapy milieu to train pragmatic skills.

Individual Focus

The clinical experience of the authors is consistent with these findings. In a day-treatment postacute head injury rehabilitation setting, group therapy targeting pragmatic skills has been successfully completed with over 25 patients. In this setting, however, a more individualized approach has been adopted, which allows for the targeting of particular pragmatic behaviors that are deficient in individual patients.

Initially, patients are videotaped in conversation with the therapist. The tapes are reviewed in group, and pragmatic goals and objectives are identified for each patient. Two therapists independently rate each patient on the Pragmatic Protocol, which serves as a baseline measure of communication ability. Different patients have different goals, but all are encouraged to assist each other in working on the specific communication objectives.

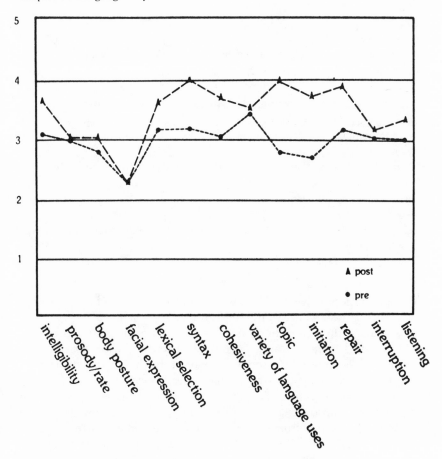

FIGURE 9.1. Clients' mean pre- and posttreatment scores for each scale item. Reprinted with permission from Ehrlich & Sipes (1985).

Role-play activities are carried out during group therapy to target relevant pragmatic skills.

The authors feel that the key to success in working on restricted pragmatic abilities is to provide remediation across a broad range of naturalistic communication environments. Thus, it is important that patients receive feedback not only during group therapy but in individual therapy sessions and outside clinical settings as well. Other therapists working with the patient, as well as those individuals within the home environment, receive descriptions of the communication goals and suggestions for providing appropriate feedback to the head-injured patient.

Periodically, videotapes using the same therapist as a communication partner are recorded and again rated using the Pragmatic Protocol. The

TABLE 9.1. Remediation of Pragmatic Deficits

Ten-minute conversation between patient and therapist is videotaped.

Two therapists independently rate videotape samples using an appropriate pragmatic observational protocol. The most prominent areas of concern are identified.

Videotapes are reviewed in group, and individual goals and objectives are assigned.

Group members, adjunct therapists, and individuals in the home environment receive information on patient communication goals and ways to give constructive feedback.

Role-play exercises targeting specific communication goals are conducted in regular group therapy sessions.

Periodic videotape samples are recorded, rated, and discussed in group. Progress is discussed.

Progress is monitored in extraclinic settings by individual reports elicited from relevant persons.

group provides peer feedback regarding improvements and residual problems. Table 9.1 summarizes the steps of this approach.

In summary, the treatment of pragmatic deficits requires structured feedback regarding communication performance across a wide variety of environments. Patients need intensive opportunity to practice appropriate behaviors and to modify existing problem areas as well as to establish new, effective modes of communication. Appropriate treatment goals are an extension of a thorough analysis of communication in naturalistic social situations. Peer input from a group therapy environment can provide a powerful clinical tool for assisting patients in understanding problem areas and for offering methods to improve their communication. Videotapes and role-play exercises allow patients to practice and evaluate target behaviors.

SUMMARY

Persons who have sustained head injuries may exhibit a variety of communication disorders. Although classic aphasias, apraxias, and dysarthrias are possible sequelae of head trauma, these do not represent the most common communication problems within this population. When patients do exhibit such deficits, intervention designed for these impairments should be implemented.

The greatest communication concern within the head-injured population is addressed by a relatively new branch of speech/language pathology called pragmatics. Pragmatics refers to how meaning is communicated between people (the social role of language). Head-injured persons often have difficulty with such pragmatic behaviors as appropriate topic selection and maintenance of and turn-taking in conversation.

Assessment of pragmatic abilities should include observing patients in conversation and rating communication performance on a variety of behaviors. In this chapter, three sample pragmatic protocols were reviewed.

Both assessment and treatment of pragmatic deficits need to be conducted within the context of natural communication. Group therapy, utilizing videotaped communication samples to establish communication objectives and written role-play exercises to practice appropriate pragmatic skills, is valuable as a clinical approach. However, remediation of pragmatic deficits must extend beyond the clinical environment and include monitoring and feedback in a variety of natural communication settings.

STUDY QUESTIONS

1. What are the most common types of aphasic disturbances in the head-injured population?
2. What three areas need to be considered when evaluating communication ability in the head-injured population?
3. Define pragmatics. What are the most common pragmatic deficits in individuals who have sustained brain trauma?
4. How does one assess pragmatics?
5. What are the important components of remediating pragmatic impairments?

REFERENCES

Austin, J. (1962). *How to do things with words.* Cambridge: Harvard University Press.

Bates, E. (1979). *The emergence of symbols.* New York: Academic Press

Bloom, L., & Lahey, M. (1978). *Language development and language disorders.* New York: John Wiley.

Bolton, S. O., & Dashiell, S. E. (1984). *Interaction checklist for augmentative communication: An observational tool to assess interactive behavior.* Idyllwild, CA: Imaginart Communication Products.

Buck, R., & Duffy, R. (1980). Nonverbal communication of affect in brain damaged patients. *Cortex 16:*351–362.

Chapey, R. (1981). *Language intervention strategies in adult aphasia.* Baltimore/London: Williams & Wilkins.

Constantinovici, A., Arseni, C., Iliesciu, A., Debrota, L., & Gorgea, A. (1970). Considerations on past traumatic aphasia in peacetime. *Psychiatric Neurolo-Neurochirurgy 73*:105–115.

Darley, F. L., Aronson, A. E., & Brown, J. R. (1975). *Motor speech disorders.* Philadelphia: W. B. Saunders.

Davis, A. (1983). *A survey of adult aphasia.* Englewood Cliffs, NJ: Prentice-Hall.

Ehrlich, J., & Spies, A. (1985). Group treatment of communication skills for head trauma patients. *Cognitive Rehabilitation 3*:32–37.

Ekman, P., Hager, J., & Friesman, W. (1981). The symmetry of emotional and deliberate facial expression. *Psychophysiology 18*:101–106.

Groher, M. (1977). Language and memory disorders following closed head trauma. *Journal of Speech and Hearing Research 20*:212–223.

Halpern, H., Darley, F., & Brown, J. R. (1973). Differential language and neurologic characteristics in cerebral involvement. *Journal of Speech and Hearing Disorders 38*:162–173.

Heilman, K., Safran, A., & Geschwind, N. (1971). Closed head trauma and aphasia. *Journal of Neurology, Neurosurgery, and Psychiatry 34*:265–269.

Holland, A. L. (1977). Practical considerations in aphasia rehabilitation. In M. Sullivan & M. S. Kommeara (Eds.), *Rationale for adult aphasic therapy.* Omaha: University of Nebraska Medical Center.

Levin, H., Grossman, R., & Kelly, P. (1976). Aphasia disorder in patients with closed head injury. *Journal of Neurology, Neurosurgery, and Psychiatry 39*:1062–1070.

Lund, N., & Duchan, J. (1983). *Assessing children's language in naturalistic contexts.* Engelwood Cliffs, NJ: Prentice-Hall.

Milton, S. B., Prutting, C. A., & Binder, G. (1984). Appraisal of communicative competence in head injured adults. In R. H. Brookshire (Ed.), *Proceedings from the clinical aphasiology conference* (pp. 114–123). Minneapolis: BRK Publishers.

Porch, B. E. (1967). *Porch Index of Communicative Ability.* Palo Alto: Consulting Psychologists Press.

Prigatano, G. (1986). *Neuropsychological rehabilitation after brain injury.* Baltimore: Johns Hopkins University Press.

Prutting, C., & Kirchner, D. (1983). Applied pragmatics. In: T. Gallagher & C. Prutting (Eds.), *Pragmatic assessment and intervention issues in language* (pp. 29–68). San Diego: College-Hill Press.

Ross, E. D. (1983). Right hemisphere lesion in disorders of affective language. In: A. Kertesz (Ed.), *Localization in neuropsychology* (pp. 493–508). New York: Academic Press.

Sarno, M. T. (1980). The nature of verbal impairment after closed head injury. *Journal of Nervous and Mental Disease 168*:685–692.

Schuell, N. M. (1965). *Differential diagnosis of aphasia with the Minnesota test.* Minneapolis: University of Minnesota Press.

Searle, J. (1969). *Speech acts: An essay in the philosophy of language.* Cambridge: University Park Press.

Strauss, E., & Moscovitch, M. (1981). Perception of facial expression. *Brain and Language 13*:308–332.

Thompson, I. V. (1975). Evaluation and outcoming of aphasia in patients with severe closed head trauma. *Journal of Neurology, Neurosurgery, and Psychiatry 38*:713–718.

Tomkins, C., & Mateer, C. A. (1985). Right hemisphere appreciation of prosodic and linguistic indication of implicit attitude. *Brain and Language, 24*:185–203.

Wapner, W., Hamby, S., & Garner, H. (1981). The role of the right hemisphere in the apprehension of complex linguistic materials. *Brain and Language 14*:15–33.

Wechsler, D. (1945). A standardized memory scale for clinical use. *Journal of Psychology 19*:87–95.

Weinstein, D., & Keller, W. (1963). Linguistic patterns of misnaming in brain injury. *Neuropsychologia 1*:79–90.

APPENDIX A: POOL OF PRAGMATIC BEHAVIORS[a]

TAXONOMY	MODALITY	DESCRIPTION AND CODING
Utterance act	Verbal/para-linguistic	The trappings by which the act is accomplished
1. Intelligibility		The extent to which the message is understood
2. Vocal intensity		The loudness or softness of the message
3. Voice quality		The resonance and/or laryngeal characteristics of the vocal tract
4. Prosody		The intonation and stress patterns of the message; variations of loudness, pitch, and duration
5. Fluency		The smoothness, consistency, and rate of the message
6. Physical proximity	Nonverbal	The distance from which speaker and listener sit or stand from one another
7. Physical contacts		The number of times and placement of contacts between speaker and listener
8. Body posture		Forward lean is when the speaker or listener moves away from a 90° angle toward other person; recline is when one party slouches down from waist to head and moves away from the partner; side to side is when a person moves to the right or left.
9. Foot/leg movements		Any movement of foot/leg

Appendix A (*continued*)

TAXONOMY	MODALITY	DESCRIPTION AND CODING
10. Hand/arm movements		Any movement with hand/arm (touching or moving an object or touching part of the body or clothing)
11. Gestures		Any movements that support, complement, or replace verbal behavior
12. Facial expression		A positive expression is when the corners of the mouth are turned upward; negative is a downward turn; neutral expression is when face is in a resting position
13. Eye gaze		When one looks directly at the other's facial region; mutual gaze is when both members of the dyad look at each other
Propositional act	Verbal	Linguistic dimensions of the meaning of the sentence
1. Lexical selection/ use		
A. Specificity/ accuracy		Lexical items of best fit considering the context
2. Specifying relationships between words		
A. Word order		Grammatical word order for conveying message
B. Given and new information		Given information is that information already known to the listener; new information is information not already known to the listener.
a. Pronominalization		Pronouns permit the listener to identify the referent and form one of the devices used to mark givenness
b. Ellipses		Given information may be deleted
c. Emphatic stress		New information may be marked by stressing various items
d. Indefinite/ definite article		If new information is signaled, the indefinite article is used; if old information, then the definite article is used
e. Initialization		Given information is stated prior to new information
3. Stylistic variations		
A. The varying of communicative style	Verbal, paralinguistic, nonverbal	Adaptations used by the speaker under various dyadic conditions, e.g., polite forms, different syntax, vocal quality changes

TAXONOMY	MODALITY	DESCRIPTION AND CODING
Illocutionary and per-locutionary acts	Verbal	Illocutionary (intentions of the speaker) and perlocutionary (effects on the listener)
1. Speech act pair analysis		The ability to take both speaker and listener role appropriate to the context
		Directive/compliance: personal need, imperatives, embedded imperatives, permissions, directives, questions, directives, hints
		Query/response: requests for confirmation, neutral requests for repetition, requests for specific constituent repetition
		Request/response: direct requests, indirect requests, inferred requests, request for clarification, acknowledgement of the request, perform the desired action
		Comment/acknowledgment: descriptions of ongoing activities in immediate subsequent activity, of state or condition of objects, persons, naming, acknowledgments that are positive, negative, expletive, indicative
2. Variety of speech acts		The variety of speech acts or what one can do with language, such as comment, assert, request, promise, etc.
A. Topic		
a. Selection		The selection of a topic appropriate to the context
b. Introduction		Introduction of a new topic in the discourse
c. Maintenance		Maintenance of topic across the discourse
B. Turn-taking		Smooth interchanges between speaker and listener
a. Initiation		Initiation of speech acts
b. Response		The responding as a listener to speech acts
c. Repair/ revision		The ability to repair a conversation when a breakdown occurs and the ability to ask for a repair when misunderstanding, ambiquity, etc. has occurred
d. Pause time		When pause time is excessive or too short between words or in response to a question or between sentences

Appendix A (*continued*)

TAXONOMY	MODALITY	DESCRIPTION AND CODING
e. Interruption/ overlap		Interruptions between speaker and listener; overlap is when two people talk at the same time
f. Feedback to speaker		Verbal behavior to give the speaker feedback such as "yea," "really"; nonverbal behavior such as head nods up and down can be positive; side to side can express negative effect or disbelief
g. Adjacency		Utterances that occur immediately after the partner's utterance
h. Contingency		Utterances that share the same topic with the preceding utterance and that add information to the prior communicative act
i. Quantity/ conciseness		The contribution should be as informative as required but not too informative

[a] From Prutting and Kircher (1983). Reproduced by permission.

APPENDIX B: COMMUNICATION PERFORMANCE SCALE*

1. Intelligibility
Difficult to understand; requires repetition   1 2 3 4 5
                                                     Always understandable

2. Prosody/Rate
Choppy rhythm, uneven; too fast or slow   1 2 3 4 5
                                                     Appropriate stress patterns

3. Body posture
away from others; limited gestures   1 2 3 4 5
                                                     Body oriented towards others; appropriate gestures

4. Facial expression
Limited affect and eye gaze   1 2 3 4 5
                                                     Shows emotions and appropriate eye gaze

5. Lexical selection
Limited word selection; ambiguous words   1 2 3 4 5
                                                     Good variety of words; clear referents

6. Syntax Ungrammatical; uses only short phrases	1	2	3	4	5		Uses mature sentence pat- terns, phrases, clauses, and conjunctions
7. Cohesiveness Random, diffuse, and disjointed ver- bal style	1	2	3	4	5		Planned, sequential expres- sion of ideas; concise
8. Variety of language uses Limited use of lan- guage; stereotypic- al language	1	2	3	4	5		Uses language to express feelings, share information, social interaction
9. Topic Abrupt shift of topic; perseveration	1	2	3	4	5		Can appropriately introduce, maintain, and change topic
10. Initiation of conversation Lim- ited initiation of talk; restricted re- sponse to con- versation	1	2	3	4	5		Freely initiates and responds to conversational leads
11. Repair Inflexibile, unable to change message when communica- tion failure occurs	1	2	3	4	5		Able to revise message to facilitate listener com- prehension; flexible
12. Interruption Frequently in- terrupts others	1	2	3	4	5		Appropriate interruption; good conversation flow
13. Listening Limited listening; listener shows res- tricted reaction to the speaker	1	2	3	4	5		Attends well; listener pro- vides verbal and nonverbal feedback to speaker

*From Ehrlich and Sipes (1985). Reprinted by permission.

APPENDIX C. Interaction Checklist for Augmentation Communication (INCH) [a]

SYMBOL KEY:

Scoring	Modes	Color Code
+ Present	L Linguistic	—— Initial
~ Emerging	PA Paralinguistic	—— Follow-up
− Absent	K Kinesic	
■ Not Applicable	PR Proxemic	
	C Chronemic	

STRATEGIES	CONTEXTS														
	1 (Notes)				2 (Notes)				3 (Notes)						
	MODES														
1.0 INITIATION	L	PA	K	PR	C	L	PA	K	PR	C	L	PA	K	PR	C
As Sender:															
1.1 Gains attention and/or designates receiver															
1.2 Uses social greetings															
1.3 Introduces self (when appropriate)															
1.4 Asks questions to gain information															
1.5 Initiates topics consistent with place, role, and social situation															
As Receiver:															
1.6 Responds to greetings from others															
2.0 FACILITATION	L	PA	K	PR	C	L	PA	K	PR	C	L	PA	K	PR	C
2.1 Indicates physical state and emotion															
2.2 Maintains optimal physical distance for communication															
2.3 Positions self for optimal communicative exchange															
2.4 Uses polite social forms															
2.5 Uses vocabulary appropriate to receiver's needs															
2.6 Defines sentence types and indicates tense															
2.7 Seeks help when needed															

			L	PA	K	PR	C		L	PA	K	PR	C		L	PA	K	PR	C
2.8	Gives receiver instructions when necessary																		
2.9	Uses augmentative system without prompting																		
	When receiver doesn't understand, the sender:																		
2.10	Re-states (paraphrases) message																		
2.11	Adds detail; expands on message																		
2.12	Replaces a word with another word																		
2.13	Adjusts rate of production																		
2.14	Adjusts volume as appropriate																		
2.15	Keeps trying; persists; repeats if necessary																		
3.0	REGULATION		L	PA	K	PR	C		L	PA	K	PR	C		L	PA	K	PR	C
	As Sender:																		
3.1	Alerts receiver that more time is needed when composing																		
3.2	Shifts topics smoothly; uses transitional forms																		
3.3	Uses pauses or spaces for greater clarity																		
3.4	Maintains interest and monitors understanding																		
3.5	Gives feedback when message is not understood																		
	As Receiver:																		
3.6	Uses eye contact to indicate attention to sender																		
3.7	Gives feedback to indicate comprehension of message																		
3.8	Stays on topic consistent with place, role and social situation																		
4.0	TERMINATION		L	PA	K	PR	C		L	PA	K	PR	C		L	PA	K	PR	C
4.1	Uses farewells																		
4.2	Indicates when finished with message																		

10
Remediation of Executive Function Impairments

Deficits in executive functions, perhaps more than any other cognitive process, determine the extent of social and vocational recovery. Although impairments in such functions as anticipation, goal selection, planning, self-regulation, incorporating feedback, and completion of intended activities are very prevalent following head injury, remediation efforts have been fairly minimal. This chapter begins with a review of relevant neuroanatomic and neuropsychologic issues and then presents a model for describing, assessing, and retraining executive functions. Topics covered include neuroanatomy of the frontal lobes, frontal lobe susceptibility to trauma and associated psychoemotional changes, tests of executive function, examples of retraining tasks, the executive function treatment model (selection and execution of cognitive plans, time management, and self-regulation), and environmental modification.

NEUROANATOMIC/NEUROPATHOLOGIC CONSIDERATIONS*

The human frontal lobes are unique. They are very large structures and constitute approximately 30% of the total cortical surface (Goldman-Rakic, 1984). Phylogenetically, as one moves up the animal chain, an increasing proportion of the cortex is devoted to the prefrontal structures. Thus, primates have more prefrontal cortex than dogs, which have more than cats, which have more than rodents (Stuss & Benson, 1986). This region of the cerebral cortex is the most recently developed part of the brain in an evolutionary sense and is the latest to develop in a maturing

---

*Many of the facts about frontal lobe functions reviewed in this chapter were gleaned from the Stuss and Benson (1986) text, which represents one of the more complete and scholarly works on the nature of the frontal lobes.

individual. The relatively massive growth of the prefrontal cortex is considered to be a major contribution to human beings' superior mental capacity.

In addition to their size, the frontal lobes are also distinguished by their neuroanatomic diversity. This region has numerous rich connections to other parts of the brain, and the functions it carries out are products of information collected from widespread locations in the central nervous system. Damage in one or more of the many different loci within the frontal lobes can result in very different behavioral changes.

The size and diversity of these anterior structures present several practical obstacles to research. Because they are unique structures to humankind, relevant animal research opportunities are limited. For the most part, valid study of frontal lobe function must utilize human research subjects. The ethical restrictions on experimental study have been previously addressed. However, even when examining human case studies of frontal lobe damage, there are research obstacles. In many head trauma cases, damage to the frontal lobes is diffuse and simultaneously affects multiple brain structures, making it difficult to isolate specific frontal lobe functions. There are limited studies providing clear-cut correlations between anterior frontal lobe impairment and specific behavioral changes. Disturbances to one frontal lobe usually result in disturbances in the other lobe (except in cases of tumors and strokes). Thus, there is a high propensity for bilateral damage.

Susceptibility to Trauma

The frontal lobes are especially susceptible to substantial damage from trauma caused by open or closed head injuries. Open head injuries are less common and may be caused by such accidents as gunshot wounds or other penetrating injuries. Many of the early localization studies in frontal lobes were done with persons who received open head injuries in military accidents. Closed head injuries often result in frontal lobe damage, presumably because of the lobes' location in relation to the frontal bones. When the head strikes an object, such as a windshield in a car accident, the brain is thrust forward against these bony protrusions. Figure 10.1 shows the position of the orbital regions of the frontal lobe within the skull relative to the bony processes and stiff membranes which surround it. Figure 10.2 shows the tendency for traumatic brain injury to result in pathology in the orbital and frontal as well as temporal regions. Given the propensity for injury, it is important for clinicians to be aware of the different cognitive and behavioral manifestations of frontal lobe pathology.

The Nature of Frontal Impairments

Current research has not resulted in the identification of one specific classic behavior pattern that could be termed a frontal syndrome. However, when

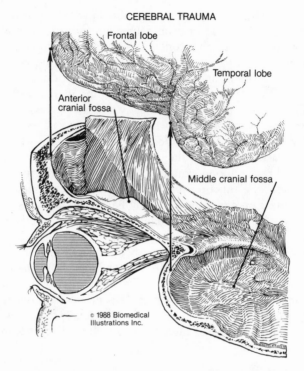

FIGURE 10.1. Schematic pull-away illustrating the position of the orbital and anterior frontal regions and the anterior temporal lobe relative to bony processes. Copyright © 1988 by Biomedical Illustrations, Inc.

there is substantial damage to this region, experienced clinicians readily recognize impairments that they identify as "frontal" in nature. The types of impairments that clinicians and researchers attribute to frontal lobe damage include a mixture of behavioral and emotional deficits as well as cognitive problems, specifically decreased executive functions. Common problems in the psychoemotional realm include apathy, disinhibition, restricted range of affect, emotional lability, and disorders in awareness (denial, unconcern, decreased insight).

The classic case of Phineas Gage described by Harlow (1868) provides a compelling example of the altered personality following frontal damage. Harlow reported that this man suffered a severe frontal

> . . . injury when an iron tamping bar was blown upward into this brain region while he was working on a railroad construction crew. Although he appeared to make a complete physical recovery, his emotional behavior and personality were greatly changed. Following his accident, he was described as fitful and irreverent, indulging at times in the grossest profanity (which was not previous-

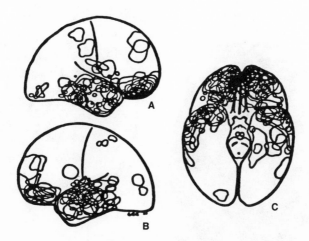

FIGURE 10.2. Drawing of contusions after traumatic brain injury based on 40 consecutive cases. Depicts the tendency for maximum pathology in the orbital frontal and temporal regions. From Courville (1937). Reprinted by permission.

ly his custom), manifesting but little deference for his fellows, impatient of restraint or advice when it conflicts with his desires. . . .

Blumer and Benson (1975) described two separate syndromes of frontal personality alteration. One, termed pseudodepression, is characterized by a reduced activity level, including apathy, unconcern, decreased drive, and lack of emotional responsiveness. The authors suggested that this syndrome occurred with damage involving the anterior convexity and/or the medial regions of one of both hemispheres. The second syndrome, termed pseudopsychopathic, features disinhibition with inappropriate focus on sexual pursuits, egocentricity, and lack of concern for others. Pathology in the orbital frontal region was associated with this personality change. Should a clinician recognize these sorts of behavioral characteristics in a patient, he or she might suspect frontal pathology and look for some of the cognitive problems that relate to frontal lobe damage. (See Chapter 14 for further discussion on the role of frontal lobes in psychosocial functioning.)

Effect on Cognition

Stuss and Benson (1986) suggest that perhaps the greatest confusion regarding the function of the frontal lobes involves their role in cognition. A multitude of case studies demonstrate that patients with frontal lobe pathology may suffer severe deficits in functional abilities despite normal IQ levels on psychologic tests. Figure 10.3 shows the CT scan of a patient who

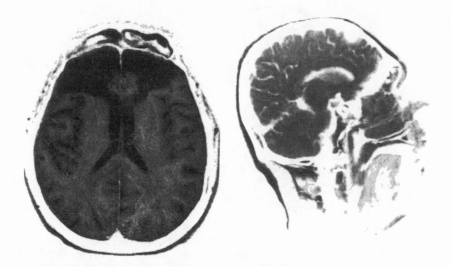

FIGURE 10.3. Computed tomographic scan of a 48-year-old male 20 months after a fall from a scaffold showing observable frontal pathology from the closed head injury. Many neuropsychologic measures were within normal limits: WAIS-R, 108; verbal IQ, 104; performance IQ, 106; Wechsler Memory Quotient, 99; Category Test, 35; Impairment Index, 10. However, Finger-Tapping Scores (left and right) were 2 SD below mean, Paced Auditory Serial Addition Test was 3 SD below mean, verbal fluency was below the 15th percentile, design fluency was below the 10th percentile, and the Wisconsin Card-Sorting Test showed 70% perseverative errors.

sustained observable bilateral frontal lobe damage with corresponding neuropsychologic test scores. Intellectual skills remained relatively intact, yet this patient was completely dysfunctional in his daily living because of inappropriate behaviors and poor executive functions.

It appears that the frontal lobes are responsible for coordinating and actualizing the activities involved in cognitive processing, but they are not necessarily responsible for primary cognitive functions. For example, frontal lobe damage does not interfere with the storage of information but may affect other activities related to memory such as attention, motivation, regulation, and self-monitoring (Stuss & Benson, 1986). Luria (1973) suggests that the frontal lobes may be involved in organizing storage and recall and comparing results of one's actions with original intention. Similarly, research examining the role of frontal lobes in visual processing has suggested that they do not have a primary function in visuospatial processing but may affect behaviors requisite for dealing with visual information. Thus, if a task simply requires straightforward understanding of spatial relationships, frontal lobe functions may not be relevant. If, however, a task involves selection of information, initiation, planning, flexibility, monitoring, or other executive functions, the frontal lobes may be significant.

Role of Executive Functions

In summary, much of the frontal lobe involvement in coginition may be understood through examination of executive functions. The rest of this chapter specifically addresses the assessment and treatment of impairments in these functions. Unlike cognitive processes such as memory and visual processing, executive functions do not represent a discrete process. Instead, they operate as an umbrella function that comes into play with all realms of cognitive processing.

As stated previously, the frontal lobes coordinate input from other parts of the brain. When executive functions are impaired, all other cognitive systems have the potential to be affected, even though they may remain individually intact. Executive functions may be considered a composite of the following activities related to goal completion: anticipation, goal selection, planning, initiation of activity, self-regulation or self-monitoring, and use of feedback.

Luria (1966) described how executive functions relate to problem-solving ability. He investigated a number of patients with lesions to the frontal lobes of the brain and noted that most were unable to analyze systematically the conditions of a problem and select the important connections and relationships. The system of operations that would normally lead to solution of a problem appeared disintegrated; instead, isolated fragmentary connections unrelated to a general plan were evident. Typical of patients with frontal lobe damage was the absence of a plan for solving a problem, the omission of the phase of preliminary investigation of conditions and constraints of the problem, and a replacement of true intellectual operations by unrelated, impulsive actions.

The case of a 30-year-old businessman who suffered extensive bilateral frontal lobe pathology in a motor vehicle accident provides an illustration of the importance of intact executive functions for successful operation in the daily world. The patient's wife noted that her husband could successfully perform one-step operations but was unable to plan, sequence, and monitor multistep activities. This patient could prepare one item, such as a salad, but was unable to plan and cook a whole meal or do multistep activities such as the laundry (which was his habit prior to the accident). Relatively intact general intellectual functioning and old learning may mislead families and less-experienced clinicians regarding a patient's ability to complete purposeful activities successfully. It is an important challenge to the cognitive remediation specialist to rehabilitate impaired executive functions because they present such devastating barriers to successful reintegration into society.

ASSESSMENT OF EXECUTIVE FUNCTIONS

For the most part, standard psychologic and neuropsychologic tests are not sensitive to the effects of frontal lobe damage. There are three basic approaches to the evaluation of executive functions:

- Specific tests of the executive system
- Experimental procedures
- Analysis of task completion for nonspecific tests or activities

Specific Tests for Evaluation of Executive Functions

There are several standardized tests that are specifically designed to assess executive functions. These include sorting, category, and maze tests, all of which examine planning ability. Two of the most common classification and sorting tests are the Halstead Category Test (Halstead, 1947) and the Wisconsin Card-Sorting Test (WCST) (Grant & Berg, 1948). Both of these tests require that the patient utilize examiner feedback regarding whether or not the correct sorting principle is used to classify the test stimuli. The WCST has an added feature—once the patient has correctly indentified one way of classifying the test cards, the examiner switches the sorting principle, and the patient must deduce the new rule. This addition demands that the patient shift cognitive sets.

The research examining whether the above tests are particularly sensitive to deficits in frontal lobe functioning is equivocal. The ability to group and categorize is intact in some but not all frontal lobe patients. Most of the research does support that such patients have difficulty performing category tasks that require shifting; they tend to demonstrate difficulty maintaining correct responses to a particular sorting principle, and they frequently perseverate on erroneous responses, showing that they do not incorporate feedback very well (Milner, 1964). In general, sorting tests appear to be sensitive to frontal lobe damage, although they do not necessarily indicate damage to this region. Diffuse brain damage may produce similar difficulties. Thus, the clinician needs to examine whether or not patients perform poorly on these types of tests and relatively well on other "nonfrontal" measures. Also, even if patients do not show impairment on sorting tasks, impairments in executive functions should not be ruled out, and further tests should be administered.

Tests requiring solution of a maze are also a common measure of frontal lobe involvement. The Porteus Maze Test (Porteus, 1950) is the best known measure of this type. The patient is presented with a series of mazes that increase in difficulty. The task is to find the most direct route from beginning to end without encountering dead ends or violating boundaries of the maze. The patient cannot lift the pencil while tracing the route, and if an error is committed, the same maze is presented for another trial. The test measures visuospatial planning ability. As with the aforementioned sorting and category tests, the Porteus Maze appears to be sensitive to executive functions, given relative lack of damage in other cognitive areas.

Experimental Procedures

There are several tasks originally used for research on frontal lobe pathology that have been adopted as measures of executive functions. One such procedure is the Tower of London Puzzle (Shallice, 1982) which requires sequencing and planning. It consists of three pegs of different lengths and three differently colored rings. The subjects must move the rings from an initial starting position to a specified end position in the fewest moves possible. Subnormal performance is believed to reflect a specific deficit in planning.

Believing that more structured neuropsychologic testing may not be sensitive to deficits in initiation and goal-directed behavior, Lezak (1983) advocates the use of unstructured tasks in the assessment of executive functions. In her Tinkertoy Test, the patient is presented with dowels and rods that fit together and is asked to construct a structure. The product is scored for the number of pieces used and for its complexity (e.g., whether it is three-dimensional or has moving parts). By analyzing the manner is which the subject builds the structure, the examiner can evaluate initiation and planning ability.

Although the clinical value of such procedures has yet to be established, they appear to hold some potential for testing executive functions. Much work remains to be done, however, in the standardization and norming of these procedures.

Analysis of Task Completion

Often tests that have been designed for other purposes or tasks and are not standard neuropsychologic measures may be adapted to measure executive functions. Assessment in this form usually involves a qualitative evaluation approach in which the examiner evaluates the process of task completion for any sign of decreased executive functions. Stuss and Benson (1986) offer the use of analogies as an example. Luria (1969) indicates that frontal lobe patients do not have difficulty with the simple abstraction ability required to complete basic analogy problems such as, "father is to mother as boy is to _____." However, he points out, these patients will have difficulty if an automatic or overlearned response is not known or if a previous response must be overcome. Analysis of error responses can show a tendency to revert to familiar associations and thus indicate frontal pathology. Patients with frontal damage also show difficulty on block design tests (e.g., the Block Design subtest from the WAIS-R) in the absence of any primary impairment in visual processing. They have a tendency to pay selective attention to the most salient features of the design and correctly reproduce the inside design but modify the external configuration (Goodglass & Kaplan, 1979). They may also demonstrate specific difficulty with planning or with self-monitoring and neglect to compare their model with the original. Again, careful analysis of the process of responding is important to capture these qualitative indices of executive function impairment.

Another informal measure of executive functions is to provide patients with a multistep task in which success depends on intact executive functions and to observe their performance. For example, a patient might be asked to cook a dish, plan an inpromptu event, or organize a cupboard. Use of a standardized scoring system such as the one described later in this chapter by Boyd (1987) might facilitate collection of quantitative data from these tasks and help document executive function ability.

TREATMENT OF EXECUTIVE FUNCTION IMPAIRMENT

The guiding treatment principle in the rehabilitation of executive functions involves *structure*. This applies both to retraining executive functions and to teaching compensation for deficits in this area. Organization and structure appear to be important variables for all executive functions. Anticipation, goal selection, initiation, planning, self-monitoring, and use of feedback all incorporate some degree of organized, purposeful behavior. In rehabilitation, clinicians first identify which of the functions appear deficient and then provide the structure necessary for practicing them successfully. (See principles of the process-specific approach to cognitive rehabilitation outlined in Chapter 3.) If the deficit does not appear to be amenable to treatment, the clinician may structure the environment or modify situational variables to compensate for the problem rather than continue with actual retraining methods. For example, if a patient had difficulty starting activities (i.e., an initiation deficit) that was resistant to treatment, the clinician might implement an external cuing system such as an alarm or light system in the work or living setting that would trigger the patient to engage in target activities. Thus, the structuring of exercises that activate specific executive functions and/or the structuring of the environment to compensate for deficit functioning in this area are critical to the remediation of these important functions.

A Self-Instructional Approach

Although there is a dearth of information in the literature pertaining to the rehabilitation of executive functions, there are several initial reports of techniques that appear to have potential for addressing impairments in executive functions. One such study was conducted by Cicerone and Wood (1987). These authors reported successful treatment of a patient who exhibited impaired planning ability and poor self-control 4 years after closed head injury. The rehabilitation technique involved a self-instructional procedure that required the patient to verbalize a plan of behavior before and during execution of the training task. Gradually, overt verbalization was faded. The training task was a modified version of the Tower of London Puzzle.

Training in the self-instructional technique involved three distinct phases. In the first phase, the patient was instructed to verbalize out loud each move he was going to make and the reason for the move. He then verbalized each move while actually performing it (overt self-guidance). The next phase was exactly the same except the client was told to whisper rather than verbalize aloud (faded overt self-cuing). Finally, in the last phase, the client was told to perform the task again, but to talk to himself (covert internalized self-monitoring).

In their report, the authors also noted the importance of generalization training to ensure transfer of treatment effects to everyday behavior. The following procedure for promoting generalization was implemented subsequent to the above three-stage training procedure. The client was presented with a structured interpersonal problem and asked to solve it applying principles learned in the self-instructional training. Emphasis was placed on real-life problems and ways of using the treatment strategy outside the clinical context.

The success of these procedures was evaluated through (1) pre- and postadministration of neuropsychologic tests thought to be sensitive to executive functions and (2) assessment of generalization of the principles to functioning in everyday tasks. The results clearly supported the clinical efficacy of verbal mediation training for treating executive functions. (The authors noted that generalization of training occurred only after direct, extended training using real-life situations.) Although this is only one case study, the Cicerone and Wood (1987) procedure does provide a training model for patients who exhibit poor planning.*

The Executive Function Route-Finding Task (EFRT) developed by Boyd, Sautter, Bailey, Echols, and Douglas (1987) is also designed to target frontal lobe functions. Route finding is highly dependent on the integration of information and the selection and execution of cognitive plans; it thereby provides a relevant training (or assessment) task in which to target executive functions. The authors initially conducted a pilot study in which they observed over 200 patients' route-finding behavior. They gave the patients open-ended instructions, indicating that they were to find the location of a particular office on the hospital campus in as efficient a manner as possible and that the examiner could not give them any cues but would accompany them. In their observations, they authors noted four distinct approaches to

---

*Luria (1981) also supports the use of verbal mediation. He suggests that the formulation of a plan and execution of corresponding behaviors is based on the verbal self-regulation of volunteer activity in a form of "inner speech."

route finding. One they called the "wandering aimlessly approach"; this was nondirected, nonsystematic walking around the facility. Another was a "trial-and-error method" characterized by continuous guessing and a gradual process of elimination. The "step-by-step approach" suggested that patients were recognizing their limitations. These patients systematically narrowed in on the target location by asking for information limited to the next closest location so that they did not tax their information-processing system with too much data to remember. Finally, there were those patients who used a "strategy approach" in which they took notes, asked for a map, or performed some other higher level strategy to maximize their chances for successful route finding.

The EFRT is a route-finding task like the one used in the pilot study and rates performance on the following parameters: (1) Task Understanding, (2) Incorporation of Information Seeking, (3) Retaining Directions, (4) Error Detection, (5) Error Correction, and (6) On-Task Behavior. (The second, fourth, fifth, and sixth parameters directly relate to the executive functions of planning, self-monitoring, and use of feedback.) Contributory problems related to emotional, interpersonal, communication, and perceptual barriers are recorded to note any variables that might confound the direct testing of executive functions.

The EFRT utilizes a unique cuing system that might be applied to any task that tests executive functions. The cuing is divided into nonspecific and specific cues. *Nonspecific cues* are used to remind the patient to self-monitor. An example might be, "What should you do now?" A *specific cue* provides information relevant to how actually to execute the task. These two cue levels provide an excellent hierarchy for training executive functions. The ability to self-monitor and the ability to incorporate feedback correspond to the constellation of executive functions necessary for planning and executing a task (see task protocol in Appendix A). Although this task has yet to be standardized and to undergo efficacy studies, it provides a useful initial procedure and protocol for clinicians attempting to retrain executive functions.

Currently, there is no available overall treatment approach to assist individuals with the broad range of executive function deficits exhibited in so many victims of traumatic brain injury. There are a few descriptions of isolated procedures as previously described, but these do not address the full range of executive functions. What is lacking is a theoretical model with associated treatment tasks backed by empirical research. The aforementioned procedures provide useful beginnings and assist with task development, but they are not derived from an overall model of the executive system.

The next section presents a model for conceptualizing executive functions; it provides a schema for organizing assessment and treatment activities. Empirical support for these training techniques is still lacking. Currently, the only available support is from case studies, one of which is presented at the end of this chapter.

A MODEL FOR THE ASSESSMENT AND TREATMENT OF EXECUTIVE FUNCTIONS

Sohlberg and Geyer (1986) developed the Executive Function Behavioral Rating Scale based on a model of executive functions useful for the conceptualization of the full range of frontal lobe behaviors (see Appendix B). The development process began with an examination of available literature on frontal lobe functions to establish the theoretical basis for the model. Second, a two-year study of the disorders in executive functions manifested in patients who had sustained traumatic brain injury was conducted. The greatest impetus for the development of the scale stemmed from the authors' frustration with the lack of a comprehensive method for approaching problems in executive functions. They noted that problems in this area were often what kept patients from realizing maximum levels in independent living and vocational pursuit.

The model consists of three major treatment and assessment areas:

- The Selection and Execution of Cognitive Plans
- Time Management
- Self-Regulation

The first area, the Selection and Execution of Cognitive Plans, includes those behaviors and processes required for initiating and completing purposeful, goal-directed activity. Much of its theoretical support is derived from the case-study literature discussed in the initial portion of this chapter. The second area, Time Management, includes abilities related to the understanding, awareness, and regulation of activity according to time constraints. The need for this arose from the observation that patients' poor time management was often part of the complex of decreased executive functioning and frequently resulted in an inability to pursue meaningful vocational activity. The last area, Self-Regulation, emphasizes those behaviors in the social–emotional realm that affect adequate executive functions. Each of these three main areas has corresponding subcomponents. They are described in the next section.

Selection and Execution of Cognitive Plans

This area has six subcomponents. These comprise the behaviors required to select, execute, and complete purposeful goal-directed activity. They are:

1. *Knowledge of appropriate steps:* In order to complete a plan, individuals must have some knowledge of the appropriate steps to be taken whether or not they initiate and follow through with the corresponding activity. This area refers to the simple awareness of the range of steps involved in a multicomponent activity.
2. *Sequencing:* In addition to knowing the correct steps, an individual must be able to order them appropriately.
3. *Initiation:* It is not uncommon for an individual with significant impairments in executive function to sit quietly without apparent interest in or curiosity about the environment until someone specifically directs him or her to do something. Thus, initiation is an important part of carrying out goal-directed activity.
4. *High-level organization skills:* This subcomponent refers specifically to planning ability and the capacity to orchestrate a multistep, multicomponent scheme.
5. *Repair:* An essential feature of executive functions is the ability to revise a plan or develop alternatives in the face of new information.
6. *Speed of response:* In order for goal completion to be functional, it must be accomplished within a reasonable time (this will, of course, vary among activities).

Time Management

Time Management refers to the ability to judge units of time accurately and regulate behavior according to time constraints. It consists of the following four subcomponents:

- *Time estimation:* This refers to judgments of time. Often, persons with frontal lobe damage have difficulty estimating the amount of time that has elapsed.
- *Creating time schedules:* This is the capacity to generate an accurate and realistic time schedule for activities to be completed.
- *Performance of scheduled activities:* It is important not only to have the capacity to plan a timetable appropriately but also to be able to execute a plan within given time constraints.
- *Repair:* This is the ability to revise a time schedule effectively when new information is presented.

Self-Regulation

Self-Regulation refers to the ability to utilize internal and external feedback to control the variety and quality of behaviors exhibited. It has four subcomponents:

- *Awareness:* This is the ability to make insightful statements about one's own or others' behavior as well as to modify behavior in response to internal and external feedback.
- *Impulse control:* This is the capacity for reflective, logical behavior. Impulse control is demonstrated when there is an absence of disinhibition or "acting before thinking."
- *Perseveration:* Perseveration refers to inappropriate, repetitious behaviors. A person who does not exhibit this problem will demonstrate an appropriate variety of behaviors.
- *Environmental dependency:* This problem is exhibited when an individual demonstrates mechanical, automatic, or reflexive behavior in response to the environment. For example, individuals who are environmentally dependent or "stimulus bound" may automatically fill a glass of water or take a drink when passing by a faucet, whether or not they are thirsty. The person who does not have this problem would exhibit consistent, appropriate, and autonomous behavior relative to each particular setting.

The *Executive Functions Behavioral Rating Scale,* based on the preceding model, is designed to be used by a clinician who would assess and treat cognitive impairments in this area. The assessment protocol is presented in Appendix B.

In considering clinical treatment of executive function problems, the schedule of therapy is important. The remediation of executive functions requires intensive practice of appropriate behaviors; this implies consistent and regular remediation sessions. Regular contact over a number of sessions is also required for assessment.

On the rating scale, the clinician rates each of the subcomponents on a 1-to-5 "severity of impairment" scale in which 1 indicates a profound degree of impairment and 5 indicates normal functioning. Usually a clinician needs to create the opportunity to observe the patient performing multistep activities in multiple settings. For example, the clinician might ask the client to perform a two-step errand in the hospital or community or to complete the route-finding task described earlier in this chapter. In observing behavior on these and other tasks under varying conditions, the clinician would begin to acquire an adequate understanding of the status of the individual's executive functions. At this point, the Executive Functions Behavioral Rating Scale would be filled out. The authors recommend that a second clinician work with the patient (or perhaps obtain the information by interviewing a family member) in order to gather interrater reliability measures. The clinician can then target those areas that both parties deem to be significantly impaired.

Treatment is then carried out through tasks corresponding to the different subcomponent abilities of the model. Task descriptions for several sample treatment activities are outlined in the next section. Corresponding task protocols and data-collection sheets are presented in Appendix C.

SELECTION AND EXECUTION OF COGNITIVE PLANS

Listing-Steps Activity

This is a simple task to assist the patient with the knowledge of appropriate steps in a multicomponent activity. It addresses cognitive knowledge and is not concerned with active demonstration of a task. The client lists the steps involved in an activity and is scored plus/minus on the completeness of the list that is generated. (A sample of multistep tasks and scoresheet is provided in Appendix C.)

Sequencing Activity

The same task and data collection sheet for the Listing-Steps Activity can be used with the additional requirement that the steps be ordered properly.

Initiation of Conversation

In this task, the patient is told that he or she will be practicing initiating conversation. The patient is provided with samples of how to carry out this activity. For example, the clinician might provide a list of typical phrases that are useful for initiating conversations (e.g., How is it going today? What are you doing this weekend? What hobbies do you have?) as well as sample conversational situations (e.g., sitting at a cafeteria table in the hospital or waiting for group therapy to begin). The clinician then chooses a situation in which this behavior will be monitored (e.g., accompanying the patient to a cafeteria or engaging the patient in one-to-one conversation) and then gathers data on the Initiation-of-Conversation scoresheet. Analogous initiation activities are easily developed for other behaviors. The important steps are first to increase the patient's awareness of the initiation problem and then to provide structured opportunities to practice the initiation of activity.

Errand Completion

This task addresses both initiation and organization skills. The patient is given an errand either within the hospital or in the community (see sample errand list). The patient is then scored on his or her ability to complete the errand. Additional training in such strategies as recording the errand in whatever memory system is being used (e.g., To Do list in the memory notebook) may be necessary. This exercise provides the opportunity for the patient to initiate, plan, and organize activities. It will, of course, be important for the clinician to organize errands hierarchically from easiest to hardest and to address problem areas as they arise for individuals.

Group Planning Activity

This activity is designed to move from hypothetical planning to actually carrying out the planning for a real-life activity. It targets on high-level organization skills. The Group Planning scenarios provide sample situations for which a patient might make a planning scheme. Initially, a patient can write or dictate the steps and tasks involved in planning a particular activity. Once a patient has mastered this stage, he or she is provided with the opportunity and resources to carry out a plan. The clinician needs to be creative in providing opportunities that meet the constraints of the particular work setting. For example, if a clinician is working one-on-one in a private practice, he or she might suggest that the patient plan the order of therapy tasks for the next session and arrange for refreshments. In a group setting, the clinician can ask the patient to plan an activity for the group. Again, a hierarchic organization from simple to more elaborate planning is important in order to increase the level of planning ability systematically. Data collection pertaining to the ability to plan hypothetical and/or real activities is scored on the Group Planning chart.

Planning/Repair Activity

The above planning activity is repeated for this task, but the clinician provides an obstacle that forces the patient to modify the plan. Again, this is done in a therapy format that moves from hypothetical situations to actual tasks. For example, if the patient was planning a hypothetical surprise party, the clinician might announce that the recipient was sick on the day of the party and inquire as to how the plan should be revised. In a real-life task, if the patient were organizing refreshments, for example, the clinician might say (after the planning had been done) that he or she was allergic to the particular food that had been planned. Of course it takes creativity and ingenuity to adapt to the specific cognitive level and environmental variables for each patient/clinician situation, but the provision of structured opportunities to plan and revise goal-directed activity can result in improved executive functions.

TIME MANAGEMENT

All of the preceding tasks are designed to give the patient an opportunity to practice planning and executing goal-directed activity. Since decreasing amounts of structure are provided as the executive system improves, the patient becomes more independent. Another important feature is the use of naturalistic tasks that promote carryover to real-life behaviors. Similar therapy principles hold true for training Time Management, an equally critical part of executive functions. Below are two sample tasks that address this area.

Time Estimation

An important component of Time Management is the ability to gauge the passage of time accurately. This can be practiced in both a single- (without distractions) or dual-task (with intervening distractions) format. The patient is told to keep track of a specified number of minutes and to inform the therapist when the target amount of time has elapsed. In the intervening time period, the patient can either do other therapy activities (distractor paradigm) or simply sit quietly (nondistractor format). The clinician collects data on the time estimation scoresheet as shown in Appendix C.

Scheduling Activity

In this activity, the patient is given a worksheet adapted to his or her particular ability level (such as the schedule worksheet in Appendix C). The patient is then provided with a number of therapy tasks to do in a particular time period. The patient schedules activities with appropriate time allowances and then tries to stick to the outlined schedule and complete the activities within the designed time frame. The clinician collects relevant data on the scheduling chart (shown in Appendix C) to mark progress and get information regarding problem areas.

SELF-REGULATION

The last main area of executive functions, Self-Regulation, is usually treated with various behavior modification programs charting desirable and/or undesirable behaviors. The patient is initially provided with examples and feedback to increase awareness of target areas and then receives structured feedback whereby less and less cuing is provided. It is most clinicians' experience that persons with frontal lobe damage have limited insight into their problems and require explicit behavioral objectives, which are outlined with structured cuing systems in order to understand and progress in therapy. A sample task for the first subcomponent of self-regulation, awareness, is presented below.

Awareness Task

The patient is informed of the particular behavior (either desirable or undesirable) that he or she has a tendency to exhibit. The patient is then told to mark a piece of paper every time he or she exhibits the behavior during a designated time frame. This recording can be done during a spontaneous conversation, in a one-on-one session, or during a group therapy session. The clinician simultaneously keeps track of the behavior, and the patient's awareness is increased by comparing his or her observations to those of the clinician.

The tasks reviewed above represent a few samples of therapy activities that can target important objectives within the executive function system.* They illustrate the types of activities that are effective in increasing executive functions. They have the advantage of being based on a comprehensive model of executive functions, such that specific goal areas can be examined and targeted. Patients with poor executive functions need to be provided with the opportunities to practice all three functional areas: to select and execute cognitive plans, to meet given time constraints, and to demonstrate appropriate self-regulation in order to be able to carry out the tasks.

As discussed in Chapter 3 on the Process-Specific Approach to cognitive rehabilitation, a clinician must hierarchically organize tasks, repetitively administer the exercises that target the same type of processing, and concurrently take objective and subjective data to record information on performance.

In summary, tasks such as those presented allow a patient to successfully initiate and complete goal-directed behaviors. The belief is that this repetitive activation of target executive functions will result in improved ability in the corresponding frontal lobe behaviors. As stressed in the report by Cicerone and Wood (1987), direct training and generalization to real-life situations are important for achieving functional transfer of learning.

COMPENSATION

For some patients whose executive functions are severely impaired or for whom therapy is not successful, training in compensatory strategies or environmental modification may be the most appropriate approach for

---

*For more information regarding other tasks, interested readers should contact the authors.

accommodating the impairment. There is some support in the literature for this. Luria (1963) remarked on the benefits of a behavioral approach for managing executive function deficits. He also advocated modification of the work environment such that behavior is directed by another person or setting and does not depend on intact executive functions (e.g., working in a product assembly line). Craine (1982) recommended setting up a daily schedule that may be memorized and that becomes automatic after training, thereby eliminating the demand on the executive system. External cuing systems and predictable work environments involving repetitive structured tasks might facilitate successful functioning despite poor executive functions. In a sense, when designing compensatory strategies, the clinician needs to orchestrate the environment so that it can act as the patient's frontal lobes, the functioning of which remains impaired.

Case Study

To date, approximately eight patients have completed treatment using the assessment and treatment model described in this chapter, and all have shown corresponding improvement in executive functions in naturalistic settings. The following is a case study of one of these eight patients and provides a representative example. J.K. is a 30-year-old male who sustained a closed head injury in a motor vehicle accident. He was a patient at Good Samaritan Hospital's Center for Cognitive Rehabilitation, a postmedical day-treatment brain injury program. At the time of treatment, he was 13 months post-injury. Demographic and neuropsychological findings from testing completed 1 week prior to the initiation of the executive function treatment are displayed in Table 10.1. Prior to his accident, J.K. owned a factory and was a successful businessman. School records indicate he was of average or above-average intelligence.

A CT scan performed 2 weeks after the subject's accident revealed multiple focal hemorrhages in both frontal lobes, consistent with a white matter shearing injury. Behaviorally, J.K. exhibited a restricted range of affect and appeared apathetic, without motivation or drive. He initiated little movement of any kind. He rarely initiated conversation or exhibited body movements while talking or listening to conversation (little eye contact or adjustment of body to indicate participation in a conversation as well as reduced initiation of verbal behavior). In addition to poor initiation, J.K. had great difficulty with sequencing and planning abilities. He was unable to plan hypothetically the steps for even simple activities such as making a cup of tea (which he was accustomed to drinking). Substantial problems in self-monitoring and use of feedback were also noted. The patient was unable to detect obvious errors in performance on simple math problems independently but easily noted them when they were pointed out. Overall, the patient was judged to have severe impairments in the full range of executive functions. J.K. received intensive daily treatment in the

TABLE 10.1. Neuropsychologic and Demographic Data for Subject JK

Age	38
Sex	Male
Education (years)	16
Time post-onset (months)	13
Etiology	Closed head injury
Preinjury vocational status	Owned a small business
WAIS-R	
Verbal IQ	90
Performance IQ	73
Full-scale IQ	81
Wechsler Memory Scale	
Paragraph recall:	
immediate/delayed	5/2
Design reproduction:	
immediate/delayed	8/6
Digits (forward/backward)	4/3
Wisconsin Card-Sorting Test	
Number of categories completed	0
Percentage perseverative errors	30

areas of Selection and Execution of Cognitive Plans, Time Management, and Self-Regulation. After 6 months of targeted remediation in executive functions, he was able to perform the following:

Conduct a meeting at his factory and keep adequate notes using structured forms with spaces for writing down "new business" and "old business."

Independently initiate and keep appointments for speech therapy, his health club, and social dinners.

Plan a birthday party for his best friend with minimal assistance.

The area that improved most significantly was initiation ability. Planning, including the ability to "repair" or adjust plans, remained the most impaired area and the least responsive to remediation. Overall, practice in initiation, planning, and organizing activities, managing time variables, and increasing awareness of deficits resulted in substantial gains in executive functions. J.K. successfully returned to work as a manager in his own factory with a special supported work system whereby a colleague provided additional structure as needed. J.K. also went from having 24-hour attendant care to living independently in his own house with weekly assistance for money management, yard work, and heavy housekeeping (e.g., cleaning of floors and windows).

SUMMARY

The chapter began with a discussion of the frontal lobes, which house the executive functions. These anterior structures constitute a huge portion of the cerebral cortex and are located just behind the forehead. They are the most recently developed part of the brain in an evolutionary sense and are the latest to develop in the maturing individual. It has been well established that this region has rich connections to many other parts of the brain, but only in recent years has the importance of the frontal lobes begun to be appreciated. Research correlating frontal lobe functions with specific localization sites has not revealed clear-cut relationships.

Clinically, it is accepted that the frontal lobes play a critical role in controlling emotional and psychosocial behaviors and in regulating executive functions. Frontal lobe damage may result in psychoemotional disturbances such as apathy, disinhibition, restricted affect, and disorders in awareness and in damage to executive functions, which allow human beings to accomplish goal-directed activities such as anticipation, goal selection, initiation, self-monitoring, use of feedback, and goal completion. Impairment in one or all of these abilities may be present in spite of intact intellectual skills. People who have executive function impairments are unable to put their intelligence to work without assistance; thus, every aspect of cognitive functioning is affected.

There are different approaches available for the assessment of executive functions. One includes specific tasks for evaluating executive functions—including sorting, category, and maze tests—all of which require planning ability. Adoption of experimental procedures originally designed for research purposes has been another approach. The *Tinkertoy Test* and *Tower of London* Puzzle are examples. Finally, analysis of task completion—either with tests originally designed for other purposes or with situations presented by the clinician for observational purposes—have been utilized.

Structure is an extremely important treatment principle in the remediation of executive function impairments. Two types of training tasks were presented. One involved a verbal self-instructional technique and the other a route-finding exercise.

One model for executive function was presented in response to the need for a more comprehensive model that incorporates the full range of executive functions and provides an organization schema for test, assessment, and treatment activities. This model has three main components: the selection and execution of cognitive plans, time management, and self-regulation. A behavioral rating scale and sample treatment tasks were reviewed. Case study evidence was also provided with an acknowledgment of the lack of experimental efficacy studies supporting executive function treatment. Finally, the need for environmental modification and compensation in addition to retraining was discussed.

STUDY QUESTIONS

1. How is the importance of the frontal lobes reflected in their neuroanatomy?
2. Why do we consider the frontal lobes to contribute to the uniqueness of the human species?
3. What are executive functions, and how do they relate to other areas of cognition?
4. What are some of the psychoemotional problems that commonly correspond to frontal lobe pathology?
5. What are the three most common ways of evaluating executive functioning?
6. Describe the EFRT. How might the cuing system developed for this task be utilized for other executive-function-training exercises?
7. Describe the three-pronged model of executive functions including Selection and Execution of Cognitive Plans, Time Management, and Self-Regulation.
8. How can the above treatment model be implemented according to the Process-Specific Approach to cognitive rehabilitation?

REFERENCES

Blumer, D., & Benson, D. F. (1975). Personality changes with frontal and temporal lobe lesions. pp. 151–170. In D. F. Benson & D. Blumer (Eds), *Psychiatric aspects of neurologic diverse* (Vol 1). New York: Gyvne & Stratton.

Boyd, T. M., Sautter, S., Bailey, M. B., Echols, L. D., & Douglas, J. W. (1987, February). *Reliability and validity of a measure of everyday problem solving.* Paper presented at the annual meeting of the International Neuropsychological Society. Washington, DC.

Cicerone, K. D., & Wood J. C. (1987). Planning disorder after closed head injury: A case study. *Archives of Physical Medicine and Rehabilitation, 68:* 111–115.

Courville, C. B., (1937). *Pathology of the central nervous system, Part 4.* Mountain View, CA: Pacific Publishers.

Craine, S. F. (1982). The retraining of frontal lobe dysfunction. In L. E. Trexler (Ed), *Cognitive rehabilitation: Conceptualization and intervention* (pp. 239–262). New York: Plenum.

Goldman-Rakic, P. S. (1984). The frontal lobes: Uncharted provinces of the brain. *Trends in Neuroscience, 7:* 425–429.

Goodglass, H., & Kaplan, E. (1979). Assessment of cognitive deficit in the brain-injured patient. In M. S. Gazzaniga (Ed). *Handbook of behavioral neurology* (Vol. 2., pp. 3–22). New York: Plenum.

Grant, D. A., & Berg, E. A. (1984). A behavioral analysis of reinforcement and ease of shifting to new responses in a Weigl-type card-sorting problem. *Journal of Experimental Psychology, 38:* 404–411.

Halstead, W. C. (1947). *Brain and intelligence.* Chicago: University of Chicago Press.

Harlow, J. M. (1868). Recovery after severe injury to the head. *Publication of the Massachusetts Medical Society*, 2: 327–346.

Lezak, M. D. (1983). *Neuropsychological assessment* (2nd ed). New York: Oxford University Press.

Luria, A. R. (1963). *Restoration of function after brain injury*. New York: Pergamon Press.

Luria, A. R. (1966). *Human brain and psychological processes*. New York: Harper & Row.

Luria, A. R. (1973). *The working brain*. New York: Basic Books.

Luria, A. R. (1981). *Language and cognition*. Washington, DC: Winston.

Luria, A. R. (1969). Frontal lobe syndrome. In P. J. Vinker & G. W. Bruyn (Eds), *Handbook of clinical neurology* (Vol. 2, pp. 725–767). Amsterdam: North Holland.

Milner, D. (1964). Some effects of frontal lobectomy in men. In J. M. Warren & A. Akert (Eds), *The frontal granular cortex and behavior* (pp. 313–334). New York: McGraw-Hill.

Nanta, W. J. N. (1973). Connections of the frontal lobe with the limbic system. In C. V. Lastinen & K. E. Livingston (Eds), *Surgical Approaches in Psychiatry* (pp. 303–314). Baltimore: University Park Press.

Porteus, S. D. (1950). *The Porteus Maze Test and intelligence*. Palo Alto, California: Pacific Books.

Shallice, T. (1982). Specific impairments of planning. In P. Broadbent & L. Weisknartz (Eds), *The Neuropsychology of Cognitive Function* (pp. 199–209). London: The Royal Society.

Sohlberg, M. M., & Geyer, S. (1986). *Executive Function Behavioral Rating Scale*. Paper presented at Whittier College Conference Series, Whittier, California.

Stuss, D. & Benson F. (1986). *The frontal lobes*. New York: Raven Press.

APPENDIX A: WOODROW WILSON REHABILITATION CENTER EXECUTIVE FUNCTION ROUTE-FINDING TASK

Client's name:_____ Date of evaluation:_____

Disability:__/__/__Examiner:_____

Instructions: "I am going to give you an exercise that involves your finding an unfamiliar office,_____. How you do this is up to you. I will go with you but cannot answer questions about how to find_____. I want you to do this exercise as quickly and efficiently as possible. Before you begin, I would like you to tell me what I have asked you to do."

I. Task understanding

1. Failure to grasp nature of task despite several elaborations.
2. Faulty understanding of important element requiring specific or explanatory cuing and elaboration (e.g., "How am I supposed to know where it is?")

3. Distorts peripheral detail requiring slight clarification or a nonspecific cue (e.g., "Can you tell me where it is?")
4. Shows a clear grasp or asks for clarification appropriately (e.g., "Can I get someone to take me there?"). Initiates task spontaneously.

II. Incorporation of information seeking

1. Aimless wandering.
2. Follows a hunch without gathering information first (unless shows prior knowledge of destination) or exhaustive door-to-door search.
3. Gathers information before commencing search, but without appraisal of information source.
4. Shows judgment in use of information sources (e.g., selects staff over clients; clarifies confusing directions; verifies information with another person).

III. Retaining directions (functional memory)

1. Continual forgetting of directions or name of destination and failure to use suggested means of compensating (e.g., note taking) unless cued repeatedly.
2. Needs repeated nonspecific cuing or provision of concrete strategy for coping with memory deficits.
3. Forgets detail(s) but compensates after nonspecific cue (e.g., "How might you keep yourself from forgetting the destination?")
4. Paraphrasing or clarification sufficient for remembering, or spontaneous compensation (e.g., note taking).

IV. Error detection (self-monitoring)

1. Continued errors without self-detection even after repeated examiner cues.
2. Some spontaneous awareness of errors, but more instances of cuing required.
3. Some cuing required, but more instances of spontaneous error detection shown.
4. Verifies correctness independently when appropriate; may exploit incidental information (e.g., signs) to prevent errors.

V. Error correction (troubleshooting)

1. Helpless or perseverative behavior.
2. Inefficient strategy (e.g., returns to original information source).
3. Seeks help immediately once aware of error.
4. Reasons efficiently (e.g., looks for signs; considers where he or she may have erred in following directions to self-correct independently).

VI. On-task behavior

1. Must be held to task in ongoing fashion (e.g., distractible, stimulus-bound).
2. Digression from task requiring cues to redirect attention to task needed.
3. Incidental behaviors (e.g., small talk) interfere with efficiency.
4. Any incidental behaviors (e.g., waving to a friend) do not hinder performance observably.

Contributory problems

Emotional
_____ Indifference, lack of effort
_____ Frustration, intolerance
_____ Self-criticism, depression
_____ Defensiveness
_____ Thought disturbance
_____ Euphoria, mania
_____ Other
_____
_____
_____

Interpersonal
_____ Self-consciousness, shyness
_____ Social skills
_____ Setting context for requested
        information
_____ Flirting
_____ Interrupting
_____ Other
_____
_____
_____

Communication
_____ Speech reception
_____ Expressive speech
_____ Reading ability
_____ Writing ability
_____ Other
_____
_____
_____

Perceptual
_____ Visual acuity
_____ Auditory acuity
_____ Right/left confusion
_____ Neglect
_____ Other visuospatial problem
_____
_____
_____

Motor
Manual limitations
Ambulation
Other comments:_____
_____
_____
_____
_____

Evaluation of overall independence

	Client's rating	Examiner rating	Overall
Extensive cuing required	—	—	—
Appreciable cuing required (Specific cues or several nonspecific cues)	—	—	—
Occasional nonspecific cuing required			
Independent of cuing	—	—	—

SCORING SUMMARY

Task understanding	1	2	3	4
Information seeking	1	2	3	4
Retraining directions	1	2	3	4
Error detection	1	2	3	4
Error correction	1	2	3	4
On-task behavior	1	2	3	4

Overall average _____

Rules for cuing

1. When to cue
   a. *A nonspecific cue* is given when client deviates from path approaching goal (not necessarily most direct) and passes up a subsequent opportunity for correction (e.g., sign, staff person, office doorway that might lead to information, path leading toward goal).
   b. *A specific cue* is given following a nonspecific cue after client fails to attempt correction or passes another opportunity for correction in doing so.
2. Nature of cues
   a. *A nonspecific cue* alerts the client to monitor performance (i.e., "Tell me what you need to do now.").
   b. *A specific cue* provides information on how to execute the task.

APPENDIX B: GOOD SAMARITAN HOSPITAL CENTER FOR COGNITIVE REHABILITATION EXECUTIVE FUNCTIONS BEHAVIORAL RATING SCALE

Selection and Execution of Cognitive Plans

The ability to *plan* and *follow through* with the necessary steps to achieve a desired goal.

1. Generation and selection of appropriate goals and methods

Unable to state appropriate goals and/or methods to accomplish goals	1 2 3 4 5 +--+--+--+--+	Able to spontaneously state appropriate goals and suitable methods for goal attainment

2. Initiation

Minimal spontaneous activity	1 2 3 4 5 +--+--+--+--+	Spontaneously takes goal-directed action in group and individual settings

3. *Sequencing*

	1	2	3	4	5	
Not able to order steps to complete familiar tasks			+--+--+--+--+			Temporal ordering of steps to complete familiar tasks intact

4. *High level of organizational skills*

	1	2	3	4	5	
Limited ability to complete multistep, multitasks activities			+--+--+--+--+			Ability to orchestrate multistep, multitask planning scheme

5. *Repair*

	1	2	3	4	5	
Unable to revise plan or develop alternatives			+--+--+--+--+			Able to revise plans given new information

6. *Speed of Response*

	1	2	3	4	5	
Unable to complete plan in a functional time frame			+--+--+--+--+			Completes plan in reasonable time frame

7. *Follow-through/ persistence*

	1	2	3	4	5	
Does not maintain effort on task, loses interest over time			+--+--+--+--+			Independently maintains effort until task is completed

Time Management

The ability to accurately judge the passage of units of time and regulate behavior in terms of time constraints.

1. *Time estimation*

	1	2	3	4	5	
Unable to gauge units of time accurately			+--+--+--+--+			Able to estimate units of time up to one hour

2. *Creating time schedules*

	1	2	3	4	5	
Unable to create an accurate time schedule for activities			+--+--+--+--+			Able to create a reasonable time schedule for daily activities

3. *Performance of scheduled activities*

	1	2	3	4	5	
Unable to carry out scheduled activities without external prompts			+--+--+--+--+			Able to carry out scheduled activities in a timely fashion

4. *Repair*

	1	2	3	4	5	
Unable to effectively revise time schedule when new information is presented			+--+--+--+--+			Able to revise plan and remain on schedule when new information is provided

Self-Regulation

The ability to utilize internal and external feedback to control the variety and quality of behaviors exhibited.

1. *Self-awareness*

   Makes no independent statements evaluating own behavior

   1 2 3 4 5
   +--+--+--+--+

   Spontaneously evaluates and discusses own behavior

2. *Behavioral self-management*

   Requires specific directions from others to modify behavior in familiar situations

   1 2 3 4 5
   +--+--+--+--+

   Spontaneously modifies own behavior to match diverse situations

3. *Impulse control*

   Unable to inhibit response to impulses

   1 2 3 4 5
   +--+--+--+--+

   Anticipates consequences of behavior and controls impulses accordingly

4. *Perseveration*

   Demonstrates inappropriate, repetitious behaviors

   1 2 3 4 5
   +--+--+--+--+

   Demonstrates appropriate variety of behaviors

5. *Enviromental dependency*

   Consistently exhibits mechanical, automatic, or reflexive behavior in response to the environment

   1 2 3 4 5
   +--+--+--+--+

   Exhibits consistent appropriate and autonomous behavior relative to the setting

6. *Social dependency*

   Seeks frequent reassurance and/or assistance from others on tasks within capabilities

   1 2 3 4 5
   +--+--+--+--+

   Only seeks reassurance/assurance after displaying significant independent effort

APPENDIX C: LISTING-STEPS ACTIVITY

State each of the steps involved to complete each task in detail. The order of steps is not important.

1. Making a can of soup
2. Carving a pumpkin
3. Putting up and decorating a Christmas tree
4. Shaving a beard
5. Making popcorn
6. Grocery shopping
7. Defrosting a freezer
8. Making hot chocolate
9. Changing an appointment
10. Frying an egg
11. Setting a watch
12. Writing a check
13. Getting ready for bed
14. Finding a job
15. Applying for a credit card
16. Planting a garden
17. Washing a car
18. Painting a house
19. Parking a car
20. Raking the leaves

Listing Steps Activity Data Collection Sheet

Format: Any order
In order
(Circle one)

Date	Activity	Was list complete? (+/–)	Were steps in proper order? (+/–)	Comments

Initiation of Conversation Score Sheet

Goal:

Date	Situation	Initiation	Cues	Comments

Independent Completion of Errands (One-Step Directions)

Date	Errand	Recorded in Things To Do	Task Completed Correctly?	Cross off To Do list	Comments

Sample Errand List

1. Go to the gift shop and see what the hours are.
2. Go to the cafeteria and see what the special is for lunch.
3. Go to Safeway and buy a _____.
4. Get a business card from a (travel agent, bank, etc.).
5. Find out the price for a hamburger at Cattin's
6. Buy three post-card stamps.
7. Get something free.

8. Get something printed.
9. Get a travel brochure.
10. Find the price of jeans at Penney's.
11. Find the price of aspirin at Beall's or Safeway.
12. Get a bus schedule.
13. Find out the cost of a savings account at Rainier Bank.
14. Find out the brand name of a waterproof digital watch.
15. Find out the Saturday hours of a store or business.
16. Get income tax forms from the Post Office.
17. Find out the price of a model at the hobby shop.

Group Planning Scenarios

Task: Write out a plan for the following event. You are the event leader and can give jobs to other patients to do.

1. Plan a surprise birthday party for_____. The party will be next week. Staff and patients should attend.
2. Plan a graduation party for one of the patients. Make this a special event for that person.
3. Plan a Christmas party. Include some way to have a gift exchange that would not embarrass anyone.
4. Plan a barbecue for 10 people.

Group Planning Activity Data Collection Sheet

Date	Task real/ hypothetical	Time used to plan	Performance cues (note problems with sequencing, initiation, follow-through, and cues provided)

Time Estimation with Distractions Scoresheet

Date	Duration of time estimated	Clock (Y or N)	Distraction used	Response On time	Early	Late

Scheduling Worksheet

Date: _____
Time slot: _____
Tasks: _____
_____
_____
_____
_____

Plan

Time: Task   _/_/_Completed _____
                                                                    Time

_____ _____

Time: Task   _/_/_Completed _____
                                                                    Time

_____ _____

Time: Task   _/_/_Completed _____
                                                                    Time

_____ _____

Time: Task   _/_/_Completed _____
                                                                    Time

_____ _____

Time: Task   _/_/_Completed _____
                                                                    Time

_____ _____

Scheduling Chart

Date	Hours Planned	Time to plan	Ability to stay within schedule	Repair

Planning–Repair Activity Data Collection Sheet

Date	Task	Stage interrupted	Type of change	Responses/cues needed

Awareness Charting/Agreement

Date	Target behavior	# Times observed per_____unit of time	Patient's count	Agreement

11

Assessment and Treatment of Deficits in Reasoning and Problem Solving

A multitude of models and taxonomies are found in the literature describing the process of human reasoning and problem solving (e.g., Bourne, Dominowski, & Loftus, 1979; Luria, 1966a). Reasoning ability is a complicated area to define because this cognitive process depends on the intact functioning of other fundamental neuropsychologic processes. There are many possible contributing factors that may explain why a person is unable to solve a particular problem. Disruption of motivational systems, memory, attention, or visuospatial ability as well as impairment in primary reasoning/problem-solving processes can all weaken a person's ability to generate a successful solution to a prescribed problem. Discussion of reasoning/problem solving is further complicated by the fact that the nature of this capacity is defined by the particular activity that is targeted. Some problems, for example, require creative divergent production of solutions, whereas for others, successful solution demands a systematic convergent approach. Furthermore, problem-solving ability is a highly individualized function; people bring unique problem-solving styles to the problem situation.

All of the above factors contribute to the lack of well-established approaches to the treatment of reasoning deficits within the brain-injured population. Comparatively more attention has been devoted to other process areas such as memory, attention, and visual processing. Currently, there are no available theoretical frameworks on which to organize treatment of reasoning skills and very little empirical data to support treatment efficacy.

This chapter begins by describing some of the terms and related areas that make up the cognitive process of reasoning/problem solving and attempting to organize them in a framework useful for rehabilitation. Assessment and treatment of deficits in reasoning/problem-solving ability are reviewed in the latter portion of this chapter. Topics covered include concept formation, reasoning, problem solving, deductive reasoning, inductive reasoning, convergent thinking, divergent thinking, abstraction, core cognitive abilities, standardized neuropsychological tests, informal measures, generalization, and lack of efficacy studies.

WHAT IS REASONING AND PROBLEM-SOLVING ABILITY?

Higher level thinking in humans is the product of complex interactions among many cognitive functions. This section defines three categories of higher thinking: problem solving, reasoning, and concept formation. Such a division provides useful insights into cognitive theory, but it must be recognized as somewhat arbitrary.

Problem Solving

Problem-solving ability is perhaps the easiest area to understand since it directly relates to daily living. All of us actively engage in problem solving each day, whether in sequencing the steps of our morning routine as we get off to work or seeking out leisure activities such as crossword puzzles or chess. It is not difficult to imagine how impairment in the ability to solve problems could profoundly impact daily living.

Luria (1966b) describes problem solving as a special form of cognitive activity arising when a goal or problem is placed before a subject in certain conditions and no prepared solution is available. According to Luria, there are three phases of problem solving. The first is *strategy selection*. This preliminary phase involves the discovery of conditions, creation of hypotheses, and selection of strategies for generating a solution to the problem. The second two phases are executive in nature and consist of the *application of operations* and the *evaluation of outcomes*.

Vygotski (1934) and Bruner (1957) support Luria's conceptualization. They also view problem solving as an investigatory activity in which conditions are analyzed and the central relationships used to formulate hypotheses are identified. These hypotheses determine the course of subsequent reasoning involved in the carrying out and evaluation of operations.

In a similar and somewhat more current approach, Bourne and colleagues (1979) present problem solving as a multicomponent process. Like Luria (1966a, b), these authors conceptualize problem solving as a three-stage process. They identify the stages as *preparation, production,* and *judgment*. The preparation stage includes activities oriented toward the construction of a representation of the problem and the determination of constraints imposed on the solution of the problem. The production phase is geared toward generating possible solutions by such activities as retrieving previously acquired information from memory or scanning the environment for available information and then operating on the content. The judgment phase allows a decision to be made as to whether the problem was adequately solved or whether more work is required. This is done by comparing the generated solution with the solution criteria. The authors note that although much of the processing may be serial in nature (i.e., preparation activity followed by production and judgment processes, respectively), complex problem solving requires considerable recycling through the three stages.

Deficits in Problem Solving

As considered thus far, problem solving relates closely to the executive functions described in Chapter 10. In that chapter, deficits in such functions as anticipation, goal selection, planning, initiation, self-regulation, and use of feedback (all of which are essential for the completion of goal-directed activity) were shown to be frequently associated with damage to the frontal regions of the brain. Luria (1966a), for example, evaluated a number of patients with pathology to the frontal lobes of the brain and described the disturbances in their intellectual processes. He noted that patients were unable to analyze the conditions of a problem systematically and select out the important connections and relationships. The system of cognitive operations that would normally lead to the solution of a problem appeared disintegrated; instead, isolated, fragmentary connections unrelated to a general plan were evident. Also typical of patients with frontal lobe lesions were the omission of the phase of preliminary investigation of conditions and constraints of the problems and a replacement of true intellectual operations by unrelated, impulsive actions. Goldstein (1944) and Halstead (1947) also examined patients with frontal lobe damage, and both noted lowering of the abstraction orientation (categorical behavior) and difficulty understanding logical relationships.

Although much work has been done relating problem-solving ability to the frontal regions of the brain (Levin, Benton, & Grossman, 1982), Luria (1966a) reminds us that complex mental processes are not localized to circumscribed areas of the cortex. Instead, higher mental processes exist as constellations of interrelated functional subsystems diffusely represented in the brain. Thus, significant disruption of any number of neurological systems can be responsible for decreased problem-solving ability. Prescribed neurological correlates for reasoning and problem-solving ability are difficult to envision (Levin et al., 1982).

Reasoning*

Reasoning is the branch of thinking that specifically concerns the drawing of inferences or conclusions from known or assumed facts. It essentially

---

*Definitions and descriptions of reasoning and concept formation were abstracted from Bourne et al. (1979), which provides an excellent overview of the theoretical basis of reasoning and problem-solving ability.

refs to the process of determining "what follows from what." There are three types of reasoning that have been extensively studied and that represent the spectrum of reasoning skills. These are syllogistic reasoning, proposition testing, and statistical reasoning.

Syllogistic reasoning refers to the process of relating premises to conclusions. It involves the examination of the internal consistency of an argument. It is a type of deductive reasoning. An example of a syllogistic argument might be the following: all mammals are covered with hair; a dog is a mammal; therefore, a dog is covered with hair. *Proposition testing* involves relating evidence to the truth or falseness of a statement or proposition. In the same metaphor, to test the proposition that a particular animal is a mammal, one might first identify whether it has hair.

Syllogistic reasoning and proposition testing are usually related to absolute standards of truth or falsehood. *Statistical reasoning,* on the other hand, concerns the treatment of uncertain information and deals with how a person interprets and uses uncertain information in drawing conclusions. In order to determine the number of domesticated dogs in a particular city, one would conduct a survey or review public records.

Logic is a *formal system* of reasoning and often serves as the standard against which human reasoning is evaluated. Since logic systems are the creation of human thinking, we know that people can and do reason in accordance with formal logic principles. However, it is important to note that people also deviate from logical reasoning. For example, it has been discovered that one of the reasons people make logical errors in syllogistic reasoning is that they fail to consider all the possible combinations of premises and accept an invalid conclusion because the contradicting combinations were not generated.

In studying human reasoning, it is important to understand how people reach their conclusions when they do not conform to the dictates of logic. Research has shown, for instance, that people have a tendency to confirm rather than disprove their hypotheses. Thus, when performing a reasoning task, they will be more likely to check whether their conclusion is consistent with the premises than to try and disprove it. This confirmation-seeking approach gives us insight into why people might arrive at invalid conclusions when reasoning out a problem.

Concept Formation

Concept formation is the capacity to analyze relationships between objects and their properties. The forming of a concept requires that an individual identify the critical features of instances of that concept and also determine how those features interrelate. The definition of a concept involves both features and the rules or relationships among those features. Rules are learnable components of concepts.

The basic format of concept formation tasks used in most experiments is inductive. The learner is given certain defining features of a concept and then provided with stimuli, some of which illustrate the concept and some of which do not. The learner categorizes each stimulus and receives feedback regarding the accuracy of the categorization. Each trial thus provides a learning opportunity because it gives examples and new information about the target concept. When the subject learns the defining characteristics and rules and can assign stimuli to appropriate categories without errors, it may be said that he or she has learned the concept.

Laboratory studies of concept formation are limited, however, because they have typically used arbitrary tasks in which concepts bear little resemblance to ordinary, natural concepts. Research on natural concepts suggests that their representation may take the form of a prototype or best example; membership in a natural category is evaluated in terms of how well an item matches the prototype. This seems to be true of a wide variety of concepts, from simple perceptual stimuli such as colors to semantic categories such as plants. Categorization reduces the vast numbers of stimuli in our world to a manageable size.

Deficits in concept formation are manifested by the adoption of a "stimulus-bound," or "concrete," approach to problem solving (Goodglass & Kaplan, 1979). A concrete attitude is characterized by the tendency to be bound to the stimulus properties of an activity and the inability to remove oneself from the immediate task. Persons with brain injury have a difficult time forming and utilizing superordinant categories, which is a manifestation of decreased concept formation ability. For example, they might have difficulty organizing a cupboard or drawer and grouping items in a logical fashion.

Rule difficulty is an important factor to consider when measuring concept formation. The degree of rule difficulty is heavily dependent on the subject's initial response tendencies. Difficulty of a given concept is a function of how many of the subject's initial tendencies are accurate and how many have to be changed. For example, an individual given a group of objects to classify will move rapidly to figure out the rule if it is based on gross visual features (e.g., color or size) rather than abstract properties (e.g., use of object or initial letter of name).

The division of higher level thinking into the categories of reasoning, problem solving, and concept formation, although somewhat arbitrary, illustrates some of the theoretical foundations in this area. These categories are derived from the multitude of studies performed in the field of cognitive and educational psychology investigating how people approach various reasoning and problem-solving activities. Again, these activities represent much integration and assimilation of other cognitive abilities and thus do not stand as discrete functions. The distinction between problem solving and reasoning, for example, is purely theoretical and mostly relates to how these entities have been studied. As mentioned in the initial portion of this chapter, reasoning and problem solving are best defined by the particular target problems or tasks; the nature of the problem-solving, reasoning, or concept formation skills that will be applied to a particular situation or activity will vary dependent on the specific task. In addition to illustrating the different subcomponents related to reasoning and problem solving, a general review of these three broad categories offers ideas for the assessment and treatment of impairments in reasoning and problem-solving ability.

CLINICAL MANIFESTATIONS OF DECREASED REASONING AND PROBLEM-SOLVING ABILITY

What are the clinical manifestations of reduced reasoning and problem-solving ability in the head-trauma population? Adamovich, Henderson, and Auerbach (1985) list the following high-level thought processes as subject to disruption following closed head injury: convergent thinking, divergent thinking, deductive reasoning, and inductive reasoning. These specific areas of impairment affect problem solving because patients tend to have a narrow perspective, which results in a concrete and incomplete analysis of problems. They do not take time to analyze problems and have difficulty deciding how to approach a problem. Overall, patients' ability to generate hypotheses and employ strategies is reduced.

Similarly, Prigatano (1986) lists the following cognitive dysfunctions related to problem solving and reasoning secondary to traumatic head injury: impairment of abstract attitude (tendency toward literal interpretation of information), impulsivity, confusion as to where to start solving a problem, difficulty sequencing information, and trouble learning from mistakes as well as successes.

Ben-Yishay and Diller (1983a) note impairments in the following parts of the complex they term "high-level or complex problem solving": convergent reasoning, divergent reasoning, and executive abilities. These authors also report that the head-injured population exhibits an inability to exercise good judgment regarding what is appropriate in different social situations. Similarly, Szekeres, Ylvisaker, and Halland (1985) delineate component skills of what they term "organizing processes" that are vulnerable to disruption following a head injury: analyzing, classifying, integrating sequences, identification of relevant features of objects and events, comparing similarities or differences, integrating concepts into propositions, and imposing organization on unstructured stimuli.

Goldstein and Levin (1987) divide deficits involved in reasoning and problem-solving ability into the following four categories: motivational disturbances, impairments in reasoning and concept formation, impairments in the productive aspect of thought, and impairments in cue utilization and the ability to shift response sets. They also indicate that deficits in problem-solving behavior can result from impairments of more fundamental aspects of attention and memory. In some patients, reasoning and general intellectual functioning may be intact, but the executive functions (as in the frontal lobe syndrome) are impaired. From a remediation standpoint, they argue that it is critical to conduct a detailed process analysis to determine where performance is breaking down and then to design programs that address the level and nature of impairment.

Goldstein and Levin's (1987) "levels of impairment" approach provides a useful model with which to view problem solving and reasoning. If disruption of problem-solving ability is attributable to impairments in "core deficits" such as memory or attentional disturbances, remediation programs specifically designed for these processes may be implemented. Similarly, remediation techniques for deficient executive functions (see Chapter 10) may be initiated when these represent the cause of a breakdown. Difficulties arise, however, when the primary impairment lies with the integration/assimilation processes. There is no theoretical model for conceptualizing the deficits in the highest-level skills involved in reasoning and problem solving that are manifested in patients who have suffered head trauma.

A review of the major clinical works in head injury reveals the following compilation, or master list, of cognitive skills directly related to reasoning and problem solving that are reported to be commonly disrupted in persons with head injury:

Convergent thinking	Recognition and analysis of information relevant to a central theme or main point.
Divergent thinking	Includes thought production and idea fluency; the generation of unique abstract concepts or hypotheses that deviate from known or standard concepts and ideas.
Deductive reasoning	The process of drawing conclusions based on premises or general principles; requires analysis that progresses from the whole situation to specific parts or features.
Inductive reasoning	Process of formulating solutions given information that leads to, but does not necessarily support, a general conclusion; requires an analysis of parts or details to formulate an overall gestalt or whole concept.
Abstract attitude	The ability to transcend the immediate environment, to appreciate different aspects of the situation or problem, and to think symbolically.
Sequencing	The ability to order information properly.
Classification	The ability to discriminate between relevant features of objects or concepts and to group them in categories appropriately.

This list suggests that persons who have sustained brain injury may potentially experience difficulty with all aspects of reasoning and problem-solving ability. As is discussed under assessment and treatment, the clinician's task is to identify which aspects are disrupted in individual patients and to implement specific remediation programs for target skill areas.

A Model of Reasoning/Problem Solving

Currently, descriptions of reasoning and problem-solving deficits in the head-injured population are restricted to a pathognomonic sign- or deficit-listing approach. Lists of impaired component processes of reasoning and problem solving such as those reviewed above are not adequate from a rehabilitation standpoint. Such lists are neither empirically based nor theoretically motivated. Usually they are generated from observations of brain-injured patients with a resultant mixture of neuropsychologic processes, psychosocial deficits, and behavioral problems that have no inherent validity other than that authors have observed them in their patients. What is lacking is an organizational structure for these deficit areas. From a remediation perspective, it is essential to have a conceptualization or framework on which to organize assessment and treatment activities. A review of the brain injury and cognitive psychology literature suggests the following four-pronged model of reasoning and problem solving ability (see Table 11.1): *reasoning skills, thought production, problem solving,* and *social comprehension and reasoning.*

The first component, *reasoning,* incorporates both the primary types of reasoning noted to be disrupted in the head-injury population and the fundamental skill areas of classification and sequencing. Most reasoning

---

TABLE 11.1. Model of Reasoning/Problem-Solving Ability

I. Reasoning
   A. Skill fundamentals (sequencing, classification)
   B. Deductive reasoning
   C. Inductive reasoning
   D. Convergent thinking

II. Thought Production
   A. Divergent thinking
   B. Abstraction ability

III. Problem Solving
   A. Strategy selection (i.e., identification of problem conditions and creation of solution hypotheses)
   B. Application of operations (i.e., applying strategies)
   C. Evaluation of outcome (comparing actual outcome with desired outcome)

IV. Social Comprehension and Judgment

---

therapy tasks can be classified into deductive reasoning, inductive reasoning, and convergent thinking.

The second area, *thought production,* refers to those skills involved in the generation of thought. Divergent thinking incorporates fluency or ease of producing multiple ideas as well as creativity or the capacity to generate novel ideas. Abstraction refers to the capacity to represent information symbolically.

The third component, *problem solving,* is broken down into the stages of preparation, production, and judgment, as discussed earlier. Problem-solving skills correspond to those executive functions involved in the selection and execution of cognitive plans (see Chapter 10). Impaired problem-solving ability may be the result of faulty reasoning skills or deficit thought production; this can be determined by examining the three stages separately.

The final category, *social comprehension and judgment,* is probably the least examined in brain injury literature. Many descriptions of the cognitive and psychosocial sequelae of head injury (e.g., Ben-Yishay & Diller, 1983a, b; Prigatano, 1986) mention problems related to poor judgment and decreased interpersonal skills. There is a gray zone, however, between clearly cognitive problems and clearly psychosocial deficits. Often individuals exhibit psychosocial problems that are really manifestations of cognitive problems. The category of social comprehension and judgment refers to the cognitive aspects of social judgment and reasoning, that is, the understanding of social situations. It does not describe action or behavior; rather, it involves knowing what is appropriate and inappropriate and being able to apply reasoning to social situations.

These four categories—reasoning, thought production, problem solving, and social comprehension and judgment—do not represent discrete or equivalent processes. There is much overlap among areas. For example, difficulty with divergent thinking (generating multiple ideas) will necessarily affect the first stage of problem solving, generating solutions. However, it is important to consider both categories. Recognizing which phase of problem solving is most disrupted and identifying the particular deficit thinking process, such as reduction of divergent thinking ability, allows the clinician to target the particular impaired subskill(s) responsible for a breakdown in the process.

The model thus serves as an organizational structure to guide assessment and treatment. It is comprehensive, incorporating the various components of reasoning, problem solving, and concept formation that are reported to be vulnerable to disruption in head injury. It allows conceptualization of the gestalt, or overall process, of problem solving and also delineates the different subskills related to reasoning and problem-solving ability. Assessment and treatment approaches are presented according to this model.

ASSESSMENT

Assessment Models

The assessment of reasoning and problem-solving skills has taken many forms. There are standardized measures of concept formation and reasoning ability as well as informal measures that evaluate an individual's problem-solving capacity. It is important for the clinician to remember that these skills represent the integration of many other cognitive abilities. Thus, when assessing reasoning and problem-solving ability, the examiner is simultaneously viewing the effects of other cognitive functions such as attention, memory, and perceptual abilities. The key is to make the correct attributions for any observed breakdowns in performance.

Goldstein and Levin (1987) designed a three-stage decision tree for guiding the assessment and remediation of reasoning and problem-solving disorders. This system provides a procedural hierarchy for organizing assessment/remediation of problem solving and reasoning (see Figure 11.1). The initial step involves a comprehensive neuropsychological assessment, which examines functioning in other fundamental cognitive process core areas such as language, attention, memory, and visual processing. If deficits are evident in these related areas, remediation is initiated. If no impairments are demonstrated in core cognitive areas, a detailed reasoning or problem-solving assessment is administered. Again, if problems are identified, intervention is initiated. The third phase involves remediation and treatment of executive functions.

One benefit of the Goldstein and Levin system is that it promotes an individualized approach to assessment and treatment that allows the clinician to target relevant areas for each patient. Other models utilize a standard format in which patients receive treatment in all areas regardless of their particular neuropsychological profile (e.g., Ben-Yishay & Diller, 1983b). The decision tree, presented in Figure 11.1, encourages clinicians to evaluate the potential underlying causes for decreased reasoning and problem-solving ability. One disadvantage lies in the serial testing separated by treatment. The clinician is unable to determine what effects any initial remediation implemented in the first stage may have had on results of testing reasoning and problem-solving ability in the second stage.

An alternative assessment model is to test simultaneously all areas including both fundamental cognitive processes such as attention, memory, language, and visual processing as well as the integrated processes of problem solving, reasoning, and executive functions. Treatment may then be organized so that intervention is initiated first for core cognitive areas, followed by treatment of executive functions and/or reasoning and problem-solving ability, as appropriate (see Figure 11.2).

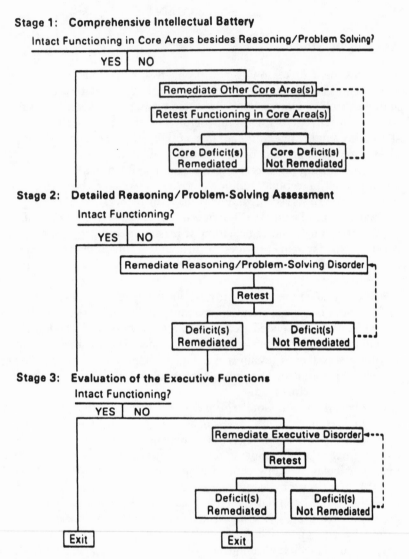

Stage 1: **Comprehensive Intellectual Battery**

Intact Functioning in Core Areas besides Reasoning/Problem Solving?

Stage 2: **Detailed Reasoning/Problem-Solving Assessment**

Intact Functioning?

Stage 3: **Evaluation of the Executive Functions**

Intact Functioning?

FIGURE 11.1. Stages for assessment of Reasoning/Problem Solving. From Goldstein and Levin (1987). Reprinted by permission.

Selected Tests of Reasoning/Problem Solving

Standardized Measures

Lezak (1983) divides higher-level thinking assessments into tests of concept formation and reasoning. She notes that tests of concept formation may be distinguished from other mental tests by the fact that they focus on the

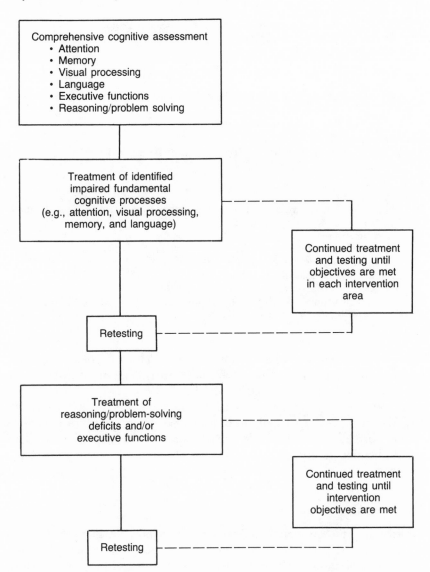

FIGURE 11.2. Sequence for assessment and treatment of Reasoning and Problem Solving.

quality of thinking rather than on response accuracy. Tests of concept formation include tests of interpretation of proverbs, word usage, and sorting tests (see Table 11.2). Scores on most of the tests represent qualitative judgments about the level of abstractness, complexity, or relevance of responses.

According to Lezak, reasoning tests evaluate logical thinking, comprehen-

TABLE 11.2. Selected Standardized Tests of Reasoning/Problem Solving

---

I. Proverb interpretation
   A. The Proverbs Test (Gorham, 1956)
II. Word usage tests
   A. Similarities Subtest from the Wechsler Adult Intelligence Scale—Revised (WAIS-R) (Wechsler, 1981)
   B. The Category Test (Halstead, 1947)
III. Sorting tests
   A. The Wisconsin Card-Sorting Test (Grant & Berg, 1948)
   B. The Color Form-Sorting Test (Weigl, 1941)
IV. Tests of reasoning
   A. Verbal reasoning
      1. Verbal Reasoning Subtest from the Differential Aptitude Test (Bennett, Seashore, & Wesman, 1982)
   B. Arithmetic reasoning
      1. Arithmetic Subtest from the WAIS-R (Wechsler, 1981)
      2. *Cube Analysis* (Newcombe, 1969)
   C. Design/spatial reasoning
      1. Raven's Progressive Matrices (Raven, 1960)
      2. Paper-Cutting Subtests from the Stanford–Binet (Terman & Merrill, 1973)

---

sion of relationships, and practical judgments. This category of tests includes verbal reasoning problems, arithmetic reasoning problems, and design/spatial reasoning tests (see Table 11.2).

Several of the assessments of executive functions (see Chapter 10) might also be categorized as evaluations of problem-solving ability. (An example is the Porteus Maze Test, (Porteus, 1965.) These tests provide data about planning ability and would supply information relevant to problem solving.

Informal Measures

In discussing the evaluation of executive functions, Lezak notes the difficulty of utilizing standardized neuropsychological tests to measure such abilities as initiation and planning. Most testing situations impose structure and may not reveal disorders and skills related to goal completion. She encourages the administration of constructional tasks such as the Tinkertoy Test, which requires the patient to construct a structure from Tinkertoy pieces without guidance from the examiner regarding what to build. The product can be scored for such features as complexity and the number of pieces utilized.

The opportunity to observe the *process* of solving a problem or performance of a multiple-step task can be very useful in the evaluation of integrated cognitive functions such as the executive system and reasoning ability. Provided the clinician has either previously ruled out potential confounding impairments in fundamental cognitive processes (e.g., attention disorders) or administered relevant intervention programs and remediated existing underlying deficits, informal tasks may be utilized that require the patient to apply reasoning and problem-solving skills. The key to a successful evaluation is for the examiner to have a clear idea of the parameters he or she is interested in observing. For example, the route-finding task provides a structure for evaluating and scoring various executive functions that are involved in route finding. The same task might be administered using a different observational protocol that would focus the clinician's attention on performance related to reasoning ability. Information gleaned from these sorts of activities, combined with the results from standardized tests of reasoning ability, will provide the examiner with a good understanding of the patient's overall reasoning and problem-solving abilities.

Relationship of the Assessment and Treatment Model

The model outlined in Table 11.1 helps to direct and organize the assessment of reasoning and problem-solving ability. Reasoning components may best be tested using the standardized measures listed in Table 11.2, particularly the sorting tests and all of the reasoning measures. Thought production may be evaluated using verbal and design fluency tests such as the Controlled Word Association Test (Benton & Hamsher, 1978) and the Design Fluency Test (Jones-Gotman & Milner, 1977) in addition to the Proverbs Interpretation and word usage tests listed in Table 11.2, which require abstraction ability. Problem-solving ability may be evaluated along the same lines as executive functions (see Chapter 10). Informal testing by observing as the patient solves a naturalistic task is an excellent format for looking at the three stages of problem-solving ability.

Social comprehension and judgment deserve special attention because although these skills are very commonly disrupted in persons who have sustained head injury, there are no established assessment and treatment tools available. One preliminary screening and treatment program (Corey, 1987), now in a pilot stage, may have some utility in managing deficits in the understanding and interpretation of social situations. Called the Social Comprehension Screening Test (Appendix A), it provides questions about different situations or behaviors. Answers are scored using a point system modeled after the Similarities Subtest on the Wechsler Adult Intelligence Scale—Revised. As discussed in the next section, treatment is an extension of the screening test: It involves multiple practice and feedback to help patients deal with situations analogous to those listed in the screening protocol.

TREATMENT

Despite the fact that we currently have neither a good grasp of the neuroanatomic correlates nor a clear conceptualization of the mechanisms involved in the integrated functions of reasoning and problem-solving ability, educational and rehabilitation fields have developed a healthy library of materials designed to target reasoning and problem-solving skills. Because of the lack of a theoretical basis, the clinician has the following responsibilities: (1) organizing and grouping similar tasks that target identified impaired processes in order that repetitive activation of deficit areas may be stimulated, and (2) determining what response information needs to be collected in order that desired performance parameters can be measured and progress gauged.

In the next section, published therapy materials that address reasoning and problem-solving ability are categorized according to the four-pronged model presented in Table 11.2. Tasks that, in the authors' experience, have been particularly useful in improving these abilities are reviewed in more detail. (Administration of tasks should be done in accordance with the therapy principles outlined in the process-specific approach of cognitive rehabilitation discussed in Chapter 3.)

Treatment of Reasoning Deficits

In their text on cognitive rehabilitation, Adamovich and colleagues (1985) have organized available published therapy materials into the categories of reasoning presented earlier (sequencing and classification, deductive reasoning, inductive reasoning, and convergent thinking). Their resource list may be combined with other sources to provide clinicians with a library of materials that target reasoning impairments (see Appendix B). However, these materials lack methods for data collection and strategy analysis. They do not provide the clinicians with methods for analyzing task completion in order that therapy can be appropriately modified and progress measured. Where possible, suggestions are offered about ways to expand existing tasks to make them more therapeutic.

Fundamental Skills (Sequencing and Classification)

There are a myriad of tasks from the educational arena that address sequencing and classification. These are also skill areas for which the clinician can easily invent tasks using common objects. Examples of published therapy materials (Appendix B) include:

1. *Basic Thinking Skills Workbook* (Midwest Publication Company) Verbal Classification Exercises

    Patterns
    Associations, Set 1 and 2
2. *Developmental Learning Materials*
    Association Picture Cards
    Career Association Cards
    Category Cards
    Picture-Sequencing Cards
3. *Brubaker Workbook for Aphasia* (Wayne State University Press)
    Associations
    Similarities and Differences
4. *Structure of Intellect* (Meeker & Meeker)
    Cognition of Figural Classes Workbook
    Evaluation of Figural Units Workbook
    Evaluation of Figural Classes Workbook
5. *Teaching Resources*
    People, Places, and Things
    Categories—Food and Animals, Clothing and Household Items
    Associations, Sets 1 and 2
    Categories, Varied
6. *Therapy Guide for Adult with Language and Speech Disorders* Volumes I and II (Visiting Nurse Service, Inc.)
    Categories
    Associations
    Object Description

Samples of easy-to-develop tasks include the following:

Sequencing alphabet or word cards.
Connecting randomly placed dots representing sequentially ordered strings of information (e.g., alphabet, numbers, months, days of the week).
Sequencing steps of activities in daily living (e.g., cooking, laundry, cleaning).
Sorting blocks by color, shape, and size or sorting contents of drawers or cupboards by designated features.

Task Administration

Published therapy materials, particularly workbook exercises, often do not provide enough examples to allow the repetitive administration of exercises necessary for achieving an increase in cognitive function. Also, as discussed, they do not provide a means for evaluating performance. Whenever a clinician purchases or develops a therapy exercise, the following steps need to be followed to ensure that the tasks are used in a therapeutic manner:

1. Designate a sampling of problems that will serve as the baseline and pre-/posttraining measure. Do not provide the patient with corrective feedback on these particular exercise problems. These problems should not be administered during training.
2. Identify what parameters of performance would be relevant to score using both objective and subjective measures (see Chapter 4). For reasoning and problem-solving tasks, the following information might be useful: time needed to complete problems, number of errors, type of errors, type of strategy used, and amount and type of cuing required. Gather this information each time the task is administered.
3. Make up extra analogous problems so that multiple practice opportunities will be available.
4. When the patient appears to have mastered the task, readminister the baseline problems and see if initial errors have been corrected.
5. Administer neuropsychological tests of reasoning and problem-solving ability when therapy objectives have been met in order to evaluate the generalization of improved reasoning and problem-solving ability to untrained tasks.

An excellent set of therapy activities that target the highest level of classification or concept formation and illustrate the therapy principles just mentioned are presented in *Attribute Activities* published by Creative Publications. These materials include a set of blocks in three shapes (circles, triangles, and squares), four colors (red, green, blue, and yellow), and two sizes (big and small). Activities include sorting the blocks into sets that are different by one, two, or three designated attributes. (See Figures 11.3 and 11.4 for sample therapy activities.) The directions for the difference activity (Figure 11.3) might be: "I want you to place all the blocks that are different by one characteristic inside this box." These tasks were developed as educational tools, not as cognitive rehabilitation materials; thus, they require adaptation (such as developing a scoresheet) to make the task more therapeutic. Speech/language pathologist S. Geyer, at Good Samaritan Hospital's Center for Cognitive Rehabilitation, developed the scoresheet shown in Figure 11.5, which allows the clinician to examine relevant performance data. For example, in the classification task, it is important not only to rate accuracy but also to know the type of strategy employed (trial and error, process of elimination, etc.). It is important to note further the type of cuing required. The suggested scoresheet allows convenient recording of performance information as well as a means for analyzing task performance over time.

For the patient who displays impairments in classification ability or concept formation, the clinician might utilize this task in conjunction with several others targeting the same process area. When therapy criteria are

DIFFERENCE ACTIVITY

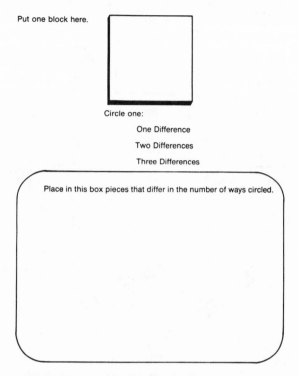

Put one block here.

Circle one:

One Difference

Two Differences

Three Differences

Place in this box pieces that differ in the number of ways circled.

FIGURE 11.3. Concept Formation therapy activities. Reprinted with permission from Creative Publications, Inc.. Pacific Grove, CA.

met, a test such as the Wisconsin Card-Sorting Test can be readministered to assess potential changes on untrained standardized measures.

Deductive Reasoning Tasks

Deductive reasoning is the process of drawing conclusions based on premises or general principles. The following are commercially available therapy tasks (see Appendix B for sources) that target deductive reasoning:

1. *Basic Thinking Skills* (Midwest Publications)
    Mind Benders Series A-1 through A-3, B-1 through B-4, C-1 through C-3
    Word Benders Series
    Think About It
    What Would You Do? and True to Life or Fantasy?

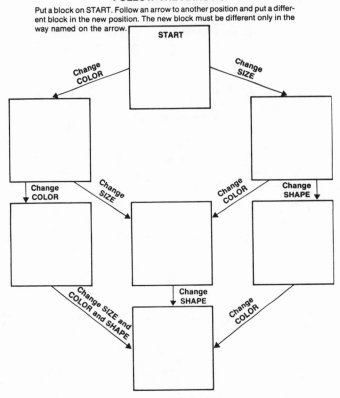

FIGURE 11.4. Concept formation therapy activities. Reprinted with permission from Creative Publications, Inc., Pacific Grove, CA.

2. *Brubaker Workbook for Aphasia* (Wayne State University Press)
   Making Conclusions
3. *Creative Play: Problem-Solving Activities with the Computer* (Lawrence Hall of Science)
   Function Machine
4. Atari Computer Programs
   Code-Breaker
   Manual for Expressive Reasoning
   Determining Missing Information

Once more, a description of a sample task serves to illustrate the therapy principles. The computer program *Function Machine* presents a task in which the user is shown three trials; in each one, a digit is fed into a "machine" and a different digit emerges. The user's task is to determine the arithmetic rule that is operating on the first number to product the second.

# Differ- ences 1, 2, or 3	Trial	# Correct sorts	#Incorr/ omitted	Percent correct	Cue level	Strategy used	Behavioral observa- tions/other cues used (Baseline each differ- ence type without cues)

Strategies: 1, trial/error; 2, process of elimination.
Cue level: 1. Verbal prompting and written cards used, manipulated by therapist.
　　　　　2. Verbal prompting and written cards used, manipulated by participant.
　　　　　3. Verbal prompts/cues by therapist.
　　　　　4. Therapist models task with verbal explanations.
　　　　　5. Participant asks for help as needed.
　　　　　6. No cues.
　　　　　7. Other (specify).

FIGURE 11.5. Scoresheet for activity shown in Figure 11.3.

The user can choose numbers to feed into the machine and try to anticipate the resulting answer numbers. The computer then provides feedback regarding the accuracy of the answers. The difficulty level can be controlled from very easy addition rules to more complex algebraic equations. An example of a Level 1 problem might be: The user sees the digits 3, 5, and 8 fed into the machine, and 4, 6, and 9 emerge, respectively. The user's task is to determine the arithmetic rule of "plus 1." This task provides a good therapy activity, but it requires a scoresheet that permits examination of performance parameters and measurement of progress over time. The scoresheet presented in Figure 11.6 was developed by S. Geyer at Good Samaritan Hospital's Center for Cognitive Rehabilitation to provide performance information.

Inductive Reasoning

Inductive reasoning exercises include tasks that require the patient to formulate solutions based on partial or indirect information. Samples of published therapy materials are listed below:

1. *Brubaker Workbook for Aphasia* (Wayne State University Press)
   Antonyms
   Homonyms

Date	Difficulty level	Rule	Strategy used[a]	No. of guesses before looking at answers	Correct? (Y/N)

[a] Strategies:
  1. Process of elimination.
  2. Hypothesis testing: jots down possible rules and then tries numbers.
  3. Trial and error: to get more data, randomly tries numbers.

FIGURE 11.6. Sample scoresheet developed for computer program *Function Machine*.

2. *Developmental Learning Material*
     Antonym Cards
     Word Master
3. *Logic, Anyone?* (Pitman Learning, Inc.)
     Circle Logic Problems
     Table Logic Problems
     Matrix Logic Problems
4. *The Thinking Skills Workbook: A Cognitive Skills Remediation Manual for Adults*
     Decision-Making Task
5. *Therapy Guide for the Adult with Language and Speech Disorders*, Volume II (Visiting Nurse Service, Inc.)
     Word Associations
     Analogies
     Cause and Effect
     Story Completion
     Decision-Making Task
     Sentence Completion

Again, a description of a particular exercise serves to highlight task administration principles. The logic problems from *Logic, Anyone?* (samples shown in Figures 11.7–11.9) provide an excellent therapy sequence to target inductive reasoning ability. They may be organized hierarchically from circle logic to table logic to matrix logic in order of increasing difficulty. Therapy goals may be set up so that the patient needs to complete the last four problems in each series independently without error. The fifth-to-the-last problem in each series might be used as a baseline, pre-/posttreatment measure. The scoresheet shown in Figure 11.10 allows the clinician to look at objective accuracy data and subjective performance

7. ARE YOU HUNGRY?

The categories in this problem are *sweets, vegetables,* and *cereals.* Into which areas of the circles do the following children fit?

1. Bill is a vegetarian._____
2. Mary will eat anything except vegetables._____
3. There is nothing that Derek doesn't eat._____
4. Don likes sweets but he will also eat cereals._____
5. Tom has given up eating sweets but he will eat anything else._____

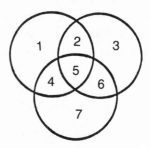

FIGURE 11.7. Sample treatment activities targeting indictive reasoning ability. Reprinted with permission from Pitman and Learning, Inc., Belmont, CA.

15. DINNER PARTY

Teri has a fancy dinner party for eight friends. Cindy, Judi, and Lyn don't sit next to any boys. Where does the hostess seat each of her eight guests?

1. John and Jeff sit next to each other.
2. Karen sits next to Miss Adams, and DeDe sits next to Paul.
3. Teri Moss enjoys sitting to the right of Jeff and also next to Paul.
4. The Thompson girl sits to the right of DeDe.
5. Judi Johnson sits between two girls.
6. Cindy does not sit next to Karen.
7. Paul and Jeff are twins.
8. The Beaver boys do not often see John.
9. The Fillmore girl sits to the right of the Adams girl.
10. The King girl is delighted to be invited to the gathering.
11. John and Judi are not related but do have the same last name.

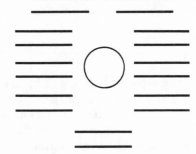

˙If you have trouble working this problem, be sure to reread the upper portion (situation) *very* carefully.

FIGURE 11.8. Sample treatment activities targeting indictive reasoning ability. Reprinted with permission from Pitman and Learning, Inc., Belmont, CA.

17. OCCUPATIONS

Four people have the following occupations: police officer, dress shop owner, teacher, and candy store owner. Match the person to his or her correct occupation. In this matrix, making notes above the boxes may help you solve the problem.

1. Kay and Jason met in a dress shop while one of them was buying a dress from the other.

2. Bill and Don met each other when one of them was buying candy from the other for his class.

3. Don and Kay met while one was giving the other a traffic ticket.

4. Don meets a friend at the Country Club every Tuesday at 10:00 a.m.

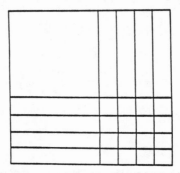

FIGURE 11.9. Sample treatment activities targeting indictive reasoning ability. Reprinted with permission from Pitman and Learning, Inc., Belmont, CA.

data. Problems may be readministered until performance criteria are met; this allows repetitive activation of the same type of processing.

Convergent Thinking

In convergent thinking tasks, the patient analyzes information in order to identify the central or main point. Tasks that require the learner to reduce information to its most salient features and to abstract the main idea are examples. This category of thinking requires discrimination between relevant and irrelevant information (Adamovich et al., 1985). Examples of published therapy materials (see Appendix B for sources) include:

1. *Brubaker Workbook for Aphasia* (Wayne State University Press)
   Why? What? When? Where? Who? How? Questions
2. *Davidson and Associates* (computer software)
   Word Attack
3. *Manual of Exercises for Expressive Reasoning* (Lingui Systems, Inc.)
   Interpolative Thinking

Date	Page number	Number of errors	Type of errors	Suggested strategies

FIGURE 11.10. Sample scoresheet for treatment activities in Figures 11.7–11.9.

4. *Therapy Guide for the Adult with Language and Speech Disorders* (Visiting Nurse Service), Vols. I and II
    Who? What? Where? Activity
    Paragraph's Central Theme
    Given Clues, Come Up With Conclusion
5. *Sunset Software* (computer software)
    Understanding Questions
    Understanding Sentences

Treatment of Deficits in Thought Production

Tasks targeting divergent thinking and abstraction ability are grouped together because these two areas are not different enough to be easily separated. Thought production includes those processing capabilities related to fluency (the ability to generate multiple ideas) as well as creativity (the ability to think of novel ideas). Commercially available tasks that target abstract/divergent thinking include the following:

1. *Teaching Resources*
    What's Wrong Here? (Level I and Level II)
    Visual Absurdities
2. *Therapy Guide for the Adult with Language and Speech Disorders, Vols. I and II*
    Multi-Meaning Words
    Verbal Absurdities
    Idioms: Sentence, Idiom Interpretation
    Abstracting a Meaning
    Homophones

Many informal tasks also may be developed to address divergent thinking. Luria (1963) described an intervention for a patient who had sustained frontal lobe injury and was unable to generate a story independently. The intervention program involved giving the patient transitional words on a card, such as "however," "then," and "although." The clinician read the patient a story and then asked him to retell it. The transition cards were used to cue to patient on the next component in the story. Luria reported success with this program and noted generalization to other activities, such as the spontaneous description of a picture.

Other tasks targeting idea production that would be relatively easy to administer and for which scoresheets could be developed include the following:

1. Listing Object Uses, e.g., "Tell me as many things as you can think of to do with a tin can." Scoring might include the number of total items generated in a prescribed period of time as well as number of unusual (but realistic) items.
2. Interpreting Abstract Designs, e.g., "List as many things as you can see in this picture." Scoring might consist of the number of pictures identified in the target design (fluency) as well as the ability (scored +/–) to describe the features of the picture that are identified.
3. Drawing, e.g., "Make this _____ (circle or geometric figure) into a recognizable object." Scoring might consist of a creativity rating as well as a +/– score reflecting the ability to incorporate the original line or geometric figure into a recognizable object.
4. Story Completion, e.g., "I am going to tell you the beginning (end) of a story and I want you to provide an ending (beginning)." Scoring might consist of rating the presence or absence of a logical relationship between the generated story and the initial given part of the story as well as the number of idea units (fluency).

Treatment of Deficits in Social Comprehension and Judgment*

Deficits in social comprehension and judgment may be treated by providing multiple opportunities for the patient to practice interpreting and understanding social situations with corrective feedback from therapists. Corey and Sprunk (1987) developed lists of hypothetical situations for five types of social comprehension and judgment questions:

- What are two good reasons why most people . . . ?
- What are two different things that would be likely to happen if . . . ?
- When would it be socially appropriate to . . . ?
- When would it be socially inappropriate to . . . ?
- What are two different things that would be good to do (or say) if . . . ?
- When would it be a good idea to . . . ?
  When would it be a bad idea to . . . ?

---

*Treatment of problem solving is not detailed in this chapter since interventions in this area are analogous to the treatment procedures outlined in Chapter 10 for executive functions.

Samples of each of these questions are provided in Appendix C. The Social Comprehension and Judgment Screening Test (shown in Appendix A) contains a mixture of the above questions and permits the clinician to identify whether or not social comprehension and judgment are impaired. The questions used in a treatment program are scored like those in the screening protocol (0, 1, or 2 points based on the quality of the answer; see Appendix A). The use of a quantitative scoring system permits the clinician to track progress.

TREATMENT ISSUES

Generalization

Because the available published workbooks and computer programs are not tied to neuropsychologic models, they tend to address isolated, fragmented components of reasoning and problem solving. A review of the literature accompanying available published tasks suggests a narrow focus on the mechanics of the respective exercises without attention to increasing overall reasoning processes within the brain. (The materials do not attempt to move the learner beyond the task.) To be effective, therapy must move beyond the clinic and ensure that gains made on clinical activities are being reflected in the patient's everyday life. However, the lack of a theoretical model and limited consideration of the ecologic validity of tasks weaken the chance for generalization of therapy to naturalistic settings.

The model described in this chapter addresses both of these issues. First, it provides a theoretical model and organizational structure to guide assessment and treatment. Second, in the last two categories of the model, treatment is carried out using real-life situations. Thus, any related skills treated in the first two areas (reasoning and thought production) are later applied to naturalistic training tasks.

Efficacy

Interventions in reasoning and problem-solving ability, perhaps more than in any other cognitive process area, lack empirical validation of efficacy. There are several reasons why this unfortunate situation may exist. Reasoning/Problem Solving is not a well defined process. It exists as the constellation and integration of a number of related cognitive processes. It is therefore difficult to measure. Neuropsychologic tests may be sensitive to certain aspects of reasoning and problem solving but not necessarily to those aspects that have changed as a result of intervention. Furthermore, the experimental population is difficult to describe. It is very difficult to find two subjects who exhibit parallel impairments in reasoning and problem-solving ability, which, unlike memory and attention deficits, are too illusive and complex.

Because of these constraints, and with the methodologic problems of conducting treatment efficacy studies in any applied field, few researchers have attempted to evaluate program efficacy for interventions in reasoning and problem-solving skills. Some of the single-subject designs reviewed in Chapter 4 could be very useful in the effort to collect data examining treatment outcomes. Certainly documentation of treatment efficacy in reasoning and problem solving warrants increased research attention.

SUMMARY

Reasoning and problem solving represent the highly complex integration of a number of other cognitive functions. A discussion of the clinical manifestations of reduced reasoning and problem solving seen in individuals who have sustained brain trauma has been provided. A master list cataloging the reasoning and problem-solving deficits that have been noted in this population has been generated.

Based on the problem-solving literature for both normal and brain-injured individuals, a four-pronged model of this cognitive process area was proposed for the purpose of providing clinicians with a conceptualization of reasoning and problem-solving ability and a structure to guide assessment and treatment practices. The model consisted of the following: skills related to reasoning ability, thought production, problem solving, and social comprehension and judgment. It was noted that these categories do not represent discrete areas but instead have much overlap. The categories, however, provide an appropriate focus for evaluation and treatment of reasoning/problem-solving ability.

Assessment of reasoning and problem-solving deficits necessarily must include a comprehensive cognitive evaluation to determine potential contributors to decreased problem-solving ability (e.g., impairments in attention and memory). Assessment of reasoning/problem solving is best served by a combination of standardized and informal measures. There are standardized tests of concept formation that include tests of proverb interpretation, word usage, and sorting/categorization ability as well as tests of reasoning ability, which include measurements of verbal, arithmetic, and design/spatial reasoning. Informal measures allow the clinician to evaluate the overall reasoning process as the patient applies reasoning and problem-solving abilities to complete naturalistic, multistep activities.

Treatment activities for each of the four areas—Reasoning, Thought Production, Problem Solving, and Social Comprehension and Judgment—were discussed. Currently available published therapy materials were listed in each of the areas. Suggestions for how to conduct treatment in accordance with the principles of the Process-Specific Approach to cognitive rehabilitation were offered, including methods for collecting essential data relevant to task performance.

Finally, issues related to generalization and treatment efficacy were discussed. The importance of moving a learner beyond the clinic task and ensuring generalization of improved reasoning and problem-solving ability to a naturalistic setting was reviewed. The lack of treatment efficacy studies was also noted. It was suggested that single-subject designs be utilized to reduce some of the current research obstacles.

STUDY QUESTIONS

1. Write down all the steps involved in grocery shopping including putting away groceries in the cupboard. Identify which aspects of the steps fall into the categories of Problem Solving, Reasoning, and Concept Formation.
2. Describe how the integration of other cognitive process areas (e.g., Attention and Memory) relates to Reasoning and Problem Solving ability.
3. Make up an informal measure for evaluating problem-solving ability that includes a description of the task and scoresheet.
4. What principles of the Process-Specific Approach to cognitive rehabilitation permit evaluating generalization of treatment to real-life functioning?
5. What factors have contributed to a lack of efficacy studies in this area? Suggest a single-subject design to evaluate treatment outcome.

REFERENCES

Adamovich, B., Henderson, J., & Auerbach, S. (1985). *Cognitive rehabilitation of closed head injured patients.* San Diego: College Hill Press.

Bennett, G. K., Seashore, N. G., & Wesman, A. G. (1982). *Differential aptitude tests.* New York: Psychological Corporation.

Benton, A. L., & Hamsher, K. (1978). *Multilingual aphasia examination.* Iowa City: University of Iowa.

Ben-Yishay, V., & Diller, L. (1983a). Cognitive deficits. In M. Rosenthal, E. Griffith, M. Bond, & J. D. Miller (Eds.), *Rehabilitation of the head injured adult* (pp. 167–183). Philadelphia: F. A. Davis.

Ben-Yishay, Y., & Diller, L. (1983b). Cognitive remediation. In M. Rosenthal, E. Griffith, M. Bond, & J. D. Miller (Eds.), *Rehabilitation of the head injured adult* (pp. 367–380). Philadelphia: F. A. Davis.

Bourne, L. E., Dominowski, R. L., & Loftus, E. (1979). *Cognitive processes.* Englewood Cliffs, NJ: Prentice-Hall.

Bruner, J. (1957). On perceptual readiness. *Psychology Review 64*:10–41.

Corey, M. and Sprunk, H.S. (1987). *Social comprehension and reasoning.* Puyallup, WA: Good Samaritan Hospital Center for Cognitive Rehabilitation.

Goldstein, R. (1944). The mental changes due to frontal lobe damage. *Journal of Psychology 17*:58–72.

Goldstein, F. L., & Levin, H. S. (1987). Disorders of reasoning and problem solving ability. In M. Manfred, A. Benton, & L. Diller (Eds.), *Neuropsychological rehabilitation* (pp. 327–354). New York: Guilford Press.

Goodglass, H., & Kaplan, E. (1979). Assessment of cognitive deficits in the brain-injured patient. In M. S. Gazzaniga (Ed.), *Handbook of behavioral neurobiology, Vol. 2: Neuropsychology* (p. 22). New York: Plenum.

Gorham, D. R. (1956). A proverbs test for clinical and experimental use. *Psychological Reports 1*:1–12.

Grant, D. A., & Berg, E. A. (1948). A behavioral analysis of degree of reinforcement and ease of shifting to view responses in a weigh-type-and-sorting problem. *Journal of Experimental Psychology 38*:404–411.

Halstead, W. C. (1947). *Brain and intelligence.* Chicago: University of Chicago Press.

Jones-Gotman, M. & Milner, B. (1977). Design fluency: The invention of nonsense drawings after focal cortical lesions. *Neuropsychologia, 15*:653–674.

Levin, H. S., Benton, D. L., & Grossman, R. G. (1982). *Neurobehavioral consequences of closed head injury.* New York: Oxford University Press.

Lezak, M. (1983). *Neuropsychological assessment* (2nd ed.). New York, Oxford: Oxford University Press.

Luria, A. R. (1963). *Restoration of function after brain injury.* New York: Pergamon.

Luria, A. R. (1966a). *Higher cortical functions in man.* New York: Basic Books.

Luria, A. R. (1966b). *Human brain and psychological processes.* New York: Harper & Row.

Newcombe, F. (1969). *Missile wounds of the brain.* London: Oxford University Press.

Porteus, S. D. (1965). *Porteus Maze Test. Fifty years' application.* Palo Alto, CA: Pacific Books.

Prigatano, G. P. (1986). *Neuropsychological rehabilitation after brain injury.* Baltimore: Johns Hopkins University Press.

Raven, J. C. (1960). *Guide to the standard progressive matrices.* London: N. K. Lewis. New York: Psychological Corporation.

Szekeres, S., Ylvisaker, M., & Halland, A. (1985). Cognitive rehabilitation. In M. Ylvisaker (Ed.), *Head injury rehabilitation: Children and adolescents* (pp. 219–246). San Diego: College-Hill Press.

Terman, L. M., & Merrill, M. A. (1973). *Stanford–Binet Intelligence Scale. Manual for the third revision, form L-M.* Boston: Houghton-Mifflin.

Vygotski, L. S. (1934). *Intellectual activity and speech.* Moscow: Satsekgiz.

Wechsler, D. (1981). *The Wechsler Adult Intelligence Scale—Revised.* New York: Psychological Corporation.

Weigl, E. (1941). On the psychology of so-called processes of abstraction. *Journal of Abnormal Social Psychology 36:3–33.*

APPENDIX A: SCORING SOCIAL COMPREHENSION QUESTIONS

Answers to social comprehension questions will be scored either 0, 1, or 2, based on the quality of the answers.

2 points: In general, a 2-point answer is one that clearly states an important reason or solution, is basically logical and well explained, and shows a good understanding of social norms. In order to get credit for two responses of 2 points each, the two responses must be totally different.

1 point: In general, a 1-point answer gives some information but is incomplete, vague, only partly logical, an incidental reason, similar to another response (but not the same), and/or shows a limited understanding of social norms.

0 point: In general, a 0-point answer is one that does not answer the question, does not make sense, is overly personal, is essentially the same as another answer, and/or shows poor understanding of social norms.

If the question was: "What are two good reasons why most people wash their plates, before they put them away in the cupboard?"

2-point examples:
a. So they will not get other dishes dirty.
b. Because they are easier to wash when the food has not dried on them.
c. Because the plates could have germs or bacteria on them which would continue to grow and could make you sick (if you didn't wash them).
d. Because dirty plates would look bad and start to smell bad in the cupboard.

1-point examples:
a. Everything would get dirty. (Vague)
b. People could get sick. (Not well explained)
c. My mother would get mad at me. (Overly personal and not a general social reason)
d. They might stick to each other. (Incidental reason)

0-point examples:
a. It's just dumb. (No reason given)
b. They would be dirty. (Does not explain why it's a problem)
c. Because it would get other glasses dirty, given after, Because it would get other plates dirty. (Answers are basically the same)
d. They would probably fall on top of you. (Not sensible)

Good Samaritan Hospital Center for Cognitive Rehabilitation Social Comprehension Screening Test (Corey, 1987)

Below are several items that look at your social reasoning ability. Make sure that all of your answers are *clear, specific,* and *well explained.* (Administer orally for individuals with impaired reading or writing ability.)

What are two *different* things that would be good to do if the toilet at your apartment is not flushing properly and almost overflows? You will be gone when your room-mate gets home this afternoon.

    1. _____

       _____

    2. _____

       _____

What are two *different* things that would be good to do (or say) if you got to the checkout stand to pay for your groceries, and you did not have your wallet?

    1. _____

       _____

    2. _____

       _____

What are two *different* good reasons why most people do not hit others, even when angry?

    1. _____

       _____

    2. _____

       _____

What are two *different* good reasons why most people drive cars that are less than 15 years old (whether you do or not)?

    1. _____

       _____

    2. _____

       _____

What are two *different* things that would be likely to happen if you borrowed your friend's car and wrecked it?

    1. _____

       _____

    2. _____

       _____

What are two *different* things that would be likely to happen if you are always passive and do not speak up for yourself?

1. _____

_____

2. _____

_____

When would it be socially appropriate and socially inappropriate to look into your neighbor's window?

1. Appropriate:_____

_____

2. Inappropriate:_____

_____

When would it be a good idea and when would it be a bad idea to babysit your friend's children?

1. Good Idea:_____

_____

2. Bad Idea:_____

_____

APPENDIX B: PUBLISHED THERAPY MATERIALS

Atari, Inc., 1195 Burregas Ave., Sunnyvale, CA 94086.

Attribute Games and Problems Set, Creative Publications, Inc., P. O. Box 10328, Palo Alto, CA 94303.

Basic Thinking Skills, Midwest Publication Co., P. O. Box 448, Pacific Grove, CA 93980.

Brubaker Workbook for Aphasia, Wayne State University Press, Detroit, MI 48202.

Creative Play: Problem Solving Activities with the Computer, Lawrence Hall of Science, Berkeley, CA 94720.

Davidson and Associates, 6069 Grove Oak Place, ' 12, Rancho Palos Verdes, CA 90274.

Developmental Learning Materials, One DLM Park, Allen, TX 75002.

Logic, Anyone? by B. Post & S. Eads, Pitman, Learning, Inc., Belmont, CA 94002.

Manual of Exercises for Expressive Reasoning, Lingui Systems, Inc., Ste. 806, 1630 Fifth Avenue, Moline, IL 61265.

Structure of Intellect Workbooks, by M. Meeker & R. Meeker, Structure of Intellect Institute, 343 Richmond Street, El Segundo, CA 90245.

Sunset Software, 11750 Sunset Boulevard, Ste. 914, Los Angeles, CA 90049.

Teaching Resources, *Fokes Sentence Builder,* 50 Pond Street, Hingham, MA 02043

Therapy Guide for the Adult with Language and Speech Disorders, Vols. I & II. Visiting Nurse Service, Inc., 1200 McArthur Drive, Akron, OH 44320.
The Thinking Skills Workbook: A Cognitive Skills Remediation Manual for Adults, by C. Carter, J. Caruso, M. Languirand, & M. A. Berard. Charles C. Thomas, 2600 S. First St., Springfield, IL 62717.

APPENDIX C: SAMPLE SOCIAL COMPREHENSION AND JUDGMENT QUESTIONS USED IN TREATMENT

What are *two* good reasons why most people:

1. Cover their mouths when sneezing? _____
   _____

2. Work? _____
   _____

3. Give gifts to close friends or relatives on their birthday?_____
   _____

4. Turn on their headlights when driving at night?_____
   _____

5. Don't smoke or would like to stop smoking?
   _____

6. Cover an open wound?_____
   _____

7. Get seven or more hours of sleep per night?_____
   _____

8. Wear shoes outdoors in the wintertime?_____
   _____

9. Answer the phone when it rings?_____
   _____

10. Look at a menu before ordering when in a new restaurant?_____
    _____

11. Don't have several serious boyfriends or girlfriends at the same time?_____
    _____

12. Make sure that stove burners are off before leaving the kitchen when cooking has been completed?_____

_____

13. Wave back if a person they know waves at them?_____

_____

14. Get to know another person fairly well before arranging to spend a weekend alone with them?_____

_____

15. Take out the trash?_____

_____

16. Buckle a child in a car seat when traveling?_____

_____

17. Praise others when they do a good job?_____

_____

What are two different things that would be likely to happen if . . .

1. You drank too much at a party and drove home anyway?

_____

_____

2. You ran a stoplight at a very busy intersection during rush hour traffic?

_____

_____

3. You forgot to pick your friends up to go to work and it was your week to drive in your carpool? (So you were at work without your friends.)

_____

_____

4. You are a supervisor and you yell at your workers a lot?

_____

_____

5. You walked into an interview an hour late?

_____

_____

6. You were preparing food for a group of people and they saw you sticking your fingers in your mouth?

_____

_____

When would it be socially appropriate to:
When would it be socially inappropriate to:

1. Give an associate advice on a problem?

   Appropriate:_____

   _____

   Inappropriate:_____

   _____

2. Cry?

   Appropriate:_____

   _____

   Inappropriate:_____

   _____

3. Make a collect phone call?

   Appropriate:_____

   _____

   Inappropriate:_____

   _____

4. Take off your shoes?

   Appropriate:_____

   _____

   Inappropriate:_____

   _____

5. Take a photo of someone with your camera?

   Appropriate:_____

   _____

   Inappropriate:_____

   _____

6. Cancel a dinner engagement?

   Appropriate:_____

   _____

   Inappropriate:_____

   _____

What would be appropriate action to take when . . .

1. A friend tells you that his or her dog just died.

   _____

   _____

2. You have firm plans to get together for dinner with a friend and an emergency comes up so that you can't make it.

_____

_____

3. A telephone salesperson calls you a second time after you said you weren't interested in the product.

_____

_____

4. You have just finished dinner in a restaurant and want to pay the check. You haven't seen your waiter in a long time.

_____

_____

When would it be a good idea to . . .
When would it be a bad idea to . . .

1. Flag down a passing vehicle when you have car trouble on the freeway?

   Good Idea:_____

   _____

   Bad Idea:_____

   _____

2. Sleep in until noon?

   Good Idea:_____

   _____

   Bad Idea:_____

   _____

3. Lend a friend $100?

   Good Idea:_____

   _____

   Bad Idea:_____

   _____

4. Exchange house keys with a friend?

   Good Idea:_____

   _____

   Bad Idea:_____

   _____

5. Take a plane versus a car to reach a destination?

Good Idea:_____

_____

Bad Idea:_____

_____

Part III
ADJUNCT APPROACHES

12
Conducting Group Therapy with Head-Injured Adults

Much has been written about the benefits of the group therapy process (e.g., Cartwright & Zander, 1953; Sampson & Marthas, 1977; Yalom, 1975). In most cities, one can find groups designed to assist overeaters, undereaters, compulsive shoppers, and compulsive gamblers, as well as support groups for almost any type of health or medical problem. With the advent of self-help and support groups in the 1960's, the benefits and principles of the group therapy process have become well established.

Group cognitive and psychosocial treatment with the head-injured population offers some of the advantages common to all group therapy situations and draws on already established principles of group treatment. However, there are some factors unique to managing group therapy with individuals who have sustained brain injury. In this chapter, the benefits of group therapy for this population are outlined, followed by an explanation of specific management and leadership techniques for therapists. A description of the different types of groups that can be conducted with head-injured patients is also given. Appendix A provides a catalogue of sample group activities that have been successfully implemented with the head-injured population. Speech/language pathologists or occupational therapists are often the clinicians responsible for leading groups, and they may not have received formal training in group process as part of their education. This chapter is designed to provide some background and practical intervention techniques for group leaders, including the following topics: modeling, generalization, feedback techniques (support, confrontation, advice/suggestions, summarizing, clarifying, probing/questioning, repeating/paraphrasing, reflecting, interpreting, and listening), leadership style (democratic versus autocratic), group heterogeneity, group resistance, cooperation, establishing group goals, and preparation procedures for conducting group therapy.

BENEFITS OF GROUP THERAPY

Human beings are social animals. In order to function successfully in society, an individual must possess a minimal level of interpersonal skills. Following a head injury, there is often a disruption of the cognitive and psychosocial systems that are responsible for successful interaction in our complex societal matrix. Group therapy provides an excellent clinical tool to address these impairments. Individual cognitive therapy may increase a person's cognitive status, but without the abilities to relate appropriately to others in one's environment, such gains may not be functional.

There are many advantages to working in a group format, including cost effectiveness and specific psychosocial benefits (Carberry & Burd, 1983). Some are outlined below.

Support. A group environment can provide needed support to individuals who have sustained head trauma. As with any support group, the opportunity to be with other individuals who may have experienced similar problems and fears decreases feelings of isolation. Groups provide a source of identification. They can also instill hope. Witnessing the successes of others who have similar handicaps encourages a more optimistic view of the future. The process of sharing and helping others overcome disappointments also increases self-esteem and self-confidence.

Modeling. Group therapy provides an opportunity to model appropriate behaviors. Therapists can demostrate the types of target behaviors they wish to encourage in the group participants. Vicarious reinforcement, whereby the therapist reinforces one participant for exhibiting a behavior he or she wishes to see in another participant, is another example of modeling.

Generalization. Group therapy can provide an effective context for applying skills established in therapy to naturalistic situations. Groups provide a controlled microcosm of society. Therapists can systematically introduce the interactional components that are found in the interpersonal dynamics of society at large and, in so doing, can facilitate generalization or transfer of skills outside the clinical environment.

Accurate self-perception. The group format provides opportunities for participants to gain a realistic perception of their strengths and weaknesses. Individuals who have sustained brain injuries may have a tendency to underestimate their cognitive and psychosocial deficits and deny the existence of impairments. The converse of denial, the tendency to exaggerate the magnitude and amount of deficits and to be overly focused on impairments, can also be present. Groups can provide reality testing by offering individuals honest feedback.

Economic therapy ratio. A more pragmatic advantage to group therapy is the economic benefit of a reduced staff/patient ratio. Obviously, it is more cost effective to provide rehabilitation services to many persons than to one at a time.

GENERAL LEADERSHIP TECHNIQUES

Sampson and Marthas (1977) write that the act of leading or facilitating a group demands a sophisticated, high-level corrdination of cognitive and interpersonal skills. It requires the ability to reflect on and evaluate actions and behaviors rapidly as they occur. The group leader must focus on the immediate situation; this requires an ability to distance oneself from the immediate ongoing task while actively participating in it. This distance is essential for appropriate modification of ongoing activity or provision of constructive direction in the group process. Good interpersonal skills are critical for intervening appropriately and providing group members with feedback based on reflective evaluation.

Argyris (1976) uses the analogy of a thermostat to describe the functions of a group leader. Just as a thermostat receives information about room temperature, compares that information against the present temperature goal, and makes heat adjustments accordingly, a group leader must have an accurate perception of the ongoing pattern of interaction, compare perceptions with group target goals, and provide appropriate direction and feedback so the group can modify itself and thereby better accomplish its objectives.

There are specific techniques that the group leader can use to provide group participants with appropriate feedback and to direct the group process effectively. Sampson and Marthas developed a list of techniques of group leadership, which are summarized in Table 12.1. A brief description of each feedback technique is provided below:

Support. Support comes from feedback that reinforces the behavior of an individual group member or of the entire group. Supportive comments may (1) inform persons about behaviors the leader feels are on target and helpful and (2) create an atmosphere of trust so that all group members feel comfortable sharing their ideas.

Confrontation. Confrontation occurs when the group leader challenges a member about a particular behavior or idea. The goal is to encourage an individual to view a situation or thought in a way that is different from his and her current perceptions. The combination of confrontation and support can be one of the most effective methods of inducing change. Without a supportive environment, confrontation is more likely to result in feelings of defensiveness than in growth and learning.

TABLE 12.1. A Summary of Leader Interventions[a]

Type of intervention	Goals of intervention
Support	Provides supportive climate for expressing ideas and opinions, including unpopular or unusual points of view
	Facilitates members continuing with their ongoing behavior
	Helps reinforce positive forms of behavior
	Creates a climate in which silent members may feel secure enough to participate
Confrontation	Aids in growth and development; helps unfreeze members from being stuck in one mode of functioning
Advice and suggestions	Shares expertise; offers new perspectives
	Helps focus group on its task and goals
Summarizing	Helps keep group on its task by reviewing past actions and by setting agenda for future sessions
	Brings to focus still unresolved issues
	Organizes past in ways that help clarify; brings into focus themes and patterns of interaction
Clarifying	Helps reduce distortion in communication
	Facilitates focus on substantive issues rather than allowing members to be sidetracked into misunderstandings
Probing and questioning	Helps expand a point that may have been left incomplete
	Gets at more extensive and wider range of information
	Invites members to explore their ideas in greater detail
Repeating, paraphrasing, and highlighting	Helps members continue with their ongoing behavior; invites further exploration and examination of what is being said
	Clarifies and helps focus on the specific, important, or key aspect of a communication
	Sharpens members' understanding of what is being said or done
Reflecting: feelings	Orients members to the feelings that may lie behind what is being said or done
	Helps members deal with issues they might otherwise avoid or miss
Reflecting: behavior	Gives members the opportunity to see how their behavior appears to others and to see and evaluate its consequences
	Helps members to understand others' perceptions and responses to them
Interpretation and analysis	Renders behavior meaningful by locating it in a larger context in which a casual explanation is provided

	Helps members understand both the likely bases of their behavior and its meaning
	Summarizes a pattern of behavior and provides a useful way of examining it and working to modify it through the insights gained
Listening	Provides an attentive and responsive audience for those who participate
	Models a helpful way for members to relate to one another; gives a feeling of sharing and mutual concern
	Helps members sharpen their own ideas and thinking as they realize that, indeed, others are listening and concerned about what they are saying

[a]From Sampson and Marthas (1977). Reprinted by permission.

Advice and suggestions. When a leader has greater expertise and knowledge about a subject area than group members, an important intervention tool is the offering of advice or suggestions. It is important, however, that advice be provided in the form of recommendations rather than directives.

Summarizing. Summarizing is the process of organizing recollections of recent events. The leader may take a range of behaviors or activities occurring over a past time period and organize and summarize them for the group. He or she may also enlist the group's assistance in summarizing what has taken place. The process of summarizing organizes group actions and helps focus the group by highlighting key points and issues.

Clarifying. The leader can check on the meanings of interaction and communication by summarizing and verifying the information (e.g., "Is what you are saying...?") or by asking group members to clarify what they mean (e.g., "I am not sure I understand what you meant. . . ."). This intervention serves to reduce distortion and confusion in communication.

Probing and questioning. These techniques are used to elicit increased sharing and information from group members. The group leader can directly ask a question such as, "Can you tell us more about that?" or use a less direct tactic, such as repeating the last few comments made by a group participant in order to facilitate a continuation of the person's commentary.

Repeating paraphrasing/highlighting. These feedback techniques are components of the aforementioned interventions and offer specific methods for carrying out such processes as summarizing, clarifying, and probing. In using repetition, a leader simply reiterates what he or she has heard; this serves either to correct inaccurate communication or to emphasize accurate communication. With paraphrasing or highlighting, the leader can clarify by restating what has been said in a different form and, in so doing, highlight what the leader considers to be the key message. (The more the paraphrasing becomes removed from the actual content of the original message, the closer it is to being an interpretation rather than a paraphrase.)

Reflection. Reflection occurs when the leader focuses the attention of the individual or group on the predominant feelings or behaviors that are demonstrated in the group. A reflection of feelings requires that the group leader go beyond the face value of the message and respond to the feelings that are being communicated (either through the actual message content or through the manner in which the message is presented). Phrases such as "You sound angry about this situation," or "I sense you feel frustrated with these circumstances" are examples. The reflection of *behavior* is much less interpretive and involves informing group participants about behavior(s) the leader has observed in the group.

Interpretation and analysis. These processes extend beyond observations. The leader essentially shares his or her impressions of a situation and, in so doing, uncovers deeper levels of meaning. The leader identifies themes and patterns that are useful for group members to understand.

Listening. Attentive listening is an important technique for group leaders. It lets group participants know that what they have to say is important and encourages them to communicate their ideas more clearly. Good listening on the part of the leader models desirable communication behavior that is important for successful group therapy. Groups can become simply a chain of talkers, none of whom listens to what the others have to say. An attentive, listening leader can prevent this problem by demonstrating good listening skills and modeling them for the entire group.

These ten feedback techniques are general tools appropriate for the management of any type of therapy group. The next section reviews group therapy techniques for brain-injured patients specifically. Appendix A describes various group activities that a clinician might try to implement in head injury rehabilitation groups. They represent a sampling of different types of cognitive group activities. Each activity has been successfully implemented numerous times with groups of head-injured patients with a full range of disability.

CONDUCTING GROUP THERAPY WITH BRAIN-INJURED PARTICIPANTS

There are certain unique problems with which the cognitive remediation specialist is confronted in trying to conduct effective group therapy. These include the enormous heterogeneity within the population and within most therapy group settings, the problems encountered when conducting group therapy with individuals who have compromised intellectual functioning, and the difficulties produced by conducting groups for persons who may not have voluntarily sought out membership in the group.

Dealing with Heterogeneity

The one characteristic that leaders of head-injury groups can count on is heterogeneity within the population. This is not surprising because everyone begins with a unique personality and individual set of strengths and weaknesses and the mechanisms, extent, and location of brain injury are never the same in any two people. This diversity can be problematic for clinicians trying to conduct group therapy, however, because patients will have differing levels of cognitive and psychosocial abilities. The following are some techniques for managing the heterogeneity within a group.

The Buddy System

Pairing two participants such that one can assist the other with particular problems can be mutually beneficial for both group members. An increase in confidence, self-esteem, and empathy and a decrease in egocentricity (which is common in this population) can occur when a higher-level patient helps a more needy colleague. The buddy system helps the lower-level patient participate more fully in the group as he or she receives one-on-one attention. For example, a pair might include one patient whose injury has left him or her with an inability to write and the other who possesses intact writing skills. If a particular group activity requires writing, the patient with preserved writing ability may be asked to assist the disabled writer by acting as the secretary or scribe.

Therapist Coach

At the New York University Brain Injury Rehabilitation Center, groups are conducted with two therapists, one of whom acts as a patient advocate or "coach" assigned to the particular participant whose turn it is to perform an individual task within the group. It is the coach's responsibility to make sure that the target group member understands the activity and to assist him or her as needed in the group. Each of the group participants is aware of the role of the coach.

Establishing Individual Goals within the Group

Another technique useful for managing the heterogeneity of a brain-injury therapy group is to establish individual therapy goals within the group format. Managing group activities such that success is measured by whether or not group members improve their own individual performance and organizing group activities so that participants compete against themselves rather than each other can be a useful method for coping with groups that display a wide range of abilities. For example, if a cognitive group activity consists of a task working on Speed of Information Processing, the therapy exercise might be organized such that individuals try to beat their own previous times.

Coping with Decreased Cognitive Abilities

Conducting effective group therapy with individuals who have decreased attention, memory, and reasoning capacity presents a unique challenge to the group facilitator. The following techniques are useful for lessening the impact of cognitive impairments.

Increase the Predictability of Group

Following the same general agenda during each group session allows individuals who suffer memory and organization deficits to predict and follow the activities of the group. It provides an organizational schema that can assist group members to feel more comfortable and participate more fully because they are less confused and more aware of upcoming events. Predictability increases independence and task initiation; as group members become more familiar with the schedule, they can start to conduct sections of the group on their own. This is a sample agenda for a morning cognitive group that meets daily:

9:00–9:10   Patients trade events diaries (the section of their notebook in which they make hourly entries recording their therapist's name and the activities that were performed) and quiz each other on their memory of the previous day.

9:10–9:15   Announcements: Personal announcements by both participants and therapists, including any special accomplishments, birthdays, upcoming events, etc. This serves to increase feelings of cohesiveness and ownership within the group.

9:15–9:45   A therapy activity (corresponding to whatever unit the group is working on) is introduced and carried out.

9:45–9:55   The purpose of that day's group therapy activity is reviewed. Any special problems or incidents, as well as any particular successes, are noted. The therapist tries to achieve closure within the group.

9:55–10:00 Participants are reminded to record a statement in their events diary about what occurred during group.

Although the general agenda remains the same, the therapeutic activity changes from day to day, which prevents the group from becoming boring or monotonous.

Providing Patients with a Method for Recording Group Activities

In situations in which the same participants are coming to group each day, systems may be developed to provide participants with a means to remember information from therapy. At Good Samaritan Hospital's Center for Cognitive Rehabilitation, participants keep an hourly record of whom they had for therapy and what they did during their therapy in an "events diary" (see Figure 12.1). (They are provided with a notebook which contains an Events Diary section. See Chapter 7.) Systems such as these that are implemented across therapies (each therapist cues participants to make an hourly record of their session) allow patients to remember information from earlier sessions and can assist with carryover from one group to the next.

Managing the Involuntary Nature of Therapy

Group therapy with head-injured individuals can be more difficult than with other types of groups because often patients have not sought out the therapy or are not attending under purely voluntary circumstances. The groups may be part of an inpatient rehabilitation program or an intensive outpatient rehabilitation program. Sometimes patients object to attending group therapy as part of their rehabilitation package. Resistance to the group process is not uncommon and may be reflected in uncooperative and unproductive behavior. Techniques useful for managing this therapy obstacle, based on the authors' experience, are listed below.

Having Group Members Determine Group Goals

The therapist can have the group at large outline acceptable group behavior. Assigning the responsibility for setting rules of appropriate group behavior to the participants can be an effective method for achieving cooperation. Listed below is an example of "group rules" that were generated in a cognitive group therapy session. (A therapist facilitated the group and acted as a moderator and secretary while the group members produced the list.)

No sleeping during group.
No leaving the group except for urgent reasons.
Every group member has the right not to talk on a certain subject if he or she feels uncomfortable.
No one should laugh at or unkindly criticize another person in the group.
No interrupting.

DATE:	3/4	
8:30 – 9:30	Had cognitive group. We discussed yesterday's events.
	Did an activity to work on communication.
9:30 – 10:30	Worked on attention computer programs. I improved.
10:30 – 11:30	Did cooking. Still hard to follow directions.
11:30 – 12:30	I ate lunch with all of the participants. We played
	Trivial Pursuit.
12:30 – 1:30	
1:30 – 2:30	
2:30 – 3:30	
3:30 – 4:30	
4:30 – 5:30	
5:30 – 6:30	
6:30 – 7:30	
7:30 – 8:30	
8:30 – 9:30	

FIGURE 12.1. Sample of an Events Diary used to record daily events. It is reviewed each morning during cognitive group.

Some of these rules were a direct response to particular problems that were occurring within the group. For example, there was one individual who would close his eyes and appear to be sleeping during the group and who refused to participate in the discussion. After the rule was generated, if the particular participant attempted to close his eyes, different group members would remind him of the rule. In this way, the therapist was taken out of the role of disciplinarian, and peer therapy operated as an effective means for increasing the individual's level of participation.

Appropriate Leadership Style

A second method for decreasing or avoiding resistant behavior is the implementation of a democratic leadership style. Sampson and Marthas (1977) discuss research that differentiates among a participant-oriented, problem-solving style of leadership (democratic), a leader-centered, directive style (autocratic), and a noncentered style of group leadership *(laissez faire)*. They note that the democratic leadership style is the most effective and results in the greatest group satisfaction. The mission of a democratic leader is to facilitate the group members' participation in decisions regarding the goals and outcomes of the group. A democratic leadership style encourages participation of all group members. It is more effective in facilitating changes in cognitive or psychosocial functioning, and it also decreases resistance to the group therapy process. Individuals feel that they have more control and more ownership for the group process.

Therapists can implement this leadership style by such activities as allowing group members the freedom to choose among certain activities and by demonstrating a willingness to change the direction of a group based on feedback from group participants. One particularly effective method is for the therapist to participate fully in all group activities and to require any visitors (e.g., other therapists, family members, students) also to take part in discussion and activities. It is important that groups promote the patients' adjustment to normal living environments as well as achieve specific therapy goals. Therapists who need to have a great deal of control (e.g., autocratic group leaders) and are unwilling to participate as a group member may not only experience more resistance on the part of group participants but may do a disservice by perpetuating the patient–therapist distinction, which is not a normalizing function. Effective leaders of head-injury groups need to be secure and willing to take risks by making themselves vulnerable to the group process and by sharing their personal selves while participating fully in discussions and activities.

In addition to these general management techniques there are other key interventions that, while not unique to head injury rehabilitation, are useful to review in the context of this population. These two interventions are (1) defining the goals of the group and (2) promoting cohesiveness and cooperation.

Defining Group Goals

In working with individuals who have reduced cognitive faculties, it is important that the goals of group be carefully identified and outlined. A clear definition of goals allows the clinician to develop specific group activities and evaluate group and individual progress and outcomes. There are three types of goals. One involves improvement within specific cognitive or psychosocial therapy arenas (e.g., increasing interpersonal skills or increasing attention). These sorts of goals extend over many therapy sessions and may be measured by objective neuropsychologic tests or data collected on specific observational protocols. A second type of group goal involves the particular activity or discussion being conducted within one session. Thus, the goal for a problem-solving group may be to generate a solution to a particular problem experienced within the group. Such objectives would not extend beyond the particular therapy session. A third type of objective for group therapy simply involves the process of completing a shared activity or discussion together. The only expectation for carryover would be increased positive feelings about the group and group members. For example, celebrating a group member's birthday during a group session might not have specific individual therapy goals, but the process of sharing that time would have therapeutic value in terms of promoting good feelings.

The same activity may contain all three types of goals. For example, an "Open Group," in which the group chooses a general topic and everyone shares his or her thoughts on the topic, might have individually specified therapy objectives, goals related to the discussion topic, and the goal of participating in a shared experience with other individuals. A clinician might be targeting increased initiation in conversations for one particular group member and orchestrate that person's participation in the Open Group to coincide with this therapy objective, whereas for another person the goal might be increased information processing as measured by the ability to attend to and remember the contents of previous statements.

If the goal of therapy is to increase specific cognitive processes, the group activities should be organized according to the Process-Specific Approach to cognitive rehabilitation. As discussed throughout this text, this approach requires repetitive administration of tasks. In a group setting, the clinician can choose group activities that activate targeted cognitive process. Similar therapy tasks can be done multiple times, with patients trying to improve on earlier scores.

Cooperation

Cooperation is, of course, important to any group process. It is perhaps more difficult to foster in groups with head-injured members than in other types of groups because many of the psychosocial and cognitive sequelae suffered by this population interfere with the ability to demonstrate cooperative behavior. Choosing activities that promote cohesiveness and cooperation is an important part of establishing a unified group. Examples of such activities include having the group members challenge therapists to a recreational activity (e.g., ping-pong or cognitive games) or organizing a celebration for a particular participant or therapist who has achieved something special. These activities provide an excellent means to increase group cohesiveness. At the Center for Cognitive Rehabilitation at Good Samaritan Hospital, participants meet daily for a cognitive group. Once a week, one member is chosen "Participant of the Week." A certificate is awarded, and the member's picture is posted in the Center. Similarly, participants are given an opportunity to choose an individual for "Staff of the Week." Such activities give group members an investment in each other's successes and help promote cooperation. Cooperation is perhaps the clinician's best tool for conducting effective cognitive groups; it is worth the time and effort required to foster cohesiveness in a group therapy process.

TYPES OF GROUPS

The specific goals of therapy discussed earlier will be reflected, in part, in the type of group that is being conducted. The type of group, in turn, will depend on the rehabilitation setting. Intensive outpatient programs, where the same group of patients attend each day, allow more flexibility and intensity than an acute setting, where group members change day to day and may possess lower level skills.

Listed below are sample types of groups that might be conducted within various head injury rehabilitation settings:

Orientation group: designed to assist patients in increasing orientation to person, place, and time.

Cognitive group: designed to increase specific cognitive processes, including attention, memory, reasoning, visuospatial skills, and executive functions. It may also be used to educate individuals about head injury.

Communication group: designed to increase communication skills or pragmatic abilities (see Chapter 9).

Psychosocial group: designed to increase adjustment to disability and to provide a forum for sharing feelings.

Although groups may be organized around any rehabilitation need (e.g., Activities of Daily Living groups or Vocational groups), these are the most common in head injury rehabilitation settings.

There are numerous ways of orchestrating group activities that may vary according to the type of group. In cognitive groups, units of similar activities are grouped together (see the list that follows). For psychosocial groups, different components of psychosocial functioning might be simultaneously addressed.

Cognitive group activities may be organized into the following units:

Attention: activities targeting attentional processing.
Memory: group tasks addressing memory ability.
Reasoning: exercises addressing reasoning and problem solving.
Visual processing: group therapy tasks involving visual–perceptual ability.
Brain injury education: activities designed to increase knowledge regarding general issues of head injury.

A three-times-weekly psychosocial group might be organized according to the following schedule.

Day 1 and Day 3: Open Groups—The group chooses a specific topic (e.g., a social problem), and the therapist assists in the generation of a productive discussion.
Day 2: Interpersonal Skills Group—Activities/discussions designed to increase social skills are implemented.

PREPARATION FOR GROUP THERAPY

Regardless of the type of group, it is important that the clinician plan and organize the therapy session in advance of the group meeting. The following serves as a checklist for preparing for a group session:

1. Decide on the agenda (e.g., introduction, explanation of group activity, closure of the group meeting). This will vary, of course, depending on the type of group, but the clinician should have a good idea of the time allocated for different portions of the group meeting and be able to outline the intended plan at the beginning of the meeting. This will increase the predictability of the group (see above for sample group schedule).

2. Reflect on the goals for the group session. These may be ongoing group objectives to increase cognitive processes, or they may be one-time goals such as an activity to increase group cohesiveness.
3. Choose the group activity or discussion format.
4. Gather any materials needed.
5. Arrange for the collection of any data that will be useful. (Other therapists can perform this task.) Frequency measures of behavior targeted in group might be taken in settings outside of group to assess generalization of skills.
6. Decide on a method for evaluating the success of group sessions. A system for noting any changes that would be useful to remember in subsequent group sessions and a method for documenting observations during the group are important for increasing the efficacy of group therapy.

Once a therapist builds up a repertoire of successful group activities, the preparation process may take only a matter of minutes.

SUMMARY

Group therapy has several advantages over individual therapy, including the opportunity to provide patients with a support network, the opportunity to model and reinforce appropriate behaviors, the ability to encourage generalization of skills in therapy to naturalistic settings, the opportunity to increase the accuracy of patients' self-perception by providing reality testing, and, finally, the provision of an economic staff/patient therapy ratio.

A number of feedback techniques are useful to group leaders facilitating any type of group process. The ten described in this chapter were supportive feedback, confrontation, advice/suggestions, summarizing, clarifying, probing/questioning, repeating/paraphrasing, reflecting, interpreting, and listening.

Group therapy with head-injured patients presents specific challenges to the group leader. One such challenge is the tremendous heterogeneity found within this population. Techniques for coping with this problem include pairing participants (a buddy system) or pairing a therapist with a patient in a coaching format. Establishing individual objectives within the group also helps to deal with the diverse patient population. Techniques for managing group therapy with members who have decreased cognitive capacity or who may be resistant to the group process were also outlined.

Research suggests that a democratic leadership style is most effective in increasing group members' therapeutic progress and satisfaction. Democratic group leaders encourage all members to participate in decisions and in the direction of the group process. Establishing group goals and facilitating cooperation and cohesiveness are other methods for increasing the therapeutic value of the group therapy.

There are different types of head injury rehabilitation groups, including cognitive, psychosocial, and communication groups. Activities may be organized according to the type of group and/or specific group goals. It is important that the clinician leading the group prepare for the group session by setting an agenda, reflecting on the goals of the group, gathering the group materials, arranging for data collection, and preparing a system for evaluating the success of the group.

STUDY QUESTIONS

1. Why would a mix of individual and group therapy be most beneficial to a head-injured person undergoing rehabilitation? What does each therapy format offer that the other cannot provide?
2. Using the scenario of providing patient Joe Smith with feedback regarding his difficulty initiating conversation and his low participation in group, develop sample statements that illustrate each of the ten feedback statements described in the chapter.
3. Choose an activity in the Appendix and describe how it might be conducted using a democratic and an autocratic leadership style.
4. Choose a different activity from the Appendix and go through the checklist in the text, describing how you might prepare for the group.

REFERENCES

Argyris, C. (1976). Theories of action that inhibit individual learning. *American Psychologist* 31:638–654.

Carberry, H., & Burd, B. (1983). Social aspects of cognitive retraining in an outpatient group setting for head trauma patients. *Cognitive Rehabilitation* 1:5–7.

Cartwright, D., & Zander, A. (1953). *Group dynamics: Research and theory.* Evanston, IL, White Plains, NY: Row, Peterson.

Sampson, E., and Marthas, M. S. (1977). *Group process in the health professions.* New York, London, Sydney, Toronto: John Wiley & Sons.

Yalom, I. D. (1975). *The theory and practice of group psychotherapy.* New York: Basic Books.

APPENDIX

Verbal Drawing Task

Unit: *Communication*

Activity: Give/receive directions for drawing a multishaped form.

Goals: Improve ability to follow and give accurate directions.

Materials: Three pieces of blank paper per person and two colored pens per person.

Preparation: None.

Procedure: Divide participants into pairs. Instruct one participant in each pair to make a drawing involving three different kinds of shapes (e.g., rectangle, triangle, square) and two colors. Do not let the other person in the pair see the drawings. The participant who drew the picture gives instructions to the partner so that he or she can reproduce the drawing without seeing it. Participants then compare drawings and see if/where communication and/or direction following broke down. The pairs then switch roles. The person who received directions now gives directions to the other person. The therapist can then lead a discussion about accuracy of communication. He or she might ask participants which role they found more difficult and generate a discussion surrounding the answers.

Hat Communication Activity

Unit: *Communication*

Activity: Group communication activity in which people respond to each other in a specified style of communication.

Goals: Increase communication skills; increase perspective taking and empathy.

Materials: Communication hats. These are paper hats (the sort a fast food service worker wears) with different directions written on the outside. Sample directions for five hats include: "Talk down to me," "Ignore me," "Interrupt me," "Compliment me," and "Ask me questions about myself."

Preparation: Make communication hats.

Procedure: Therapist hands out paper communication hats and instructs participants to put them on without looking at them. Time is given for everyone to review each other's hats. A topic is introduced, and the group begins talking and responding to each other as indicated on people's hats. After each topic, people try and guess what their hat said. Therapist directs discussion about how individuals felt when people responded to them in the specified manner. The group can trade hats and repeat activity. The activity can be broken down and done in pairs. The rest of the group watches while one communication pair role-plays a discussion and responds to each other according to the manner indicated on the hat. The group can make up a hat message for the group leader so that he or she can participate as well.

Party Activity

Unit: *Communication*

Activity: Individuals assume hypothetical identities and role play a party situation trying to meet everyone in the room.

Goals: Increase communication and social skills; increase memory for names and people.

Materials: Identity cards listing hypothetical name, age, occupation, and family situation (e.g., marriage status, children) for each member in the group.

Preparation: Make identity cards.

Procedure: Participants receive cards with identity. Everyone then role-plays being at a party and introducing self. Individuals may embellish on their life situation and provide additional information other than that on the card. At the end of the designated time, the group tries to recall everyone's identity. The group generates a discussion on social skills and initiating conversation. Group might discuss what was hard or easy about the activity.
              A variation for a higher-level group is to write identities for each other (including group leader).

Extemporaneous Speeches

Unit: *Communication*

Activity: Participants present extemporaneous speeches to group.

Goals: Increase verbal expression skills, speed of processing, and verbal organization.

Materials: None.

Preparation: None.

Procedure: Therapist helps participants generate a master list of speech topics on board. Each person chooses a topic and has 4 minutes to prepare a minimum 2-minute speech. After each speech, the group offers information concerning strengths and weaknesses (e.g., "need better eye contact").

To make the task easier, therapist can present speech structure that each participant should follow. For example, therapist may write on board:

1. Introduce topic.
2. Give information about topic.
3. Summarize your information.

Give examples of short speeches following this structure.

Head Injury Film

Unit:	*Brain Injury Education*
Activity:	Presentation of film on head injury.
Goals:	Increase awareness about the effects of brain injury.
Materials:	Film, discussion sheet (see below).
Preparation:	None.
Procedure:	Review discussion sheet with participants prior to film. View film and fill out discussion sheets together.

Sample Discussion Sheet

1. What was the purpose of this film?
2. What things did you relate to from your own experiences?
3. What did you like best about the film?
4. Did anything in the film bother you?

Problem Lists

Unit:	*Brain Injury Education*
Activity:	Participants fill out personal lists identifying changes resulting from the brain injury.
Goals:	Increase awareness of the effects of brain injury. Decrease denial of deficits.
Materials:	Problem lists (see below for sample).
Preparation:	None.
Procedure:	The group leader leads an initial discussion about the common cognitive and psychosocial effects of head injury. Then participants are asked to think about their own situation and what effects they notice from their head injury. The group is given time and assistance to fill out problem lists. People then share their information with the group.

Brain Injury Education

Name: _____

Check any cognitive or language problems you have as a result of your brain injury.

————decreased attention
————memory problems
————visual spatial problems
————problems in reasoning and judgment
————slowed thinking
————trouble thinking of words
————speech problems
————problems with organization and planning
————other (describe) _____

Check any psychosocial problems you have as a result of your brain injury.

————problems controlling anger
————easily irritated
————depressed
————fatigue
————denial (trouble admitting you have problems)
————labile (cry or laugh too easily)
————trouble initiating or starting up activities
————poor social skills (can't relate well to people)
————anxiety
————other (describe) _____

Summary List

Impairments	Strengths
Write a list of your cognitive problems	Write a list of those cognitive skills that were NOT affected by your head injury.
1.	
2.	1.
3.	2.
	3.
Write a list of your psychosocial problems.	Write a list of those psychosocial skills that were NOT affected by your head injury.
1.	
2.	1.
3.	2.
	3.

Feelings about Brain Injury

Unit: *Brain Injury Education*

Activity: Sentence completion for feelings about brain injury.

Goal: Share feelings about brain injury; build empathy for others' situations.

Materials: Sentence completion sheet (see below).

Preparation: None.

Procedure: Using a round-robin approach, have each group member take a turn completing each sentence. Discuss responses, noting how people have different feelings about what has happened to them.

Complete the sentences so they tell *how* you really feel.

1. Since I've had this brain injury, I feel . . .

2. A question I have about brain injury is . . .

3. One frustrating thing about brain injury is . . .

4. One good thing that has resulted from my brain injury is . . .

5. Being at this rehabilitation center makes me feel . . .

6. I decided to come to this rehabilitation facility because . . .

7. Having to do homework and go to "school" again makes me feel . . .

8. When I think of a brain-injured person, I think of someone . . .

9. In therapy, I wish we could . . .

10. When friends ask why I am going to therapy, I say . . .

11. Having my family listen and talk about my progress in therapy makes me feel . . .

Number Identification

Unit: *Reasoning*

Activity: Participants try to guess target number given clues.

Goals: Improve reasoning and questioning strategies.

Materials: Blackboard.

Preparation: None.

Procedure: Ask participant to think of a number between 1 and 50. Group tries to guess what it is, but the other person can only say "too high" or "too low" when a guess is suggested. Count how many guesses it takes the group to discover the number. The leader helps the group devise a strategy to guess the number more quickly.

Sequence Race

Unit:	*Reasoning*
Activity:	Participants arrange the steps of activity in proper sequence.
Goals:	Improve sequencing skills.
Materials:	3 × 5 cards.
Preparation:	None.
Procedure:	Choose one of these activities:

Making a peanut butter and jelly sandwich
Washing the car
Changing a tire
Wrapping a present
Making scrambled eggs
Giving the dog a bath

Have participants list each step in sequence needed to carry out the activity. Try to have no fewer than seven and no more than 12 steps. The group leader prints each step on a separate 3 × 5 card and shuffles the cards thoroughly. Several participants get stacks of cards and race to see who can put their cards into correct order first.

A variation is to leave one card out of each stack when it is handed out to participants. The participants then race to figure out the content of their missing card.

Card Story

Unit:	*Reasoning*
Activity:	Participant create a story from unrelated words.
Goals:	Improve sequencing skills and divergent thinking.
Materials:	Cards with nouns on them.
Preparation:	Therapist writes each of the following words on small cards:

key	guitar
calendar	letter
flashlight	bag
parrot	coin
glove	

Procedure: Have participants arrange the cards in any order they wish and then write a story that includes each item in sequence and connects them into a plot. May use two teams and divide cards.

Variations: (1) Deal the cards out and write the story using the sequence as dealt, or (2) deal the cards face down and write the story as you turn up one card at a time.

Photo Activity

Unit: *Reasoning*

Activity: Suggesting what might have occurred in pictures right before they were taken.

Goals: Improve divergent thinking; improve verbal expression skills.

Materials: Pictures (e.g., photographs, magazine pictures).

Preparations: None.

Procedure: Therapist presents pictures, and each participant tells in a few sentences what might have occurred right before a picture was taken of each scene. Creativity and the ability to generate different ideas is emphasized. Therapist should also participate in the activity.

Drawing Add-On

Unit: *Reasoning*

Activity: Participants take turns adding one line/part to a drawing and try to create something.

Goals: Improve divergent thinking and group cooperation.

Materials: Blackboard.

Preparation: None.

Procedures: Have one person start off with a line/curve on the board. Each person takes turns adding on until the group is able to define a picture.

Continuation Story

Unit: *Reasoning*

Activity: Build on each others' story.

Goals: Improve sequencing, divergent thinking skills, and verbal expression.

Materials: None.

Preparation: None.

Procedure: Therapist lays out guidelines and tells group that one person will start a story and everybody will have a chance to add on to and expand on the story, and one person will do the conclusion. Guidelines include: story "add-on" must logically follow the preceding part, no inappropriate scenes, and a time limit of 4 minutes per person. Can tape-record story and play back for group.

Word Fluency Activity

Unit: *Reasoning*

Activity: Participants try to think of as many words as they can in a category.

Goals: Improve speed of information processing and divergent thinking (fluency).

Materials: Blackboard and paper.

Preparation: None.

Procedure: Group comes up with a category and people write down as many words as they can in 1 minute. Participants try to increase their individual scores over trials. The group may compare answers to provide models. Difficulty levels may be increased by using more abstract categories or by changing task to "name everything you could do with a piece of string" using the same format.

13
Beyond Cognitive Rehabilitation: Achieving Community Reintegration

Cognitive remediation is only one piece of the rehabilitation puzzle. If results were limited to improved scores on clinical measures of intellectual processes, with no provision for applying improved cognitive status to real-world activities, then most people would question the utility of the retraining program. Acute care and early inpatient rehabilitation are relatively firmly established phases in the treatment process, but it has only been in the past decade that postacute rehabilitation programs have been developed to assist head-injured individuals in achieving maximal levels of independent living and vocational pursuit.

It is important for professionals delivering cognitive rehabilitation services in both early acute-care hospitals and postmedical rehabilitation programs to be aware of the barriers that face head-injured persons trying to reintegrate into society. If everyone were cognizant of the end goals of community integration, more appropriate treatment objectives might be targeted from the beginning.

This chapter reviews a number of issues essential to promoting community integration, including community reintegration, community reentry, postacute rehabilitation, use of a multidisciplinary team, levels of independence, rehabilitation outcome, and cost effectiveness.

RELATED DISCIPLINES

Other disciplines that typically treat patients in more functional contexts provide valuable assistance to the cognitive rehabilitation specialist in promoting the application of cognitive gains to naturalistic tasks. These disciplines include *occupational therapy, vocational rehabilitation,* and *therapeutic recreation.* They can provide information on how a patient functions within different environments and on different tasks and thus help the cognitive rehabilitation specialist develop appropriate therapy. The

327

professional responsible for managing the cognitive deficits can work with other specialists to promote transfer of improved cognitive function to real-world activities and can help these other professionals to manage residual cognitive impairments that might affect therapeutic activities. Below are brief descriptions of occupational therapy, vocational rehabilitation, and therapeutic recreation, with suggestions for how these disciplines might work in conjunction with the cognitive rehabilitation specialist to promote maximal community reentry.

Occupational Therapy

In their education, occupational therapists receive training in task analysis, kinesiology, design and use of adaptive equipment, and visuoperceptual functioning, all with a focus on learning to assist individuals to achieve their highest level of functioning in home, work, and leisure settings. In some work environments, occupational therapists deliver cognitive rehabilitation services; however, in many head injury treatment settings, they are responsible for training related to daily living skills such as dressing, feeding, shopping, cooking, and money management. If not responsible for cognitive therapy themselves, they can serve as valuable resources in training head-injured patients to apply cognitive skills to everyday functional tasks.

What information might the cognitive rehabilitation specialist seek from the occupational therapist? The following are sample questions:

- What is the patient's attention span during independent living activities such as cooking and shopping?
- Does the therapist note any problems in executive functions, such as poor initiation or difficulty sequencing and planning the steps involved in meal preparation, dressing, and shopping, for example?
- Is the patient using compensatory memory techniques to manage memory impairment during functional tasks?

The occupational therapist, in turn, might pose the following sorts of questions to the cognitive rehabilitation professional the better to plan appropriate treatment:

- What is the nature of the patient's memory functioning? Does he or she have good procedural memory?
- What is the rate of new learning, and what are suggested ways to present new information to maximize learning?
- Is the patient using a memory notebook or being trained in the use of any other specific compensatory techniques?

- Do neuropsychological test results indicate any deficits in reasoning and problem solving that might suggest poor safety or judgment in an independent living situation?
- Are the patient's mathematics ability and executive functions adequate for balancing a bank statement?

An exchange of information and mutual consultation between clinicians training functional activities and those managing retraining of deficit cognitive processes can result in assisting patients to achieve their maximum level of independence.

Therapeutic Recreation

Therapeutic recreation focuses on changing behaviors through specific activities so that an individual can enjoy independent and satisfying leisure time. Therapeutic recreation specialists receive training in how to teach individuals to utilize community and personal resources in order to pursue leisure activities. Within the rehabilitation team, the therapeutic recreation specialist's role is to increase the patient's leisure awareness, social interaction, and leisure participation. There has been a recent movement within this discipline away from serving a purely diversionary function toward taking a more active role in the rehabilitation process. For example, within most rehabilitation settings, the therapeutic recreation specialist is responsible for taking patients out into the community on recreational outings. Rather than viewing these events simply as field trips or one-time leisure experiences, the "state of the art" in therapeutic recreation is to encourage community outings as training opportunities in which therapy objectives targeted within the clinic can be transferred to naturalistic contexts.

Sample questions that a cognitive rehabilitation specialist might ask the therapeutic recreation specialist include the following:

- Did the patient have difficulty with route finding or orientation to place on the outing.
- Did the patient appropriately record information in his or her memory system while out in the community?
- Could the patient process information given by any tour guides, sign boards, or brochures?
- How well is the patient able to plan, initiate, and carry out leisure activities?

Questions that the therapeutic recreation specialist might be interested in having the cognitive specialist address include the following:

- Does the patient's neuropsychologic profile suggest that he or she is able to pursue a particular hobby or activity?
- What system is the patient using to compensate for deficits in episodic memory (i.e., ability to recall personally experienced events)?
- What cognitive goals are being addressed that the therapeutic recreation specialist might target in naturalistic settings?

Vocational Rehabilitation

Return to work is a realistic goal for many head-injured persons. The vocational rehabilitation counselor is a critical member of a rehabilitation team that assists patients in reaching maximal levels of employment. Vocational rehabilitation counselors (VRCs) are trained in methods for assessing work tolerance, examining past work history to identify transferrable skills that are compatible with existing cognitive and physical limitations, identifying appropriate vocational goals, performing job analyses, and conducting labor market surveys to determine the feasibility of employment goals. The VRC often assists the patient with coordinating whatever government or disability monies he or she may be receiving and may also work with state and federal agencies to identify and apply any available employer incentives or specific return-to-work programs that might be options for particular patients in specific regions. Perhaps the most critical task of the VRC working with head-injured patients is job placement. Often, too much emphasis is placed on prevocational readiness and too little effort is applied to actual job identification. Finding employers willing to hire disabled persons and adapt existing jobs takes a great deal of time and energy. Preparing patients for employment without placing them in appropriate jobs can result in long-term unemployment.

Information that a cognitive therapist might glean from the VRC to assist in planning appropriate treatment includes the following:

- What are the cognitive demands of the particular jobs being considered?
- Is there an opportunity to educate the potential employer about existing cognitive deficits and how to manage them?
- Will current memory systems or trained compensatory strategies be adaptable to the types of work environments being considered?

The VRC will need the cognitive rehabilitation professional to supply information about the projected cognitive levels so that suitable employment can be identified. Questions such as these might be posed:

- How well can the patient learn new information?
- What types of strategies or techniques can be developed for managing residual cognitive deficits within the work setting?

Once again, a mutual exchange of information between the cognitive rehabilitation professional and the VRC is crucial for meeting the patient's needs. The VRC depends on the cognitive therapist to assist a patient in maximizing cognitive functions that might be needed on a job. Likewise, the clinician managing the cognitive deficits is dependent on the VRC to communicate possible job options and corresponding cognitive requirements so that the major obstacles to success in the work setting might be addressed.

The following section provides a sample discharge report describing the treatment of a patient who completed a 6-month postacute intensive day-treatment program at Good Samaritan Hospital's Center for Cognitive Rehabilitation. It is included to illustrate how the different disciplines work together to maximize a patient's functioning in living, work, and leisure settings. (In addition to the types of therapy discussed in this chapter, the report documents contributions of psychosocial treatment, which is discussed separately in Chapter 14.)

The multidisciplinary team model is appropriate because of the complexity of overcoming and adjusting to residual disabilities at a level that allows successful functioning in today's society. The following discharge report has been preserved in its original form. It was chosen because it is representative of an average patient at the clinic and because it serves as a good introduction to the following section, which describes community reintegration programs.

SAMPLE DISCHARGE REPORT

Pertinent History

Mr. G. is a 21-year-old single male who sustained a closed-head injury in a single motor vehicle accident on August 23, 1985. He was hospitalized in three different facilities prior to treatment at Good Samaritan Hospital's Center for Cognitive Rehabilitation. He initially received acute-care treatment followed by inpatient rehabilitation. He was then transferred to a nursing facility for a total of 8 months. He was initially comatose for approximately 1 week. Posttraumatic amnesia (PTA) was present, but of unknown duration.

Prior to his injury, Mr. G. attended high school through the 10th grade, but dropped out at this point to obtain employment. Mr. G.'s grade point average was 2.0. He left school to begin working as a painter and had been working as an insulation and glass installer for 6 months prior to his injury. At the time of program entry, Mr. G. was unemployed and living with his mother in her home.

Course of Treatment

Mr. G. entered Good Samaritan Hospital's Center for Cognitive Rehabilitation (CCR) on February 2, 1987. During the first 2 weeks of the program, comprehensive testing in the areas of cognition, psychosocial adjustment, independent living skills, physical abilities, recreational skills, and vocational potential was performed. Based on the findings from this assessment, goals for each of the above disciplines were established. Overall rehabilitation goals were set for ultimate return to independent living and entry-level competitive employment.

In addition to his work in the above areas, Mr. G. participated in a transitional living experience to retrain independent living skills and a community work station to improve vocational behaviors.

Progress and Current Level of Functioning

Cognition

Results from initial testing indicated that when Mr. G. entered the CCR program he suffered the following impairments: (1) a mild to moderate deficit in attention, (2) a moderate to severe decline in memory ability, (3) a mild to moderate compromise in concept formation and reasoning skills, and (4) reduced speech intelligibility.

Treatment consisted of group and individual cognitive rehabilitation sessions targeting attention, memory, and concept formation. Hierarchically organized treatment tasks designed to activate target components of deficit cognitive process areas repetitively were administered.

Posttesting performed on June 3, 1987, indicated substantial gains in attention, memory, and reasoning/problem-solving ability. Scores from the Paced Auditory Serial Addition Task (PASAT), a sensitive measure of attention, improved significantly over initial testing levels. At the time of program entry, PASAT scores ranged from the mildly to moderately impaired range. Posttest scores on all three trials now appear in the high-average to superior range of functioning.

Mr. G. also demonstrated substantial gains in memory, although this remains an area of residual concern. Initially the Memory Index on the Randt Memory Test appeared 3 standard deviations below the mean. At the time of discharge, it is less than 1 standard deviation below the mean. It should be noted that Mr. G. exhibits particular difficulty with the delayed recall of verbal information. On the Rey Auditory Verbal Learning Test, a measure of new verbal learning, Mr. G. continues to demonstrate major deficits. On this measure, he exhibited moderate to severe deficits in the rate of new learning and considerable confabulation. Improvement was noted, however, in the retention of new information following distraction (estimated in the moderately impaired range as compared to the severely impaired range previously). On the Prospective Memory Screening (PRO-MS), Mr. G. did improve from the mildly impaired range to the normal range, suggesting a good ability to remember into the future and perform target tasks at specified future times.

Mr. G. worked on two aspects of reasoning and problem solving. One was logical reasoning and abstract thinking, and the other involved social comprehension. Improvements in this area were documented by gains on the Comprehension and Similarities subtests from the Wechsler Adult Intelligence Scale—Revised (WAIS-R), both of which emphasize social comprehension and abstract reasoning. It should be noted that Mr. G. continues to exhibit some rigidity and concreteness in his approach to practical problem solving. He has a difficult time generating alternative solutions and thinking in a flexible manner.

Slight improvement was noted on general IQ testing. Initial scores in the WAIS-R revealed a Verbal IQ in the average range, a Performance IQ between the Low-Average range and the borderline mentally compromised range, and a Full Scale IQ in the low-average range. At discharge, Mr. G. showed modest changes in intellectual functioning, with the current Verbal IQ still in the average range, the Performance IQ now in the low-average range, and Full-Scale IQ remaining in the low-average range.

Initially, reduced speech intelligibility was noted in conversational speech in all contexts. The Assessment of Intelligibility of Dysarthric Speech was administered with the results suggesting single-word intelligibility of 75% and sentence intelligibility rated at 95%. However, these data overestimated Mr. G.'s intelligibility since this test uses written word stimuli rather than spontaneous speech, and his intelligibility significantly decreased during conversational speech. Improved speech was addressed through an intelligibility training program that began with in-clinic exercises and advanced to speech training in naturalistic settings. At the conclusion of the speech program, Mr. G. was able to participate in a 10-minute conversation with an intelligibility rating of 100%. Residual speech impairments exist when Mr. G. loses concentration and no longer effortfully produces quality speech. He can increase his level of intelligibility by making a conscious, concerted effort to decrease rate of speech and exaggerate pronunciation.

Overall, Mr. G. demonstrates excellent improvements in the cognitive abilities addressed in this program. Residual areas of cognitive concern include decreased rate of new learning, reduced speed of processing, and a tendency toward concreteness in thought. Mr. G. was taught to compensate for residual deficits by implementing the following strategies: (1) utilization of his Day-Timer (memory notebook) to record new information, appointments, and errands and (2) requests for repetition of directions and attempts to summarize information to be remembered to ensure correct recall of the target information. Additionally, it will be important for those individuals working closely with Mr. G. to be aware of the above deficits and to structure the environment to maximize his potential for success. This will include reducing demands for speeded performance as well as heavy demands on memory.

Psychosocial Adjustment

When Mr. G. entered the CCR program, he displayed moderate deficits in interpersonal skills, including a range of socially immature behaviors, a self-centered approach in conversations, and a limited repertoire of appropriate social skills for making friends with others. In the area of self-regulation, Mr. G. demonstrated mild to moderate deficits in terms of behaving childishly and sometimes making tactless statements before thinking about their impact. Mr. G. displayed mild to moderate deficits in stimulus-bound behavior including an unnecessary degree of practical and emotional dependence on others. This meant that he rarely initiated or followed through with activities unless others provided considerable direction and/or assistance. In the area of depression, Mr. G. scored within the normal range on the Beck Depression Inventory. Mr. G. displayed mild deficits in the area of adjustment to disability in terms of some unrealistic statements about financial expectations and general plans for the future following completion of the CCR program. Finally, within the area of family stress, Mr. G. demonstrated some discomfort with receiving direction and guidance from his mother.

During the course of his 6-month program at the CCR, Mr. G. participated in once-weekly individual psychosocial treatment sessions and in three-times-weekly psychosocial groups. Individual treatment focused on decreasing immature and inappropriate social behaviors and replacing them with more desirable social skills as well as on establishing more realistic expectations for the short-term future. Group psychosocial treatment focused on improving problem-solving skills, values clarification, extensive practice with communication skills in a wide variety of situations, and discussion of personal adjustment issues. In addition to the above, family counseling was also provided to facilitate carryover and maintenance of therapy objectives to naturalistic family contexts as well as to provide the family with information about Mr. G.'s deficits and needs. Mr. G. participated fully in all aspects of the program and demonstrated very good psychosocial progress.

In the area of interpersonal skills following discharge, Mr. G. displays mild difficulties. In most circumstances, Mr. G. behaves in ways appropriate for his age. He is much more serious than before, takes a greater interest in others, can accept compliments, and can initiate appropriate conversations with others. Mr. G.'s mild difficulties are only apparent when he is in an unfamiliar situation or when he is fairly anxious. At these times, Mr. G. tends to withdraw, behave less maturely, or act somewhat defensively. However, Mr. G. generally responds well to feedback and makes appropriate changes. In the area of self-regulation, Mr. G. improved his ability to interact in an appropriately mature manner. Mr. G. no longer displays the degree of silliness and giggling that he did at the time of program entry and is no longer overreacting in an irritable or tactless way as was reported previously, except on a very occasional basis. Final functioning in this area is judged to be between the normal and mildly impaired range. Mr. G. also demonstrates functioning in the area of stimulus-bound behavior between the normal and mildly impaired ranges. He is considerably more confident and resourceful in his independence and displays the ability to initiate and follow through with a wide range of tasks with little or no assistance. However, Mr. G. still tends to seek ways to complete chores that included dependency on others. It will be important to make sure that Mr. G. is set up in a fully independent situation (e.g., find a residence on a bus line) as soon as he moves to a new location.

Depression at discharge is in the normal range. In the area of adjustment to disability, Mr. G. made significant improvement in terms of more realistic expectations for the future. Mr. G. is better able to treat the current situation as a "new start," meaning that he will have to "start at the bottom and work his way up again." Mr. G.'s functioning at program completion in this area is judged to be between the mildly impaired and the normal range. Finally, there is improvement in the area of family stress. Mr. G. and his mother are able to work together more effectively, and his mother appears to have a clearer idea of Mr. G.'s needs and limitations. Mr. G. reportedly still finds it difficult to accept direction and advice from his mother in some situations, but only to a degree that is fairly typical in families. Overall, family stress is considered to be within the normal range at the time of discharge.

In summary, Mr. G. made excellent progress in psychosocial adjustment during his program. Continued attention should be given to the two following areas: (1) emphasis should be placed by Mr. G., his family, and employers on mature and appropriate social behavior, especially when in new or stressful situations, and (2) CCR, Mr. G., and Ms. G. (mother) should ensure that Mr. G. establishes fully independent ways of completing functional tasks from the very beginning in his new living situation.

Independent Living Skills

At the time of program entry, Mr. G. completed a 2-week assessment of independent living skills in the areas of safety knowledge, meal planning and preparation, transportation, community access, and money management. Results from the evaluation suggested mild to moderate deficits in safety knowledge, ability to use public transportation, money management, and skills to access community resources in an organized manner. Mr. G. was not driving and expressed a desire to be relicensed. He had been living with his family following his discharge from rehabilitation facilities prior to entering the CCR program.

The treatment program focused on providing structured and supervised tasks in the impaired functional process areas to increase skills, followed by practice in naturalistic settings. Mr. G. moved into a transitional-living apartment and received daily monitoring to promote carryover of newly learned or relearned skills in the home setting.

At discharge, Mr. G. has met all objectives in the independent living skills program. He demonstrates good safety knowledge and procedures, excellent meal planning/preparation skills, and increased organizational skills in accessing community resources through the use of his Day-Timer. He was opened an individual checking account and is managing his routine financial matters independently. He is relicensed to drive but is strongly encouraged to be accompanied while driving for several weeks. He is competent in using the public transportation system independently. Mr. G. is prepared to move from the transitional-living apartment to his own independent apartment at the completion of his CCR program and has located an appropriate residence.

Physical Abilities

Mr. G. participated in the community-based physical program throughout his CCR program. Initial goals included increasing cardiovascular fitness, increasing weight, increasing general strength, and improving flexibility, especially in the trunk. Mr. G.'s program included aqua-aerobics and low-impact aerobics classes for improving both cardiovascular fitness and gross motor coordination, a stationary bicycling program for strength and cardiovascular fitness, and specific stretching exercises for flexibility. Objective measures taken monthly showed a steadily decreasing resting heart rate, suggesting improved cardiovascular fitness. A weight gain of 8 pounds and an increase of 0.9% in body fat suggest an increase in muscle mass (i.e., strength), while body fat percentage remains in the low range.

Mr. G. was also seen by a physical therapist for training in posture, gait, and balance. He now has a right ankle–foot orthosis (AFO) to aid in his gait, which has resulted in good improvement in walking while wearing the brace. Mr. G. did not demonstrate gains in posture, however, and probably will continue to exhibit problems in this area because of decreased proprioception. Excellent improvement was noted in balance. Mr. G. can now walk on a balance beam and was unable to do this at the initiation of treatment. Finally, Mr. G. independently follows a walking program. It is recommened that he continue with this activity and with physical therapy services to address gait and posture.

Therapeutic Recreation

On entrance to the Center, Mr. G.'s leisure interests focused primarily on passive activities such as listening to music, reading the newspaper, collecting coins, and table games (i.e., backgammon, chess, and cards). Results from the initial assessment suggested that Mr. G. demonstrated limited knowledge and poor utilization of community resources and reduced speech intelligibility for social and telephone situations. It was also noted that he displayed difficulty with self-motivated leisure participation. In terms of leisure strengths, Mr. G. demonstrated enthusiasm and determination as he began treatment in the therapeutic recreation area.

Treatment included both paper/pencil and functional community tasks. These tasks focused on the identification and utilization of community resources in the planning and organization of both individual and group community recreational outings. Treatment also promoted community reintegration by assisting Mr. G. with signing up for community classes. He participated in a community cooking course, recreation class, and guitar lessons while in the CCR program. Leisure education focused on the development of leisure alternatives, the elimination of barriers to leisure participation, and increased leisure awareness.

Quantitative measures including Weekend Leisure Scores and Recreation Log Statistics supported improved functioning in the appropriate use of leisure time. Initially, Mr. G. achieved an average Weekend Leisure Score of 5 (out of 12 possible) over the first 2 weeks of his CCR program, suggesting moderate impairment in the areas of the initiation of recreational activities and knowledge of community resources. Posttreatment level of performance consisted of an average score of 12 for the final 2 weeks of the CCR program. The average score in the Weekly Recreation Log for the first month consisted of 10 recreational activities, and the final month ended with 20 independently initiated activities. Overall, Mr. G. demonstrates significant improvements in the area of therapeutic recreation.

At discharge, Mr. G. utilizes a Day-Timer for planning daily activities and pursues both passive and active recreational activities, some of which include painting, guitar playing, reading, and participation in community classes. Mr. G. demonstrates excellent abilities in establishing new friendships to broaden his social outlets and increase the frequency and quality of his recreational pursuits. It is recommended that once Mr. G. settles into his new apartment, he continue his appropriate use of free time and community involvement. If Mr. G. is assisted with the initial development of a leisure program, he could now independently follow through with the suggested structure. The CCR's therapeutic recreation specialist will assist with the establishment of a leisure program once Mr. G. has relocated to his new residence.

Vocational Abilities

At the time of program entry, Mr. G. was unemployed. Prior to his injury, he left school to begin working as a painter for a 36-month period. Subsequently, he was offered a higher pay rate as a glazier and went to work in that occupation. Mr. G. was employed as a glazier for a 7-month period until the date of injury, August 23, 1985. In 1987, Mr. G. attended a community college for completion of a G.E.D.

Initial obstacles to competitive employment included impairment in the following cognitive processes: decreased memory/new learning ability, reduced executive functions (e.g., organization, planning, and follow-through), decreased speed of information processing, deficits in attention and concentration, reduced speech intelligibility, and problems in reasoning and judgment. Additional areas of concern were noted regarding anger management, balance and coordination, motor speed, and physical restrictions for lifting/carrying, bending, climbing, reaching, and standing for extended periods of time. There was also a high degree of unrealistic vocational expectations.

Throughout his CCR program, Mr. G. received individual and group vocational counseling and participated in a volunteer work station at Good Samaritan Hospital's print shop. The work station provided a method for measuring cognitive levels of performance in a naturalistic setting, physical tolerance/capability, and work behavior. Excellent gains were noted in all areas of vocational ability. Specifically, Mr. G. was observed as (1) maintaining a medium speed of performance with good quality control, (2) maintaining a good attendance record including good punctuality, (3) demonstrating good tolerance to frustration and working well under stress and emergency situations, (4) demonstrating good self-initiation, self-motivation, and a consistent work effort, (5) exhibiting good dexterity and manipulative skills, and, finally, (6) working well with others and having a friendly disposition. During the program's placement phase, Mr. G. worked on interviewing techniques and application procedures. Employers were contacted and in-person interviews arranged. A general list of realistic occupational possibilities was developed with the relevant agencies to contact. Possibilities for formal training, on-the-job training, or direct placement were examined.

In the process of job development, Mr. G.'s former employer in the painting industry was contacted, and specific proposals were established. Mr. G. interviewed, was offered a position, and accepted the job offer. Tentative start date is August 17, 1987. The position offers a large degree of flexibility to ensure Mr. G.'s successful reestablishment of his work career.

The job accommodates Mr. G.'s physical and cognitive impairments. There will be no heavy lifting; he can alternate among sitting, standing, and walking. Hours will be gradually increased to suit stamina and endurance. The pay rate is initially $4.25 per hour with the possibility of regular merit increases. Mr. G. will be supervised by the owner. Duties include warehouse tasks, inventory responsibility, delivery work, prefinish work, marking, packaging, bundling, and sanding. Mr. G. can work at his own pace.

The CCR vocational placement specialist will continue to monitor placement activity and follow up with Mr. G. for a minimum period of 1 year.

Summary and Recommendations

Mr. G. demonstrates excellent improvements in the areas of cognition, psychosocial adjustment, independent living skills, management of leisure time, physical abilities, and vocational adjustment. He achieved his overall rehabilitation goals of return to independent living and gainful employment. Residual areas of concern include decreased memory and new learning, a decline in social maturity, and remaining deficits in coordination and balance. Based on Mr. G.'s progress and current levels of functioning, the following recommendations are offered:

1. Mr. G. accept the job position proposed at the paint company.
2. Mr. G. continue to utilize his Day-Timer and other compensatory memory strategies.
3. Mr. G. continue to wear his orthotic and receive follow-up physical therapy.
4. Mr. G. continue with his walking program.
5. Mr. G. relocate to the identified apartment near his place of employment.

The clinical staff at Good Samaritan Hospital's Center for Cognitive Rehabilitation has enjoyed working with Mr. G. and has been encouraged by his excellent progress in all areas. Follow-up calls and visits by the staff will occur on a regular and as-needed basis for a minimum period of 1 year to ensure maintenance of and continued progress in gains demonstrated throughout Mr. G.'s rehabilitation program.

This report illustrates the intensity and breadth of treatment as well as the coordination among disciplines that must occur to facilitate successful community reentry. Although all cognitive rehabilitation was administered within the clinic, coordination with other disciplines allowed gains to be extended beyond the treatment setting. In the next section, community reintegration treatment programs are described in more detail.

COMMUNITY REINTEGRATION PROGRAMS

Until recently, the early stages of head injury rehabilitation treatment—emergency care, coma care, inpatient and outpatient rehabilitation—were all that were available for brain-injured individuals. However, as increasing numbers of patients were discharged from hospitals to their homes or into institutions, unable to live independently and unable to work, the need for treatment specifically directed at community reentry was recognized. Since the early 1980s, more and more community reentry programs or postmedical head injury rehabilitation programs have been established. Most major cities and all of the states have facilities that can treat the initial phases of head injury recovery. Community reentry programs, however, are still scarce.

It is important to include a description of this final stage of rehabilitation since many students and professionals will not have opportunities to do internships or to experience this treatment setting. In this next section, examples of postacute or community reintegration programs are provided in order to introduce the structure and nature of current program models.

Bay Area Head Injury Recovery Center

The Bay Area Head Injury Recovery Center has a facility known as the Transition's House located in Berkeley, California. The following is an excerpt of a description of the program written by Berlanger, Berrol, Cole, Fryer, and Lock (1985):

> The Transition's House offers a highly structured regime of individualized daily treatment provided by a skilled, interdisciplinary team of specialists. Transition's staff comprise a complete rehabilitation team including a neuropsychologist, a speech and language pathologist, an occupational therapist, a physical therapist, a recreation therapist, consultants, case managers, and counselors/attendants. The program is based on an educational model utilizing a modularized approach that is developed within the framework of the therapeutic community.
>
> The weekday program consists of individual therapy utilizing computerized rehabilitation programs and various learning and educational materials. The emphasis of the day program is on cognitive restructuring, a method specifically designed for retraining in basic cognitive skills underlying information processing. These skills include attention, vigilance, perceptual consistency, behavioral control, and memory. This is a prescriptive program based on extensive neuropsychological testing and applied through individualized contracting with each client. Specific training is provided in the areas of memory, perceptual organization, problem-solving strategy development, mental flexibility, and language development. The individualized therapy program is scheduled from 9:00 A.M. to 3:00 P.M. Monday through Friday.
>
> The recreation therapist coordinates the afternoon, evening, and weekend programs. These programs focus on group activities and development of in-

dividual leisure interests and leisure planning skills. The evening program has been designed to address the needs of the whole person through a broad range of recreational activities that are cognitively stimulating, physical and social in nature, foster personal growth and exploration, and are designed to enhance environmental awareness. Over 50% of the recreational programming occurs in a community setting, continually exposing residents to mainstream activities. Residents swim in public pools, play softball in local parks, attend local movie theaters, and learn to participate as members of the general public. In addition to the scheduled recreation program, the home itself is used to promote group cohesiveness.

A peer-counseling group meets on a weekly basis to discuss issues of concern among the residents. The session provides the opportunity to learn problem-solving strategies from each other and to appreciate the fact that others share their same problems and frustrations.

A menu-planning meeting is held on a weekly basis, and all residents have a voice in selecting meals for the upcoming week. Residents participate in the meal-preparation responsibility and rotate this responsibility on a weekly basis. One resident is assigned the role of head chef for each meal, and another is assigned the role of assistant. Clean-up is done by the remaining residents.

One of the most significant values of a residential program in a community setting is that residents are continually challenged to develop, expand, and reintegrate functional abilities and skills of daily living. The overall goal is for residents to develop self-initiation and responsibility. Residents must be responsible for following their daily schedules, completing their work assignments, maintaining their own bank accounts, planning ahead to get a weekend pass, and washing their own laundry. Our premise is that functional skills and abilities learned can be generalized and integrated into the resident's own lifestyle. One aspect of encouraging residents toward maximum levels of independence is educating them regarding the life-long residual problems they will face. Residents are taught techniques of behavioral change and compensation for their cognitive deficits. The average length of stay at Transition's House is four to six months. The case managers, families, and rehabilitation team begin developing discharge plans and long-range treatment plans from the time the resident enters Transition's House. Plans are continually modified and refined to best serve the needs of the client and his or her family. The goal upon discharge is to create the most optimal environment for the individual as possible, given the constraints of the individual's situation and abilities. By the end of their stay, many residents have established daily programs outside the facility, at local community colleges, or in volunteer job placements. A hallmark of an individual's readiness to leave occurs when he or she can continue to make gains outside the program. Thus, he or she can continue to perform successfully with less structure and less supervision. (pp. 6–7)

Community Reentry

Below is an excerpt from another article (Schmidt, 1984) describing a community reentry program in a different part of the nation.

Community Reentry Services, Inc. (CRS) of Lynn, Massachusetts, functions as an outpatient rehabilitation program in which several housing options are available in the community for individuals who live outside of commuting distance. . . .

Cognitive functions are the focal point from which all general and specific skills are taught. In order to achieve these goals, CRS is divided into two phases. Phase 1 focuses on the reacquisition of functional independent living skills. Phase 2 focuses on vocational exploration, work evaluation, prevocational and vocational training. Each student progresses through both Phase 1 and Phase 2 at their own pace. Students are given a check list of skill requirements necessary for completion of Phase 1 and Phase 2. Specific performance criteria must be met as students progress from Phase 1 to Phase 2. Students continuously evaluate their own performance with feedback from staff.

Students admitted to CRS are preselected from an intensive evaluation which takes at least 2 weeks. The program, which functions much like a school, offers a variety of classes. Core classes are required for all students, and elective classes are optional selections by the student. Each student has a program adviser who acts as a coordinator for the student's program. In Phase 1, classes begin at 9:00 A.M. and end at 4:30 P.M. In additional to group classes, all students are engaged in individual tutoring or cognitive remediation work. Any area in which the student demonstrates special needs that cannot be adequately addressed in a class situation is addressed through individual tutoring. Students are given the opportunity to tutor their peers in a variety of areas, depending on their individual strengths. . . .

In addition to class work, the student is given the opportunity to practice in the community what is being taught through the Independent Living Skills class, a required class for students in Phase 1. In all class situations, the community becomes the training laboratory for what is taught within the classroom. With Phase 1 laying the foundation, Phase 2 begins when a student has reached criterion for graduation into Phase 2. For most students, this takes approximately four to six months. Phase 2 begins for all students with a vocational exploration seminar lasting one full week. This seminar defines and discusses a variety of community-based jobs. It also helps the student self-define, through a variety of exercises, areas of vocational interests and aptitude. Each student concludes the seminar by selecting an "Internal" Work Evaluation Station. Internal indicates that the work station is physically based within the program.

The purpose of the Internal Work Evaluation is to assess the student's work-related behavior, i.e., ability to report to work on time, follow instructions, demonstrate carryover from day to day, etc. Following a 4-week period of satisfactory performance, the student is placed on an "External" Work Evaluation and Training Site. External refers to a work station outside the program and within the community. This experience purposely reduces the structure offered within the CRS program and promotes adaptation to a new, less-structured work environment. Job sites are community based and provide a graduated step from the Internal Work Evaluation to an actual competitive work environment. . . .

Students completing Phase 2 are assisted in residential and job placement within the community in which they choose to live. It should be noted that direct entry into Phase 2 is optional for individuals who are assessed as not requiring the intensive cognitive remediation work provided by Phase 1. (pp. 10–12)

Tangram

Some programs have utilized rural environments as a means of promoting community reintegration. Tangram Rehabilitation Network, located in Texas (Seaton, 1985), is an example. The program uses a behavioral approach; there is a token economy system in which clients earn money for daily accomplishments such as completing physical therapy, chores, or community activities. Clients can use their money to buy goods at the Token Store.

> Tangram Rehabilitation Network currently provides four separate yet interrelated facilities. These facilities include the Therapeutic Camping Facility, Ranch Treatment Facility, Nursery Treatment Facility, and the Townhouse Facility. The programs begin at 6:30 A.M. and are active and structured until 10:00 P.M. seven days a week. Group activities such as softball, bowling league, volleyball, and group outings, etc., occur many times a week. This crossover provides the clients with exposures to other facilities, clients, and staff, thus enhancing the transitional process.
>
> The Camp is located on the Ranch property and offers a "back-to-basics" approach in a calm, relaxing environment. The primary daily chores are planning and preparing three meals a day, participating in the ongoing construction of the campsite area, cutting firewood, and participating in group projects and outings. Each task is performed within a "group process" approach that allows personal and physical achievement, develops appropriate behaviors, and builds relationships and self-esteem. This program has proven to be invaluable to clients as a steppingstone to the Ranch or Nursery Treatment Program.
>
> The Ranch facility is located on 155 acres, 15 miles south of San Marcos, Texas. The program is highly structured and consistent. It promotes the development of basic living skills, socially appropriate behaviors, cognitive orientation, functional physical capabilities, and responsible work and personal habits. The client learns predominantly through daily living experiences and work programs.
>
> The program begins with the clients meeting at the barn to take care of the animals. This program is one of the most successful and enjoyable. Each client has responsibility for his or her farm animals. The animals provide more than a warm and affectionate relationship; they are a valuable learning resource, teaching respect for other living creatures, as well as teaching responsibility, planning, and organizing. Client also assumes responsibility for their own 12-foot garden plot where they are able to grow vegetables and sell them to the Ranch for token money. Thus, the treatment philosophy at the Ranch promotes individual success, personal responsibility, group interaction, and reality-based activities. In doing so, cognitive retraining, physical, speech, and occupational therapies are taught with a "hands-on" approach in the normal routine of the day's activities. This approach ensures the greatest degree of transferability and functional use of the skills in everyday living.
>
> The Nursery facility continues the transitional concept of the rehabilitation process as it incorporates a residential treatment program into a real business setting.

The Nursery dorms are located 100 yards from the greenhouses, providing easy access to the Tangram Nursery Business. This program provides increased opportunity for earning and budgeting money, developing vocational and independent living skills, and acquiring responsible work habits as it enhances self-esteem through accomplishments.

The clients have daily involvement with the Nursery Business to propagate new plants, to landscape, or to help make deliveries. This involvement has proven to be vital to clients as a prevocational tool prior to their applying for a job. In addition, it is a valuable cognitive, physical, and occupational exercise. . . .

The business setting provides vocational training and job skills so that the clients can reenter the work world. Each client applying for a job is involved in a normal job-seeking procedure such as filling out an application and being interviewed. When hired, they receive a job title and a written job description listing daily responsibilities. All employees work for a salary on an 8:00 A.M. to 5:00 P.M. schedule. This program provides clients with excellent job-oriented learning experiences. . . .

The Tangram Townhouse, a historical home located within the San Marcos city limits, is designed for the client who can benefit from a relatively independent living situation and from increased community involvement. The program is available to the client who has a full-time job and demonstrates a high level of maturity and responsibility. Each client pays rent and utility bills and also buys groceries and personal items with the money earned as an employee at the Nursery or at a job in the community. All residents are expected to share household chores and responsibilities similar to those of most families (cooking, cleaning, yard work). Meals are cooperatively planned on a weekly basis. The clients also have an increased opportunity for shopping and employment and to utilize the social and recreational activities of the community. By providing minimal supervision and direction, clients have an opportunity to practice and experience "living independently" within a supportive environment. This environment offers a normalized home-like setting in which adults can share living responsibilities with peers. Thus, clients learn how to live independently by practicing independent living. Most residents have progressed through the Ranch or Nursery Program before coming to the Townhouse. Usually this is the last phase of the program before the client moves into Tangram's Independent Living Program. (pp. 5–6)

Good Samaritan

The authors of this text assisted in the development of Good Samaritan Hospital's Center for Cognitive Rehabilitation (CCR), a postacute rehabilitation program, located in Puyallup, Washington. There are three separate facilities, designed to accommodate the full range of disabilities possible following traumatic brain injury. The rehabilitation spectrum extends from a program for participants who have sustained severe head injury with resultant handicaps requiring 24-hour supervision to a program for those with mild head injuries who may not need training in independent living but who require cognitive rehabilitation, psychosocial treatment, and vocational rehabilitation. The program is designed to assist persons with head injury in achieving their maximum levels of independent living and employment.

Figure 13.1 shows a sample weekly schedule for the middle program, which is tailored for individuals with moderate to severe head injuries. Initially, patients receive:

- intensive cognitive rehabilitation, using the Process-Specific Approach
- independent living skills training, designed to apply improved cognitive status to functional tasks
- physical therapy including both traditional services and therapy geared toward achieving maximal fitness in order to build tolerance for working a full work day
- treatment is psychosocial adjustment
- therapeutic recreation designed to encourage people to become productive and adjusted in their free time as well as to promote carry-over of

Hours	Monday	Tuesday	Wednesday	Thursday	Friday
8:30 – 9:30	Recreation Group: review weekend; plan outings	Cognitive Group	Cognitive Group	Cognitive Group	Work Station |
9:30 – 10:30	Individual Cognitive Tx	Individual Psychosocial Tx	Individual Cognitive Tx	Individual Cognitive Tx	|
10:30 – 11:30	Individual Occupational Tx	Individual Vocational Tx	Individual Cognitive Tx	Individual Occupational Tx	|
11:30 – 12:30	Lunch	Lunch	Lunch	Lunch	Lunch
12:30 – 1:30	Individual Cognitive Tx	Individual Occupational Tx	Individual Occupational Tx	Individual Cognitive Tx	|
1:30 – 2:30	Psychosocial Group	Psychosocial Group	Psychosocial Group	Psychosocial Group	|
2:30 – 4:00	Aquacise Swimming Class	Aerobics at Gym	Recreation Outing	Aerobics at Gym	|

FIGURE 13.1. Sample schedule of weekly treatment activities of CCR-1, a post-acute community reentry program for individuals with moderate to severe head injury.

• goals in the cognitive and psychosocial therapies to naturalistic contexts.

Examples of how gains are transferred from the clinic to real-life functioning and community reintegration may be seen in the following.

Physical Training Program

Each CCR participant automatically receives membership in a health club facility and pool in the community. Modified aerobics classes and individual physical therapy and fitness plans are designed and presented by physical therapists, occupational therapists, and recreational therapists at the health club. In addition to meeting physical therapy needs, the community health club promotes social reintegration by encouraging participants to interact in a normal community setting.

Training in Independent Living Skills

The occupational therapists coordinate closely with the speech/language pathologists who work on cognitive rehabilitation. The occupational therapists provide independent living training for meal preparation, money management, transportation (public or preparing for licensure to drive), community access (e.g., use of post office, phone book, bank, library), and housekeeping. Initially, the therapists use tasks within the clinic that incorporate cognitive skills being targeted in the cognitive rehabilitation discipline. Gradually, therapy is moved out into the community. Participants move from their initial supervised setting (e.g., a nursing home or family residence) to a transitional living situation. Transitional living apartments are normal apartments within the community. The CCR staff provides monitoring and training within the apartment setting as necessary. Finally, at the end of the program, most participants move into their own independent residences near their intended place of employment. Thus, training in independent living skills begins in the clinic and is systematically moved into the community. Graded, hierarchical tasks that increasingly approximate independent real-world activities of daily living are implemented until the participant has achieved his or her maximal level of independence.

Vocational Model

Midway through their program, participants have usually achieved enough gains in cognition and psychosocial functioning to begin volunteer work stations, which offer simulated work-trial experiences. In addition to providing opportunities for applying improved cognitive and psychosocial facilities to a naturalistic work setting, the work station may target general work behavior, depending on an individual patient's needs. Goals may include improving punctuality and attendance, building up physical tolerance for an 8-hour work day, improving speed of performance or productivity, or promoting the use of trained compensatory cognitive strategies in a vocational setting. When possible, participants are placed in work stations that relate closely to their actual vocational goals either in local businesses or factories or in hospital departments within Good Samaritan Hospital. Job stations have included work in printing, child care, library work, maintenance, groundskeeping, dietetics, shipping and receiving, accounting, and many other skilled and unskilled positions. The participant continues with other therapies (cognitive, psychosocial, occupational therapy, and recreation) on the days when he or she is not in the work station.

Toward the last weeks of the program, the participant enters the intensive vocational placement phase. The vocational rehabilitation counselor uses data collected from other disciplines as well as data from the work station—with consideration of the patient's interests and prior work history—to develop a vocational goal. Potential job positions in the individual's labor market area are identified, and interviews are arranged. For most participants, the goal is to complete their CCR program on Friday and begin work the following Monday.

The commitment of the Center for Cognitive Rehabilitation program is to promote normality and to assist an individual recovering from brain injury to achieve the highest possible level of independent living and work. One critical component of this effort is the interdependent, multidisciplinary team of rehabilitation professionals, all of whom are aware of the vocational and independent-living goals, who design programs that support each other.

Several different program models have been presented here to assist the reader in understanding the comprehensive nature of community training, which is a necessary step in the rehabilitation process to maximize recovery from head injury. The following is a list of concepts fundamental to most community reintegration programs:

1. Therapy goals in disciplines such as cognitive rehabilitation, psychosocial counseling and treatment, and occupational therapy must be actively generalized to the individual's everyday life.
2. The community serves as a valuable treatment medium as a participant advances in independent living or work abilities.
3. Participants require programs that are individually tailored to accommodate their profile of cognitive and psychosocial strengths and weaknesses and rate of learning in order to allow each participant to realize optimal levels of functioning within the community.

LEVELS OF INDEPENDENCE

Having acknowledged that for many patients it takes a multidisciplinary team of professionals and a program model specifically geared toward community reentry to assist them in achieving maximal reintegration into society, we next turn the discussion toward identifying the range of options available for maximizing independence. It was not too long ago that most severely head-injured individuals were placed within institutions after a period of acute care or discharged to the homes of relatives who then acted as full-time caretakers. Return to work was often not even considered a viable option. Since that time, head injury rehabilitation has been extended and refined. At the same time, the disabilities movement has been educating society about persons with handicaps; there are now an increased number of living and work options for those with disabilities.

Because not every person who sustains a head injury needs to be cared for in an institutional setting, and also not every person can recover to complete independence in managing his or her own residence, what are some of the options between institutionalization and total independence?

Attendant Care

For the patient who still requires 24-hour, one-on-one supervision, an attendant model might be one step toward normalization. In this model, an individual lives in a regular residence within the community and has an attendant who is hired to make sure his or her daily needs are met.

Group Home

Still another step toward independence is a group home setting where a number of disabled individuals live together and receive assistance from a person hired to provide necessary monitoring. Ideally, this situation is set up as a family unit. In the past several years, group homes specifically designed for head-injured persons have been established. Within the group home setting, the resident can potentially have access to the community to the extent to which his or her disability allows.

Selective Monitoring

Frequently, individuals recover to the extent that they can manage most of their daily needs and do not require constant supervision, although they may need assistance with selected tasks. In such cases, it is important for the professionals involved to identify the tasks with which an individual requires assistance and then to explore resources to accommodate those needs. We term this level of independent living "selective monitoring." For example, if a person can live in his or her own residence, given assistance with money management and grocery shopping, systems can be put into place that allow this. There are agencies and some banks that will provide money management services for handicapped persons at little or no cost. A friend might be enlisted, or a therapy aide hired, to do weekly grocery shopping. Another individual might have physical problems that make it difficult to perform any heavy housekeeping. Chore services can be set up by agencies to meet this need. Projecting how residual deficits, whether they are cognitive, physical, or psychologic in nature, will affect a person's ability to live independently and arranging for needs to be met may allow many head-injured individuals to live on their own in independent residences. Table 13.1 provides a list of levels of independence within the residential realm.

TABLE 13.1. Levels of Independence

Model	Description
Residential options	
1. Maximal independence	Occupies own residence with no assistance for daily needs
2. Selected monitoring	Receives assistance with daily needs (e.g., money management or housekeeping) as needed
3. Group home	Lives in community with other disabled persons and a monitor hired to supervise the household
4. Attendant care	One-on-one supervision in noninstitutional setting
5. Institutional setting	Includes nursing homes or extended-care facilities that are not community based
Vocational options	
1. Competitive employment	Regular position with no modification for worker
2. Modification of competitive job	Employer willing to modify job position selectively to accommodate handicapped worker
3. Supported work	Another employee receives extra pay to assist disabled worker
4. Sheltered workshop	A business designed for disabled workers who usually produce a business product and receive on-the-job monitoring
5. Avocational pursuits	Volunteer position
6. Unemployed/nonproductive	No productive use of time for an outside agency or business

Similar levels of independence exist in the vocational arena. If a person is unable to pursue gainful employment because of the injury, one option is to arrange an avocational placement in a volunteer capacity. All people, regardless of handicap, need to feel productive. The incidence of substance abuse, depression, and suicide is higher for the unemployed than the employed population, which includes individuals who have sustained head injury. Identifying an avocational position where a person can contribute however much he or she is able can prevent feelings of despair and worthlessness.

Sheltered Workshops

This type of work setting, initially designed for the developmentally disabled population, may provide a means for head-injured individuals to pursue gainful work. In this model, individuals typically receive payment based on their productivity (i.e., piece work), and there are a number of workshop supervisors specifically trained to assist workers to be productive. Currently, however, there are very few sheltered workshops specifically designed for the head-injured population. This is problematic because developmentally disabled and head-injured persons have different problems and needs; mixed programs have not been very effective.

Supported Work

This vocational option involves an assisted work situation that can allow a disabled individual to be productive. In this model, another employee in the work environment receives payment for assisting the disabled individual, as needed, on the job. This is a relatively new work concept and holds much promise for the head injury population. As the head-injured person learns the job and becomes more independent, the support can be withdrawn.

Modified Work Setting

Finally, many employers are willing to modify existing jobs to accommodate an individual's particular cognitive or physical disability. Vocational rehabilitation counselors can work with employers to develop appropriate job situations.

With vocational as with independent living goals, professionals assisting patients in reintegrating into society need to anticipate potential barriers produced by residual deficits, develop a strategy to accommodate them, and aim for the highest level of independence in vocational pursuits possible. See Table 13.1 for a summary of vocational options.

It is important to realize that patient's abilities may change and that they may be able to achieve higher levels of independence as they gain experience. Professionals need to build the ability to increase independence in work or living needs into the discharge plan.

OUTCOMES

As noted throughout this text, there has been both a rapid expansion in the number of programs that treat head injury survivors and an extension of services to include community reintegration training. This expansion has grown out of the recognition that maximal levels of independence at home, work, and leisure were not realized following discharge from inpatient rehabilitation programs.

Perhaps the most important question that a professional or family trying to determine the quality of a rehabilitation program can ask is, "What are the program's independent living and vocational outcomes?" Postmedical community readaptation programs now have enough data to examine trends and patterns and are beginning to look at this questions.

Of course, there are a number of ways in which a program might measure outcomes. The Disability Rating Scale (Rappaport, Hall, Hopkins, Belleza, & Cope, 1982) incorporates the Glasgow Coma Scale (a four-point scale rating cognitive ability for feeding, toileting, and grooming), an overall rating of cognitive independence scaled on a six-point continuum, and a four-point scale of employability ranging from "not restricted" to "not employable." Surveys and structured interviews offer alternative means to rating scales for gathering information about a patient's level of functioning after program participation (Jacobs, 1987). Regardless of the methodology employed, the key is whether or not gains were demonstrated that resulted in functional changes in the life of the head-injured patient. It is important to measure not only changes in neuropsychological status and psychosocial adjustment but also actual gains in independent living and vocational pursuits.

It is essential that information on residential and vocational outcomes be collected and carefully analyzed. These data allow programs to examine trends and make improvement in service delivery. Given the newness of the field, accountability issues are primary. Professionals need to be able to justify the tremendous cost involved in head injury treatment, especially during the postacute and community-retraining stages.

Articles reporting outcomes for postacute rehabilitation programs have only recently begun to be published. Findings in such articles suggest that increases in cognitive and psychosocial functioning have yielded better community reintegration for many brain-injured patients (Fryer & Haffey, 1987; Prigatano, Fordyce, Zeimer, Roveche, Pepping, Wood, 1984; Ben-Yishay, Silver, Piasetsky, & Rattok, 1987). What is misleading, however, is that in some reports, outcomes are measured according to an individual's capability rather than actual realized gains. In other words, a patient might be deemed capable of competitive employment but not be placed in a job and thus remain unemployed. Under some measures, such a patient would be considered successful. At CCR the primary measure of outcome is the percentage of patients who return to work and independent living. Outcome statistics for program graduates at the facility for 28 patients with moderate to severe head injury served between 1986 and 1988 are shown in Tables 13.2 and 13.3.

Recent literature is also building a case for cost effectiveness of cognitive rehabilitation programs. A study by Aronow (1987) examining the benefits to society of such programs showed that inpatients who were provided with rehabilitation were returned to productive or nonburdensome levels of functioning at the same rate as a less severe nontreatment group. Among patients with similar severity of disabilities, those receiving rehabilitation had better average cost outcomes than a comparison no-treatment group. The saving for a group of 50 patients was estimated to be $335,842. Aronow suggests that once the resources are committed to save the life of a severely injured traumatic brain-injured victim in the emergency room, the most cost-effective measure is to provide rehabilitation services and prevent long-term disability payments by government or private disability funds.

Similar findings regarding the cost effectiveness of rehabilitation were found in a study by Sohlberg and Brock (1985), who performed a hypothetical cost comparison of postacute rehabilitation services with long-term

TABLE 13.2. CCR Residential Outcomes (N = 28)

	Entry	Discharge
Maximal independence	0	10
Selected monitoring	8	17
Group home	1	0
Attendant care	13	1
Institutional setting	6	0

TABLE 13.3. CCR Vocational Outcomes (N = 28)

	Entry	Discharge
Competitive employment	0	14
Modification of competitive job	0	8
Supported work	0	1
Sheltered workshop	4	2
Avocational pursuits	5	1
Unemployed, nonproductive	19	2

disability/welfare payments (assuming only a 40% success rate for returning head-injured patients to productive work and independent living). Results showed that substantial savings, on the order of millions of dollars, would be achieved by financing postmedical cognitive rehabilitation as opposed to disability and social welfare payments.

SUMMARY

Professionals delivering cognitive rehabilitation services need to be aware of the causes of problems that face head-injured persons trying to reintegrate into society in order that they can do their part in helping patients achieve maximal levels of independence in work, home, and leisure. One important means for achieving this goal is to work closely with other disciplines that more commonly treat the patient in naturalistic, community settings. These disciplines include occupational therapy, therapeutic recreation, and vocational rehabilitation. The sharing of information between disciplines and mutual targeting of goals allows appropriate objectives to be addressed within the clinic and transfer of clinical gains to real-life settings.

Because many patients did not successfully reintegrate into society following discharge from early inpatient rehabilitation programs, a number of postacute treatment facilities focusing on community reentry have been established. Several sample programs are described in this chapter. Such programs utilize the community as a therapy medium in which generalized learned skills are applied to real-life settings.

In focusing on community reintegration, it is important to realize that there are many levels of independence in work and residential situations. Creative and thorough planning for discharge from rehabilitation is required to allow patients maximal independence. It is the professionals' obligation to project how residual deficits will affect living and work situations and to design systems to accommodate any handicaps.

Recent reports of outcomes of postacute rehabilitation suggest that such programs are successful in helping patients achieve productive lives. Studies also indicate that rehabilitation is cost effective, considering the expense of long-term disability and social welfare costs for individuals who do not return to gainful employment or independent residential situations.

STUDY QUESTIONS

1. Review the sample discharge report for Mr. G. presented in this chapter and determine the levels of independence reached in residential and vocational outcomes.

2. Suggest goals that the recreational therapist and cognitive therapist might mutually work on within their own disciplines and describe how each professional's therapy enhances and supports the others.
3. Write a brief hypothetical description for a program designed to assist head-injured individuals in achieving community reintegration. Include information regarding the types of disciplines and how they work together.
4. Why is it important to keep statistics on the patient outcomes following rehabilitation? What sort of information should be included when gathering outcome statistics?
5. Why is rehabilitation cost effective?

REFERENCES

Aronow, H. V. (1987). Rehabilitation effectiveness with severe brain injury: Translating research into policy. *Journal of Head Trauma Rehabilitation* 2(3):24–36.

Ben-Yishay, Y., Silver, S., Piasetsky, E., & Rattok, J. (1987). Relationship between employability and vocational outcome after intensive cognitive rehabilitation. *Journal of Head Trauma Rehabilitation* 2(1):35–48.

Berlanger, S., Berrol, S., Cole, J., Fryer, J., & Lock, M. (1985). Bay area head injury recovery center: A therapeutic community. *Cognitive Rehabilitation* 3(3):4–7.

Fryer, L. J., & Haffey, W. (1987). Cognitive rehabilitation and community readaptation: Outcomes from two program models. *Journal of Head Trauma Rehabilitation* 2(3):51–63.

Jacobs, H. (1987). The Los Angeles head injury survey: Project rationale and design implications. *Journal of Head Trauma Rehabilitation* 2(3):37–50.

Prigatano, G., Fordyce, D., Zeimer, H., Roueche, J., Pepping, M., & Wood, B. (1984). Neuropsychological rehabilitation after closed head injury in young adults. *Journal of Neurology, Neurosurgery, and Psychiatry* 47:505–513.

Rappaport, M., Hall, K. M., Hopkins, K., Belleza, T., & Cope, D. N. (1982). Disability rating scale for severe head trauma. Coma to community. *Archives of Physical Medicine and Rehabilitation* 63(3):118–123.

Schmidt, N. (1984). Community Re-entry Services, Inc.: A center for cognitive and vocational adjustment. *Cognitive Rehabilitation* 2(1):10–12.

Seaton, D. (1985). Community re-entry on the head injured adult. *Cognitive Rehabilitation* 3(5):4–8.

Sohlberg, M. M., & Brock, M. (1985). Taking the final step: The importance of post-medical cognitive rehabilitation. *Cognitive Rehabilitation* 3(5):10–13.

14
Meeting Psychosocial Needs of the Brain-Injured Adult

Although most of this text has addressed approaches to the rehabilitation of cognitive disorders following neurologic injury, it must be recognized that changes in psychosocial and emotional functioning are common in individuals following neurologic damage. These changes often have at least as much impact as cognitive functions on reintegration into community living and work. They contribute to chronic disability, impose a burden on families, and present a challenge to the rehabilitation team. Furthermore, they often persist and even intensify over time.

Unraveling an individual's subjective feeling states, affective display, reactions to disability, preinjury emotional functioning, and current psychosocial environment, all in the context of acquired cognitive and physical impairment, is an enormously difficult task. This challenge is made greater by the many different models and terminologies used to describe emotional states and their reflection in behavior. The fields of psychiatry, neurology, psychology, neuropsychology, and speech pathology have all made major contributions to this area. The definitions, assessment tools, conceptual bases, and intervention models that emerge from these fields, however, are all quite different. This chapter attempts to use as consistent a terminology as possible. The topics reviewed include basic terminology, psychosocial and affective changes following brain injury, organic bases of emotional behavior, emotional changes in head-injured patients, approaches to assessment and intervention for organically based psychosocial problems, common emotional reactions to acquired disability, factors related to psychosocial functioning independent of injury, and selection of therapy techniques.

BASIC TERMINOLOGY

Mood is usually understood as the frame of mind or emotional state of a person, the internal experience of feeling (Hinsie & Campbell, 1970). Normally, it is defined by the internal state of mind, not the external behavioral manifestations.

Affect, in contrast, connotes behaviors or external manifestations of feeling, mood, or emotion. Affect can include pervasive and enduring behavioral or temperamental characteristics and/or momentary or rapidly changing manifestations of fluctuating emotional states. Characteristics ascribed to affect can include facial expression, tone of voice, and "body language"; these constitute the outward expression of the inward feeling, with comparatively little association to ideation or cognition. The fact that observed affect sometimes does not coincide with an individual's mood is well recognized in the context of many neurologic disorders. Dissociations of mood and affect are striking symptoms, for example, of pseudobulbar palsy (Lieberman & Benson, 1977), right cerebral vascular accidents (Bryden & Ley, 1983), and multiple sclerosis.

Emotion is far more difficult to define and is often used broadly and vaguely. It is usually considered as an affective state in which strong or excited mental or mood states (e.g., joy, sorrow, fear) are experienced. It links a large number of behavioral responses reflecting both physical and mental changes or activities with a strong underlying feeling tone.

Personality is usually thought of as the sum of characteristics or qualities that make an individual a unique self. It is manifested in individual and, to some extent, predictable behavior-response patterns that each person evolves both consciously and unconsciously in response to internal and external demands. "The personality functions to maintain a stable, reciprocal relationship between the person and his environment" (Hinsie & Campbell, 1970).

Psychosocial behavior and interpersonal skills are considered to be the behaviors displayed in interactions with other individuals in social situations. They incorporate verbal and nonverbal communication, adherence to social norms, and the general attitude or approach toward others.

In the following sections, we discuss some of the known organic bases of emotional or psychosocial function and their disruption following neurologic insult. Emphasis is placed on ways in which the symptoms of brain damage can be confused with more emotionally or psychiatrically based symptoms. Following that is a discussion of some of the major reactive problems seen in brain-injured patients and ways in which psychotherapeutic interventions for these patients may differ from work with a non-brain-injured individual. Finally, we discuss some general approaches to psychotherapeutic intervention with the brain-injured adult and some of the problems inherent in current approaches to their treatment.

PSYCHOSOCIAL AND AFFECTIVE CHANGES
FOLLOWING BRAIN INJURY

Many researchers have addressed the frequency and nature of psychosocial and emotional changes following brain injury. This work has largely been restricted to the generation of lists of deficits without a conceptual framework that organizes the complex symptomatology of head-injured individuals (Bond, 1975; Dikmer & Reiton, 1977; Rimel, Giordani, Barth, Boll, & Jane, 1981). The most frequently used tools and models (e.g., the Minnesota Multiphasic Personality Inventory [MMPI], Beck Depression Inventory) have originated outside the specific realm of head injury rehabilitation and are, therefore, in many cases, of limited value. Only recently have new assessment tools and theoretical models begun to emerge.

One of these is the Neurobehavioral Rating Scale (NRS) (Levin et al., 1987), presented in the Appendix. This 27-item seven-point rating scale is to be completed by staff members working with the brain-injured individual. A study of 101 head-injured patients ranging widely in severity yielded four factors on the NRS.

Factor 1 consisted of items evaluating coherence of cognition and efficiency of memory, motor retardation (slowing), and emotional withdrawal.
Factor 2 included items reflecting inaccurate self-appraisal, unrealistic planning, and disinhibition—features frequently ascribed to frontal lobe function.
Factor 3 reflected physical complaints, anxiety, depression, and irritability.
Factor 4 included ratings for expressive and receptive language deficits.

Results demonstrated satisfactory interrater reliability and reflected both the chronicity and severity of closed head injury. Use of such a standardized rating tool should prove helpful in the analysis and consistent conceptualization of such changes both in individuals and in large-scale head-injury population studies.

Corey (1987) of our own Center for Cognitive Rehabilitation has developed a model of psychosocial assessment composed of ten major areas. Five involve symptoms that are related directly to the effects of head injury: interpersonal skills, social comprehension and judgment, self-regulation, context dependency, and adjustment to disability. The other five areas involve psychosocial factors that are partially or totally independent of the injury but that affect psychosocial functioning. These areas are substance abuse, significant preinjury psychologic/psychiatric problems, endogenous clinical depression, relationship stressors, and situational stressors. This assessment is notable in its appreciation of the degree to which variables apart from head injury consequences may be influential in psychosocial/

emotional functioning. Corey argues that psychosocial assessment and intervention after head injury are likely to be incomplete and quite misleading if these factors are not attended to.

Prigatano (1986) describes three different types of psychosocial factors to be considered in head-injured patients: preinjury personality factors, organic or neuropsychologic effects of head injury, and reactive responses to head injury. Although he does not claim that these dimensions can be totally separated, he does correctly caution against assuming a singular etiology for any particular presenting symptom.

ORGANIC BASES OF EMOTIONAL BEHAVIOR

Neural Systems Involved in Emotion

Limbic System Contributions

Historically, emotion and affect have been strongly linked to a diverse group of brain structures known collectively as the limbic system (Papez, 1937; MacLean, 1949). They comprise the so-called "older" or more primitive cortices that form the medial edge of the cerebral hemispheres as well as the subcortical areas that surround the deep gray matter masses of the basal ganglia. Limbic structures are typically described as including the amygdala, septum, anterior thalamus, and hypothalamus. These structures have rich connections with the frontal lobe and with the mesial and anterior temporal cortex (Figure 14.1).

The limbic system regulates behavior through its influences on all major effector mechanisms of the brain, including endocrine and autonomic systems as well as motor systems. Input to the limbic system is largely from association areas of cortex, suggesting that the system has access to highly integrated sensory information and to memory systems. Limbic system activity thus appears to include responses not only to complex sensory events but also to the record of how such events interacted with or influenced the person in the past. Because of this, it is considered to exert specific mood and affect-related influence on all other brain functions and systems (Damasio & Van Hoesen, 1983).

Frontal Lobe Contributions

The frontal lobes, particularly their basal and orbital undersurfaces, have particularly rich connections to the limbic structures. The more "primitive" limbic structures can affect motor systems and endocrine systems—in response to environmental influences—to display rage behavior, initiate aggressive behavior, or withdraw from threatening situations (the fight-or-

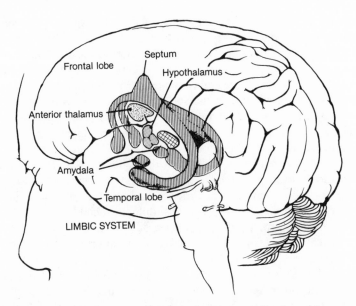

FIGURE 14.1. Major structures of the limbic system. This system receives input from all cortical association areas and from the orbitofrontal region. It influences endocrine, autonomic, and motor systems. Copyright© 1988 by Biomedical Illustrations, Inc.

flight response). With the increasing complexity of human social systems and the greater dependence on communication and cooperative behavior, basic fight/flight responses have had to be tempered, and a much more complex and variable social behavior repertoire developed. The more primitive system of response to the external environment remains, however, and the orbital frontal region is modeled as having a controlling or modulating influence on the limbic structure's ability to affect behavior. It is thus necessary for the socially appropriate expression of emotion. The disruption of this orbital system can lead to irritability, sudden and unprovoked anger or aggression, and a seeming lack of social awareness. These displays are often described as *disinhibition* of primitive responses that are normally checked or controlled.

This theoretical model of the limbic system is based on a very long history of descriptions of changes in emotional behavior following frontal lobe lesions. Holmes (1931), for example, described three likely directions of personality change in frontal disease: (1) apathy and indifference, (2) depression and automaticity, and (3) restlessness, exuberance, and euphoria. Lishman (1968), summarizing a large literature concerning abnormal emotional states following penetrating frontal lobe injury, suggested a behavioral syndrome "involving one or more of the following symptoms in severe degrees: lack of judgment, reliability or foresight, facetiousness, childlike behavior, disinhibition, and euphoria." [The earliest reports of frontal lobotomy included as consequences inertia, lack of ambition, indifference to the opinion of others, and satisfaction with the results of inferior quality or effort (Freeman & Watts, 1944)] Greenblatt, Arnot, and Solomon (1950) described these personality characteristics following frontal lobe leukotomy: a lack of inhibition, euphoria with restlessness and purposelessness, a lack of emotional expression, and display of decreased interest and drive.

More recent research has revealed that the behavioral alterations following frontal lobe injury are specific for particular locations. Damage to the orbital and/or basal frontal areas (inferior undersurface of frontal lobes) is more likely to result in inappropriate, disinhibited social behavior, irritability, and euphoria (Earp, 1979). In contrast, damage to the frontal convexity (lateral cortical surfaces) results in decreased initiation and "deficiencies in thought formation." Blumer and Benson (1975) suggested two distinct syndromes. The first, which they termed "pseudodepression," describes a distinct retardation of activity, including apathy, unconcern, lack of drive, and a lack of emotional reactivity, which is usually correlated with pathology involving the lateral convexity of the frontal lobes on one or both sides. The second syndrome, which they termed "pseudopsychopathic," was characterized by disinhibition including facetiousness, sexual and personal hedonism, irritability, and a lack of concern for others. The latter syndrome was most often associated with orbital frontal pathology. Of interest was a suggestion that the individuals derived no apparent pleasure (or other emotion) from the disinhibited behaviors. In both of these syndromes, it was unclear whether the underlying emotions are consistent with the external behavioral manifestations of mood or affect.

Right Hemisphere Contributions

[The other major brain system involved in emotional brain functioning is the right hemisphere of the brain.] For more than three decades, it has been observed that patients with left hemisphere damage appear depressed, whereas patients with right hemisphere lesions appear indifferent or emotionally flat. However, Heilman, Watson, and Bowers (1983) concluded that patients with right hemisphere damage actually fail to *comprehend* emotional information; they can neither understand nor produce emotional prosody in speech, for example, or comprehend the emotional expressions of faces. Similarly, patients with right hemisphere disease often have difficulty *expressing* emotional prosody or producing appropriate facial expressions. These patients also have decreased arousal, as determined by psychophysiologic measurements.

Heilman's and other recent studies have forced a reinterpretation of the older proposal that patients with right hemisphere lesions are indifferent or emotionally flattened. Instead, these patients are now seen as handicapped in either perceiving the emotional tone of individuals around them or in expressing emotion themselves. Indeed, there is substantial evidence that the affective display of individuals with right hemisphere disease often does not match their internal emotional state. Impaired emotional expressiveness may at one moment reflect a lowered threshold for laughing or crying and at another a disinhibited or heightened threshold for the same displays. The right-hemisphere-damaged patient who suddenly demonstrates un-controlled crying may not have had an underlying change in mood state, or only a very mild one. Such organically based alterations in affect are often characterized by extreme lability; the display may stop as quickly as it starts.

Emotional and Psychosocial Changes in Closed-Head-Injured Patients

Brain-injured patients have often been described as exhibiting socially in-appropriate behavior, outbursts of irritability, changes in attitude toward social mores, and a general lack of inhibition (Stuss & Richard, 1982). Other authors have described depression, anxiety, denial of deficits, and social withdrawal in these patients (Levin, Grossman, Rose, & Teasdale, 1979). In a previous chapter, we discussed a variety of cognitively based changes related to the so-called executive functions, manifested as im-pairments in initiating, planning, and completing activities. It is likely that different areas and degrees of frontal lobe (and potentially right hemisphere) involvement result in different types of residual affective and psychosocial symptomatology.

It is also probable that certain of the residual changes in emotional behavior reflect an interaction of organic injury with preexisting personality or mood. This notion is supported by observations of Reitman (1946), who suggested that outcome following orbital frontal leukotomy was dependent on premorbid personality. Servering of the frontal connections, he noted, was most helpful in patients with preoperative inertia, thought blockage, depersonalization, and indecision; the poorest outcomes occurred in rest-less, excited, aggressive patients.

Another fairly consistent report from the literature on both humans and animals suggests that frontal lobe damage does not change, but rather accentuates, premorbid personality. Jarvie (1954), for example, reviewed patients' past personality traits and reported that disinhibition secondary to frontal lobe damage did not cause anything new in the personality but altered self-environment relationships such that previously hidden tenden-

TABLE 14.1. Potentially Confusing "Emotional" Symptom of Brain Damage[a]

Psychogenic/psychiatric symptoms	Neurogenic symptoms
Denial	Anosognosia (lack of awareness of impairment)
Anger and irritability	Frustration, catastrophic reaction, reduced information processing, lowered anger threshold
Depression	Lack of initiative, impaired emotional expressiveness, lowered crying threshold, fatigue
Rigid compulsive/hypervigilant	Distractibility, inability to deal with more than one task at a time, dependence on external controls
Emotional lability (lability of the feeling state)	Lability of emotional expressiveness (not of the underlying feeling state)
Social withdrawal	Lack of initiative
Sense of futurelessness	Impaired planning
Thought disorder	Aphasia, anomia, or confusion
Personality or conduct disorder	Impulsivity, social disinhibition

[a]From Judd (1986). Reprinted by permission of the author.

cies were more overt. Although other researchers have not always adopted this view, further research on the role of preinjury emotional and behavioral functioning in the manifestations of symptoms following closed head injury is badly needed.

It is important to understand the ways in which neurologically based symptoms may be erroneously interpreted as psychogenic or psychiatric in origin. Table 14.1 lists some potentially confusing emotional or affective symptoms that often follow a brain injury, along with a number of labels that are primarily psychogenic or psychiatric in origin. The same behavior patterns that would give rise to these psychogenic or psychiatric labels might be natural consequences of neurologic damage; they may or may not be associated with the underlying emotional state connoted in the more traditional diagnosis.

APPROACHES TO ASSESSMENT AND INTERVENTION FOR ORGANICALLY BASED PSYCHOSOCIAL PROBLEMS

The approaches taken to remediate organically based psychosocial or emotional problems will vary, depending on the severity and level of impact of the problem and the diagnosis of the underlying cause. In the following section, we discuss several approaches to working with impairments in the areas of interpersonal skills, impaired emotional expressiveness, anger and irritability, and decreased awareness of deficits. Suggestions are gleaned from clinical experience and from the writings of many other clinicians and researchers, including Prigatano (1986), Trexler (1982), and Lezak (1983). At this stage, however, there is little or no empirical research on the efficacy of any of these approaches with the brain-injured patient. It is clinicians who are in the best position to provide the relevant data.

Interpersonal Skills

This area involves interpersonal behaviors that interfere with social success. Assessment and treatment of these problems have been discussed in Chapter 9 in relation to linguistic and pragmatic disorders, including evaluation and formal retraining of verbal and nonverbal communication (listening, turn-taking, vocal modulation, eye contact, dress, body language, etc.).

For individuals with deficits in their production or understanding of affect (facial expression, tone of voice, etc.), the first step is to determine the degree to which the problem is limited to affective display. That is, what is the degree of mismatch between affect and perception of, or internalized feeling of, underlying mood states? Table 14.2 lists suggested interview questions, observational strategies, and interventions to address diminished emotional expressiveness, diminished emotional comprehension, and lowered crying or laughing threshold.

Irritability and Anger

In working with individuals who have disruptive irritability and anger, we have had some good success with training in relaxation and in traditional anger management techniques, but only when these approaches are modified to account for the patient's cognitive level. Many individuals with even mild periorbital injury experience heightened irritability, decreased patience, and temper outbursts. A behavioral approach is the treatment of choice for these disorders. Wood (1987) provides an excellent review and discussion of these approaches. More puzzling and difficult to manage are the explosive dyscontrol syndromes that sometimes follow frontal injury or severe disorders that are associated with uncontrolled and unprovoked range. Although a variety of pharmacological interventions have been suggested in the management of these severe disorders, their use with most disruptive head-injured patients has been ill advised. This is based on the frequently reported paradoxical or exaggerated results of medication with head-injured patients. Increasingly, however, well-controlled studies are addressing the potential effectiveness of a variety of drugs on many aspects of behavior following head injury (see Cope, 1987, for a recent review).

TABLE 14.2. Evaluation of Interpersonal Skills[a]

Symptom	Interview Questions	How to observe/test	Interventions
Diminished emotional expressiveness	Do you have trouble putting feeling into your voice?	Ask the patient to produce various emotional expressions. Observe gestures. Test singing	Encourage literal expression of emotions. Attend to the patient's words about feelings. Ask about the patient's feeling state. Give feedback and use others to give feedback about the emotional tone of the patient's expressions.
Diminished emotional comprehension	Do you have trouble interpreting others' feelings? Do you fail to get jokes, or take things too literally?	Ask the patient to identify various emotional expressions	Express emotions literally to the patient. Avoid irony and sarcasm. Retrain the patient in attending to emotional cues.
Lowered crying or laughing threshold	Do you cry or laugh more often and when you don't mean to?	Observe the patient in situations with some emotional content. Inquire about feeling states at the time of laughing or crying.	Keep the conversation going. Ask what the patient is feeling. Emphasize with the problem of embarrassment over emotional expressions that exaggerate the underlying feeling state.

[a]From Judd (1986). Reprinted by permission of the author.

Impaired Awareness of Deficits

In individuals with impaired awareness of deficits and a concomitant failure to appreciate their practical impact, the clinician's best line of defense has probably been the opportunity to work in a group context. That environment, which provides opportunities for the patients both to observe the problems that others have and to get feedback on their own performance, has been extremely powerful. This is not to say that denial or unawareness changes quickly or easily, but it is more likely to change in an accepting, trusting environment that provides many opportunities for the demonstration or experience of problems in a face-saving and therapeutic fashion.

Although these last two problem areas can have an organic basis, they are likely to be exacerbated or influenced by a complex interaction with preexisting personality and with reactive responses to the individual's situation.

Table 14.3 lists some suggestions for interview, observation, and intervention in patients with these categories of problems.

It is important to recognize not only that rehabilitation specialists can sometimes easily misperceive organically based behaviors as more volitionally controlled or psychiatrically based problems, but also that the

TABLE 14.3 Evaluation of Irritability and Anger and Impaired Awareness of Deficits

Symptom	Interview questions	How to observe/test	Interventions
Irritability and anger	Are you irritable? Are you easily annoyed? Do you get frustrated at little things? Are these reactions new since your injury/illness? Have you gotten violent? Do you feel like hurting someone? Are you afraid you might hurt someone?	Observe on difficult tasks. Observe responses to interruptions, distractions and frustrations.	Recommend that patient, family, and staff back off briefly from situations producing irritation (time-outs). Avoid situations producing anger. Reintroduce those situations gradually later in recovery. Train patient in relaxation, and in calming self-talk. Restrict access to weapons, if necessary. Develop safety plan, if necessary.
Impaired awareness of deficits	How has your injury/illness affected you? What things do you have difficulty with? Do you find you are less sure of yourself? Do you make more mistakes or have more accidents? Questions for the family: Is the patient safe? Can you leave the patient alone?	Observe the patient's safety precautions. Observe self-corrections of errors on tasks. Ask the patient to make judgments about the quality of his/her performance on tasks. Ask "What would you do if . . .?"	Restrict access to dangerous situations—vehicles, sharp tools, fire, weapons. Teach the patient that they have a problem and re-educate their judgment by getting the patient to make judgments about his/her abilities immediately before and after doing a task, and giving firm feedback about judgments. Train the family in this technique. Train the patient to check out his/her judgments with others.

[a]From Judd (1986). Reprinted by permission of the author.

patients whom they treat are often facing a whole world of individuals who do just that. These may include their families, their friends, and even other medical providers. Education, not only for the individual but for others involved in his or her care, is essential for the effective management and treatment of these disorders.

COMMON EMOTIONAL REACTIONS TO ACQUIRED DISABILITY

In the next section, we discuss a variety of emotional changes following brain injury that might best be considered as normal, understandable reactions to sometimes dramatic, sometimes seemingly subtle, changes in circumstances and in capabilities. The most common reactions to traumatic brain injury, particularly in the postacute stage, include depression, anxiety, lowered self-esteem, dependency, and perplexity. The interplay of these factors often has enormous influence on what is generally termed "adjustment to disability.

Depression

The clinician evaluating psychosocial status in a person with traumatic head injury must be quite cautious about making a diagnosis of clinical or endogenous depression. Even though this syndrome can be seen in this population, there is a great deal of overlap between the symptoms of clinical depression and other psychosocial and cognitive sequelae of closed head injury. Examples of overlapping symptomatology include decreased energy, decreased initiation, irritability, difficulty with decision making, concentration and memory problems, lack of concern regarding physical appearance, decreased libido, sleep disturbance, self-criticism, and flattened affect.

In most cases, if there is a depression in the postacute state, it is a *reactive* depression—a part of the grief reaction process that typically attends may major loss. Responses to loss of function following injury are similar in some respects to grief at losing a family member or a friend to death or divorce. The stages of grief that many individuals move through have been hypothesized to include denial, anger, depression, and finally acceptance. The first is a denial or unwillingness to accept or recognize that the loss has occurred. Once the loss can no longer be denied, there are often anger and frustration. These strong emotions lessen or become more intermittent, and an individual in grief is then likely to move into a period of depression. With time and appropriate support, individuals can move on to acceptance and resume, to the extent possible, their previous lives.

Patients for whom depressive symptoms must be taken very seriously include those with suicidal feelings or actions, those with a preinjury history of a major depressive disorder or related affective disorder, and those for whom symptoms extend well beyond, or do not match, the typical reactive depression. If the depression extends to all areas of someone's life regardless of the extent of connection to the injury, if it lasts more than a year or two post-injury even if situational stressors have alleviated, or if depression continues to be moderately severe despite accomplishment of vocational goals and apparent permanence and stability of family relationships, a major clinical endogenous depression should be suspected.

The literature is not clear on the degree to which antidepressant medication affects the reactive depression that follows head injury. If depression presents major obstacles to achieving rehabilitation goals, medication might be considered, but it should be closely monitored for effects on other cognitive and behavioral capabilities.

Anxiety

Anxiety is typically manifested as nervousness, insecurity, or fear. Individuals with anxiety often appear outwardly tense, hypervigilant, and tight in their movements. They may also demonstrate nonorganically based tremor in voice and movement, nervous mannerisms, rapid speech, rapid pulse, and rapid breathing. Anxiety typically reflects an individual's difficulty in coping with stressful situations. Panic attacks and stress-induced "neurologic events" are also included in this category, although it should be noted that organic factors may precipitate such events. Symptoms include such subjective feelings as tingling or loss of sensation in fingers and toes, pseudoseizures, sweating, and skin reactions such as hives. In the nonneurologically impaired patient, an approach to anxiety disorder might be to try to correct misperceived notions about functional ability. In the brain-injured individual, anxiety may arise as a result of more realistic perceptions of reduced skills and of an actually experienced higher rate of failure. Approaches to the management of anxiety or stress disorders with this population can effectively include relaxation training, training in appropriately assertive behaviors, exercise, writing down feelings, and talking openly with others to reduce tension. Support and reassurance can also be useful, as can training of an individual to anticipate stressful situations or tasks and take actions to reduce their level of stress (e.g., modify their environment or their level of preparation).

Decreased Self-Esteem

In the non-brain-injured individual seeking psychotherapy for problems related to low self-esteem, the underlying causes typically sought are misperceptions about people's reaction to them or their performance, or a developmental history that may have lead to self-devaluation. In the case of a traumatically brain-injured individual, there has probably been a real decline in function, and the perception of capacities may not be grossly distorted. Realistic self-appraisal is typically thought to be of value in the recovery from traumatic brain injury, so treatment might include support, encouragement, and a focus on the objective nature of the impairments and spared or recovered abilities. An important concept may be that the person is not the disability, that is, allowing patients to see their value in terms of their humanness, their emotions, their relationships, etc. rather than in terms of their skills, abilities, or earning potential. It is often the case that effecting some change in the external manifestations of an individual—in appearance, clothing, posture, or hair style—will help bring about a more global change in self-esteem and perception of self-worth.

Dependency

Feelings of dependency or helplessness are primarily learned. In the non-brain-injured individual, feelings of helplessness can result when an individual sees him- or herself as less capable or more out of control than he or she actually is; psychotherapeutic efforts are designed to increase the individual's sense of competence. The traumatically brain-injured individual's feelings of helplessness may well have emerged from very real decreases in ability to control and manage the environment, particularly in the acute stages of recovery. For many of these individuals, increased feelings of capability and control will decrease subjective feelings of need for help. In other patients, excessive emotional and physical dependency on others may develop and be manifest as exaggerated fear of or distress at being alone or separated from a certain person or as reliance on others to provide constant or unneeded reassurance and assistance. Again, achieving a realistic perception of skills, abilities, and practical needs is a critical step in assisting someone to achieve a maximally independent, yet safe and supportive, living and work situation.

Perplexity

Many patients with brain injury experience confusion and bewilderment regarding their own reduced or unreliable skills and abilities. The phenomenon is often termed *perplexity*. Individuals recovering from traumatic brain injury may not necessarily feel incompetent and may not anticipate difficulty in certain situations. Suddenly, however, they find themselves at a loss for even simple words in a conversation, unable to remember an important point in a conversation held just a few moments before, unable to add the numbers in a simple game of cards, or failing to remember to pay an important bill. These problems are particularly vexing to the patient with minor head injury who has not been told to expect problems and who appears to be functioning normally. These minor but constant slips or failures often cause people to think they may be going crazy, are aging prematurely, or are developing a dementing disease. In these cases, what is needed is reassurance that the problems are real but likely to improve as the individual recovers and that there are some practical things that can be done to anticipate and accommodate for potentially problematic situations. Suggesting that these patients write down a phone message as soon as they take it, or put the letter that they intend to mail tomorrow by the door may do a great deal to reduce these feelings of perplexity.

In Table 14.4 are suggestions for interview questions, observations, and possible therapeutic techniques to deal with concerns in the areas of depression, anxiety, insomnia, and perplexity.

Adjustment to Disability

The notion of "adjustment to disability" typically refers to an individual's ability to acknowledge and accept his or her current status, including physical, cognitive, independent-living, interpersonal, vocational, and avocational strengths, as well as limitations. It also reflects the individual's ability to set appropriate goals and plans within the constraints imposed by the injury and its consequences. Specific behaviors and abilities that might be examined to evaluate the level of adjustment include the following: (1) the individual's ability to appraise current abilities and deficits realistically when reality-oriented feedback has been provided; (2) willingness to utilize compensation strategies; (3) movement through the grief process (denial, anger, depression) related to recognition of current abilities and deficits and acceptance of the situation; (4) the patient's demonstrated level of emotional stress, defensiveness, or denial when presented with current deficits or estimates of future functioning; and (5) the severity of symptoms of reactive depression, including preoccupation with loss and negativity about the present and future. If individuals seem to be "stuck" in terms of resolving certain of these areas, treatment efforts might be effectively addressed at one or more of the particular points.

In some individuals, it is important to recognize the existence of more severe and potentially longstanding symptoms of maladaptive adjustment. One such syndrome is the posttraumatic stress disorder. This term describes a set of symptoms that may be quite frequent and of little concern in the early postinjury stage but, if present in the postacute stage, many weeks, months, or even years post-injury, can become extremely problematic and disruptive. Posttraumatic stress disorder is most commonly seen in individuals who remain conscious and alert throughout an extremely stressful or life-threatening event. It is also commonly seen when significant injury to others is witnessed. The traumatic event may be experienced alone (rape or assault) or in the company of groups of people (military combat). Stressors

TABLE 14.4 Evaluation of Emotional Reactions to Disability[a]

Symptom	Interview questions	How to observe/test	Interventions
Depression	Are you depressed? How is your mood? Do you sleep well? How is your appetite? Do you feel that you have the energy to do what you want to do? Has there been any change in your sex drive? Do you feel like harming yourself?	Observe affect, sleep, appetite, energy level, motivation, responses to pleasant events, etc. Formal testing.	Support and reassure. Monitor the nature of family involvement. Acknowledge the depression. Educate about recovery. Keep the patient busy. Maximize success experiences in therapy. Depression can be a good sign of recovering judgment. Use other conventional treatments for depression, but be wary of using excessively cognitive approaches with patients who are cognitively impaired.
Anxiety	Are you anxious or nervous? Do you feel jittery, insecure, or scared? Are you easily startled or upset? Do you feel tense?	Observe on difficult tasks. Watch for tense muscles, excess movements, frustration, agitation.	Support and reassure. Train in relaxation. Limit stressful tasks.
Insomnia	Do you have any trouble falling asleep or staying asleep? Is this a problem for you?	Observation by family and nurses.	Decrease distractions at night. Keep the patient busy in the day. Train relaxation. Consider medication, including low-dose antidepressant.
Perplexity	Do you worry that you may be going crazy? Do you feel bewildered and perplexed? Do your body and mind seem suddenly unreliable?	Notice if there is unexplained pausing in the middle of tasks or conversations. Look for bewildered facial expressions.	Reassure that this is common, that patient is not crazy (if you are sure), and that it will get better as they recover and get more accustomed to their condition.

[a]From Judd (1986) Reprinted by permission of the author.

producing this disorder include natural disasters (floods, earthquakes), accidental man-made disasters (car accidents, airplane crashes), or deliberate man-made disasters (bombing, torture). The diagnostic criteria (DSM-III-R) for posttraumatic stress disorder include the existence of a recognizable stressor that would evoke significant symptoms of distress in almost everyone; reexperience of the trauma as evidenced by recurrent or intrusive recollections, recurrent dreams of the event, or sudden experience of the event in association with an environmental stimulus; numbing of responsiveness to or reduced involvement with the external world, as shown by feelings of detachment, constricted affect, or diminished interest in activities; sleep disturbance; guilt about surviving; concentration and memory problems; avoidance of activities related to the traumatic event; and/or hyperalertness. The existence of this syndrome should certainly prompt referral to a psychologist with experience in the treatment of this kind of disorder.

In this section, we have attempted to discuss the nature of a variety of reactive emotional responses to injury and to disability. We have also attempted to talk about some of the diagnostic criteria and approaches to rehabilitation that might be taken when these symptoms are present. It is important to recognize that many of these emotions or responses, depending on the point in rehabilitation during which they occur, may not be abnormal or detrimental. Support and encouragement, reality-oriented therapies, and counseling for grief and loss issues may be appropriate and sufficient. It should also be recognized that neurogenic symptoms (lack of awareness of impairment, memory problems, concentration problems, and reasoning impairments) may interfere with, slow down, and reduce the consistency with which more reactive emotional changes can resolve. Thus, for example, an individual with frontal lobe involvement will have a harder time moving through a grief reaction related to loss of a family member in an accident than someone without such cognitive impairments.

In addition, it must be recognized that other behavioral and psychosocial variables can have an enormous impact on recovery and rehabilitation. The next section presents information on issues related to substance abuse, significant preinjury psychologic or psychiatric problems, relationship stressors, and major situational stressors (Corey, 1987).

FACTORS RELATED TO PSYCHOSOCIAL FUNCTIONING INDEPENDENT OF INJURY

Substance Abuse

For many individuals with brain injury, intake of alcohol and/or drugs (prescription or nonprescription) may have interfered with optimal functioning prior to or following brain injury. Although little can be done about the preinjury use and/or abuse of substances, the magnified impact of such chemicals on a compromised brain makes consideration of this area important. In doing an evaluation in this area, consider the following issues:

1. The level of consumption of alcohol or drugs both before and since the injury, including the degree of fluctuation in consumption.
2. The physical effects of substance use, including physiologic addiction, discoordination, and blackouts.
3. Psychosocial effects of substance abuse, including withdrawal from others, depression, hostility, defensiveness, manipulation, and dishonesty.
4. Cognitive effects of substance abuse, including impaired attention, memory, visuospatial function, reasoning, and/or judgment.
5. The vocational, legal, and/or safety effects of substance abuse, including a history of being fired, impairment of job performance, DWIs or other legal charges related to substance abuse, or accidents or other dangerous situations while under the influence of alcohol or controlled substances.
6. Attitudes toward alcohol or drugs that are suggestive of abuse and addiction potential.
7. The possibility that prescribed medications and/or injections have taken on an addictive character and are being unintentionally maintained by medical practitioners.

Although there are no easy answers to issues of substance abuse in the brain-injured population, awareness and appreciation of the potential problems are critical. It may be appropriate to obtain a formal substance abuse evaluation and/or refer the patient for targeted treatment through an in- or outpatient setting. Clinicians experienced in head injury can help alcohol professionals to tailor substance abuse treatment programs to fit the special needs (e.g., accommodating cognitive and psychosocial deficits) of head-injured individuals.

Significant Preinjury Psychologic/Psychiatric Problems

It is important to identify and describe any major psychologic problems or psychopathology that may have existed prior to an injury. To the extent possible, description should emphasize specific behaviors exhibited or problems documented premorbidly. This can be done through medical records and discussion with family or significant others. Examples of such problems or psychopathology include the following:

Personality disorder (or noteworthy personality disorder features).
Psychotic episodes or use of antipsychotic medications.

Clinical depression including suicide attempts, hospitalizations, anti-depressant medication, or vegetative signs.

Anxiety characterized by panic attacks, obsessive–compulsive disorder, or antianxiety medication.

Past counseling or psychotherapy involvement.

Anger management problems, including property destruction or physical or verbal abuse of others.

Manic–depressive disorder.

Psychosomatic/psychophysiologic reactions.

Eating disorders.

Although there are no specific recommendations that can be made regarding these possible preexisting psychologic problems, it is important to recognize the degree to which their features or antecedent events contribute to the pattern of behavioral function. Disorders that may have been "cured" or stabilized may be destabilized by either the physiologic or emotional changes associated with injury, and they must again be addressed.

Relationship Stressors

This term refers to stress and dysfunction residing within a household, family system, or friendship that appear to be primarily a consequence— direct or indirect—of changes brought about by the injury. Since the relationships are being evaluated in a very stressful context, given the injury and its effects, much of the stress may be reactive. However, it is also common for postinjury situational stress to be largely a magnification of preexisting issues. Specific aspects of the relationship that may be evaluated include:

The head-injured individual and/or another person's self-described level of stress in the context of their relationship.

Reports of destructive verbal or physical altercations, ongoing hostility, or withdrawal between the injured person and another person.

Unrealistic expectations about the injured individual or inadequate communication with the individual.

Functional and dysfunctional adjustment reactions on the part of others to the injury and to resultant changes in the injured person.

The willingness of family members to become involved in treatment and their receptiveness to treatment needs of the individual.

Indications of a marked decline in functioning on the part of others in close association with the head-injured individual, including scholastic declines, sexual "acting out," substance abuse, legal problems, avoidance of family, loss of job, depression, or anger with clear cause or target.

Background data and historical information about the previous status of
the relationship, including degree of hostility, withdrawal, effectiveness
of communication, rejection or conditionality of acceptance, and
amount of contact, with a focus on similarities and differences from the
present.

Major Situational Stressors

This category includes major situational stressors that any person might
experience and that would be at least partially separable from the head
injury per se. They are important to evaluate because a significant portion of
dysfunctional behavior may be closely related to general stress reactions and
not specifically to head-injury symptomatology. Areas that might be addressed include: chronic pain problems or the presence of other serious
medical concerns; financial difficulties; changes in vocation or employment
including loss of job; moving or other change in living situation or lifestyle;
legal difficulties or ongoing procedures; and death of a close relative or
significant friend.

Although it is again impossible to recommend specific strategies to deal
with these kinds of major situational stressors, it is critical that staff involved in managing the patient's psychosocial and general rehabilitation be
aware of these changes and their potential impact. To a large degree, a
rehabilitation team or a primary therapist will take on the role of a case
manager. This person should attempt to ease or decrease the impact of stress
associated with some of these major changes through appropriate liaisons
with other professionals or agencies.

SELECTION OF THERAPY TECHNIQUES

The combination of cognitive, psychosocial, and neurobehavioral impairments of head-injured individuals greatly affects the degree to which
therapy techniques are helpful. Many of the "standard" approaches to
psychosocial therapy are rendered impractical or ineffective by the effects of
brain injury. For example, there are many potential obstacles for verbally
mediated therapies. Severe aphasia can render "talk" therapies futile and
potentially counterproductive if they pose unrealistic expectations or demands for communication. More subtle obstacles arise when speech is left
intact but abstract language and reasoning are reduced. Verbal techniques
such as analogy and metaphor may prove confusing for the client and
frustrating for the therapist. Reasoning and memory deficits also impede
therapy. The "client-centered" techniques typically assume that clients are
intrinsically motivated and capable of solving their problems; therapists
facilitate this process by providing a supportive relationship and by guiding

patients through selective responses and comments, but the actual direction and solutions are left largely for clients to discover for themselves. Unfortunately, this approach is not well suited to many head-injured patients, since both initiative and problem-solving skills may be substantially reduced. Where deficits in initiation and problem solving pose problems for client-centered approaches, impaired abstract reasoning and memory pose major obstacles to insight-oriented and cognitive approaches. Head-injured individuals often have extreme difficulty combining the information necessary to achieve insights about the antecedents or affects of their behavior. Furthermore, insights that are reached may well be quickly forgotten because of memory deficits. It is clear that much work is needed to determine "what techniques work with head-injured individuals, with what disorders, by which therapists, in which settings, and toward what goals" (Baird, Corey, & Crinean, 1987).

Psychotherapists working with the head-injured individual need to be prepared for a flexible and potentially quite unusual therapeutic process. They must be prepared for variable levels of cooperation and potential difficulty building rapport. Many head-injured clients, because of their unawareness or denial of deficits and changes, only reluctantly come to therapy and see little need to focus on their feelings or behaviors. Concrete and straightforward education about the purposes and goals of the therapy will be important. Reduced information-processing capabilities and memory may require that treatment be modified so that only one or two points or issues are discussed in one session. It is often helpful to have the client summarize the discussion in writing and orally at the end of the session and for the therapist to make the same points in similar or different ways several times. It will be important to ask questions and generally check to see what information is being accurately understood and retained. It is also imperative to recognize that the pace of therapy and rate of change may be limited by the client's capabilities. Therapists may need to modify more traditionally held views and be willing to view their role as one that calls for didactic instruction and practical problem solving at least as much as facilitation of insight.

More than with other kinds of clients or patients, the therapist working with a brain-injured patient may need to corroborate factual data with some other source because of the possibility of memory deficits or confabulation as well as distortion and denial. This should be done in a diplomatic and supportive context so that the brain-injured individual is not made to feel dishonest or untrustworthy.

Other issues of importance include the need for innovation, appreciation of the enormous potential for family members and significant others to facilitate or sabotage treatment, the need not to personalize the behavior of a brain-injured individual, and the concept of therapy as a structured experience (Baird et al., 1987). Family members and significant others take on magnified importance as a result of a brain-injured individual's functional dependence and emotional vulnerability. Family members' support for treatment methods and goals is often facilitated by an approach that combines instruction with empathy and by interaction with family members from the beginning.

Because of their impaired social behavior, reduced cognitive ability, and emotional problems, many head-injured clients may act in irritating, inconsistent, or seemingly irrational ways. It is sometimes difficult not to react to these behaviors with frustration and irritation. (Many brain-injured individuals appear to be quite capable of managing their behavior "if they only made an effort.") It is important constantly to recognize the potential limitations and underlying impairments and to avoid rejecting or blaming the individual, while at the same time establishing firm and clear behavioral expectations.

Finally, although many therapists, for good reasons, espouse a rather open-ended and adaptable therapy style, it is important to recognize that brain-injured individuals benefit enormously from structured and predictable experience. For that reason, goals and the reasons for treatment should be clearly outlined, and sessions should have a predictable format. The ground rules and range of acceptable behaviors in treatment may need to be much more explicit and structured than would be the case for a non-brain-injured individual.

Muriel Lezak is perhaps one of the most eloquent authors who has written about the effect of an individual's cognitive and behavioral compromise on his or her family. Although many psychologic alterations can occur as the direct or indirect consequence of brain damage, several emerge as especially burdensome to families (Lezak, 1978). These include the impaired social perception and social awareness manifest in egocentricity and social insensitivity. The family may experience endless attention seeking on the part of the brain-injured family member, embarrassment, social isolation, and emotional abandonment. Other problematic behaviors include loss of control manifested as anger, impulsive eating, inappropriate sexual behavior, uncontrolled spending, and impatience. Dependency—physical, financial, and emotional—on the part of a head-injured individual also taxes family resources.

Thus, families of individuals with head injury often experience social isolation, loss of emotional supports, restricted independence, and financial strain as well as confusion, frustration, guilt, and depression (Lezak, 1987). Also problematic are often dramatic changes in familiar roles and styles of interacting. Being a head-injured individual's parent, child, spouse, or sibling may each have very different implications, frustrations, and heartaches. Treating the injured person as if he or she were unchanged may be disappointing and ineffective. Developing a new relationship is often difficult but in the long run more rewarding. Emotional evolution and the recovery from loss and grief proceed at a different pace and in a different way for each family member. Families function quite differently under conditions as stressful and burdensome as this. Some deny, some accuse or blame, some withdraw, some grow and become even closer.

Although it is beyond the scope of this discussion, it is well recognized that needs of the family and other individuals living or working with the brain-injured individual must be addressed. There is a need for early and continued provision of education, counseling, and emotional support for the family. All family members need information about the nature of head injury and its consequences, about resources available to them, and about the probable progression of recovery. They need to be supported and guided through the grief process. They also need training in specific behavioral and social management techniques.

SUMMARY

Psychosocial and emotional changes that attend neurologic disorder and disease are complex and frequently perplexing. In the case of the traumatically brain-injured adult, they are often a major factor in determining the level of return to independence and the adjustment to community and work.

In the stage of diagnosis and assessment, it is critical to have a comprehensive understanding of the possible biologic or organic bases of mood states, affective capabilities for comprehending and expressing emotion, lability of underlying emotional states and/or their expression, and the role of cognitive variables in all of the preceding functions. Effective treatment or remediation of psychosocial or emotional changes will depend on an understanding of their underlying basis. Organically based changes usually reflect dysfunction of the frontolimbic systems and their interconnection and/or impairments in the emotional processing mechanisms attributed to the right cerebral hemisphere.

Therapists working with these disorders need to gain an appreciation of the common reactive responses to injury, disability, and the changed life circumstances that such problems bring. Diagnosis, assessment, technique selection, and evaluation of progress with brain-injured clients pose a myriad of theoretical and practical issues that differ significantly from those presented by non-head-injured individuals. Failure to appreciate and respond effectively to these differences leads at best to ineffective treatment and at worst to iatrogenic effects that exacerbate conditions that were extremely difficult to begin with. Therapists working on the psychosocial needs of the head injured need to get a strong background in the neuropsychology and neurobiology of behavior and emotion and need to

ADJUNCT APPROACHES

examine and practice their therapeutic skills with a different set of assumptions and expectations than might be used with the non-brain-injured individual.

In this chapter, we have attempted to convey some models for conceptualizing organic versus reactive emotional and affective changes and have stressed the importance of addressing individual, family, and social variables that have a significant impact on the adjustment and rehabilitation of the brain-injured individual in terms of psychosocial functioning. Much work is needed in this area, and all who enter it are on the frontier.

STUDY QUESTIONS

1. How are mood and affect interrelated?
2. How are psychosocial or affective behaviors mediated by the frontolimbic system? The right hemisphere?
3. Describe differences in behavior following lateral cortex frontal injury and orbital or basal frontal injury.
4. List four of the most common reactive emotional changes following brain injury and suggest treatment approaches.
5. List distinguishing features of a posttraumatic stress disorder.
6. Discuss advantages and disadvantages of at least two major psychotherapy approaches in addressing the psychosocial problems of a brain-injured adult.

REFERENCES

Baird, B., Corey, M., & Crinean, J. (1987). Role of psychotherapy in the postmedical rehabilitation of brain injured adults. Paper presented at the Washington State Psychology Association Meetings, Tacoma, WA.

Blumer, D., & Benson, D. F. (1975). Personality changes with frontal and temporal lobe lesions. In D. F. Benson & D. Blumer (Eds.), *Psychiatric aspects of neurologic disease* (pp. 151–170). New York: Grune & Stratton.

Bond, M. R. (1975). Assessment of psychosocial outcome after severe head injury. *Abe Foundation Symposium* 34:141–159.

Bryden, M. P., & Ley, R. G. (1983). Right-hemisphere involvement in the perception and expression of emotion in normal humans. In K. M. Heilman & P. Satz (Eds.), *Neuropsychology of human emotion* (pp. 6–44). New York: Guilford Press.

Cope, N. (Ed.). (1987). Psychopharmacology. *Journal of Head Trauma Rehabilitation* 2(4):1–76.

Corey, M. R. (1987). A comprehensive model for psychosocial assessment of individuals with closed head injury. *Cognitive Rehabilitation* 5(6):28–33.

Damasio, A. R., & Van Hoesen, G. W. (1983). Emotional disturbance associated with focal lesions of the limbic frontal lobe. In K. M. Heilman & P. Satz (Eds.), *Neuropsychology of human emotion* (pp. 85–110). New York: Guilford Press.

Dikmer, S., & Reiton, A. M. (1977). Emotional sequelae of head injury. *Annals of Neurology* 2:492–494.

Earp, J. O. (1979). Psychosurgery: The position of the Canadian Psychiatric Association. *Canadian Journal of Psychiatry* 24:353–365.

Freeman, W., & Watts, J. M. (1944). Behavior and the frontal lobes. *New York Academy of Science* 6:284–310.

Greenblatt, M., Arnot, R., & Solomon, H. C. (1950). *Studies of lobotomy.* New York: Grune & Stratton.

Heilman, K. M., Watson, R. T., & Bowers, D. (1983). Affective disorders associated with hemispheric disease. In K. M. Heilman & P. Satz (Eds.), *Neuropsychology of human emotion* (pp. 45–64). New York: Guilford Press.

Hinsie, L. E., & Campbell, R. T. (1970). *Psychiatric Dictionary* (4th ed.). Toronto: Oxford University Press.

Holmes, G. (1931). Discussion on the mental symptoms associated with cerebral tumors. *Proceedings of the Royal Society of Medicine* 24:997–1000.

Jarvie, H. F. (1954). Frontal lobe wounds causing disinhibition. A study of six cases. *Journal of Neurology, Neurosurgery, and Psychiatry* 17:14–32.

Judd, T. (1986). Assessment and intervention for major symptoms of brain damage. Workshop presented in Managua, Nicaragua.

Levin, H. S., Grossman, R. C., Rose, J. E., & Teasdale, G. (1979). Long-term neuropsychological outcome of closed head injury. *Journal of Neurosurgery* 50:412–422.

Levin, H. S., High, W. M., Goethe, K. E., Sisson, R. A., Overall, J. E., Rhoades, H. M., Eisenberg, H. M., Kalisky, Z., and Gary, H. E. (1987). The neurobehavioral rating scale: Assessment of the behavioral sequelae of head injury by the clinician. *Journal of Neurology, Neurosurgery, and Psychiatry* 50:183–193.

Lezak, M. (1978). Living with the characterologically altered brain injured patient. *Journal of Clinical Psychiatry* 39:592–598.

Lezak, M. (1983). *Neuropsychological assessment* (2nd ed.). New York: Oxford University Press.

Lezak, M. (1988). Brain damage is a family affair. *Journal of Clinical and Experimental Neuropsychology* 10:111–123.

Lieberman, W. A., & Benson, D. F. (1977). Pseudobulbar palsy. *Archives of Neurology* 34:717–719.

Lishman, W. (1968). Brain damage in relation to psychiatric disability after head injury. *British Journal of Psychiatry* 114:373–410.

MacLean, P. D. (1949). Psychosomatic disease and the "visceral brain": Recent developments bearing on the Papez theory of emotion. *Psychosomatic Medicine* 11:338–353.

Papez, J. W. (1937). A proposed mechanism of emotion. *Archives of Neurology and Psychiatry* 38:725–744.

Prigatano, G. (1986). *Neuropsychological rehabilitation after brain injury.* Baltimore: The Johns Hopkins University Press.

Reitman, F. (1946). Orbital cortex syndrome following leucotomy. *American Journal of Psychiatry* 103:238–241.

Rimel, R. W., Giordani, M. A., Barth, J. T., Boll, T. J., Jane, J. A. (1987). Disability caused by minor head injury. *Neurosurgery* 9:221–228

Stuss, D. T., & Richard, M. T. (1982). Neuropsychological sequelae of coma after head injury. In L. P. Ivan & D. Bruce (Eds.), *Coma: Pathophysiology, diagnosis, and management* (pp. 193–210). Springfield, IL: Charles C. Thomas.

Trexler, L. (1982). *Cognitive rehabilitation: Conceptualization and intervention.* New York: Plenum.

Wood, R. L. (1987). Brain injury rehabilitation: A neurobehavioral approach. Rockville, MD: Aspen Publishers.

APPENDIX: Neurobehavioral Rating Scale*

Directions: Place an X in the appropriate box to represent level of severity of each symptom.

	Not present	Very mild	Mild	Moderate	Mod. severe	Severe
1. INATTENTION/REDUCED ALERTNESS—fails to sustain attention, easily distracted; fails to notice aspects of environment, difficulty directing attention, decreased alertness.	☐	☐	☐	☐	☐	☐
2. SOMATIC CONCERN—volunteers complaints or elaborates about somatic symptoms (e.g., headache, dizziness, blurred vision), and about physical health in general.	☐	☐	☐	☐	☐	☐
3. DISORIENTATION—confusion or lack of proper association for person, place, or time.	☐	☐	☐	☐	☐	☐
4. ANXIETY—worry, fear, overconcern for present or future.	☐	☐	☐	☐	☐	☐
5. EXPRESSIVE DEFICIT—word-finding disturbance, anomia, pauses in speech, effortful and agrammatic speech, circumlocution.	☐	☐	☐	☐	☐	☐
6. EMOTIONAL WITHDRAWAL—lack of spontaneous interaction, isolation, deficiency in relating to others.	☐	☐	☐	☐	☐	☐
7. CONCEPTUAL DISORGANIZATION—thought processes confused, disconnected, disorganized, disrupted, tangential social communication, perseverative.	☐	☐	☐	☐	☐	☐
8. DISINHIBITION—socially inappropriate comments and/or actions, including aggressive/sexual content, or inappropriate to the situation, outbursts of temper.	☐	☐	☐	☐	☐	☐
9. GUILT FEELINGS—self-blame, shame, remorse for past behavior	☐	☐	☐	☐	☐	☐
10. MEMORY DEFICIT—difficulty learning new information, rapidly forgets recent events, although immediate recall (forward digit span) may be intact.	☐	☐	☐	☐	☐	☐

11. AGITATION—motor manifestations of overactivation (e.g., kicking, arm flailing, picking, roaming, restlessness, talkativeness.) ☐ ☐ ☐ ☐ ☐ ☐

12. INACCURATE INSIGHT AND SELF-APPRAISAL—poor insight, exaggerated self-opinion, overrates level of ability and underrates personality change in comparison with evaluation by clinicians and family. ☐ ☐ ☐ ☐ ☐ ☐

13. DEPRESSIVE MOOD—sorrow, sadness, despondency, pessimism. ☐ ☐ ☐ ☐ ☐ ☐

14. HOSTILITY/UNCOOPERATIVENESS—animosity, irritability, belligerence, disdain for others, defiance of authority. ☐ ☐ ☐ ☐ ☐ ☐

15. DECREASED INITIATIVE/MOTIVATION—lacks normal initiative in work or leisure, fails to persist in tasks, is reluctant to accept new challenges. ☐ ☐ ☐ ☐ ☐ ☐

16. SUSPICIOUSNESS—mistrust, belief that others harbor malicious or discriminatory intent. ☐ ☐ ☐ ☐ ☐ ☐

17. FATIGABILITY—rapidly fatigues on challenging cognitive tasks or complex activities, lethargic. ☐ ☐ ☐ ☐ ☐ ☐

18. HALLUCINATORY BEHAVIOR—perceptions without normal external stimulus correspondence. ☐ ☐ ☐ ☐ ☐ ☐

19. MOTOR RETARDATION—slowed movements or speech (excluding primary weakness). ☐ ☐ ☐ ☐ ☐ ☐

20. UNUSUAL THOUGHT CONTENT—unusual, odd, strange, bizarre thought content. ☐ ☐ ☐ ☐ ☐ ☐

21. BLUNTED AFFECT—reduced emotional tone, reduction in normal intensity of feelings, flatness. ☐ ☐ ☐ ☐ ☐ ☐

22. EXCITEMENT—heightened emotional tone, increased reactivity. ☐ ☐ ☐ ☐ ☐ ☐

23. POOR PLANNING—unrealistic goals, poorly formulated plans for the future, disregards prerequisites (e.g., training), fails to take disability into account. ☐ ☐ ☐ ☐ ☐ ☐

24. LABILITY OF MOOD—sudden change in mood which is disproportionate to the situation. ☐ ☐ ☐ ☐ ☐ ☐

25. TENSION—postural and facial expression of heightened tension, without the necessity of excessive activity involving the limbs or trunk. ☐ ☐ ☐ ☐ ☐ ☐

26. COMPREHENSION DEFICIT—difficulty in understanding oral instructions on single or multistage commands. ☐ ☐ ☐ ☐ ☐ ☐

27. SPEECH ARTICULATION DEFECT—misarticulation, slurring or substitution of sounds which affect intelligibility (rating is independent of linguistic content.) ☐ ☐ ☐ ☐ ☐ ☐

*From Levin et al. (1987). Reprinted by permission.

15
Applications of Cognitive Rehabilitation in Special Populations

This book has been designed to provide models and rationales for a Process-Specific Approach to cognitive rehabilitation and to provide exposure to specific remedial strategies for the treatment of a broad range of cognitive disorders that may result from injury to the brain. The theory presented and the treatment approach described should be broadly applicable across different treatment settings and with traumatically brain-injured patients of different ages and with different levels of cognitive disability. From a theoretical perspective, they may also be applicable and of benefit to patients with other neurologic disorders and to nonpatient subjects. In this chapter, the use of cognitive rehabilitation and the special consideration that attends such treatment is addressed in several neurologic and nonneurologic populations. These include the so-called minor head injury or postconcussive syndrome, children with traumatic brain injury, children with developmental cognitive processing deficits, individuals with a variety of medical and psychiatric diagnoses, and, finally, "normal" individuals.

MINOR HEAD INJURY

Disability Related to Minor Head Injury

Minor traumatic head injury is usually defined by a loss of consciousness, if any, of less than 20 minutes, a Glasgow Coma Scale (GCS) score from 13 to 15, and no abnormality on computed tomographic scan or skull radiographs (Ommaya & Gennarelli, 1974). Mechanisms of injury can include cerebral concussion or limited intracranial pathology (e.g., small contusions). Concussion is associated with immediate, usually transient disturbance of neurologic function, typically of consciousness, memory, or speech, as a result of mechanical forces (Caveness & Walker, 1969). Of all head injuries, more than two-thirds are classified as minor; in a recent estimate, 72% of 400,000 hospital admissions for head trauma in one year in the United States were diagnosed as minor head injury (Ruff, Levin, & Marshall, 1986).

Posttraumatic symptoms themselves exhibit considerable variability. Frequent somatic or physical complaints include headache, back or neck ache, dizziness, blurred or sometimes double vision, sleep disturbance, fatigue, or increased sensitivity to noise and to medications. In the cognitive domain, frequent complains include diminished concentration, memory deficits, slowing of performance, decreased motivation, and word-finding difficulties. Anxiety, depression, irritability, and mood swings are some of the most common affective or psychosocial complaints. Although evidence for an organic etiology for posttraumatic symptoms is accumulating (Gennarelli, 1982; Jane, Rimel, & Alves, 1985), current medical and neuropsychologic techniques do not always allow definitive separation of posttraumatic symptoms into those with organic and nonorganic bases.

Despite the frequency of concussion and minor head injury, and the common report of problems such as those described above, there is still considerable debate over the genuineness of posttraumatic symptoms. Often, it is the impression of medical practitioners that the probable anatomic disruption underlying minor head injury is insufficient to account for the observed severity and duration of posttraumatic symptoms (Trimble, 1981). For some patients, few if any neurologic symptoms are present immediately after the injury. Patients may, however, begin to complain of or demonstrate deficits hours, days, or even weeks after injury. Such "late" symptoms have typically been interpreted as evidence of psychogenic etiology (Lidvall, Linderoth, & Norlin, 1974; Lishman, 1973). More recently, it has been suggested that the deficits associated with minor head injury may only become obvious as pain from other injuries or shock subsides, and the individual attempts to resume aspects of everyday functioning. It has also been suggested that the pathophysiology of minor head injury involves a much more gradual process than is currently acknowledged (Povlishock, Becker, & Miller, 1979).

Another reason postulated for the variation in onset of symptoms is the interaction between organic and psychosocial factors over the course of normal recovery. Emotional reactions to deficits on the part of the injured individuals themselves, as well as of those around them, may produce persistent and more severe symptoms than might overwise occur from the organic damage alone.

Despite the controversy surrounding the contribution of organic and nonorganic factors in cases of mild head injury, there is little doubt that these injuries can have profound implications for psychosocial adjustment and vocational stability. In a study by Rimel, Giordani, Barth, Boll, & Jane (1981), 34% of patients suffering mild head injury who were previously employed were unemployed at follow-up 3 months later. In a related study, 31% of such patients who were previously employed were not back to work at 6 weeks after injury, and 18% were still unemployed at 3 months after injury. The majority of patients (52%) did go back to work in 2 weeks or less. These researchers also suggested that involvement in litigation or potential for secondary gain appeared to bear little relationship to return to work. These reports contrast, however, with work by Wrightson and Gronwall (1981), which cited return to work in an average of 4.7 days and a total of only 8% of patients delaying return to work longer than 2 weeks. Although additional research needs to be done in exploring factors that affect return to work, it is clear that for some individuals the effects of minor head injury are substantially detrimental to adaptive functioning.

Cognitive Deficits Associated with Minor Head Injury

Individuals who have sustained minor head injury typically have difficulty concentrating under conditions of distraction or when they are called on to manage multiple demands. Selective, alternating, and/or divided attention may all be affected (Gronwall & Wrightson, 1974). Memory is often disrupted either secondary to these attention deficits or as a primary deficit (Gronwall & Wrightson, 1981). A third area commonly disrupted is that of executive functioning. Individuals with minor head injury associated with acceleration/deceleration injuries often demonstrate frontal lobe dysfunction manifest as impairments in initiation, planning, organizing, monitoring, and completing goal-directed activity.

It would be a significant mistake to assume that the deficits following minor head injury warrant only a brief assessment in comparison to those following severe brain impairment. In fact, the opposite is true. Severe deficits will quickly reveal themselves in a neurologic assessment. If, however, subtle deficits are to be delineated, the reliability of identifying deficits is enhanced by incorporating multiple measures of a very broad range of cognitive processes (Lezak, 1983). Evaluation should be particularly sensitive to the major areas of cognition that may be expected to be at risk. In the case of minor head injury, evaluation should address multiple levels of attentional capacity, multiple aspects of memory, assessment of executive functions, and evaluation of the efficiency of information processing in terms of speed and flexibility. Test selection should include a wide range of difficulty to avoid ceiling effects with repeated administration. The process-oriented neuropsychologic assessment described in Chapter 4 is suggested to fit these criterion. It must be recognized, however, that when deficits are very subtle or are only operative under the complex circumstances inherent in natural contexts, even the most assiduous testing may not reveal deficits in the laboratory setting (Mesulam, 1985). In such cases, it is important to interview extensively with the individual, the family, and/or co-workers to obtain an appreciation of potential changes in adaptive functioning in everyday circumstances.

Psychosocial Deficits Following Minor Brain Injury

Following minor head injury, most individuals expect to recover from any deficits they may experience within a short period of time. This expectation is usually endorsed by treating medical practitioners. If deficits do not resolve, emotional reactions are likely to occur. Chief among the reactive deficits are anxiety and depressive symptomatology. Anxiety disorders may be manifest as physical changes (e.g., stuttering of speech, tremor, psychogenic pain syndromes); depressive reactions may be manifest in sleep or eating disorders, social withdrawal, discomfort around people, and depressed mood (Prigatano, Pepping, & Klonoff, 1986). These disorders are thought to come about, in part, as the injured individual experiences failure in meeting previously obtainable expectations and goals, makes frequent mistakes on formerly simple activities, and experiences exhaustion following even a routine day. Such individuals often report the phenomenon of "perplexity" and find they cannot accurately anticipate or judge their capabilities in a given situation (Lezak, 1983).

Problems can also occur with interpersonal skills and interactions. After a mild head injury, the patient may demonstrate increased irritability and mood swings, frustration, impulsiveness, and outbursts of anger. Family members, friends, and colleagues may feel uncomfortable, frustrated, or confused in the person's presence and respond with rejection or avoidance. If the brain-injured individual recognizes these changes and reacts to them, a "negative spiral" of psychosocial disability may begin (Ruff et al., 1986). Deficits are thought to be particularly likely to give rise to emotional problems because of the fact that they are often not obvious. To a casual observer or even close family member, cognitive and physical deficits may not be apparent, and the individual is thought to be completely recovered or in some cases never to have been injured. Expectations are set up based on this assumption. Even the individual cannot understand the reasons underlying repeated failure and emotional dyscontrol. The clinician may be perplexed by the seemingly neurotic pettiness of patients with minor head injury when their capabilities are compared to those of severely brain-injured patients. It is postulated that impairments in psychosocial recovery, often hampered by the apparent normality of neurologic functioning, present the greatest obstacle to recovery and functional adaptation in the individual with minor head injury.

Treatment of Minor Head Injury

Perhaps the most important aspects of effectively treating mild head injury are avoidance of a potential shuffle among health care specialists and coordinated evaluative and treatment efforts. At the time of an emergency room consult, a thorough evaluation of cognitive status, neurologic function, and physical symptom review should be undertaken. In most cases of minor head injury, the individual is not admitted but should be discharged with head injury instructions. It may also be valuable to warn the individual that he or she may experience some symptomatology but that gradual recovery should be expected over days, weeks, or sometimes months. Most recovery following minor head injury will take place in the first 3 months after the trauma (Gentilini, Nichelli, & Schoenhuber, 1985; Gronwall & Wrightson, 1974). In anyone at risk for significant sequelae, a baseline evaluation taken shortly after injury is useful in establishing a cognitive and psychosocial level. If there are deficits, testing might be undertaken again after a 6- to 12-week period. Testing can be discontinued, with an invitation to return if problems arise, if there are no positive signs or symptoms in a follow-up examination.

Should continuing signs or neurologic symptoms be present, it is likely that a team approach to treatment will be necessary. A neurologic assessment is needed to assess somatic complaints; a physical therapist or chiropractor may assist in their treatment. The cognitive difficulties are most comprehensively and accurately assessed through a neuropsychologic evaluation. Affective or psychosocial symptoms are most appropriately evaluated by a psychologist or counselor who has experience with mild traumatic brain injury. Experts in these disciplines should coordinate their efforts in order to be most effective. Failure to provide the patient with an integrated approach to treatment during the early recovery process may result in chronic pain syndromes, worsening psychosocial adjustment, and misperception of cognitive deficits. Depending on the severity of injury, different recovery curves can be expected, although recovery of somatic, cognitive, and effective symptoms do not necessarily parallel each other.

Neurological signs or symptomatic complaints that extend beyond 3 months following what appeared to have been a minor brain injury suggest that a program of treatment may be necessary. Cognitive therapy approaches may be used to address deficits in attention, memory, and executive function. Within our own mild brain injury treatment program at the Center for Cognitive Rehabilitation, we have used attention process training, systematic training in the use of a memory book or organizer, and executive functioning training as described in previous chapters in this text. Physical therapy may be appropriate to promote physical recovery, to guide physical conditioning efforts, and to prevent chronic pain problems that may attend neck or back injury.

Perhaps the most important components of a minor brain injury treatment program are psychologic support and counseling for both the injured individual and family members. Following a diagnostic evaluation, specific treatment approaches may be selected to deal with anxiety and stress reactions, changes in family relationships caused by altered functional capabilities, and issues of depression, denial, and/or decreased self-esteem. If deficits do not resolve and effective return to work has not been possible, it may be necessary to involve the individual in a more intensive program of cognitive, psychosocial, and vocational assistance. Vocational counseling and guidance are often a particular challenge in this population since individuals may perform quite well in structured tests but be unable to undertake responsibilities of a complicated job. Because they are, in many respects, so close to previous levels of functioning, it is difficult to accept returning to less than full capacity or functioning at less than previous potential. At whatever level of treatment is provided, communication and interdisciplinary coordination are key features. Figure 15.1 provides a schema of recovery with appropriate interventions as needed for patients with mild head injury.

Much remains to be understood about the pathophysiology and resultant symptom complex that attend the minor brain injury or concussional syndrome. Researchers are beginning to gain a better understanding of the nature of cognitive and psychosocial impairments that impose limitations to functional recovery in some individuals with these injuries. Coordinated assessment and treatment efforts appear to be key factors in the satisfactory resolution of minor head injury.

PEDIATRIC HEAD INJURY

Cognitive and Neurobehavioral Consequences of Head Injury in Children

Because of their activity levels and their attraction to the stimulation of thrills and risk, children and young adults always have been prone to head injury and subsequent brain-related impairments. Recently, however, the numbers of young head-injured individuals are increasing. Motorized vehicles, particularly those that provide minimal protection (bikes, scooters, ATVs), have become more available. Physical abuse of children is increasingly recognized as a cause of childhood injury. Drugs and alcohol are used at an earlier age. In addition, medical technologies and sophisticated treatments allow a higher survival rate. The result has meant new problems for those institutions committed to the integration of young head-injured individuals into society's mainstream and educational network, our schools, colleges, universities, and vocational/technical institutions.

MINOR HEAD INJURY

Symptoms: Physical deficits
                 (dizziness, tinnitis, nausea, confusion)

Treatment: Patient provided with head injury instructions
                 Warned of possibility of transient deficits ─────────────────
                                                                              ►Recovery
                                    │
                                    ▼
                                    or

ACUTE CHANGE (<6 WEEKS)

Symptoms: Physical and cognitive deficits
                 (headache, blurred vision, fatigue, memory loss, irritability)

Treatment: Coordination of services
                 Evaluation
                 Reassurance
                 Physical therapy if necessary ───────────────────
                                                                   ►Recovery
                                    │
                                    ▼
                                    or

EARLY POSTACUTE CHANGES (<3–6 MONTHS)

Symptoms: Emotional reactions to physical or cognitive deficits
                 (depression, social withdrawal, anxiety)

Treatment: Cognitive rehabilitation
                 Psychosocial counseling ───────────────────
                                                            ►Recovery
                                    │
                                    ▼
                                    or

LATE POSTACUTE CHANGES (>6 MONTHS)

Symptoms: Cognitive and severe emotional deficits affecting relationships and return to
                 work

Treatment: Coordinated milieu-based cognitivepsychosocial and vocational rehabilita-
                 tion ─────────────────────
                                           ►Recovery

FIGURE 15.1.   Schema of possible recovery avenues following mild head injury.

There have been longstanding, widely held beliefs that the greater plasticity of children's nervous systems for functional reorganization provides a
measure of protection from the effects of injury (Spreen, Tupper, Risser,
Tuokko, & Edgell, 1984). Lately, however, this belief has been somewhat
modified. Although it appears that children under the age of 5 can often
accommodate quite well to focal cortical injury (such that the child appears
to recover most or all of the functions normally associated with the damaged area), the child who sustains a diffuse, widespread, or bilateral brain
injury may not have the available brain substrate to provide the takeover of
function that has been postulated. It is now thought that diffuse head injury
in children may, in fact, be even more devastating than for the adult in that

it seriously compromises the development of basic cognitive structures and psychoemotional functioning (Ewing-Cobbs, Fletcher, & Levin, 1985; Levin, Ewing-Cobbs, & Benton, 1984).

A variety of studies have shown persistent declines in intelligence test scores following head injury in children (Levin & Eisenberg, 1979). Studies of pediatric closed head injury indicate more severe and persistent Performance IQ deficits as compared with Verbal IQ deficits as measured by the Weschler Intelligence Scales (WISC-R; Wechsler, 1974) (Chadwick, Rutter, & Brown, 1981). Although Verbal IQ typically returns to within normal limits by 1 year after injury, impairment continues to be present in the Performance IQ at even 2 or more years post-injury (Winogron, Knights, & Bawder, 1984). Whereas the verbal subtests of the WISC-R tend to require retrieval and use of old or overlearned information, the performance subtests emphasize speed, motor dexterity, and new problem solving skills. Thus, the dissociation between recovery of Verbal and Performance IQ likely reflects the sensitivity of the performance scale subtests to the typical consequences of traumatic brain injury. Whether IQ scores eventually return to premorbid levels has not been established. Studies comparing posttraumatic IQ scores with premorbid estimates of intellectual functioning suggest that only a partial intellectual recovery is achieved by most severely injured children.

Evidence of both gross and subtle problems in other cognitive functions often persists for years following traumatic brain injury in children. Levin and Eisenberg (1979) found that visuospatial impairment—evaluated by construction of three-dimensional block designs and copying of geometric figures—was present in nearly one-third of children with closed head injury 1 year later. Reductions in motor speed and increased reaction time have also been identified. Although the capacity to consolidate and retrieve information is clearly critical for scholastic performance, studies have shown that memory impairment is the most common cognitive deficit following pediatric head injury; nearly one-half of patients with injuries of varying severity exhibited memory deficits (Levin & Eisenberg, 1979).

With respect to academic functions, Shaffer, Bijor, & Chadwick (1980) reported that of children who sustained unilateral depressed skull fractures, 55% were reading one or more years below their chronologic age, and 35% were performing at least 2 years below their chronologic age. Levin, Benton, and Grossman (1982) reported that arithmetic scores were significantly lower 6 months after injury than scores before injury. Furthermore, academic achievement test scores may *overestimate* the child's ability to function in the classroom. Basic academic functions, such as reading and spelling, are often not immediately affected by a closed head injury. However, difficulties with attention, memory, motor speed, and behavioral control will diminish the child's capacity to perform. The younger child who has not yet acquired reading skills may have difficulty at the point such learning is required. Problems may only become apparent years after injury, as they reflect the cumulative influence of the child's subtle learning difficulties or as new demands are placed on the child's nervous system that require integration of damaged systems (Rourke, 1983). Klonoff, Low, and Clark (1977) found that 26% of head-injured children less than 9 years of age had either failed a grade or been placed in a resource class. This finding was striking in view of the generally mild degree of head injury severity in their sample.

Typically, head-injured children and adolescents who do not manifest severe neurologic consequences (marked motor deficits or striking intellectual impairments) present the greatest challenge to educators. This is because their problems are unexpected and not readily observable. It is easy to believe that with recovery from the acute symptoms the child's healing is complete; but residual effects may linger on for months or years, even in cases of so-called "minor" head injury. Decreased attention and difficulties organizing, planning, monitoring, and generating appropriate problem-solving activities commonly pose significant impediments to learning in academic environments. The brain-injured child is also likely to demonstrate neurobehavioral deficits and psychosocial problems including irritability, depression, reduced social sensitivity, and a lack of confidence. Characteristically, these children suffer from poor self-esteem; repeated failures have made them painfully aware of the differences in their abilities, and loss of friendships and social status have isolated them. Nowhere is failure more likely than in educational situations—situations that continually demand efficient function of the abilities that are most prone to disruption by brain injury.

Listed below are some common manifestations of specific acquired cognitive deficits in the school setting.

Sustained Attention

Deficits in sustained attention make it impossible for a student to maintain attention consistently. This results in a waxing and waning effect, which interferes with information processing and with consistent high-level production. Such difficulties cause gaps in what a student receives—either visually or auditorially—and may result in fragmented and confusing perceptions. Without continuity, information is likely to lose its logical context and become incomprehensible. Retrieval of this information may be haphazard and marked by inappropriate associations. Learning, if it occurs at all, is greatly reduced. Production is also affected. Handwriting may be inconsistent; written math problems may be correctly computed one time and incorrectly computed the next; spelling may be inconsistent; written compositions may be disorganized and filled with errors of usage and style.

Selective Attention

Deficits in selective attention slow the process of reading and listening by interfering with the student's ability to inhibit competing and irrelevant visual and auditory noise. These students are "captured" by nonsalient task aspects and may engage in activities that are totally unrelated to assigned work. Often such children cannot organize themselves to begin work and cannot complete a task, even if frequently redirected to the work at hand.

Alternating Attention

Alternating attention deficits interfere with the ability to switch efficiently from one activity to another, for example, from listening to note taking, or from analyzing a math problem, to calculating or writing down the answer. Such deficits result in slowed production and increased error frequency.

Divided Attention

Divided attention is at the highest level of the attentional hierarchy. It is necessary in such activities as reading and typing a text or talking on the phone while jotting down notes. Examples of tasks requiring divided attention in the classroom include written composition and essay examinations. In these situations, the student must simultaneously attend to the accurate and complete retrieval of information, production of grammatical sentences, selection of vocabulary, and production of accurate spelling, among other activities.

Attentional deficits are difficult to understand because by nature they result in inconsistencies of performance and give the mistaken impression that if the child would just try harder to pay attention, things would be different. Children with such deficits may believe this as well, but it is not the case. When mechanisms of attention are damaged, their volitional control is severely reduced and totally unreliable. Even with extreme effort, the processes may not function as they did prior to injury.

Memory Deficits

Some failures to remember are the result of attentional deficits; information is not received or is not retrieved because concentration is interrupted. Some failures, however, are the result of injury to memory storage and/or retrieval mechanisms. These are terribly frustrating because they usually affect new learning. Information learned prior to the injury may be intact, but new information, no matter how often it is drilled, cannot be completely recalled after a brief passage of time or after interference.

Executive Functions

Problems related to frontal lobe injury (common after injuries to the forehead or face) may include impaired executive functions, reduced judgment, and lack of insight. These problems interfere with the student's ability to set appropriate goals, plan and generate strategies, monitor, and orchestrate the myriad of activities necessary for complex problem solving. They may also result in a failure to recognize limitations and in an overestimation of abilities. Practically, this can lead a student to attempt tasks that are well beyond his or her cognitive capabilities.

Educational Transition for the Brain-Injured Child

Transition of school-age individuals from hospital to school following traumatic brain injury presents one of the greatest challenges to rehabilitation. Successful transition goes beyond the transfer of hospital-based services to educational environments. It must provide follow-up services that anticipate the changing educational needs of individuals whose physical, cognitive, and social–emotional development will probably be disrupted (Begali, 1987; Rosen & Gerring, 1986).

To accomplish this, a cooperative relationship must be established by medical and educational service providers that recognizes the strengths and limitations of each. Such a cooperative relationship must consider a number of issues.

1. Rehabilation may require extended treatment, often over a period covering the entire educational process, through vocational training and establishment in an occupational setting.

2. The resources of public schools are limited. School systems are designed to best serve majority populations; individuals with special needs, such as the head injured, often get pigeonholed according to labels and funding restrictions and do not receive the services they need.

3. Practically and economically, as well as legally, parents are responsible for the education of their children. They are, therefore, the best suited to monitor rehabilitative progress and advocate for appropriate educational/ rehabilitation services. This will require a program of formal training directed at educating the parent/guardian about the needs of the traumatically brain-injured student, the legal obligations of public schools, and about community services and support systems that are available.

It is valuable to designate a professional within the rehabilitation setting to be responsible for providing parent education, coordinating school transition, and monitoring on a periodic basis to ascertain that student needs are being met. The individual or individuals who perform this role should be knowledgeable in rehabilitation services, human development, the effects of traumatic brain injury, education, special education services, and public law pertaining to the rights of handicapped individuals. This person should be knowledgeable enough in special educational curricula to make specific recommendations to teachers and therapists/counselors to meet the traumatically brain-injured student's needs as they arise. Finally, this individual should be sufficiently conversant in hospital-based service delivery to coordinate follow-up outpatient services as needs arise over the course of the educational process.

In-School Programming

In spite of the complex nature of problems attending traumatic brain injury, most schools have the resources necessary to help reintegrate the head-injured student into the educational mainstream. Of foremost importance is the employment of a team approach. Fragmented services, no matter how sophisticated they may be, only serve to make the educational experience more confusing to a mind that has suddenly lost the ability to organize or integrate experience in general.

Ideally, one member of the school staff should be responsible for closely monitoring the student's daily work load and helping the student to organize, plan, and schedule time for specific coursework. This individual may also provide tutorial instruction or supervise an aide or peer tutor in individualized instruction. In the case of older students, the staff member in this role should maintain daily contact with instructors in every course to monitor the student's progress and to help instructors modify curricula where necessary. Usually, this role is best filled by the school's special education teacher or learning disabilities specialist.

Additional key personnel may include the school nurse, social worker, school psychologist, physical therapist, speech–language pathologist, and occupational therapist. The treatment approaches of these specialists should be coordinated so that therapies serve to reinforce practical classroom needs. For example, if visuomotor efficiency is impaired, the occupational therapist may work on handwriting skills development using assignments from composition class. Speech–language therapy may involve exercises in vocabulary building using vocabulary introduced in science class. The special education teacher should see that these therapists receive information regarding specific course-related needs. In turn, therapists should provide information that will help classroom teachers to develop specific skills.

Information concerning students' levels of function and specific needs may be gained through neuropsychologic evaluation. Such an evaluation should provide insight into strengths and weaknesses that will help set general expectations for performance in a variety of academic settings. Consultation with the school psychologist may help the special education

education instructor apply the assessment results to specific classroom needs.

Frequent staff meetings should be scheduled to exchange information concerning changes in student needs. These meetings should ideally be attended by all of the student's instructors and service providers, and creative approaches to practical needs should be encouraged from all participants.

A few facts should be kept in mind concerning the child or adolescent with traumatic brain injury:

1. No two individuals are alike, and even similar injuries may produce very different effects in different persons.
2. The needs of a student recovering from traumatic brain injury may change quickly and unpredictably; recovery of functions does not follow a prescribed developmental course, and what may be measured as a deficit one day may be a strength the next.
3. Some skills may require process-specific drill over a long period of time before they are recovered.
4. Psychometric tests and academic achievement measures only sample an individual's abilities. Good test scores do not necessarily mean that a person has recovered. Factors such as decreased stamina, psychoemotional stressors, and weakened organizational abilities can severely limit a person's ability to orchestrate the systems and processes necessary for successful school performance.
5. Students' attempts to cope with physical and psychological differences may produce behaviors that disrupt learning and alienate them from the very individuals who are best suited to help with reintegration into the mainstream. Rudeness, anger, noncompliance, apathy, even physical aggression may be exhibited. Though such behaviors should be managed—to protect others as well as the students themselves— they should be managed with understanding, and more appropriate behaviors should be trained through behavior modification techniques.
6. Close communication should be maintained with the student's family, physician, and rehabilitation resources in the area to anticipate and solve problems before they become intolerable.

In this section, we have attempted to describe and discuss some of the long-term sequelae of traumatic brain injury in the adolescent and child population. We have focused the discussion largely on issues pertaining to return to the educational setting. For a more comprehensive review of educational reintegration in the school-age traumatically head-injured populations, see excellent texts by Begali (1987) and Rosen and Gerring (1986).

With regard to specific targeted retraining of cognitive skills, it is our hope that many of the procedures outlined in other chapters of this book can be effectively adapted for and applied to children with traumatic brain injury. At our own clinic, we have utilized Attention Process Training (APT) (Sohlberg & Mateer, 1986), a systematic approach to memory book training, and aspects of executive function training described in this text with school-aged children with considerable success.

COGNITIVE REHABILITATION IN CHILDREN WITH DEVELOPMENTAL PROCESSING DEFICITS

It is, of course, the case that many children who have no known history of neurologic disorder or disease manifest impairments in cognitive development and in learning. These impairments may be quite specific in nature (e.g., developmental language disorder, attention deficit disorder) or may be viewed very broadly (e.g., learning disability). In the last two decades, there has been considerable interest in developing remedial approaches to developmental language disorders and developmental visual motor impairments. Other aspects of cognition (e.g., attention, memory, reasoning, and organizational skills) have not traditionally been addressed in process-specific treatment programs.

A case in point is the diagnostic classification of attention deficit disorder (ADD). According to the DSM-III-R, the third, revised edition of the *Diagnostic and Statistical Manual of Mental Disorders* (American Psychiatric Association, 1987), the essential features of ADD are developmentally inappropriate degrees of inattention, impulsiveness, and hyperactivity. In the classroom, these deficits are evidenced by the child's not staying with tasks and having difficulty organizing and completing work. The children often give the impression that they are not listening or that they have not heard what they have been told. Their work is often messy and performed in an impulsive or careless fashion. Performance may be characterized by oversights such as omissions or insertions or misinterpretations of easy items even when the child is well motivated and not just in situations that hold little intrinsic interest. Group situations are particularly difficult for the child, and attentional difficulties are exaggerated when the child is in the classroom where sustained attention is expected. Impulsiveness may be manifest in blurting out answers to questions before they are completed, failing to take turns appropriately, interrupting during class, and failing to read directions before beginning work assignments. At home, attentional problems are shown by a failure to follow-through on parental requests and instructions and by the inability to stick to activities, including play, for the period of time appropriate for the child's age (DSM-III, 3rd Edition, 1980).

In recent years, the treatments for ADD have incorporated pharmacologic approaches (typically stimulant medication, which has a paradoxical dampening effect on behavior), classical behavior modification approaches, and metacognitive approaches that attempt to assist the child in assessing and modifying their performance on academic tasks (Barkley, 1981). Each of these approaches has been demonstrated to have some success with some children. None of them, however, address the underlying deficit in the cognitive process of attention.

Williams (1987) reported results from a preliminary study in which six children identified as ADD and learning disabled participated in a 5-week program of Attention Process Training (Sohlberg & Mateer, 1986). The children received 12 hours of training in each of the areas of sustained, selective, and alternating attention for periods of 2 hours per day, 4 days per week. Progress was documented by means of daily task performance records for each child. Generalization to nontrained treatment materials was measured by administration of a battery made up of selected higher-level attention tasks in each of the areas trained. Generalization and maintenance of attentional efficiency were measured by a battery of psychometric and educational measures sensitive to distractibility and to processing rate administered at 2½ and 5 weeks after baselines were established and 90 days after cessation of treatment. Although variability was seen among individual children, results indicated increases in processing efficiency on all measures when individual scores were averaged. Significant positive changes in classroom behavior were noted in more than half of the children on the basis of teacher evaluations. In a second, single-case study, a 9-year-old child received APT training over a 3-month period (30 hours of individual therapy). This child demonstrated significant gains on all subtests of the Kaufman Tests of Educational Achievement (Kaufman & Kaufman, 1983). In addition, this child demonstrated increased attention in the classroom, increased self-esteem, and decreased tantrum behavior at home. Williams concluded that a process-specific training approach for the remediation of attention deficits may be of considerable benefit to some children, both when conducted in a group and in an individual setting. Moreover, he suggested that gains in attentional performance may be reflected in both classroom behavior and academic achievement.

Although they are preliminary, results such as those suggested above are exciting in that they suggest the possibility and utility of training cognitive processes in children with developmental deficits. Although much additional work needs to be done in this area, it is our hope that principles and procedures for working with cognitive deficits described in this text may be applicable in their present form or modified for use with children with developmental cognitive disability.

[handwritten: unilateral— of, occuring on, or affecting one side only]

COGNITIVE REHABILITATION IN INDIVIDUALS WITH OTHER MEDICAL DIAGNOSES

[handwritten: when]

The approaches to cognitive rehabilitation described in this text have been used not only with head-injured patients but with individuals who demonstrate a variety of neurologic disorders having cognitive sequelae. Patients *[handwritten: ✱]* with unilateral cerebral vascular accidents (strokes) often benefit from training in attention skills, working on compensatory memory systems, or working on discrete visual processing deficits.

Far less certain, but of great interest, is whether or not specific cognitive remediation procedures can be used effectively in the treatment or management of progressive neurologic disorders. At present, little if any systematic work has been done in the treatment of cognitive deficits associated with such progressive disorders as multiple sclerosis or dementia. Indeed, the ethical nature of such treatment has been questioned. It is certainly not hypothesized that cognitive rehabilitation would alter the course of the underlying neuropathology. Yet, it may be that repeated, formalized orientation to person, place, and time, systematic exercise of the cognitive systems underlying attention, and/or training in a compensatory memory notebook system could potentially prolong the capacity to function with maximum independence. Positive results for studies in this area could result in enormous societal and economic benefits as we face demographic increases in both the normal aging population and the population of individuals with progressive dementing disorders.

[handwritten: Problems w/it Cognitive Therapy.]

[handwritten: demography— the statistical study of population]

COGNITIVE REHABILITATION IN INDIVIDUALS WITH PSYCHIATRIC DISORDERS

Modern researchers have been studying the association between psychiatric behavior and brain dysfunction for more than a century (Goldstein, 1978; Mirsky, 1969). However, few of the research findings to date have been translated into practical means for the effective diagnosis and treatment of psychiatric disorders (Yozawitz, 1986). Numerous neuropsychologic studies in psychiatric patients have focused on the ability of a given neuropsychologic instrument or battery to make a "neurologic versus psychiatric" discrimination (see reviews by Heaton, Baade, & Johnson, 1978; Malec, 1978). Unfortunately, tests sensitive to a wide range of neurobehavioral deficits are likely to be sensitive to motivational and behavioral limitations on performance as well, increasing the likelihood of false-positive classifications (i.e., brain injury diagnoses). Despite the problem of such false-positive classifications, some investigators were led to conclude that psychiatric patients were likely to demonstrate a global and diffuse cerebral deficit indistinguishable from chronic brain damage. Although some researchers argued for a neuropathologic substrate for psychiatric disorders, others found no difference between the neuropsychologic performance of psychiatric patients and neurologically intact controls (Barnes & Lucas, 1974; Golden, 1977).

Although any discussion of psychiatric disorder or mental illness must, by definition, incorporate a very broad spectrum of disorders, a focus on two of the more common psychiatric diagnoses having characteristic cognitive components may be fruitful.

Depression

The essential feature of a major depressive disorder includes a loss of interest in or pleasure from almost all activities and pastimes. Other symptoms are likely to include appetite disturbance, changes in weight, sleep disturbance, psychomotor slowing, decreased energy, and feelings of worthlessness. Associated with these physical manifestations and changes in mood state are cognitive disturbances, including difficulty with concentration, slowed thinking, and indecisiveness. Depressed individuals often complain of memory difficulty and appear easily distracted.

Schizophrenic Disorder

The schizophrenic disorders, which are among the most frequent of the serious psychiatric disturbances, are characterized by abnormalities in a wide variety of cognitive functions. These may include disturbances in content of form of thought, in perception, in affect, in a sense of self, in volition, and in the patient's relationship to the outside world. From a cognitive perspective, the disturbances in form and thought and in volition are most intriguing. The most common example in form of thought is what is termed a "loosening of associations," in which ideas shift from one subject to another completely unrelated subject without the speaker showing any awareness that the topics are not connected. Statements that lack a meaningful relationship may be juxtaposed, or the individual may shift idiosyncratically from one frame of reference to another. Speech may become incomprehensible or simply remain vague, overly abstract, or overly concrete. Less common disturbances include neologisms (nonwords) and persevervation. Abnormalities in volition are manifest as disturbance in self-initiated, goal-directed activity. Such deficits may grossly impair work or other role functioning. Abnormalities may take the form of inadequate interest or drive or inability to follow a course of action to its logical conclusion. Pronounced ambivalence regarding alternative courses of action can lead to near cessation of goal-directed activity. In most schizophrenic patients, the problem is not a progressive disorder but an episodic one. Individuals who, because of genetic or acquired factors, are particular susceptible to life's stress may experience episodes involving behaviors that would be charcterized as schizophrenic.

Numerous studies performed in recent years (e.g., Watson, Thomas, Anderson, & Felling, 1968) have attested to the difficulties schizophrenics have with conceptual tasks. However, many researchers argue that the apparent conceptual deficits of the schizophrenic patient may well reflect failure to attend to the task, often because of interfering ideation in combination with motivational deficits (Sutton, 1973). The problem of attention in schizophrenia has received extensive study with particular emphasis on reaction-time experiments (Zubin, 1975). Although focus has centered on the possible attention deficits of schizophrenic subjects, it is clear that they also have many other neuropsychologic impairments. And neuropsychologic impairments must be seen in the context of the broader clinical phenomenology of schizophrenia that includes intermittent bizarre behavior and sometimes unintelligible language, delusions, and hallucinations as well as a series of affective and personality characteristics including withdrawal, affective blunting, and apathy.

Despite longstanding interest in the possible neurobiologic and neuropsychologic correlates of psychiatric disease, there have been few links established between neuropsychologic assessment or neuropsychologic profiles and the treatment of psychiatric disorders. The customary regimens of pharmacologic and behavioral management for both schizophrenic and depressed patients tend to bear little relationship to the results of neuropsychologic testing, even when such testing may have been done. Instead, the neuropsychologic assessment is used to rule out the existence of structural brain diseases that would contraindicate the use of conventional pharmacologic or behavioral therapies.

Investigators in the field of psychiatric disorders have often found it useful to apply Hughlings Jackson's (1932) distinction between positive and negative symptoms. In psychopathology, negative symptoms are the signs of deficit in the cognitive or affective sphere such as blunted affect or intellectual impairment. Positive symptoms are unusual phenomena such as delusions and hallucinations. During the acute phase of schizophrenic disorders, the positive symptoms tend to become more pronounced, whereas during the quiescent phases, the patient tends to demonstrate primarily negative symptoms. Thus, the schizophrenic patient, when not in an episode of illness, may be emotionally flat and withdrawn and may demonstrate attention impairments but not exhibit florid, psychotic behavior. It has been suggested that neuropsychologic assessment and even treatment may have more to offer in regard to the negative symptoms than the positive ones.

Stress may precipitate psychiatric episodes through the mediation of environmental demands on a less than capable organism (Shields, 1978).

There are chemotherapeutic strategies that attempt to diminish the stress reaction (Iversen, 1980), and there are strategies to reduce the environmental demands on the individual (Mosher & Keith, 1980), but there has been little attempt at direct cognitive intervention (Cox & Leventhal, 1978). The few attempts that have focused on developing skills in psychiatric patients, however, have shown this approach to be the most effective intervention strategy for long-term psychiatric outcome (Anthony & Margules, 1974; Anthony, 1980). Although recidivism and employment statistics are still far from optimal, results are considered most encouraging.

Yozawitz (1986) recommends an approach to intervention with psychiatric patients in which neuropsychologic constraints on adaptive functioning are taken into account in outlining a treatment program. He suggests combining comprehensive neurodiagnostic assessment with intensive psychiatric and medical evaluation to determine a "biologically relevant course of rehabilitation" for each patient. Depending on the outcome of a comprehensive interdisciplinary screening, some patients would be directly referred to an acute-care medical facility for medical treatment; others would be directly referred to an inpatient unit for intensive management of their acute psychiatric symptoms; and others would enter the first stage of a cognitive rehabilitation program. Specific targeting of deficit cognitive processing in the areas of language function, visual–spatial processing, attention, and memory function would be available. Based on specific needs, patients might enter specific modules for training activities of daily living, community reentry skills, occupational training, or other vocational involvement. Irrespective of disposition, all patients would enter a social network where they would receive counseling and follow-up evaluations at 6-month intervals to assess their capacity to continue to function independently in the community (Marsh, Glick, & Zigler, 1981).

In almost all respects, the model proposed by Yozawitz (1986) and outlined in Figure 15.2 parallels the model for comprehensive cognitive rehabilitation and community reentry described throughout this text for persons with acquired brain injury.

Although quite different from contemporary approaches to the treatment of psychiatric disorder, the rehabilitation approach outlined by Yozawitz is not without precedent. More than 70 years ago, Adolf Meyer (1913) described conceptually a highly specialized diagnostic and treatment center that would carry out an interdisciplinary program of prevention, treatment, and aftercare for psychiatric disorders. He emphasized the importance of a cross-disciplinary training base for mental professionals to develop a theoretical model of mental health diagnosis and treatment based on both psychiatric and neurologic expertise. His model stressed the complexity of psychiatric disorder as an integration of biological and environmental forces

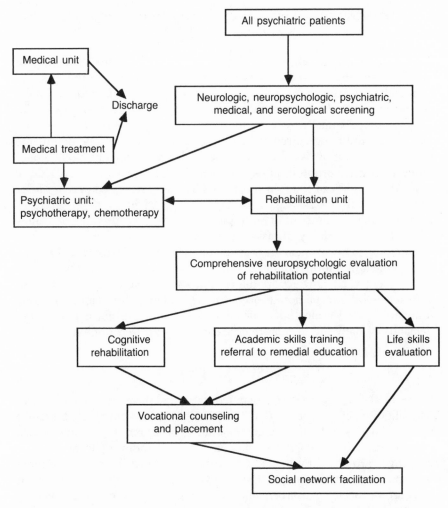

FIGURE 15.2. Flow chart for management of psychiatric patients, Adapted from Yozawitz (1986). Which incorporates rehabilitation and community reentry.

that contributed to a patient's clinical presentation. His basic objective was to help individuals make the best adaptation possible, given their constitutional resources and the demands of society, with recognition of each person's assets as well as liabilities critical to the therapeutic approach. We suggest that in attempting to approach individuals with psychiatric disorders in such a skills-orientated fashion, the models and procedures for cognitive retraining and compensation described in this text may be of value.

COGNITIVE TRAINING IN NEUROLOGICALLY NORMAL SUBJECTS

Although all of our efforts to date have focused on the retraining of individuals with acquired or developmental impairment, the theories and approaches developed may have implications for work with normally functioning individuals. From a theoretical perspective, it may be possible to enhance an individual's cognitive functioning through a series of systematic and hierarchically organized exercises and procedures. No one doubts the role of exercise in physical and cardiovascular conditioning. None would argue against the proposition that study and organized attempts to acquire new information can result in substantial learning. Repeated practice in or experience with a task (e.g., counting change, driving, typing) serves to increase efficiency in terms of both speed and accuracy. Although no claims are made for the ability of tasks described in this text to improve normal functioning, many of them are seen as foundations for learning and for the management of information. Many therapists who have worked with these procedures anecdotally report improvements in their own concentration and speed of information processing. The approaches should provide foundations for learning both information and skills and for managing the demands of daily life in a more efficient and organized fashion.

SUMMARY

In this final chapter, we have attempted to expand the horizons of cognitive rehabilitation. It is believed that the principles of cognitive rehabilitation outlined in this text and the corresponding procedures that have grown from basic models of cognitive function may be broadly applicable. Special challenges are posed by individuals with minor head injury and children with traumatic brain injuries. Not only acquired but developmental information-processing disorders may be amenable to cognitive interventions. The same is true for a wide range of both acute and progressive medical conditions. There is also a rationale for attempting the use of cognitive remediation procedures in patients with psychiatric diagnoses. Finally, there may be applications for the kind of cognitive interventions discussed in the text to normal individuals for the purpose of enhancing acquisition and efficient manipulation of information.

STUDY QUESTIONS

1. Discuss the possible interplay among cognitive, physical, and emotional symptomatology in individuals who have suffered minor head injury.

2. Describe a treatment approach for an individual who demonstrates unreliable memory, irritability, and depression 4 months after a severe concussion.
3. What cautions are necessary in making predictions from the neuropsychological evaluation of a young preschool head-injured child?
4. Describe five major principles of effective reintegration to school for the mildly to moderately head-injured child.
5. For what specific psychiatric symptomatology might cognitive rehabilitation be beneficial?
6. List four different circumstances involving nonimpaired individuals (training situations or treatment groups) for which cognitive rehabilitation approaches may be advantageous.

REFERENCES

American Psychiatric Association. (1980). *Diagnostic and statistical manual of mental disorders* (3rd ed.). revised. Washington: APA.

Anthony, W. A. (1980). *The principles of psychiatric rehabilitation.* Baltimore: University Park Press.

Anthony, W. A., & Margules, A. (1974). Toward improving the efficacy of psychiatric rehabilitation. A skills training approach. *Rehabilitation Psychology* 21:101–105.

Barkley, R. A. (1981). *Hyperactive children: A handbook for diagnosis and treatment.* New York: Guildford Press.

Barnes, G., & Lucas, G. J. (1974). Cerebral dysfunction vs. psychogenesis in the Halstead–Reitan tests. *Journal of Nervous and Mental Disease 158*:50–60.

Begali, V. (1987). *Head injury in children and adolescents.* Brandon, VT: Clinical Psychology Publishing Co.

Caveness, W. F., & Walker, A. E. (Eds.). (1969). *The late effects of head injury.* Philadelphia: Lippincott.

Chadwick, D., Rutter, M., & Brown, G. (1981). A prospective study of children with head injuries, II. Cognitive sequelae, *Psychological Medicine 11*:48–61.

Cox, M. D., & Leventhal, D. B. (1978). A multivariate analysis and modification of preattentive, perceptual dysfunction in schizophrenia. *Journal of Nervous and Mental Disease 166*:709–718.

Ewing-Cobbs, L., Fletcher, J. M., & Levin, H. (1985). Neuropsychological sequelae following pediatric head injury. In M. Ylvisaker (Ed.), *Head injury rehabilitation of children and adolescents* (pp. 3–91). San Diego: College-Hill Press.

Gennarelli, T. A. (1982). General concussion and diffuse brain injuries. In P. R. Cooper (Ed.), *Head injury* (pp. 83–98). Baltimore: Williams & Wilkins.

Gentilini, M., Nichelli, P., & Schoenhuber, R. (1985). Neuropsychological evaluation of mild head injury. *Journal of Neurology, Neurosurgery, and Psychiatry* 48:137–140.

Golden, C. J. (1977). Validity of the Halstead–Reitan neuropsychological battery in a mixed psychiatric and brain damaged population. *Journal of Consulting and Clinical Psychology 45*:1043–1051.

Goldstein, G. (1978). Cognitive and perceptual differences between schizophrenics and organics. *Schizophrenia Bulletin* 4:161–185.

Gronwall, D., & Wrightson, P. (1974). Delayed recovery of intellectual function after minor head injury. *Lancet ii:*605–609.

Gronwall, D., & Wrightson, P. (1981). Memory and information processing capacity after closed head injury. *Journal of Neurology, Neurosurgery and Psychiatry, 44:*889–895.

Heaton, R. K., Baade, L. E., & Johnson, K. L. (1978). Neuropsychological test results associated with psychiatric disorders in adults. *Psychological Bulletin 85:*141–162.

Iversen, S. D. (1980). Brain chemistry and behaviour, *Psychological Medicine 10:*527–539.

Jackson, J. H. (1932). *Selected writings of John Hughlings Jackson* (J. Taylor, Ed.). London: Hedder & Stoughton.

Jane, J. A., Rimel, R. W., and Alves, W. M. (1985). Minor head injury: Model systems. In R. G. Dacey (Ed.), *Trauma to the central nervous system.* New York: Raven Press.

Kaufman, A. S., & Kaufman, N. L. (1983). *Kaufman Assessment Battery for Children.* Circle Pines, MN: American Guidance Service.

Klonoff, H., Low, M. D., & Clark, C. (1977). Head injuries in children: A prospective five year follow-up. *Journal of Neurology, Neurosurgery, and Psychiatry 40:*1211–1219.

Levin, H. S., & Eisenberg, H. M. (1979). Neuropsychological outcome of closed head injury in children and adolescents. *Child's brain 5:*281–292.

Levin, H. S., Benton, A. L., & Grossman, R. C. (1982). *Neurobehavioral consequences of closed head injury.* New York: Oxford University Press.

Levin, H. S., Ewing-Cobbs, L., & Benton, A. L. (1984). Age and recovery from brain damage. A review of clinical studies. In S. W. Scheft (Ed.), *Aging and recovery of function in the central nervous system* (pp. 169–203). New York: Plenum.

Lezak, M. (1983). *Neuropsychological assessment.* New York: Oxford University Press.

Lidvall, H. F., Linderoth, B., & Norlin, B. (1974). Causes of the postconcussional syndrome. *Acta Neurologica Scandinavica 50 (Supplement 56):*7–144.

Lishman, W. A. (1973). The psychiatric sequelae of head injury: A review. *Psychological Medicine 3:*304–318.

Malec, J. (1978). Neuropsychological assessment of schizophrenia versus brain damage: A review. *Journal of Nervous and Mental Disease 166:*507–516.

Marsh, A., Glick, M., & Zigler, E. (1981). Premorbid social competence and the revolving door phenomenon in psychiatric hospitalization. *Journal of Nervous and Mental Disease 169:*315–319.

Mesulam, M. (1985). *Principles of behavioral neurology.* Philadelphia: F. A. Davis.

Meyer, A. (1913). The aims of a psychiatric clinic. Transactions of the Seventeenth International Congress of Medicine (Part 1, Section 12). In E. E. Winters (Ed.), *The collected papers of Adolf Meyer, Vol. 2.* Baltimore: Johns Hopkins Press, 1951.

Mirsky, A. F. (1969). Neuropsychological bases of schizophrenia. *Annual Review of Psychology, 20:*321–348.

Mosher, L. R., & Keith, S. J. (1980). Psychosocial treatment—individual, group, family, and community support approaches. *Schizophrenia Bulletin 6:*10–40.

Ommaya, A. K., & Gennarelli, T. A. (1974). Cerebral concussion and traumatic unconsciousness. *Brain 97:*633–654.

Povlishock, J. T., Becker, D. P., & Miller, J. D. (1979). The morphopathologic substrates of concussion. *Acta Neuropathologica 47:*1–11.

Prigatano, G. P., Pepping, M., & Klonoff, P. (1986). Cognitive, personality and psychosocial factors in the neuropsychological assessment of brain-injured patients. In B. Uzzell & Y. Gross (Eds.), *Clinical neuropsychology of intervention* (pp. 135–167). Boston: Martinus Nijhoff.

Rimel, R. W., Giordani, B., Barth, J. T., Boll, T. J., & Jane, J. A. (1981). Disability caused by minor head injury. *Neurosurgery 9:*221–235.

Rosen, C. D., & Gerring, J. P. (1986). *Head trauma: Educational reintegration.* San Diego: College-Hill Press.

Rourke, B. P. (1983). Reading and spelling disabilities. A developmental neuropsychological perspective. In U. Kirk (Ed.), *Neuropsychology of language, reading and spelling.* New York: Academic Press.

Ruff, R. M., Levin, H. S., & Marshall, L. F. (1986). Neurobehavioral methods of assessment and the study of outcome in minor head trauma. *Journal of Head Trauma Rehabilitation 1:*43:52.

Shaffer, D., Bijor, P., & Chadwick, O. (1980). Head injury and later reading disability. *Journal of the American Academy of Child Psychiatry 19:*592–610.

Shields, J. (1978). Genetics. In J. K. Wing (Ed.), *Schizophrenia: Towards a new synthesis.* London: Academic Press.

Sohlberg, M. M., & Mateer, C. A. (1986). Effectiveness of an attention training program. *Journal of Clinical and Experimental Neuropsychology 9:*117–130.

Spreen, O., Tupper, D., Risser, A., Tuokko, H., & Edgell, D. (1984). *Human development neuropsychology.* New York: Oxford University Press.

Sutton, S. (1973). Fact and artifact in the psychology of schizophrenia. In M. Hammer, K. Salzinger, & J. Sutton (Eds.), *Schizophrenia as a brain disease.* New York: Oxford University Press.

Trimble, M. R. (1981). *Post-traumatic neurosis: From railway spine to the whiplash.* Chichester, England: Wiley.

Wechsler, D. (1974). *Wechsler Intelligence Scale for Children–Revised.* New York: The Psychological Corporation.

Wetson, C. G., Thomas, R. W., Anderson, D., & Felling, J. (1968). Differentiation of organics from schizophrenics at two chronicity levels by use of the Reitan–Halstead organic test battery. *Journal of Clinical and Consulting Psychology 32:*679–684.

Williams, D. (1987). Effects of an attention training program on learning disabled children with attention deficits. Paper presented at the National Association for Children with Learning Disabilities, San Antonio, TX.

Winogron, H. W., Knights, R. M., & Bawder, H. N. (1984). Neuropsychological deficits following head injury in children. *Journal of Clinical Neuropsychology 6:*269–286.

Wrightson, P., & Gronwall, D. (1981). Time off work and symptoms after minor head injury. *Injury 12:*445–454.

Yozawitz, A. (1986). Applied neuropsychology in a psychiatric center. In I. Grant & K. M. Adams (Eds.), *Neuropsychological assessment of neuropsychiatric disorders* (pp. 121–146). New York: Oxford University Press.

Zubin, J. (1975). The problem of attention in schizophrenia. In M. Kietzman, S. Sutton, & J. Zubin (Eds.), *Experimental approaches to psychopathology* (pp. 139–166). New York: Academic Press.

Index

Therapy
De